# EXTRAVAGANT CROWD

## CARL VAN VECHTEN'S PORTRAITS OF WOMEN

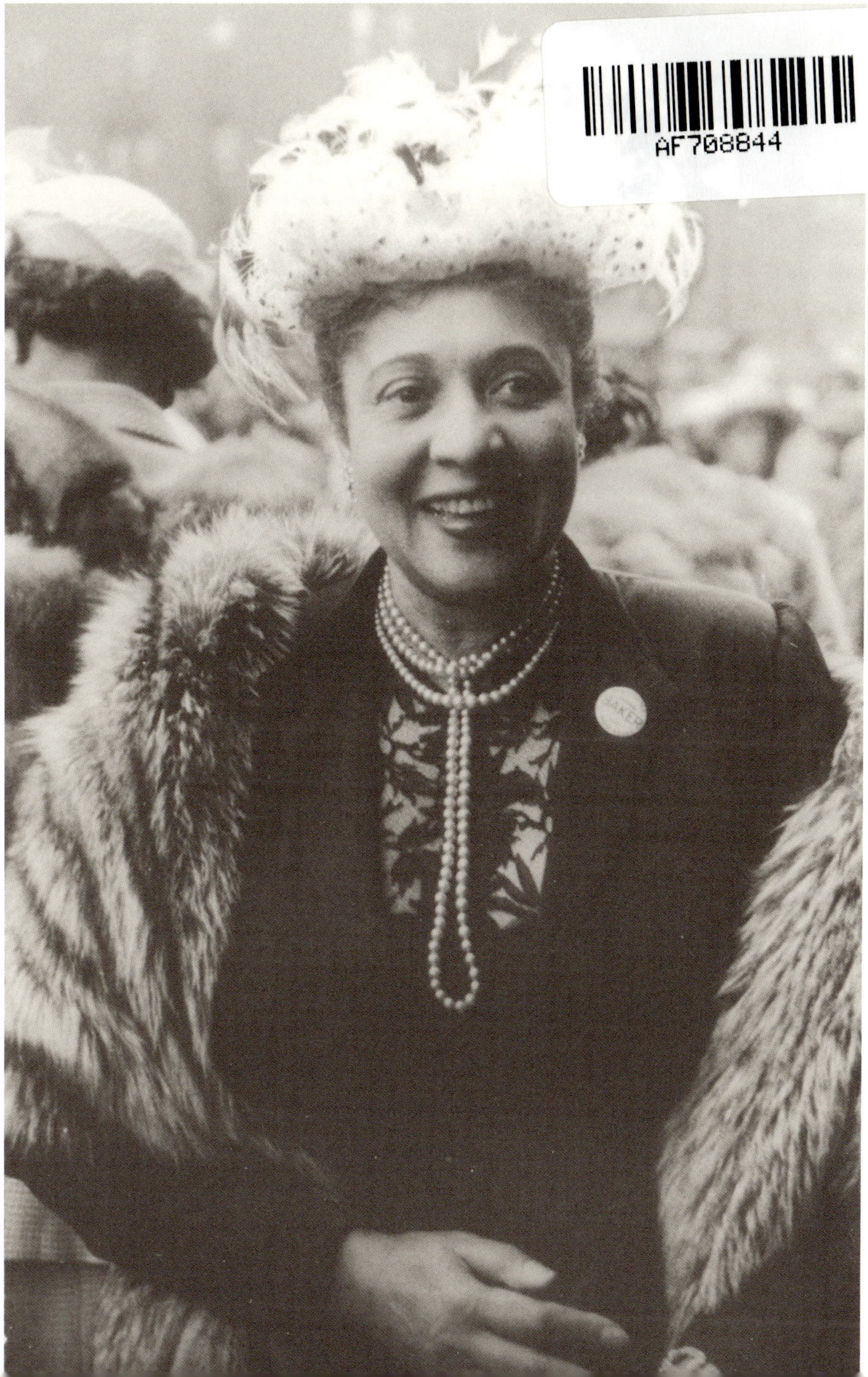

Published in the United States of America in 2003
by the Beinecke Rare Book and Manuscript Library,
Yale University, New Haven, Connecticut 06520-8240



Library of Congress Cataloging-in-Publication Data
Library of Congress Control Number: ISBN 0-8457-3148-3
Kuhl, Nancy, 1971-
Extravagant crowd : Carl Van Vechten's portraits of women / Nancy Kuhl; introduction by Bruce Kellner.
p. cm.
ISBN 0-8457-3148-3
1. Photography of women.
2. Celebrities–Portraits.
3. Portrait photography.
4. Van Vechten, Carl, 1880-1964.
I. Van Vechten, Carl, 1880-1964.
II. Title.
TR681.W6K84 2003
779'.24'092–dc21 2003006528



Special thanks to Sara Stefani for her assistance with this project.

Design and type composition by group c inc ) New Haven (BC, MM, PL)

Cover: (front) Self portrait with Gertrude Stein and Alice B. Toklas photographed January 4, 1935; (back) Mai Mai Sze photographed December 29, 1935

Inside Front Cover: Carl Van Vechten to Gertrude Stein in *Blind Bow Boy,* NY: Knopf, 1923, Beinecke Library

Title page: Geraldyn Dismond (Gerry Major) photographed in New York City, on Josephine Baker Day, May 5, 1951

Inside Back Cover: Carl Van Vechten to Grace Nail Johnson, 20 Feb. 1940, James Weldon Johnson Papers, Beinecke Library, Yale University

# EXTRAVAGANT CROWD

## CARL VAN VECHTEN'S PORTRAITS OF WOMEN

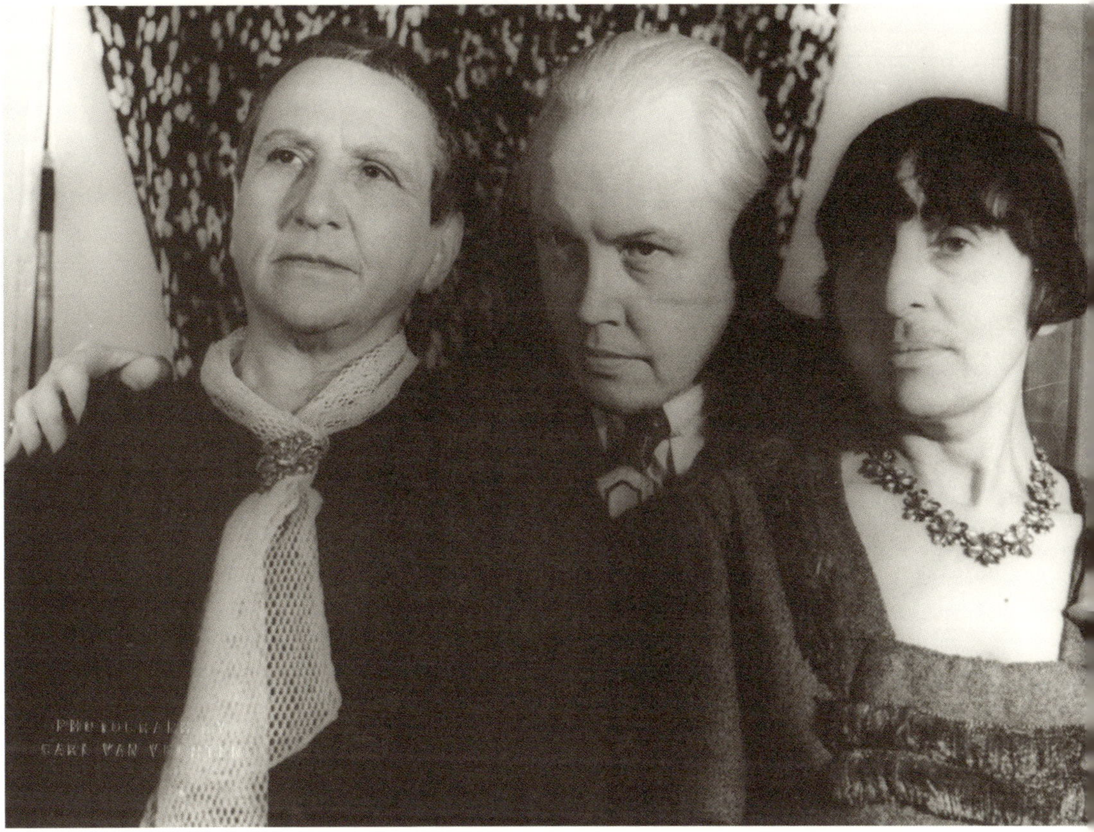

NANCY KUHL

INTRODUCTION BY BRUCE KELLNER

BEINECKE RARE BOOK AND MANUSCRIPT LIBRARY
YALE UNIVERSITY

# EXTRAVAGANT CROWD

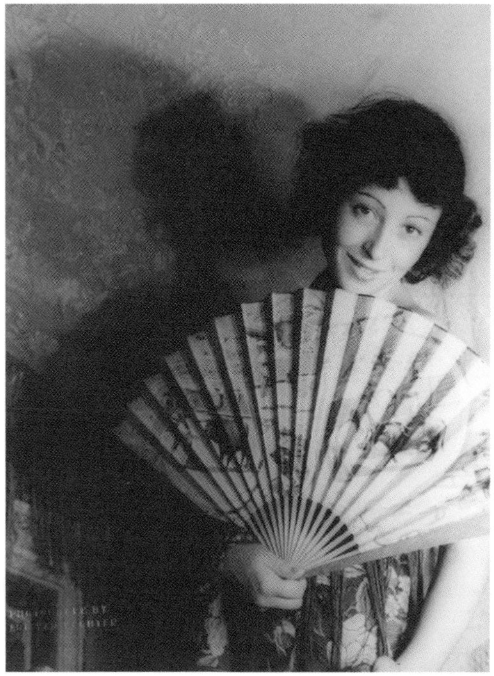

LUISE RAINER, SEPTEMBER 2, 1937

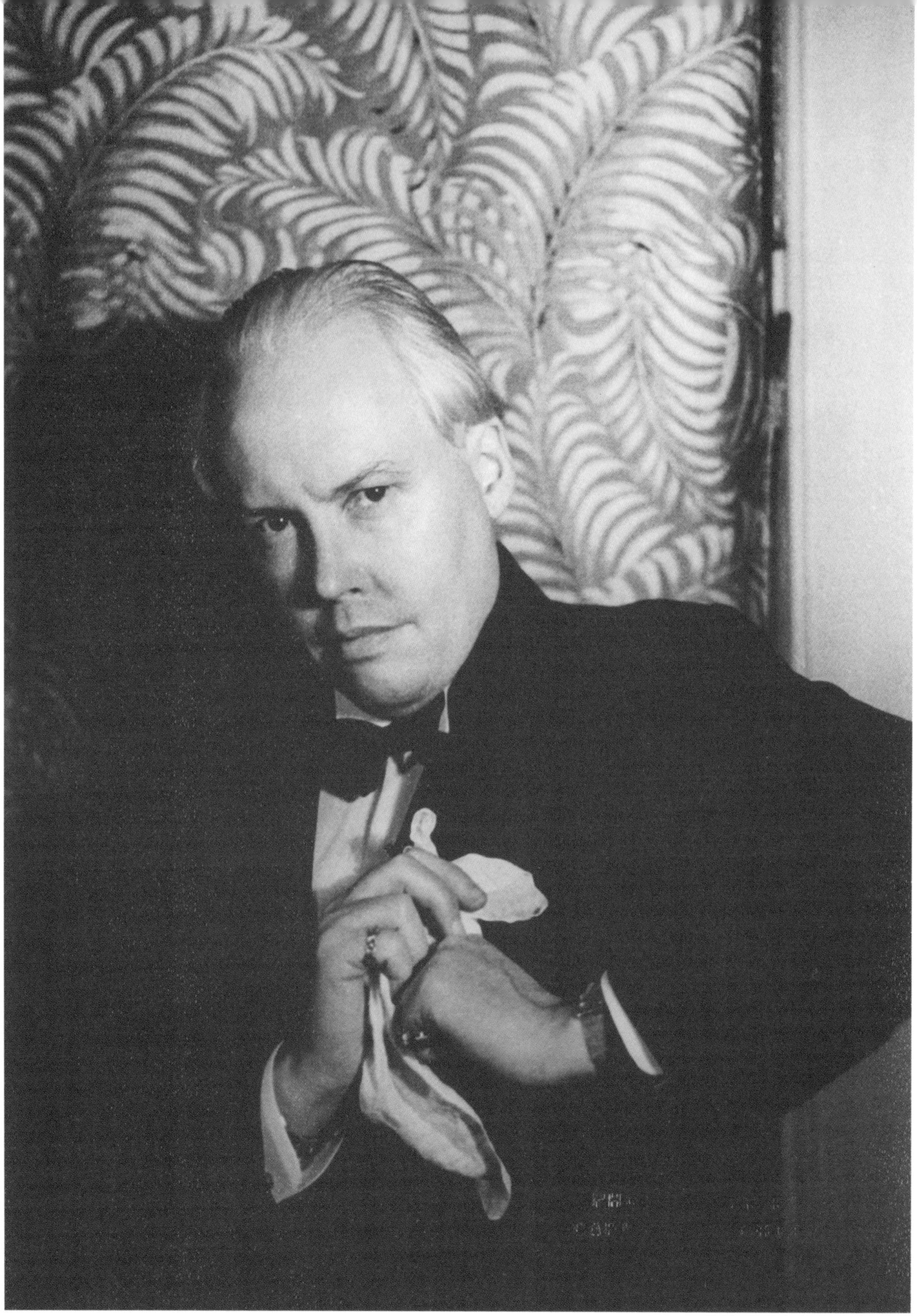

SELF-PORTRAIT, OCTOBER 2, 1934

# EXTRAVAGANT CROWD

## CARL VAN VECHTEN'S PORTRAITS OF WOMEN



The photographs in *Extravagant Crowd: Carl Van Vechten's Portraits of Women* and in the Beinecke Rare Book and Manuscript Library's exhibition of the same name represent only a fraction of those Van Vechten took of women. During his career as a photographer, Van Vechten's subjects, many of whom were his friends and social acquaintances, included dancers, actresses, writers, artists, activists, singers, costumiers, photographers, social critics, educators, journalists, socialites, and aesthetes. In the artistic and intellectual communities of his day, Van Vechten truly covered the waterfront.

Though it would be easy to compile a collection of the most famous and best-loved women of the early- to mid-twentieth century from Van Vechten's photographs, to do so would misrepresent his project. As a photographer—and as a promoter of literary talent and a critic of dance, theater, and opera—Carl Van Vechten was as interested in the cultural margin as he was in the day's most acclaimed and successful people.

This interest in the risky and risqué imaginative fringe, in fact, accounts for Van Vechten's remarkable ability to recognize and promote some of the most significant artistic figures and cultural movements of the twentieth century. It was his passionate commitment to the arts he valued, however unknown or unfashionable, that led him to become the first serious dance critic in the United States, to bring his white friends uptown to Harlem in the 1920s, and to promote the work of then marginal writers and performers including Gertrude Stein, Nella Larsen, and Bessie Smith.

*Extravagant Crowd* includes examples of Van Vechten's most familiar subjects as well as those who are now forgotten, women whose portraits are easily recognized even many years after their deaths alongside others who might have been unrecognized at the height of their achievements. That all of the portraits included here are of women who participated in shaping their cultural moment is evident in their lives and accomplishments. It is a tribute to Van Vechten's vision and foresight that he recognized their contributions and recorded what in some cases he believed to be their "truest" selves.

*Extravagant Crowd* hopes to honor Van Vechten's particular genius by taking a wide-ranging approach to the history it illustrates. If we trace a linear narrative through the portraits of the century's famous and celebrated, we get a skewed representation of the period; such a history is less a portrait of the times than an imagined ideal version of the period. To understand our cultural history more fully, we must consider as many social, intellectual, and artistic elements as possible, what has been forgotten as well as what has entered the cultural canon. This means that in addition to examining the contributions of renowned women and people of color, it is necessary to seek out the work and biographies of those around the highest achievers, those who provide a context and foundation for a more complete understanding of our history. Van Vechten, perhaps, knew something of this; maybe that is, in part, why he made thousands of photographs of hundreds of subjects, knowing that not all, that indeed quite few, would achieve lasting fame.

If the photographs collected here give a sense of both Carl Van Vechten's interests and his considerable role in defining the cultural landscape of the twentieth century, the lives of their subjects offer a glimpse of the range and development of the arts in those decades. More precisely, they demonstrate the diversity of women's contributions to the period's artistic and intellectual movements. Behind the cameras and curtains as well as in front of them, and as patrons and advocates, spokeswomen and partners, teachers and activists, the women represented here helped to shape their arts, professions, and communities.

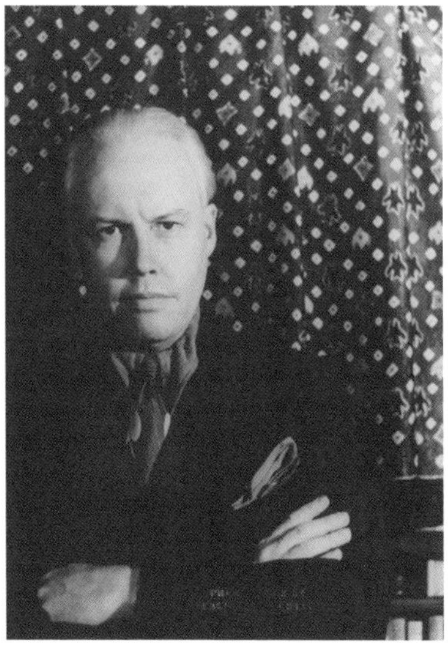

SELF-PORTRAIT, OCTOBER 1, 1934

As women working in fields dominated by men, at a time when the occupations available to women were limited by societal pressures of various kinds, it is not surprising that the work of many of these women had a political component. Among the women whose portraits are included in *Extravagant Crowd* were visible and vocal advocates on behalf of African Americans and other minority groups, immigrants, the poor, and women; others made significant political statements simply by the examples of their achievements, their successes in light of bias, prejudice, and cultural and institutional racism and misogyny. The bleak similarities in the lives and careers of many of the women pictured here—the frequency of divorce and broken relationships, the tendency toward actual or figurative exile, the racism that prevented some from achieving their full potential as artists—are evidence of the personal costs they paid as a result of breaking new ground for future generations of thinkers and artists.

While some of the photographs reproduced here are among Van Vechten's most famous portraits, others are being published for the first time. His photographs of Pearl Bailey, Emma Goldman and others are more than just well-loved images; in some cases, Van Vechten portraits have come to be the preeminent pictures of particular women. Thus, Van Vechten has helped to define the ways his subjects will be remembered, the way they will enter history and the popular imagination. On the other hand, some of Van Vechten's most compelling photographs take virtually unknown women for their subjects. Not often reproduced, these document little-known facets of Van Vechten's artistic sensibility while demonstrating his significant talent for portraiture.

Though they were pioneering and in some cases revolutionary, it seems somehow inexact to refer to Carl Van Vechten and the remarkable women represented here as "ahead of their times." They were less predictors of things to come than creators of the cultural fabric of their times. That their imprint on the cultural fabric of our times, however subtle in some cases, remains relevant and powerful is evidence of their great achievements.

Nancy Kuhl
Assistant Curator
The Yale Collection of American Literature

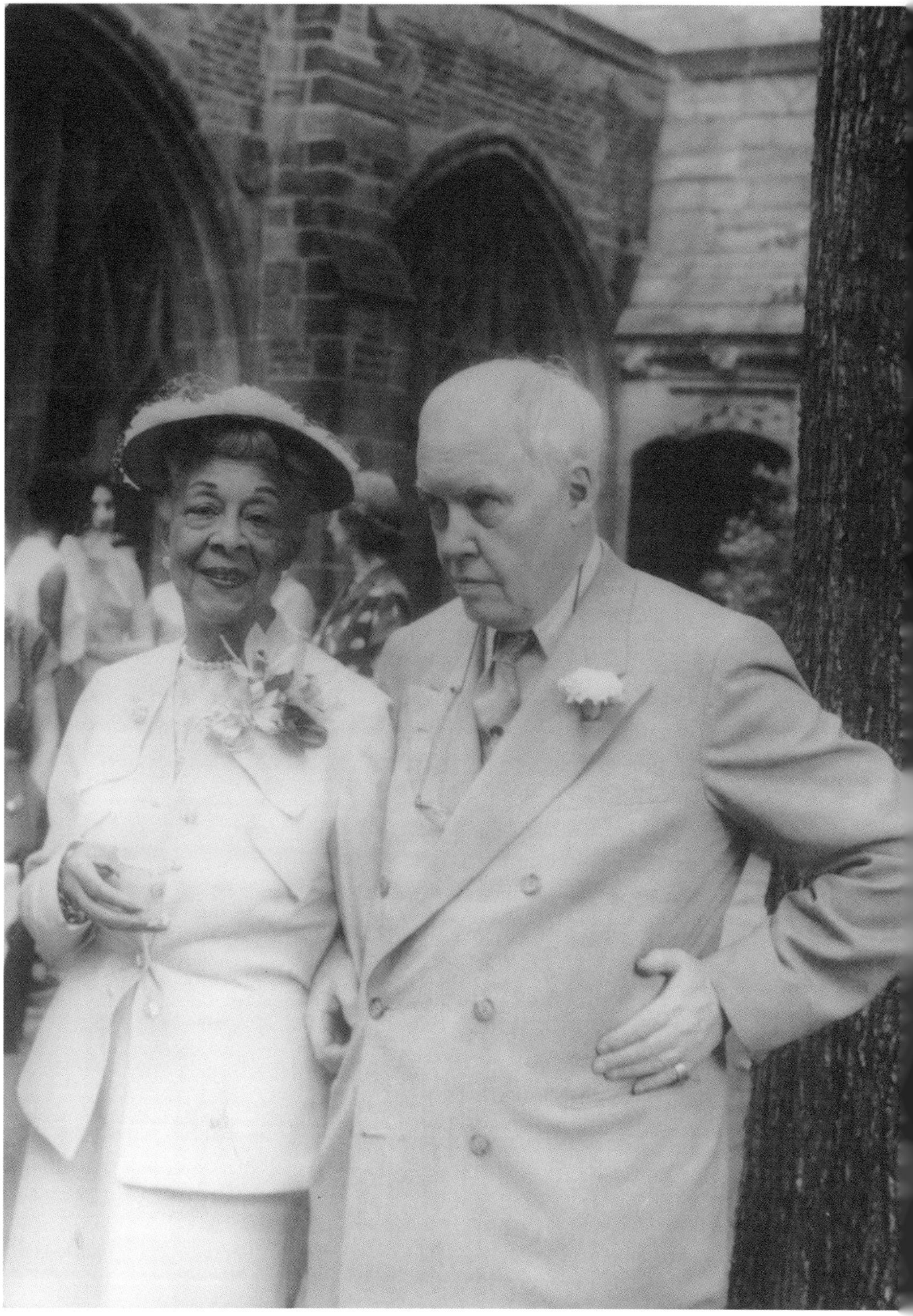

VAN VECHTEN AND NORA HOLT PHOTOGRAPHED BY SAUL MAURIBER AT YALE UNIVERSITY ON JANUARY 22, 1955

# A LOT OF APPLESAUCE



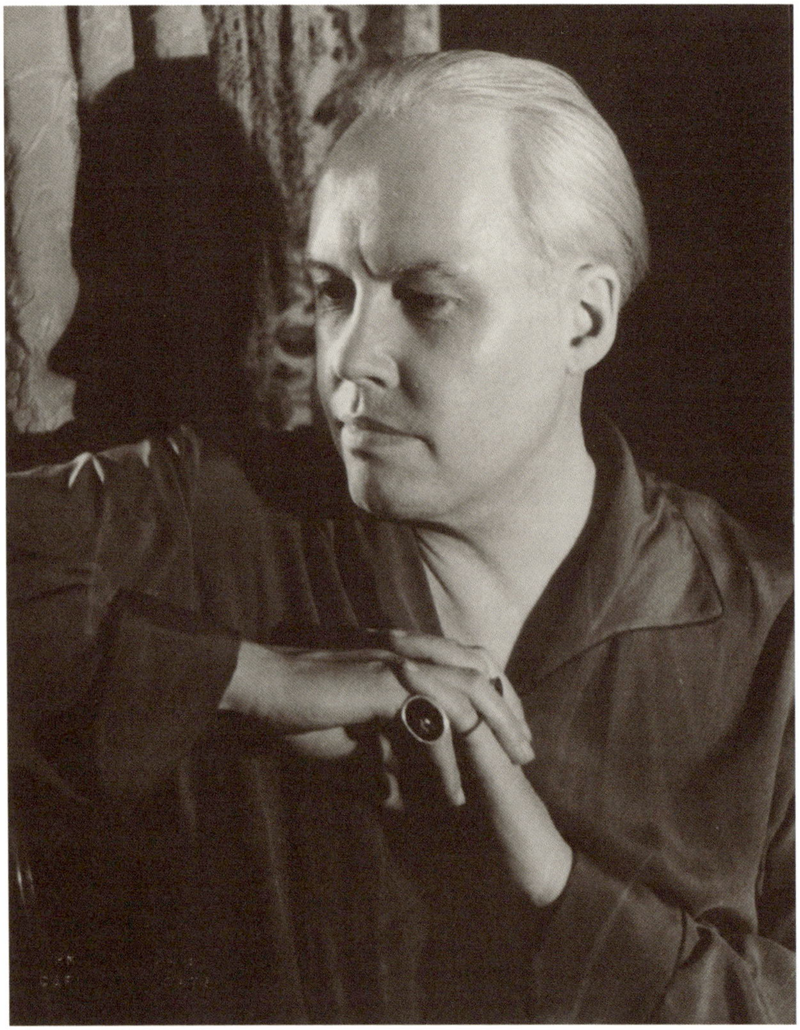

SELF-PORTRAIT, APRIL 3, 1934

Women seem always to have loomed large in Carl Van Vechten's photographic legend. During his Iowa youth in the 1890s, he began making photographs with a box camera and glass plates for blue cyanotypes, starting out with his paternal grandmother, posed rather like Whistler's mother, although he had not yet seen or even heard of that painting. Soon afterward, he photographed two little black girls sitting on the front steps of Harriet Beecher Stowe's house in Cincinnati, Ohio. Subsequently, he arranged friends—almost invariably female—for unusual compositions: as an opera singer with her mouth stretched open for a high note, as Juliet illuminated with candles in the tomb, a chorus line of Cedar Rapids girls pretending to be gypsies in makeshift costumes. A decade later, he moved on to an early Kodak, adding Metropolitan Opera singers Luisa Tetrazzini, Olive Fremstad, and others to his roster. And then he stopped taking pictures while he built a distinguished twenty-five-year career as a writer before returning to photography. He died in 1964, concluding a thirty-two-year love affair with his Leica, numbering other women among his last subjects, Frances Steloff of the Gotham Book Mart, for instance, and Gloria Vanderbilt.

His 15,000 photographs illustrated several of his avocations and interests, with broad representations of African Americans, ballet and modern dancers, theater figures, painters, musicians, and writers—a list punctuated from time

## BRUCE KELLNER

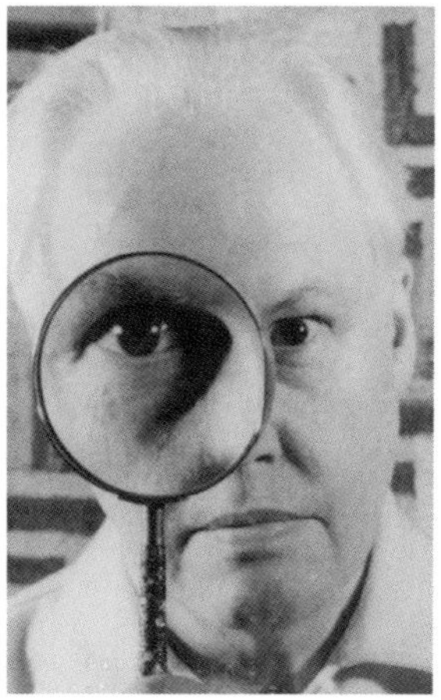

to time with athletes, politicians, educators, and silent movie queens. The Beinecke Library's current gathering, devoted exclusively to his photographs of women, is as unique as it is welcome, for it demonstrates another of Van Vechten's passionate interests.

During a 1943 radio program called "Brains for the Asking," during which listeners posed questions to celebrities, Van Vechten was asked if civilization had been dominated by men because women were not "physically, mentally, or emotionally endowed to cope with the problems involved." Some good humor and some charm allowed him to cheat a bit in replying, but he did so with more than a little truth, observing, in part:

> The premises on which this question is based seem to me unsound. I do not believe that civilization . . . has been dominated by men, and if women are not physically, mentally, and emotionally endowed to cope with the problems of the world more successfully than most men have coped with them, they must be considered very poor animals indeed. Certainly Eve dominated Adam, and since that distant day a lot of women have forced a lot of men to eat a lot of applesauce. Very often, a pretty woman with red hair and green eyes (I am choosing colors at random) who never is seen in public, has more to do with making important political decisions than the King or President or Prime Minister who sits in the front office and speaks into a microphone. . . . Was Helen of Troy a woman of power or were the wars fought so many years on her account of no import? Do names like Florence Nightingale, Margaret Sanger, Joan of Arc, Madame Curie, or Harriet Beecher Stowe . . . mean nothing in the way of evidence? Can anybody forget that Victoria, or the thing she represented, was so successful in dominating the world that practically the whole of the more or less peaceful century, during over half of which she reigned, by universal consent has come to be known as the Victorian era? Does Mrs. Roosevelt tire more quickly than the President? . . . Is Rebecca West less intelligent than [Pierre] Laval? I wonder if anyone, male or female, has ever coped successfully with the problems of this world. It is true there have been Victorias . . . but it is equally true that the public is more often at the mercy of the [Neville] Chamberlains . . . and the William Jennings Bryans.[1]

Perhaps that attitude explains, in part at least, Van Vechten's having photographed so many women. He even initiated his new career as a photographer with women—his earliest subjects were his wife, Russian-American actress Fania Marinoff, and Chinese-American actress Anna May Wong—soon after Mexican caricaturist Miguel Covarrubias returned from Germany with a Leica camera in 1932. Once Van Vechten had seen what wonders a Leica could perform, his enthusiasm was incandescent. After some rudimentary lessons from celebrity photographer Nickolas Muray, he blew out all the fuses on the floor of his apartment building at 150 West 55th Street during

PHOTOGRAPH BY SAUL MAURIBER, 1944

an early attempt at lighting. Then he had the place rewired for heavy duty and installed a darkroom in the servant's quarters of the flat he and Fania Marinoff shared.

Behind him lay several successful vocations. Before World War I he had become America's first dance critic, writing regularly about Anna Pavlova, Isadora Duncan, and Vaslav Nijinsky, and latter-day dance critics Edwin Denby and John Martin both acknowledged their debt to Van Vechten's early assessments. As a music critic, he had been first in America to endorse Igor Stravinsky and Erik Satie, and as early as January 1917 he had pronounced ragtime and jazz "the only music produced in America to-day . . . on which the musicians of this land can build . . . in the future."[2] That's about seven years before he became the first critic to champion the music of George Gershwin. As a literary critic he was Gertrude Stein's persistent advocate from 1913, and arguably he was second and maybe first to rediscover Herman Melville's *Moby-Dick* in 1920. He wrote *The Tiger in the House*, the best book ever written about the domestic cat. With the advent of the "Splendid Drunken Twenties," as he later dubbed the prohibition decade, he turned out several popular novels, including *Nigger Heaven* in 1926, which spurred interest in Harlem speakeasies as well as in young African-American writers, popularizing among white slummers and some white readers what has come to be called the Harlem Renaissance. After compiling volumes of his musical and literary criticism and of some autobiographical essays, he gave up writing almost entirely and turned to photography as a full-time occupation.

*Occupation* or *hobby*, indeed, is a more appropriate designation than *career* or *profession*, because Van Vechten never took commissions, he never sold his photographs, he only granted permission to publish them when he was assured of the quality of reproduction in periodicals and other news organs, he never photographed anybody he didn't want to photograph, and he gave away his multiple copies of his prints to their subjects and to friends. Moreover, the scope of sittings varied widely: he made four or five photographs of Myra Hess, but over a period of years he made four or five hundred photographs of Alicia Markova. A few years later, he began to establish impressive photographic archives to accompany his gifts of books and manuscripts to libraries, and he continued this activity until his death.

The archive in the Beinecke includes a number of photographs of women, some of whom comprise the library's current exhibition. Often Van Vechten printed these up as postcards—sometimes unidentified—to use for casual correspondence. "Who is the nice looking cullud lady you sent me two or three

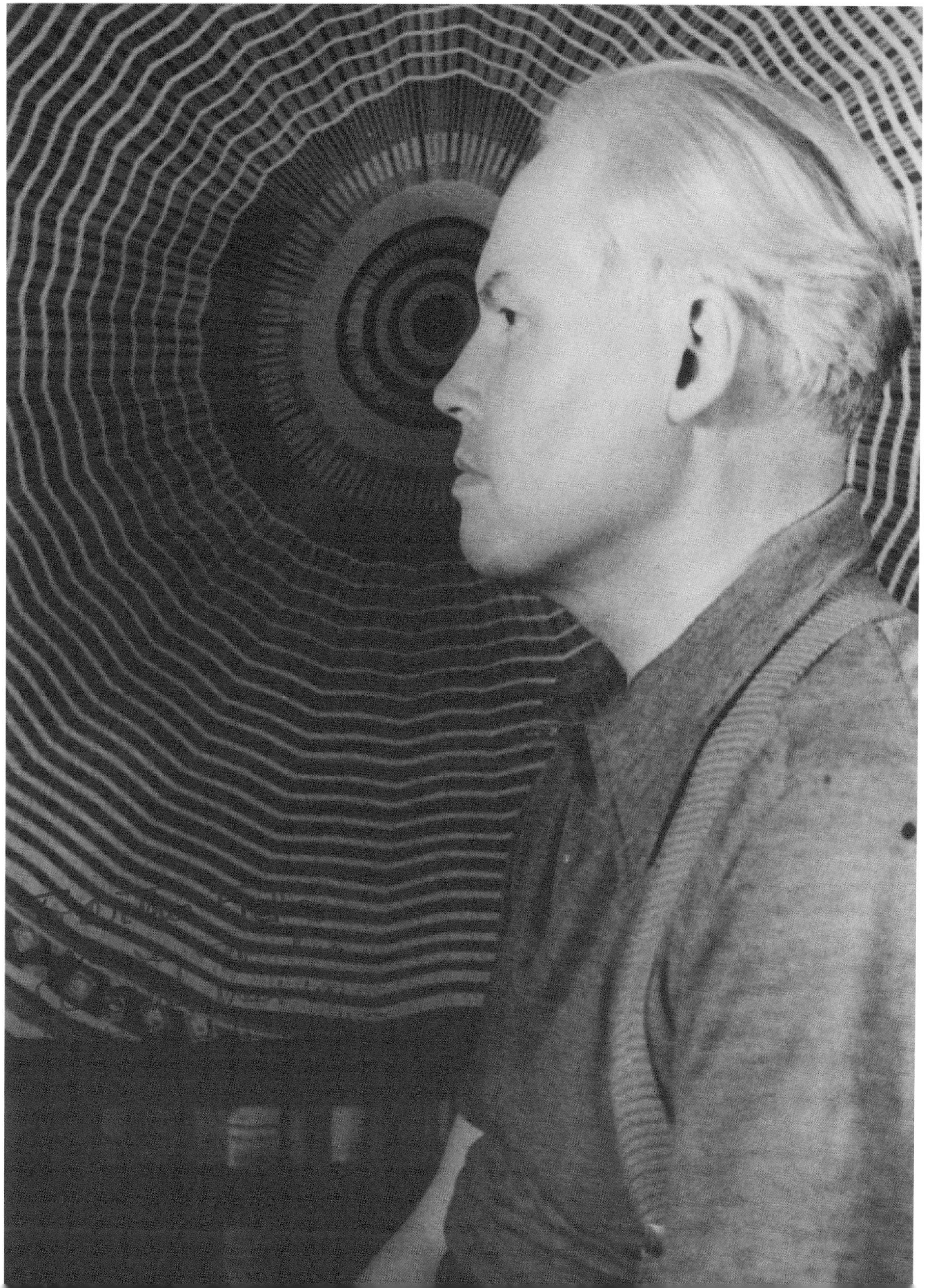

SELF-PORTRAIT, SEPTEMBER 19, 1934

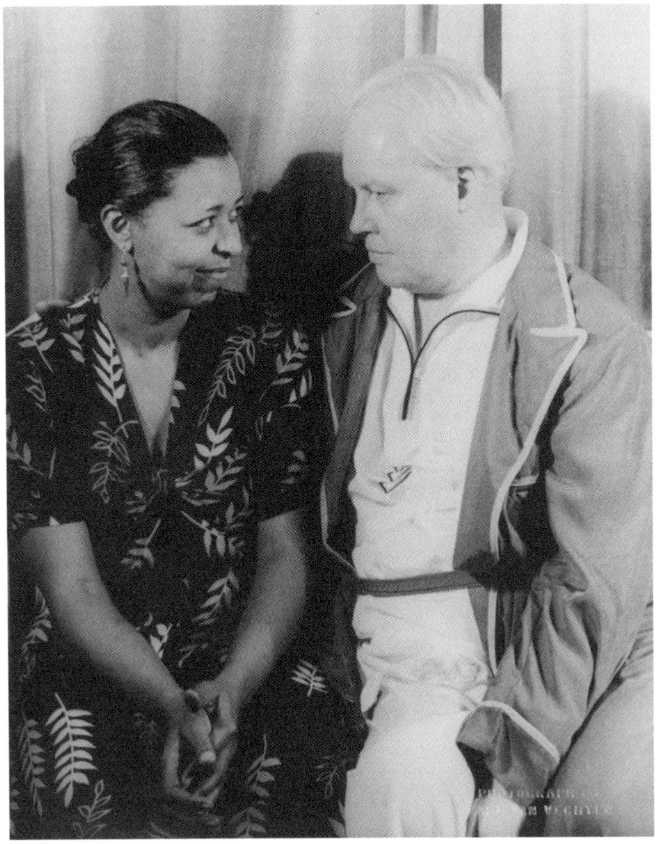

times now on a postal card . . . " Langston Hughes once queried. "Dear Langston," Van Vechten replied, "I send out so many postcards every day and 'nice cullud lady' describes a good many of them. It would even fit Lena Horne."[3] He had photographed her when she was still in her teens, as he would later photograph Diahann Carroll at about the same age.

If the identity of a Van Vechten portrait could prove temporarily mysterious, the photographer could not. There was almost always a distinctive look to his work, borne in part of his use of multi-patterned backgrounds, usually reflecting a subject's profession or personality or both. He had a fondness for profiles and pensive stares, in the beginning strong contrasts in lighting that suggest the soignée art deco that marked the Thirties, and he liked photographing women with flowers. He never retouched his photographs, and he did not approve of cropping designed to intensify some dramatic effect. Photographs were compositions in his view, and he intended them, he often claimed, to be documents.

At first, his chiaroscuro was so intense that the black and white design of the lighting often threatened to overwhelm the subject. Once past this period of experiment, however, his work did grow more documentary, as his collections grew: the James Weldon Johnson Memorial Collection of American Negro Arts and Letters at Yale University; composers and musicians for the George Gershwin Memorial Collection at Fisk University; writers for the Berg Collection in the New York Public Library; dancers for both the Lincoln Center Library of the Performing Arts and the Museum of Modern Art; actors and others connected with the theater for the Museum of the City of New York; more general collections for several other institutions, including the Moorland-Spingarn Library at Howard University, the Detroit Public Library, the Chicago Art Institute, even his high school in Cedar Rapids, Iowa, and on his death collections to Brandeis University, the Library of Congress, and a full run of his photographs to Yale, where the Beinecke Library shelters all of his negatives and contact prints.

Van Vechten once declared that he "threw away anything that isn't perfection,"[4] but his photographs often deny this claim. He could be his own worst enemy in the darkroom by not

VAN VECHTEN AND ETHEL WATERS PHOTOGRAPHED BY SAUL MAURIBER ON FEBRUARY 19, 1939 always washing his prints free of developing chemicals, in his eagerness to share his latest work with his friends. Also, he generally printed up every frame he took rather than selecting the best one from a batch of proofs. As a result of these indiscretions, borne of his enthusiasm, there are better and worse Van Vechten photographs around. But his best work justifies the admiring endorsements of two of his contemporaries who knew what they were talking about: photographer Alfred Stieglitz and art critic Henry McBride. Moreover, Van Vechten's noble profile of Gertrude Stein, his pensive Bessie Smith, and at least two of his photographs of Zora Neale Hurston—one of them on this year's Black Heritage postage stamp—are sufficiently familiar to qualify as national icons.

Other photographs in the Beinecke's collection are equally beautiful, if less familiar. Some of them in the current exhibition have never been shown or reproduced before. Many of them bear out Van Vechten's claim, "I am an intense believer in 'the exact second' and watch for it closely when I make photographs." Even so, he could be equally proud of "natural errors and fortunate accidents." Some of the latter may have occurred as the result of alarm, since Van Vechten was not always able to put his subjects at their immediate ease, despite his earnest efforts. In his youth, enormous buck teeth severely marred his handsome features; in maturity, they inspired more than one person to liken him to some member of the animal kingdom: "an amiable walrus," "a wild boar," "a scary werewolf." He barked a lot too, between photographs—"Woof! Woof!"—if he was having a good time. Often still wearing his silk pajamas under an elaborate dressing gown, or togged out in lively striped silk shirts that clashed with multi-colored neckties, and beltless trousers held in place up to his armpits by pink suspenders decorated with naked ladies, or flowered ones in red and purple, his bracelets jangling, his sparse white hair eventually combed forward into bangs above his embalmed stare, more penetrating than the eye of his Leica, he weaved and waited for that "exact second."

In his best work, Carl Van Vechten fixed time long past, and place long retired into memory, in glamorous photographs which, he insisted, were "intended primarily as documents." But he believed, too, "that is no reason they should not be beautiful."

1 "Brains for the Asking"
May 1943, manuscript
Van Vechten Papers
Beinecke Library
Yale University

2 "The Great American Composer"
*Interpreters and Interpretations*
NY: Knopf, 1917
p. 279

3 Hughes to Van Vechten
18 Sept. 1947;
Van Vechten to Hughes
19 Sept. 1947
*Remember Me to Harlem: The Letters of Langston Hughes and Carl Van Vechtan, 1925-1964*
Ed., Emily Bernard
NY: Knopf, 2001
pp. 248-49

4 "A Rudimentary Narration"
Columbia University
Oral History Collection
1962, *et seq.*

# GLADYS BENTLEY

## BLUES SINGER



There can be no doubt that Gladys Bentley was one of the more daring and dazzling figures of the Harlem Renaissance. A large woman who often dressed in a tuxedo or man's suit and tie when she performed, Gladys Bentley played piano and sang raucous, energetic, and loud blues songs in many of Harlem's best clubs. Her singular character and style made her a legend among blues aficionados.

Growing up in Philadelphia, Bentley was a muscular and masculine girl; by the time she reached adolescence, she knew that her attraction to women made her irreconcilably different from many of the people around her. As a result, she suffered harsh treatment from family, classmates, teachers, and even doctors who claimed they could "cure" her. She left home when she was sixteen.

Bentley moved to Harlem, where she found an underground social culture that included gambling, drug use, drag shows, and other behavior deemed illicit by the broader culture. In this so-called "sporting life," Bentley found the freedom to be an openly lesbian woman without risk of ridicule or abuse. She was not afraid to flaunt her lesbianism by flirting with women in her audiences and talking openly about her sexual escapades. Bentley even married a female lover in a very public ceremony.

She began performing at rent parties and in some of Harlem's marginal clubs and became a popular blues singer among Harlem's fringe community. In *The Big Sea*, Langston Hughes described her dynamic style during this period:

> Miss Bentley sat, and played a big piano all night long, literally all night, without stopping—singing songs like 'The St. James Infirmary' from ten in the evening until dawn, with scarcely a break between the notes, sliding from one song to another, with a powerful continuous underbeat of jungle rhythm."[1]

Bentley's salary increased considerably when desirable, white patrons, including Carl Van Vechten, started to come uptown to her shows. She began to play the Cotton Club and other more mainstream Harlem venues. These less "sporting" audiences didn't prevent Bentley from singing obscene songs and from creating her own salacious versions of popular tunes. Her style remained vibrant and rowdy. In *Parties*, Van Vechten modeled a blues performer on Bentley; "when she pounds the piano the dawn comes up like thunder," he wrote, "say, she rocks the box, and tosses it, you can bet, and jumps it through hoops."[2]

PHOTOGRAPHED IN HARLEM ON FEBRUARY 27, 1932

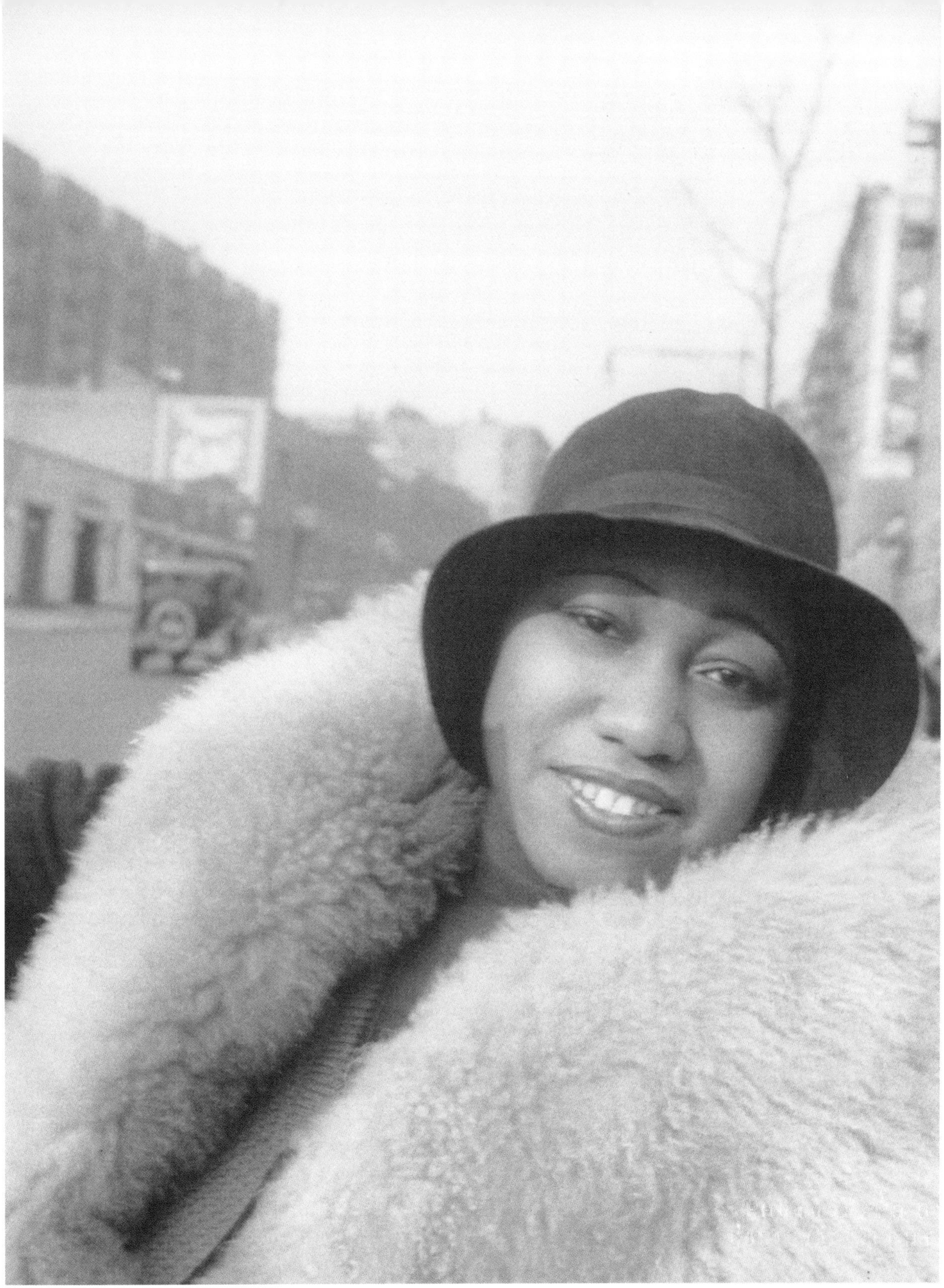

1 Langston Hughes
*The Big Sea*
NY: Knopf, 1940
pp. 225-26

2 Van Vechten
*Parties: Scenes From Contemporary New York Life*
NY: Knopf, 1930
p. 33

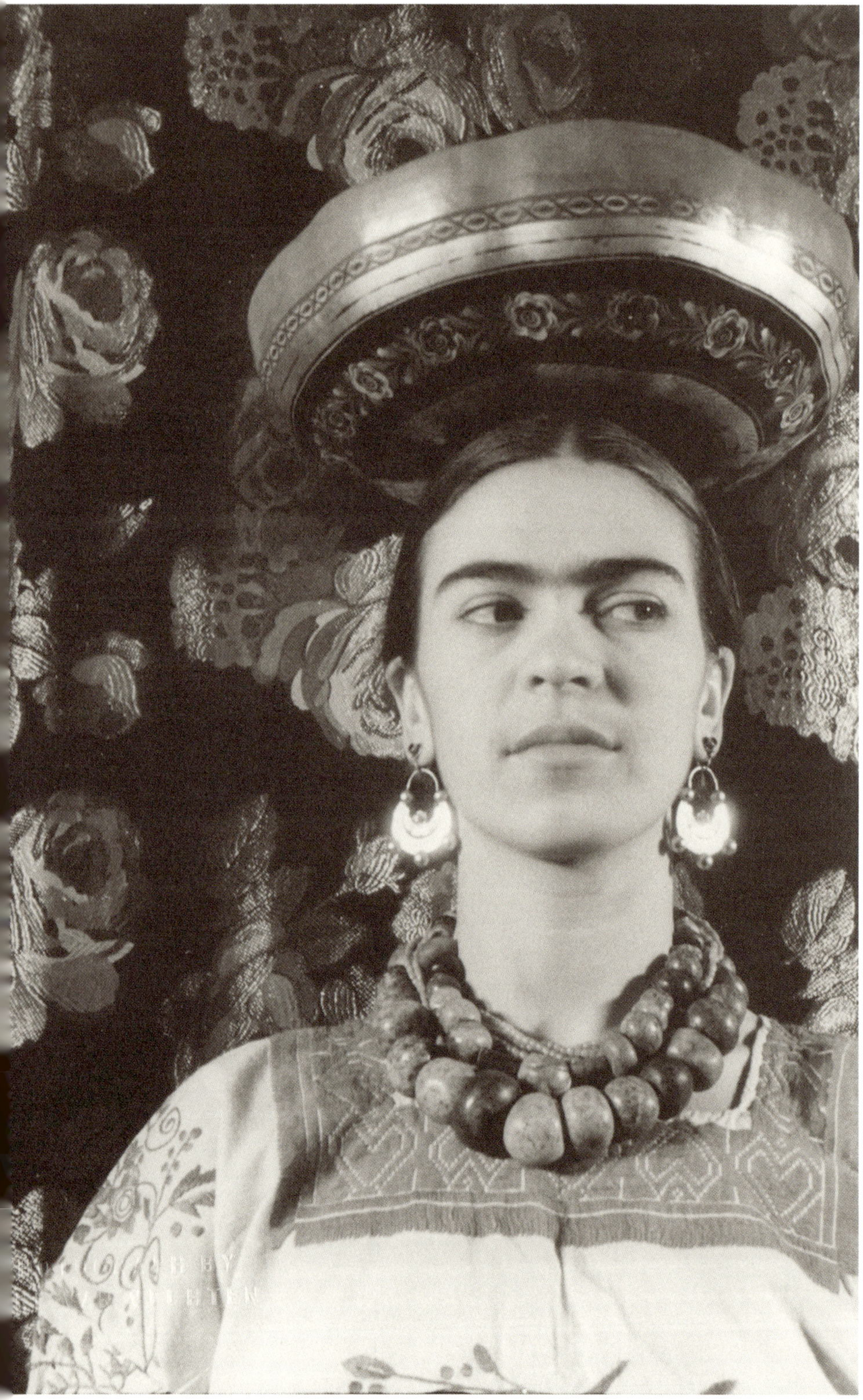

# FRIDA KAHLO

Though there were only two major public showings of her work during her lifetime, Frida Kahlo is widely admired and respected today as one of the finest painters to emerge from Mexico during the last century. Kahlo's distinctive self-portraits, which make up a significant portion of her oeuvre, have made her one of the most recognizable artists of the twentieth century. Her biography, like her work, has continually fascinated audiences and influenced artists.

Born outside Mexico City in the house where she would live for most of her life, Frida Kahlo was never formally trained as a painter. Her father, Guillermo Kahlo, was the son of Jewish immigrants from Germany; her mother, Matilde Caderòn, was of Spanish and Indian heritage. Her father, a well-known photographer, encouraged Kahlo's interest in art, her independent thinking, and her intellectual curiosity.

Kahlo suffered from significant physical pain as a result of disease and accident. A childhood bout with polio left both Kahlo's legs damaged. Ten years later, Kahlo was riding a bus that was struck by a trolley car and a piece of metal pierced her back and pelvis. Because she was bedridden for a prolonged recovery period, her parents customized an easel to allow her to paint while lying down. The injury caused Kahlo chronic pain and the need for frequent operations throughout her life, nearly forty in all.

PHOTOGRAPHED ON MARCH 19, 1932

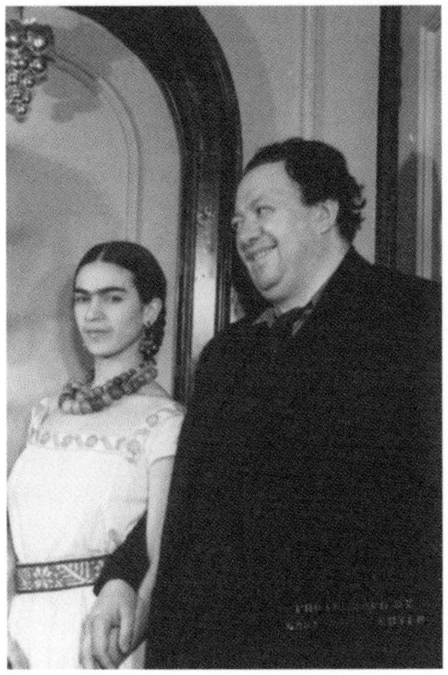

# ARTIST



Not long after her initial recovery, Kahlo joined the Young Communists League, a leftist political group that included many artists. The League was led by one of its founders, the famous Mexican mural painter, Diego Rivera. Though Rivera was nearly twice her age, Kahlo married him in 1929. Their marriage was an explosive one, full of dramatic fights, love affairs, a divorce, and a remarriage; Kahlo often referred to her union with Rivera as her second accident after the trolley car collision. She had affairs with both men and women, including a particularly famous relationship with Leon Trotsky, who briefly lived in her home. In spite of their difficulties, Kahlo longed to have children with her husband, but as a result of her complicated medical conditions she suffered numerous miscarriages. Regardless of these trials, the couple became the central figures of a circle of international artists and intellectuals in Mexico. They remained involved in leftist politics and activism throughout their lives and both painters explored their convictions in their art.

Among the artists Kahlo associated with were noted surrealists, including André Breton. Though she resisted the label, Kahlo was often linked with the surrealist painters and her work was shown in Europe in that context. Her bold, colorful paintings demonstrate her interest in indigenous traditions and Mexican culture. Her art often incorporates elements of Mexican mythologies and in many self-portraits Kahlo wears native clothing and jewelry. Her self-portraits are often described as feminist explorations of sexuality, pain, violence, and grief. Late in her life Kahlo became addicted to pain medication and her painting suffered; works from this period lack the clarity and precision of her earlier canvases.

Though many embrace Kahlo as a pioneering feminist artist, others have minimized the attention her work has achieved as merely the result of interest in her life and personality. Some contend that Kahlo was a "one painting painter," whose self-absorbed work fails to achieve anything beyond autobiographical expression. These critics claim that problematic elements in the painter's biography have been overlooked—such as her feverish devotion to Stalin and the likelihood that many of her operations were unnecessary attempts to gain her husband's attentions—in order to make her a feminist hero.

In any case, there can be no argument with the powerful influence her work has had in the art world of the late twentieth century. The subject of several major exhibitions, biographies, and a Hollywood film, Kahlo has become an icon of feminist art and Mexican cultural patriotism.

PHOTOGRAPHED WITH HER HUSBAND, DIEGO RIVERA, ON MARCH 19, 1932

# BLANCHE KNOPF

A native New Yorker, Blanche Wolf Knopf met her husband, Alfred A. Knopf, in 1911 when he was a senior at Columbia University and an aspiring publisher. Blanche shared Alfred's ambition to start a publishing house, and they were soon engaged. The two realized their goal in 1915, starting their press with five thousand dollars from Alfred A. Knopf's father and space in his New York office. The couple married in 1916. That year, they published Carl Van Vechten's book, *Music and Bad Manners*. In all, the Knopfs would publish nearly twenty books by Carl Van Vechten.

Van Vechten to Blanche Knopf 1
May 1929
*Letters of Carl Van Vechten*
Ed., Bruce Kellner
New Haven: Yale, 1987
pp. 106-7

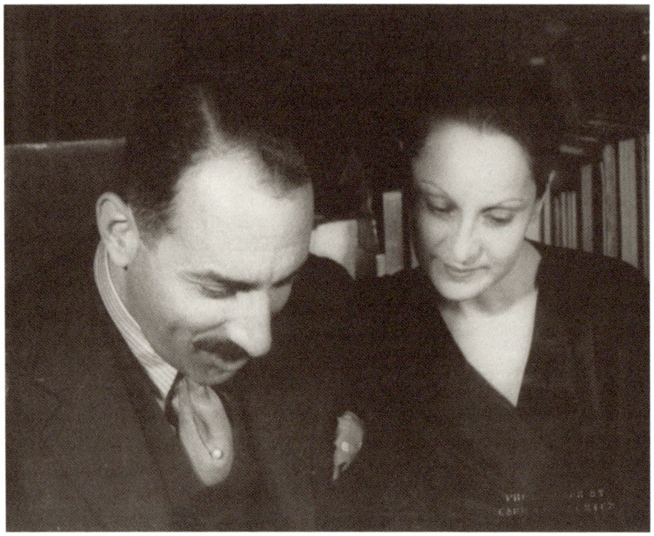

PHOTOGRAPHED WITH HER HUSBAND, ALFRED A. KNOPF, ON APRIL 4, 1932

In the press's early years, the Knopfs were involved in all aspects of the publishing process, from soliciting and editing manuscripts to designing and marketing books. From the beginning, Blanche was active in all areas of the business, including designing the Borzoi, a Russian wolfhound imprint marking Knopf titles. Blanche Knopf was soon vice president and director of the already thriving business and she earned a reputation as an influential and powerful editor. Throughout the more than fifty years Knopf worked in publishing, she was a force in shaping the American literary marketplace and the nature of American book publishing in the twentieth century. During her tenure with the firm, Knopf published the work of eleven Nobel Prize winners and eighteen Pulitzer Prize-winning titles.

Though Blanche Knopf is often associated with the European writers whose work she edited and published—Sigmund Freud, André Gide, Simone de Beauvoir and her close friend Albert Camus—she also worked closely with many American writers. These writers included Willa Cather, H.L. Mencken, Langston Hughes, and, not least, Carl Van Vechten. In the 1920s, Van Vechten encouraged the Knopfs to publish the work of a number of talented African-American writers, including Langston Hughes and Nella Larsen. By publishing the work of these influential writers, the Knopfs, like Van Vechten, were important participants in and supporters of the literature of the Harlem Renaissance.

# EDITOR & PUBLISHER

Blanche Knopf and Carl Van Vechten shared a complex, multi-faceted relationship. Though they were dear friends and collaborators, they were also editor and writer, publisher and literary promoter. Their working relationship sometimes required difficult negotiations over details of Van Vechten's books and their publication, translation, and distribution. As an advocate for the African-American poets and novelists he hoped the Knopfs would publish, Van Vechten was regularly involved with the editing and publishing of books by these writers.

Their working relationship enhanced their personal friendship; in 1918, Van Vechten dedicated his *The Music of Spain* to Knopf. His fondness for Blanche Knopf is further evident in his letters, in which he addresses her as "Grand Duchess" or "Blanchette," the endearing name he used in his dedication. In a May 1929 letter to Blanche Knopf, Van Vechten concluded with one of his unique signatures: "The carnations were long, the lilies were lovely, & so is Blanche. Carlo."[1]

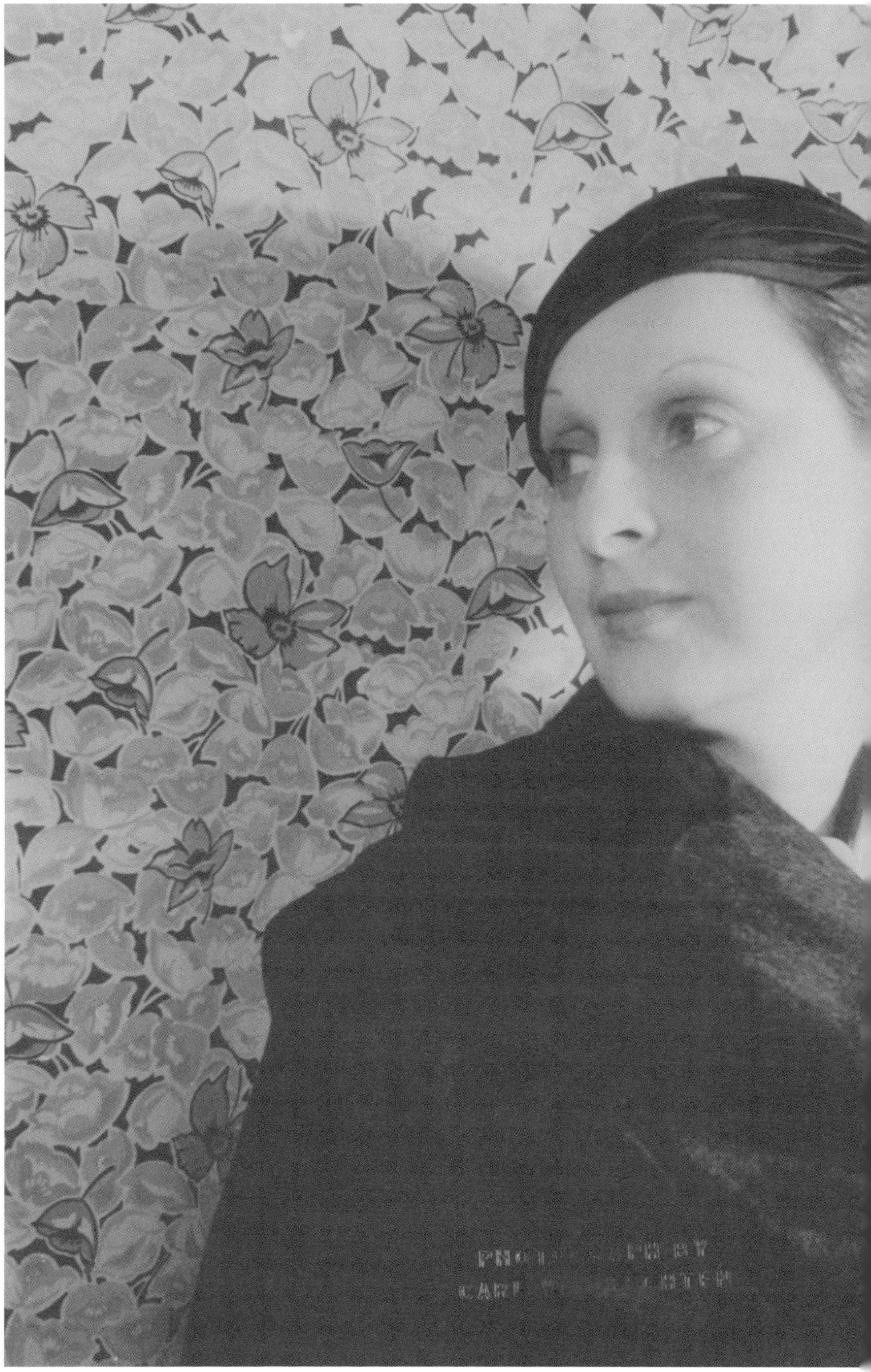

PHOTOGRAPHED ON APRIL 4, 1932

22 Anna May Wong, Hollywood's first Asian-American film star and a popular actress of the silent film era, was one of Carl Van Vechten's first subjects when he took up photography in earnest in 1932. Van Vechten, in fact, claimed that Wong was his very first subject.

Hailed as "one of the most unforgettable figures of Hollywood's great days,"[1] Anna May Wong, a native of Los Angeles, spent years skipping school to work as an extra in the movies before she was offered her first major role. In 1923 at the age of seventeen, she played Lotus Blossom, the romantic lead in *Toll of the Sea.* This film, the first Technicolor feature made in Hollywood, won Wong the attention of both critics and audiences. The part of Lotus Blossom was one of the few leading romantic roles she would play in Hollywood, where, to her great frustration, Wong was regularly offered only parts as stereotypical and unrealistic Asian characters.

The following year, Wong played an exotically beautiful slave girl in *The Thief of Baghdad* with Douglas Fairbanks. After the success of this film, Wong began to appear regularly in popular films. In spite of her increasing fame and her versatility as an actress, Wong's career was severely limited by the noxious roles she was offered—slave girls, evil dragon ladies, mysterious and exotic mistresses—all of which misrepresented Asian women. She was frustrated further by the tendency in Hollywood to cast white actresses in Asian roles. Later in her

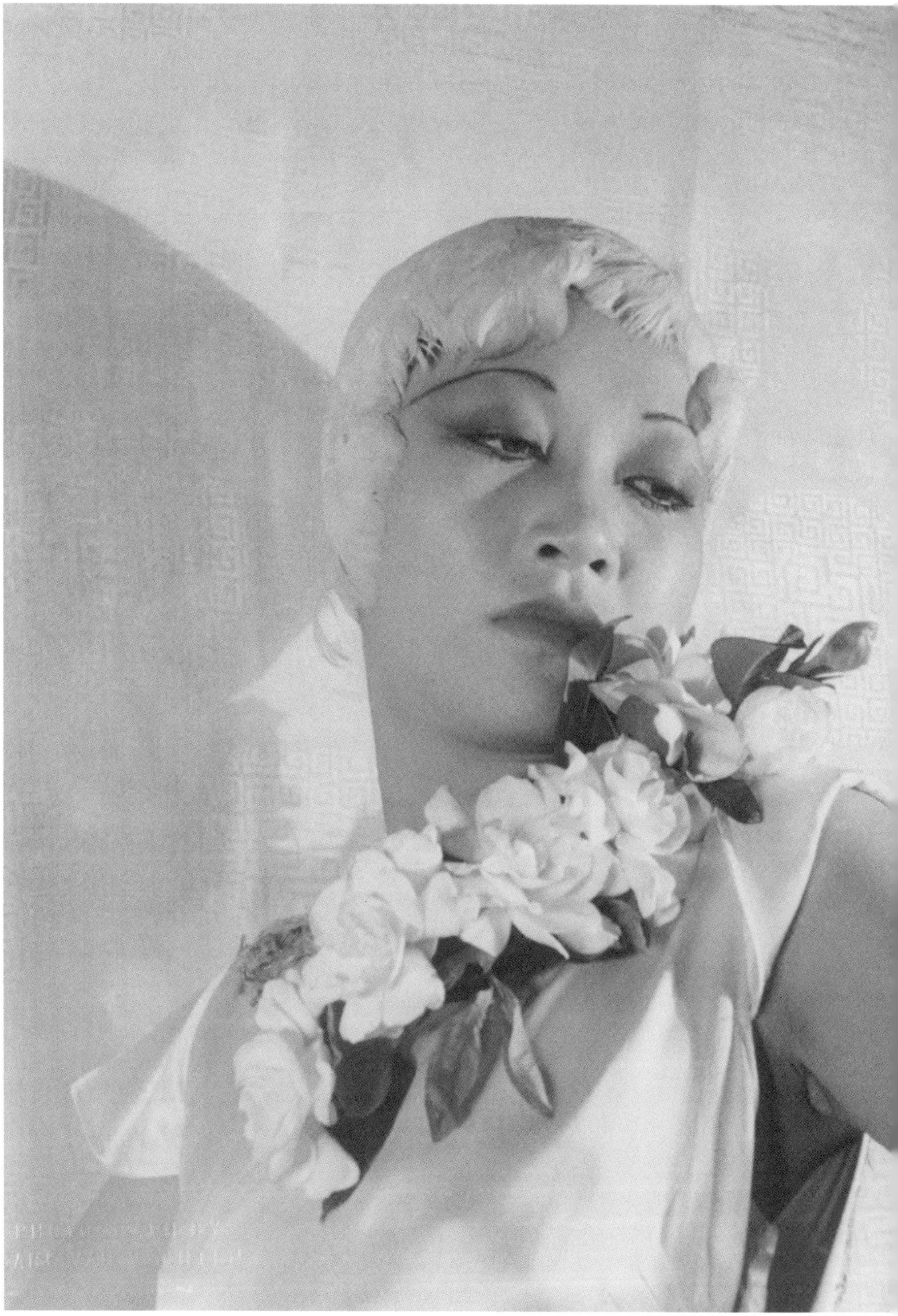

PHOTOGRAPHED ON APRIL 29, 1932

# ANNA MAY WONG

## ACTRESS

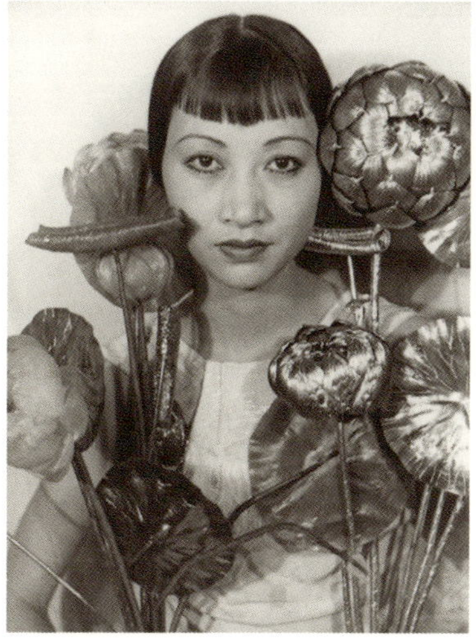

1 "Anna May Wong is Dead at 54"
*New York Times*
4 Feb. 1961

2 "Berlin Praises Miss Wong"
*New York Times*
22 Aug. 1928

3 Wong to Fania Marinoff
16 Dec. 1935
Van Vechten Papers
Beinecke Library
Yale University

4 Wong to Van Vechten
31 July 1932
Van Vechten Papers



career, Wong was sometimes hired by studios not to play Asian roles, but to coach white actresses in an effort to help them play more believable Asian women.

Disgusted with Hollywood, Wong traveled to Europe and made films in France, Germany, and England. She mastered the French and German languages so well that many thought her speech had been dubbed. European critics praised her for her "transcendent talent."[2] Throughout her career Wong pointed to the films she made in Europe, where she had the opportunity to play a wider range of characters, as evidence of her ability to play diverse roles.

When Wong returned to the United States she appeared in a number of successful films and theatrical productions, including her most celebrated film appearance, in *Shanghai Express* with Marlene Dietrich. Wong's performance was so highly praised that Dietrich was said to have complained she had been upstaged by her costar.

Wong planned to travel to China, but decided to put off the trip, hoping to play O-lan in a film adaptation of Pearl Buck's novel *The Good Earth*. The studio wanted Wong to play Lotus, the wicked concubine, while the lead role was to be played by German actress Luise Rainer. Wong was deeply disappointed by the studio's decision and refused the clichéd part. "Have made two tests for the Lotus part," Wong wrote to Fania Marinoff, "from all appearances Miss Rainer is definitely set for the part of O-lan. . . . I am still in the same frame of mind in regards to the thing and feel a strong inclination to carry out my original plans of going to China."[3]

Leaving Hollywood in frustration a second time, Wong traveled to China. There she met with harsh criticism from Chinese who felt her films degraded Chinese women. Though she studied Mandarin Chinese, Wong soon realize that she was too American to perform in the traditional Chinese theater. The irony of this, when in Hollywood's racist view she would never be American enough for many parts, was not lost on Wong. She returned to the United States, but stopped making films for many years. She was thirty-five.

Though Van Vechten's first photographs of Wong are among the most reproduced images of her, she was unsatisfied with them. "To tell you the truth," she wrote to the photographer, "I had much rather pose another time when I am not feeling so happy or when I look more fit. I am afraid I wasn't particularly interesting as a subject for your new art."[4]

PHOTOGRAPHED ON SEPTEMBER 22, 1935

# ETHEL WATERS

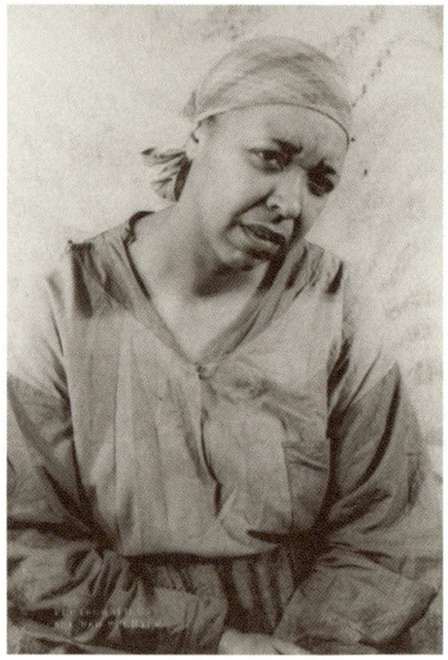

PHOTOGRAPHED ON AUGUST 28, 1938, IN "MAMBA'S DAUGHTERS"



A vibrant and versatile performer, Ethel Waters earned fame in Harlem nightclubs, on the Broadway stage, and in Hollywood films. She was so popular with audiences that at the height of her career Waters earned more money than any other woman on Broadway. Her long list of accomplishments includes many "firsts" for African Americans—she was the first African American to perform on the radio, the first to star with an all-white cast in a Broadway show, and the first to perform with white co-stars in the Deep South.

Waters's childhood in Chester, Pennsylvania, was difficult and often unhappy. Ethel Waters was conceived when her mother, twelve years old at the time, was brutally raped. Waters was sent to live with physically abusive relatives; they were devastatingly poor and she was sometimes forced to steal food rather than go hungry. When Waters was thirteen, her mother arranged her marriage to a much older man. The relationship was abusive and lasted only a year.

After making a living as a domestic worker, Waters began singing in local clubs; she was soon offered a chance to join a stage show in Baltimore, billed as "Sweet Mama Stringbean." Waters quickly distinguished herself from other popular African-American singers of the day, such as Bessie Smith and Ma Rainey, by performing the blues in a restrained, controlled manner that was nothing like the open, sweeping vocal style that was then popular.

Like Smith and other African-American performers of the time, Waters encountered the horrific effects of the Jim Crow laws while touring in the South. After a terrible car accident in Alabama, white doctors gave her only minimal treatment. Waters was unable to walk for nearly two months after the accident. In spite of a difficult recovery, she soon began to appear in popular Harlem clubs and to develop a following among their elite clientele. Waters also began to make records around this time; she would record more than two hundred songs during the course of her career.

Waters's success in clubs led to offers to perform in stage shows. Of her first major show, *Africana*, one critic wrote, "Miss Waters is a maiden of considerable personality, an all-engulfing smile and complete combination between eye and limb and admirers out front."[1] Accolades abounded for other shows as well: "Miss Ethel Waters [can] do no wrong," in *Rhapsody in Black*;[2] "The vibrant depth of Ethel Waters's voice, the perfection of her slow, poised singing, lift her scenes a notch above the comedy"[3] in a Berlin and Hart production of *As Thousands Cheer.*

Carl Van Vechten, who, Waters wrote, "was credited with knowing . . . more about Harlem than any other white man except the captain of the Harlem police station,"[4] met the singer when she was still known as Sweet Mama Stringbean; they liked one another immediately. Waters attended one of

1 "New Nubian Show at Daly's 64th Street" *New York Telegraph* 12 July 1927

2 Robert Garland "Cast and Miscast" *New York Telegraph* 5 May 1931

3 Peter Stirling Review of *As Thousands Cheer* *Philadelphia Recorder* 11 Sept. 1933

4 Ethel Waters and Charles Samuels *His Eye Is on the Sparrow* NY: Doubleday, 1951 p. 195

5 *His Eye Is on the Sparrow* p. 195

6 Bruce Kellner *Carl Van Vechten and the Irreverent Decades* Norman: Oklahoma, 1968 pp. 207-8

Van Vechten's elaborate parties, but she felt awkward amidst the fancy and expensive food and décor. "I told Carl the caviar looked like buckshot to me," she wrote, "and didn't taste much better."[5] Later she turned the tables, cooking a meal for him: "ham and mustard greens, lemon meringue pie and iced tea."[6] The two remained friends throughout their lives.

Waters continued to appear on stage and in films. She was nominated for an Academy Award in 1949 for her role in the film *Pinky*. In 1950 she starred on Broadway in *Member of the Wedding*, based on Carson McCuller's novel; many felt that this was her finest performance. She received a second Academy Award nomination for her role in the 1952 film version of that play. Just a few years later, Waters, who had always been a spiritual woman, began touring with the Billy Graham Crusade. She found evangelical performing rewarding and she sang with Graham's choir for many years.

Ethel Waters originated a vocal and performance style that would become the standard among jazz singers. Her work heavily influenced those who followed her, such as Ella Fitzgerald and Sarah Vaughan. Many of her signature songs—"Stormy Weather," "St. Louis Blues," and "His Eye Is on the Sparrow"—are still popular with jazz fans today.

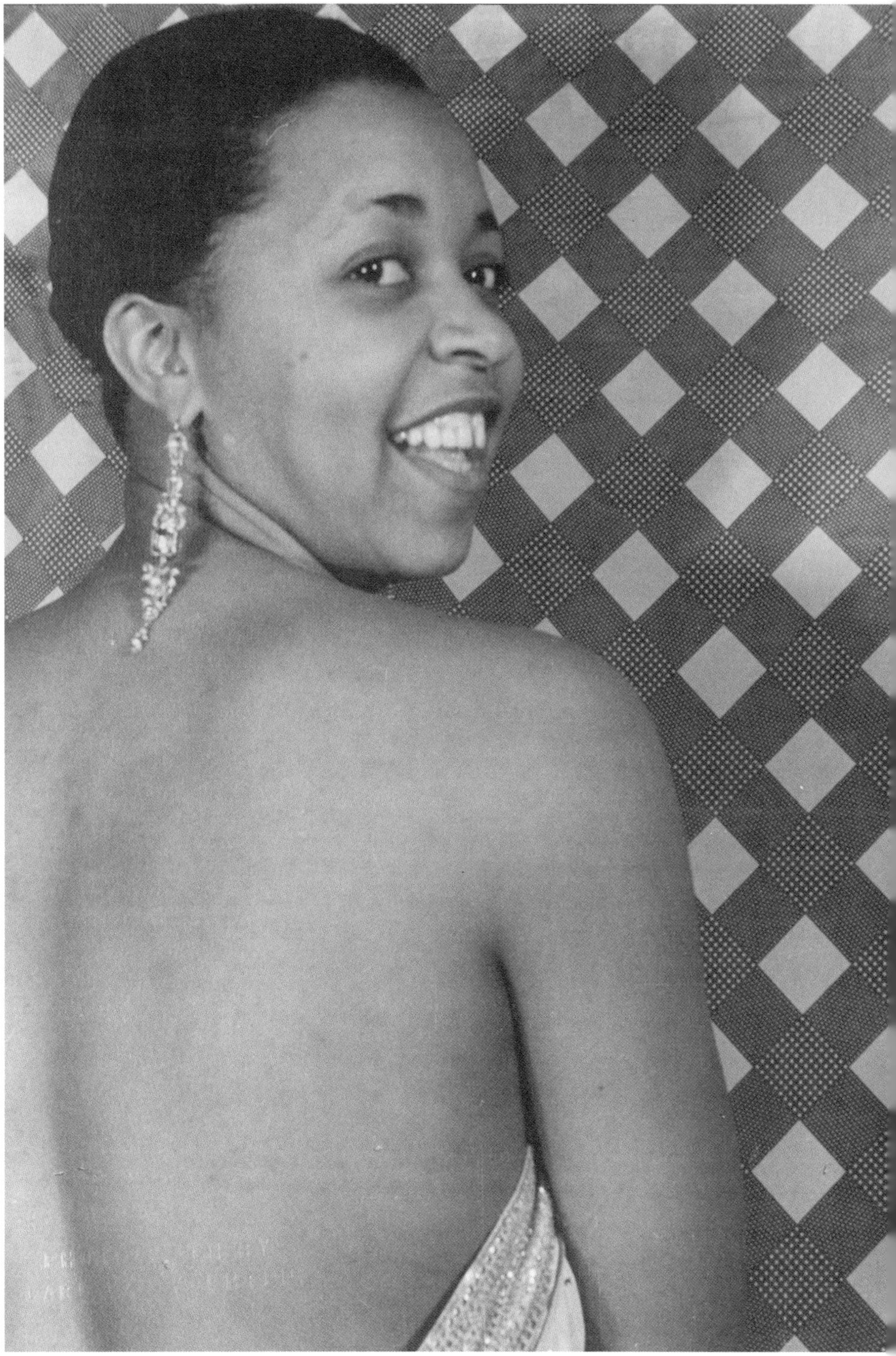

PHOTOGRAPHED ON JUNE 8, 1932

# HELEN MORGAN

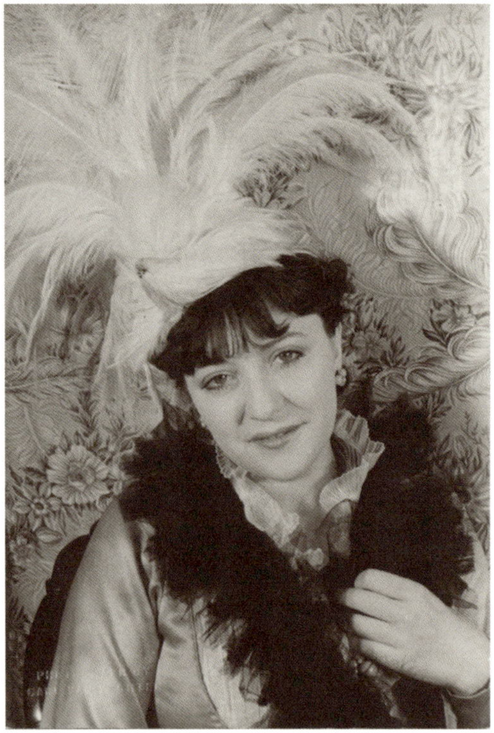



Bruce Kellner 1
*Carl Van Vechten and the Irreverent Decades*
Norman: Oklahoma, 1968
p. 260

Famous in her time as the most popular of all torch singers, Helen Morgan had a style—drinking a little too much, perching atop a piano, and singing sad songs of unrequited love—that became the model for all the others. Morgan's repertoire included many songs that have become closely associated with the performance style she perfected, songs like "Why Was I Born," "More than You Know," "Body and Soul," and "Don't Ever Leave Me."

As a young woman in Chicago, Helen Morgan worked as a manicurist to earn enough money to pay for singing lessons. She began her career singing in Chicago speakeasies before making her New York debut in a Ziegfeld production called *Sally*. She performed in clubs in both cites for several years—some of which were so small, she performed sitting on the piano because there was no room for her to stand on the stage. During this time, she developed her signature voice and performance style, which would be endlessly copied by other torch singers. In spite of her increasing popularity and financial success, Morgan drank heavily and spent money carelessly. Though on stage her boozy, grief-stricken persona was compelling to her audience, it was difficult to manage these traits in real life.

Today, Morgan is perhaps best remembered in the role of Julie in *Showboat*, a part she played on Broadway and in the 1936 film. It was in this role, after an evening performance, that Morgan became one of Carl Van Vechten's first photographic subjects. Already a little drunk when she arrived, Morgan asked her chauffeur to bring a bottle of brandy from her car after Van Vechten had taken only a few pictures. They drank and talked and Van Vechten photographed Morgan well into the night; "Helen did not depart until four-thirty in the morning," Van Vechten's friend, Donald Angus, remembered, "but during the interim Carl had captured both the bitterness and the ebullience of the story of her wretched life, which she told at length as the time passed and the brandy dwindled."[1]

PHOTOGRAPHED ON JUNE 23, 1932, AS JULIE IN "SHOWBOAT"

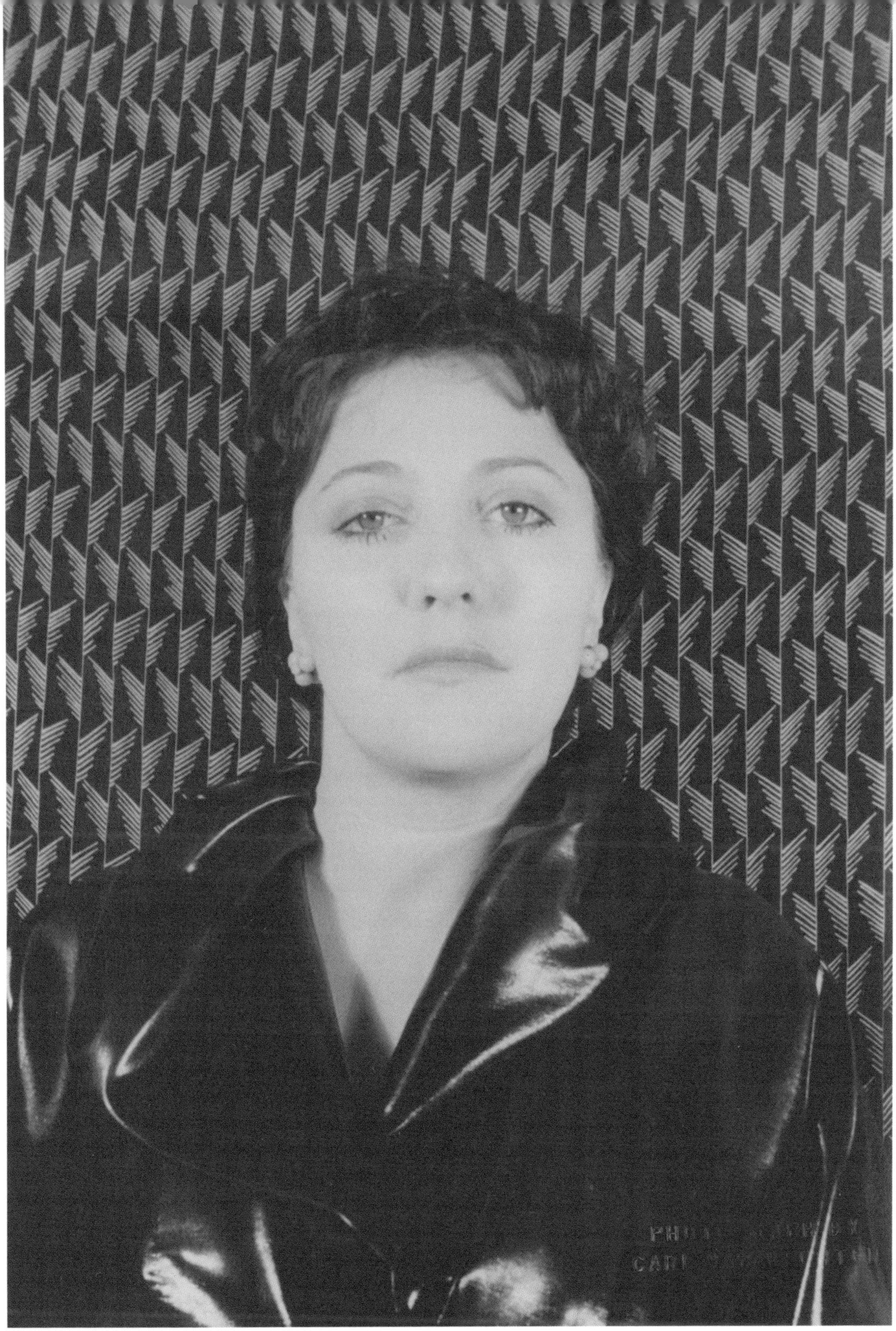

PHOTOGRAPHED ON JUNE 23, 1932

## SINGER & ACTRESS

## ACTRESS



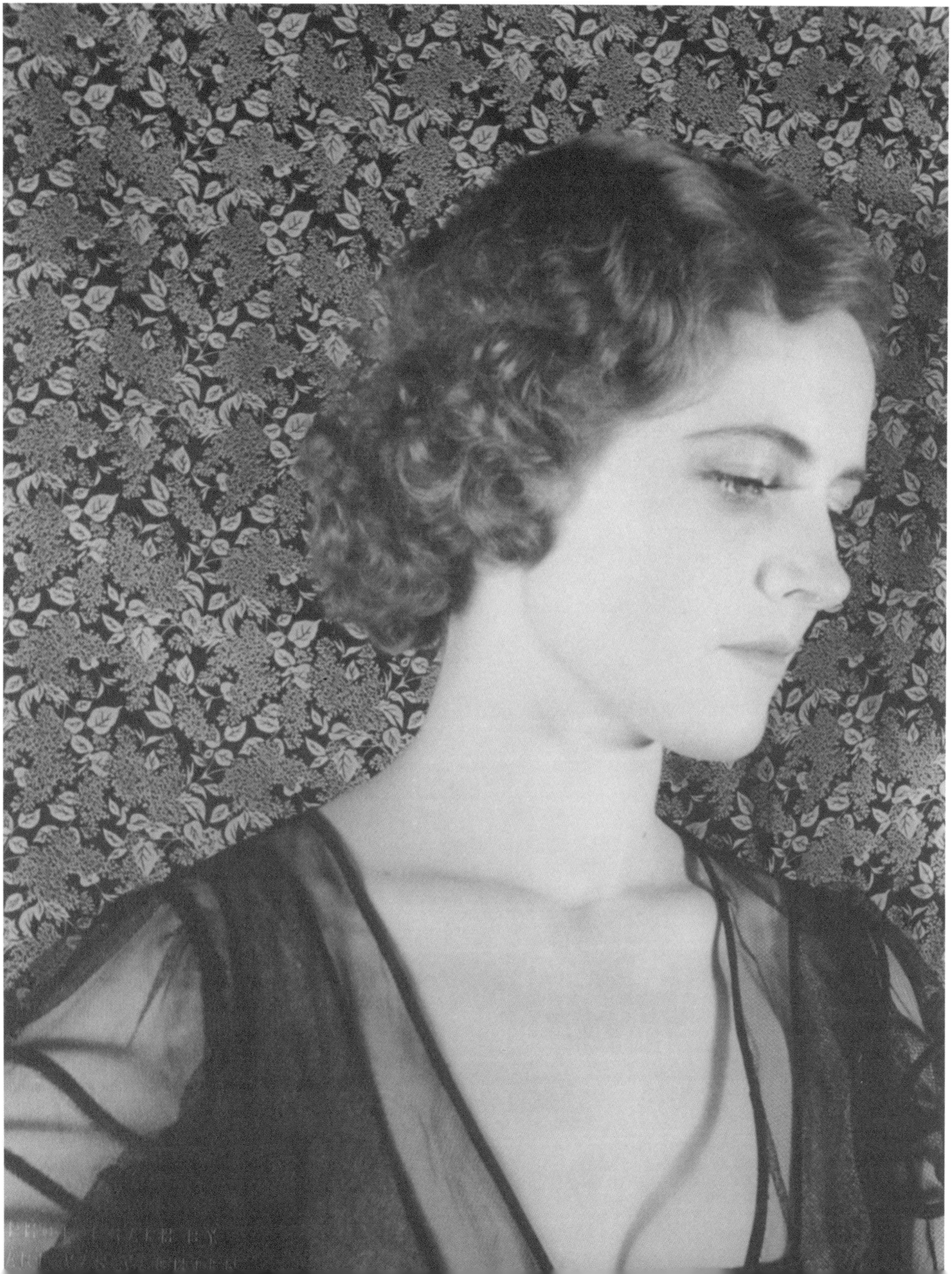

# LOIS MORAN

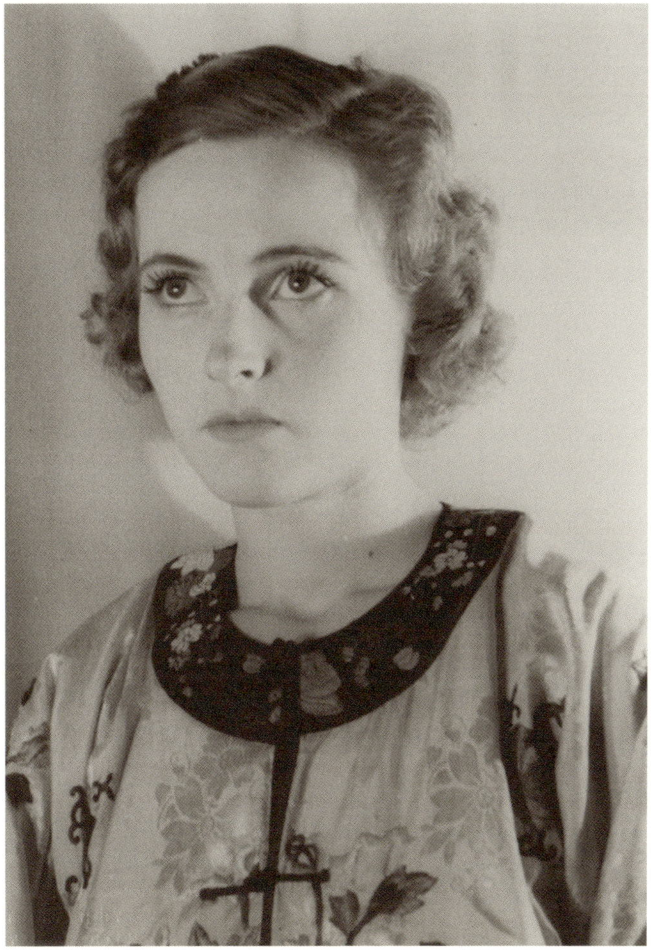

1 Mordaunt Hall
"Tears, Sighs, and Comicalities"
*New York Times*
12 June 1927

2 F. Scott Fitzgerald
*Tender is the Night*
NY: Scribner, 1933
pp. 1-2



Though she is not well known today, film and stage actress Lois Moran once epitomized the Hollywood starlet. "There is something different about her good looks," Mordaunt Hall wrote in 1927; "she is the personification of youth and beauty. She is not like the usual run of dolls' faces so prevalent in motion pictures. She is winsome, and wholesome, and earnest in her acting."[1]

Lois Moran was born and raised in Pennsylvania, but her acting career began in France, where she appeared in two films before she was discovered by American producer Sam Goldwyn. Goldwyn, who was traveling in Europe in hopes of finding a girl to play Juliet in a film adaptation of *Romeo and Juliet*, decided to make *Stella Dallas* instead and cast Moran as Laurel. She made a number of films in the late 1920s before embarking on a stage career in the early 1930s. She appeared as Emma Krull, the lead role in Robert E. Sherwood's *This is New York* and this performance was followed by successful appearances in the Gershwins' play *Of Thee I Sing* and its sequel, *Let 'Em Eat Cake*.

Despite the fact that her films have been largely forgotten, Lois Moran has been immortalized as the supreme ingénue in American literature; she was F. Scott Fitzgerald's inspiration for Rosemary, the beautiful young actress in *Tender is the Night*. Fitzgerald, with whom Moran was at one time romantically involved, provides an exact portrait of Moran in the first pages of the novel, in his description of Rosemary as she arrives with her mother on the French Riviera:

She had magic in her pink palms and her cheeks lit to a lovely flame, like the thrilling flush of children after their cold baths in the evening. Her fine forehead sloped gently up to where her hair, bordering it like an armored shield, burst into lovelocks and waves and curlicues of ash blonde and gold, her eyes were bright, big, clear, wet, and shining, the color of her cheeks was real, breaking close to the surface from the strong young pump of her heart. Her body hovered delicately on the last edge of childhood—she was almost eighteen, nearly complete, but the dew was still on her.[2]

PHOTOGRAPHED ON JULY 7, 1932

# THE STETTHEIMER SISTERS



The daughters of wealthy German Jews, the Stettheimer sisters were raised in Rochester, New York. Their father deserted the family when they were children and, after two older siblings married and moved away, the three sisters, Carrie, Ettie, and Florine, and their mother Rosetta, became a close-knit family. Together with their mother, the Stettheimers lived and traveled in Europe for several years just after the turn of the century, often socializing with other expatriate Americans.

When it became clear that World War I was approaching, the Stettheimers returned to the United States and moved to a house on New York's Upper West Side. Shortly, their home became the premier New York salon, a center of the city's artistic and intellectual life. Regular guests of the Stettheimer sisters included artists such as Francis Picabia, Marcel Duchamp, Man Ray, Charles Demuth, Marsden Hartley, and writers and critics, including Henry McBride and Carl Van Vechten. The sisters also regularly threw parties at rented mansions on the New Jersey shore or in the country, taking their friends away from the city for long weekends.

The Stettheimers were "an exotic if somewhat strange trio: Ettie in red wig, brocades, and diamonds; Carrie, who dressed never in the fashions of the day but in the elegance of a past era; Florine in white satin pants."[1] They were all extremely fashionable, though often they appeared as though they were of another age. The Stettheimer sisters typified the idea of the "new woman" of the twentieth century, they "declared men impossible but worthy of flirtation. They wore pants, smoked cigarettes, disdained marriage, romance and children, and were constantly surrounded by artists and writers who were drawn to their soigné gatherings."[2] They were also ladylike to a fault.

In addition to their friendships with many of the most significant artists and writers of the time, each of the sisters was involved in the arts in her own right. Florine Stettheimer was a painter, and she is, today, the best known of the family. During her lifetime, however, she only rarely exhibited her work publicly and refused to sell any of her paintings. Because of these limitations, her work was largely unknown for much of the twentieth century. Nevertheless, she received a great deal of attention for the innovative costumes and sets she designed for *Four Saints in Three Acts*, the Gertrude Stein and Virgil Thomson opera produced in 1934. Made in large part of cellophane, Stettheimer's costumes and sets contributed to the "spirit of inspired madness" that permeated the production; her sets and costumes were described as "fantastically absurd."[3] Exhibitions of her paintings in recent years have introduced Florine Stettheimer's work to

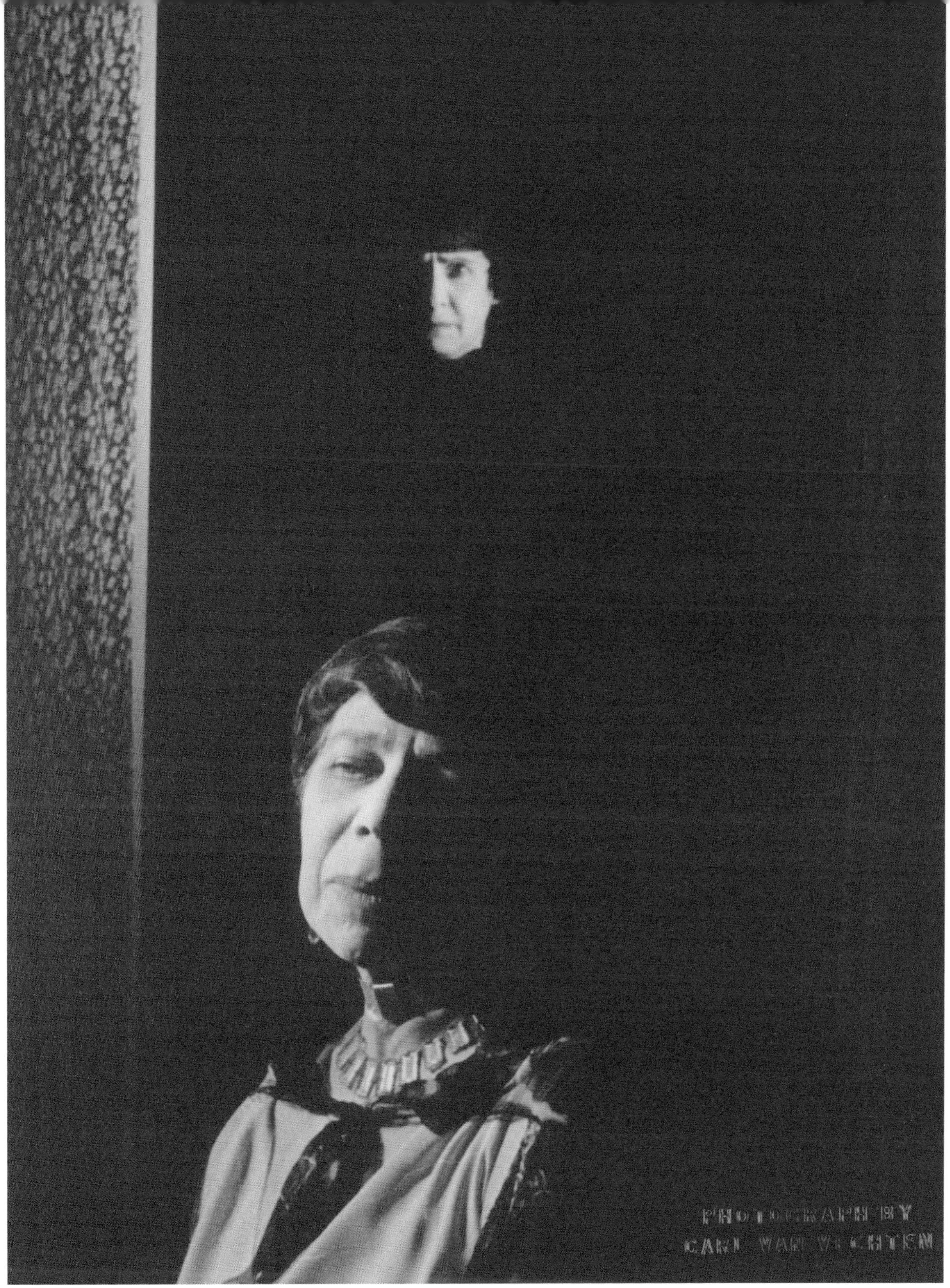

CARRIE WITH ETTIE AS MEDUSA, PHOTOGRAPHED ON OCTOBER 8, 1932

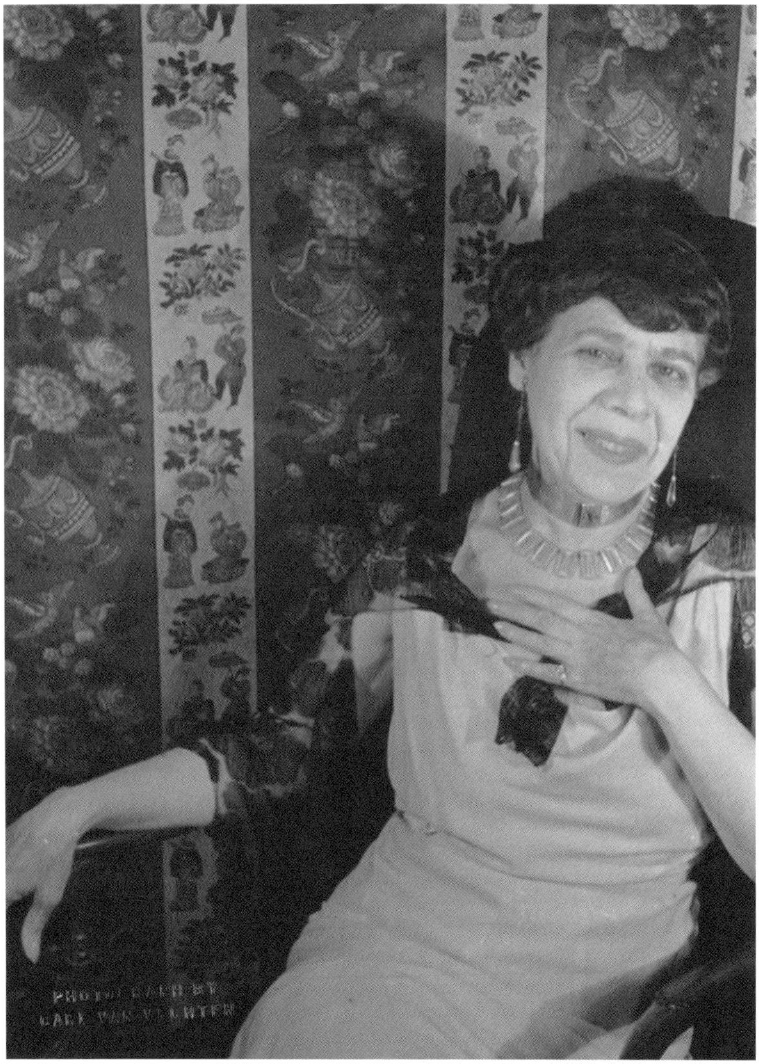

new audiences. Her witty, insightful, and vibrant portraits of her family and friends, including her portrait of Carl Van Vechten in his apartment, reveal a compelling picture of the Stettheimers, their circle, and the times in which they lived.

Ettie Stettheimer was a writer, publishing under the pseudonym Henrie Waste, a name drawn from her full name, Henrietta Walter Stettheimer. She wrote "two highly wrought novels, *Philosophy* and *Love Days* . . . that would certainly by today's standards be considered feminist in their insistence that woman's self-realization is incompatible with romantic love, and, in the case of *Love Days*, in the demonstration of the devastating results of the wrong sort of amorous attraction."[4] In his brief essay, "My Favorite Authors,"[5] Carl Van Vechten praised Ettie Stettheimer's writing and added her to his list of favorites.

In addition to the considerable artistry with which Carrie Stettheimer managed the Stettheimer household, planning imaginative meals including such unlikely dishes as feather soup, she created a replica of the sisters' home in miniature—a remarkable two story, sixteen-room dollhouse that recreated the Stettheimer's own imaginatively decorated rooms. Carrie Stettheimer worked on this project for more than twenty-five

## ETTIE STETTHEIMER, WRITER

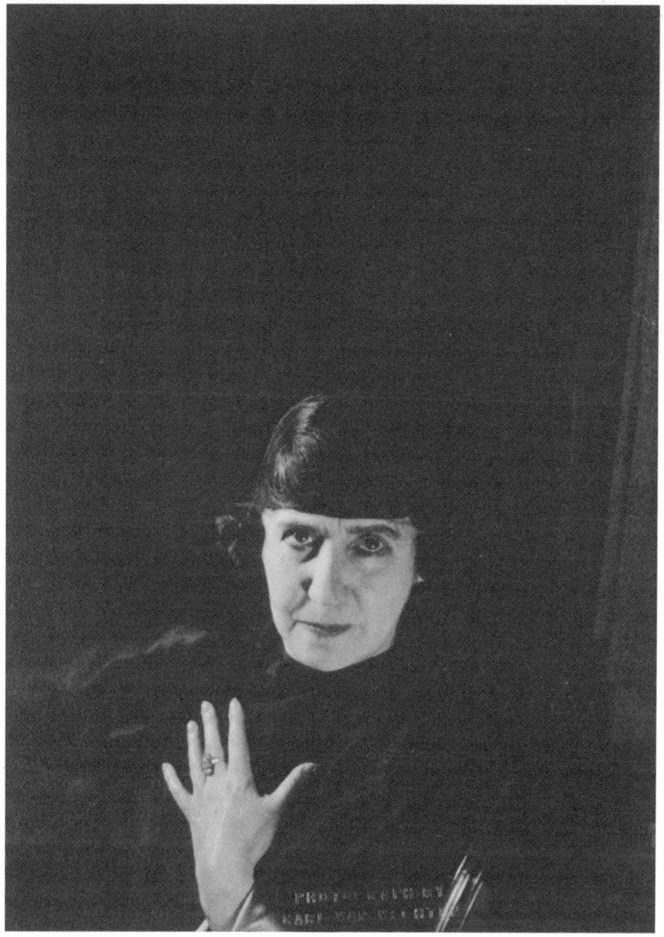

years, filling the dollhouse with detailed miniature reproductions of period furniture and replica light fixtures and lampshades. She recreated her sisters' rooms—Ettie's was painted in bright red and blue and outfitted with Chinese furniture; Florine's was draped in cellophane and lace. Artist friends made small copies of their paintings and sculptures for the dollhouse including the miniature copy Marcel Duchamp made of his *Nude Descending a Staircase*. Carrie Stettheimer's dollhouse is on permanent display at the Museum of the City of New York.

Carl Van Vechten and the Stettheimer sisters became close friends during the height of their salon in the days just after World War I. Van Vechten, in fact, dedicated his *Sacred and Profane Memories* to the sisters, a gesture that thrilled them all. Though Florine Stettheimer preferred not to be photographed, Carrie and Ettie were among Van Vechten's earliest subjects and their double portraits are among the most unusual of all his compositions.



1 Bruce Kellner
*Carl Van Vechten and the Irreverent Decades*
Norman: Oklahoma, 1968
p. 119

2 Jean Nathan
"Doll House Party"
*New York Times*
16 July 1995

3 "Stein Opera Sung by All-Negro Cast"
*New York Times*
9 Feb. 1934

4 Linda Nochlin
"Florine Stettheimer: Rococo Subversive" in
*Florine Stettheimer: Manhattan Fantastica*
NY: Whitney Museum of American Art, 1995
p. 97

5 Van Vechten
"My Favorite Authors"
Privately Published 1985

PHOTOGRAPHED ON OCTOBER 8, 1932

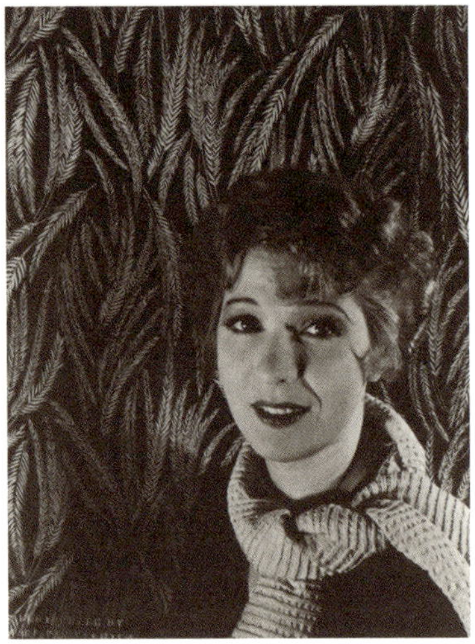

# INA CLAIRE



Ina Claire was among the first of Carl Van Vechten's subjects when he began taking portraits in 1932. The following year, *Town and Country* published four Van Vechten portraits of famous women: actress Judith Anderson, writer Fannie Hurst, Ona Munson, the wife of painter Eugène Berman, and Ina Claire.[1]

Born in 1892, Claire began her show business career in vaudeville at the age of thirteen. She eventually appeared in several musical comedies and in the Ziegfeld Follies. Her 1917 appearance in *Polly with a Past* established her as one of America's best comediennes. Claire also made several films; her most memorable roles include Grand Duchess Swana in *Ninotchka* (1939), and Ethel Barrymore in *The Royal Family* (1930).

Claire established herself as a star from her first appearances on the stage. Her 1911 performance in *The Quaker Girl* garnered her immediate attention, including from a young schoolboy, F. Scott Fitzgerald. In later years, he stated that he felt a "melancholy love" for her and Gertrude Bryan, who were intertwined in his mind as "the girl," a symbol for New York and romance.[2] When Fitzgerald decided to write a film treatment of *Tender Is the Night* in 1934, he dreamed of casting Claire as Baby Warren.[3]

During her lifetime, Claire was regarded as one of the finest comic performers on the American stage. In his review of S.N. Behrman's *Biography*, Brooks Atkinson wrote in the *New York Times* on December 13, 1932, "Miss Claire plays with dignity, wit, poise and dexterity," calling her performance "radiant [and] heady." In the *New York Post* of the same date, John Mason Brown stated, "Miss Claire is the ablest comedienne our theatre knows. . . . Her playing has about it the brilliance of a diamond. It is all sparkle and light."

Claire was known for a style that combined carefully planned stage movements with flexibility and spontaneity. She took her comic technique seriously, stating, "There is not a minute that a comedienne may rest. If she halts for a second something seems to come over the footlights to tell her that the mood is not going across. Then she must do something."[4]

PHOTOGRAPHED ON OCTOBER 31, 1932

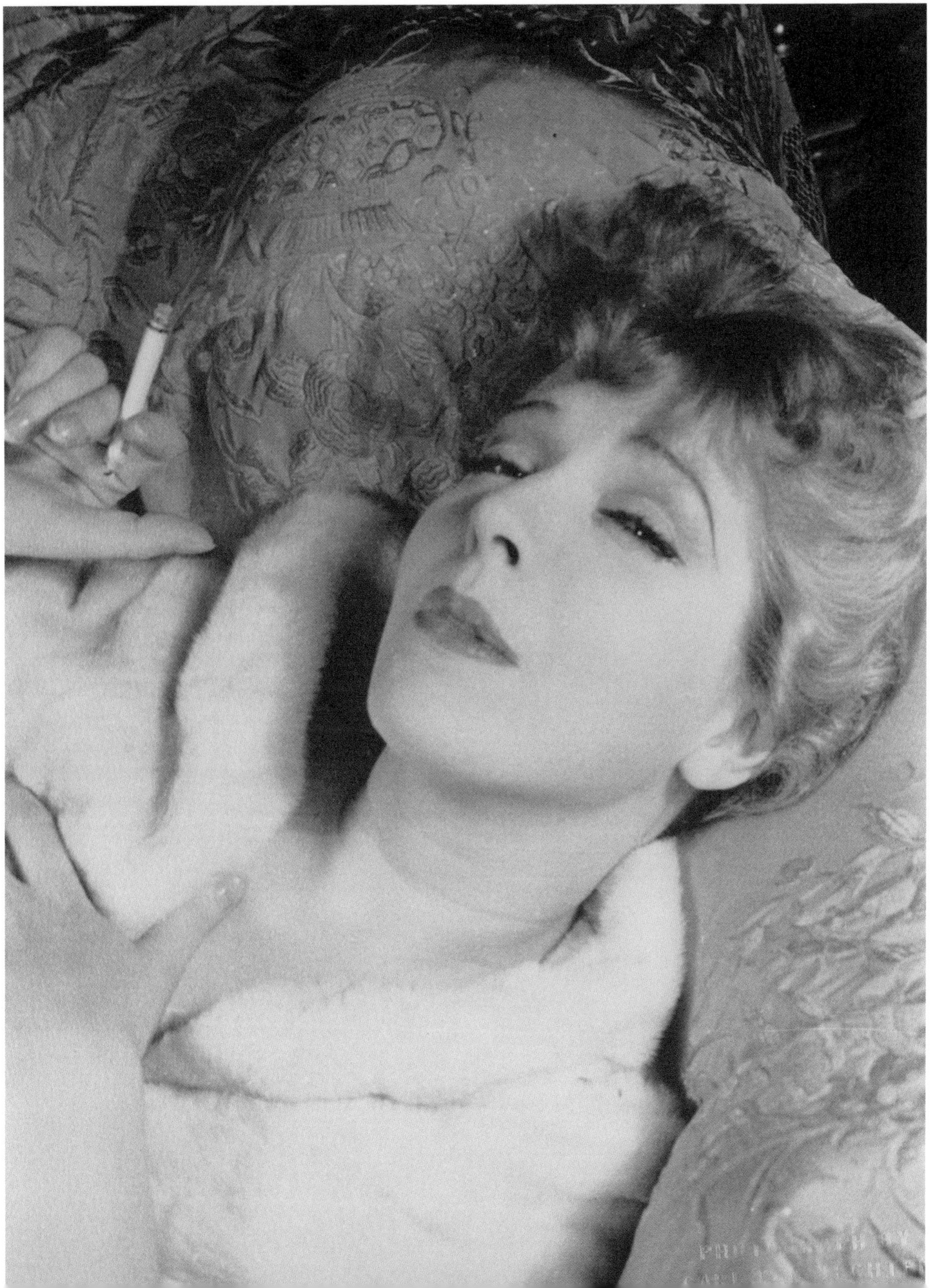

## ACTRESS




1 Bruce Kellner
*Carl Van Vechten and the Irreverent Decades*
Norman: Oklahoma, 1968
p. 261

2 James R. Mellow
*Invented Lives: F. Scott & Zelda Fitzgerald*
Boston: Houghton Mifflin 1984
p. 91

3 Aaron Latham
*Crazy Sundays: F. Scott Fitzgerald in Hollywood*
NY: Viking, 1970
p. 86

4 Peter B. Flint
"Ina Claire, 92, Who Brought Comic Artistry to Stage Roles"
*New York Times*
23 Feb. 1985

# SOCIAL ACTIVIST



Today, Grace Nail Johnson is best known as the wife of poet, essayist, and civil rights activist James Weldon Johnson. She was, however, a powerful and influential advocate for social change in her own right. Like her husband, Johnson was committed to encouraging African-American writers and artists and to supporting research in African-American culture.

Grace Nail, the daughter of a wealthy and well-respected New York family, met her future husband when she was a teenager. Fifteen years her senior, James Weldon Johnson was then living in Puerto Cabello, Venezuela, as the United States consul; they met when Johnson made a brief visit to New York City. Johnson courted Grace Nail from Puerto Cabello and later from Corinto, Nicaragua, where he became consul in 1908. After they married in New York in 1910, Grace Neil Johnson joined her husband in Nicaragua. The people of Corinto welcomed Grace Johnson with an unusual gift—a yellow parrot named LuLu. When she returned to the United States, Johnson took the bird with her and she kept the pet for the rest of her life. LuLu, in fact, outlived Johnson by some twenty years.

When they returned to New York, the Johnson's moved to Harlem, where they became central figures of the Harlem Renaissance. Grace Johnson was one of the most celebrated hostesses of the time, entertaining the African-American political and artistic elite. In addition, Mrs. Johnson worked in support

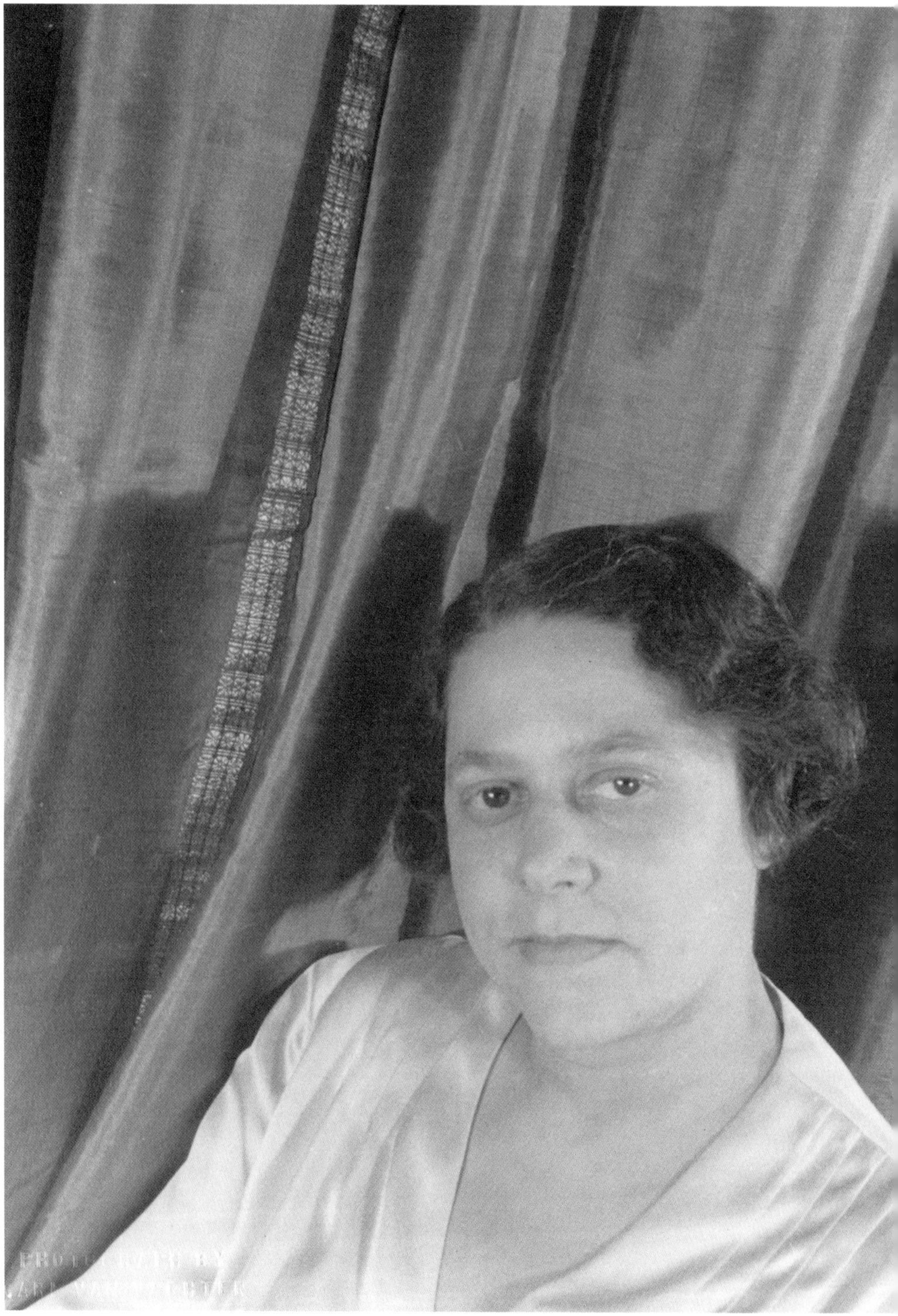

PHOTOGRAPHED ON DECEMBER 3, 1932

# GRACE NAIL JOHNSON

of a number of important civil rights groups, fighting for equal job opportunities for men and women of color, and for equal pay for African-American workers, most of whom then made significantly less than their white counterparts in the same fields. As a result of her valuable work, her high profile, and her generous spirit, Johnson became a mentor to many younger African-American women.

When James Weldon Johnson was killed in a car accident in 1938, Grace Johnson continued to promote the ideal of social justice to which he had dedicated his life. As a result of her work, many schools, community centers, and housing complexes bear his name. In support of Carl Van Vechten's idea to memorialize James Weldon Johnson by establishing an African-American research center, she made a gift of all her husband's papers, books, and correspondence to Yale University to establish the James Weldon Johnson Memorial Collection of American Negro Arts and Letters.

Other writers and artists, including Langston Hughes, Zora Neale Hurston, Jean Toomer, and Richard Wright contributed their archives to the collection as well, helping to make it one of the premier archives of materials supporting research about African-American culture in the United States. In a letter to Van Vechten, Johnson expressed her hopes for the James Weldon Johnson Memorial Collection, "May the years add to, sustain, and keep enriched the Collection, and in your lifetime see expanded the awareness and interest that supports so great a cause in human endeavor and understanding."[1]

During World War II Johnson resigned as a member of the sponsors' committee of the American Women's Voluntary Services because the group evaded her efforts to include African Americans in work projects in support of Civil Defense. She felt that she had been invited to join the group as "window dressing." In her powerful resignation letter to the organization's president, Johnson wrote:

> Token representation to hide discrimination puts further doubts into the minds of 13,000,000 American citizens, . . . this brand of democracy cannot win the war. Insistently, wise and courageous leadership must oppose the forces that would make America a laughing stock before the world.[2]

1 Johnson to Van Vechten
11 Apr. 1950
Van Vechten Papers
Beinecke Library
Yale University

2 Grace Nail Johnson
"Mrs. James Weldon Johnson Quits the AWVS"
*Pittsburgh Courier*
28 Feb. 1942

# KATHARINE CORNELL



Born in Germany and raised in Buffalo, New York, Katharine Cornell became interested in the theater as a child after seeing a production of *Peter Pan*. Her father, a doctor turned theater owner and manager, discouraged her interest in acting; however, he sent her to boarding school where, as luck would have it, Cornell participated in theater groups and was encouraged to explore all aspects of theatrical production—from acting, to directing, to script writing, even set design and construction. After graduation, Katharine Cornell moved to New York City to pursue a career in professional theater.

In 1919, after working for a few years with the Washington Square Players in New York and Jessie Bonstelle's company in Detroit and Buffalo, Cornell received one of her first major roles: she took the part of Jo in a London production of *Little Women*. Upon returning to the United States, Cornell met and fell in love with a young director named Guthrie McClintic; they were married in 1921. Later the same year, Cornell acted the role of Sydney in Clemence Dane's *A Bill of Divorcement*. This show won her the attention of the New York theater community and she was soon receiving challenging roles and brilliant notices. In Dorothy Brandon's *The Outsider*, John Corbin described her performance as "nearly perfect." He went on to say:

> Miss Cornell's method is of the simplest and is always under perfect control. Every mood is adequately voiced and no note is unduly stressed. That is all to the good; but an effect so direct and heart-searching cannot be achieved without more than a touch of histrionic genius.[1]

In 1931, Cornell and her husband founded the Cornell-McClintic Corporation and began producing plays. Their first venture, Rudolph Besier's *The Barretts of Wimpole Street*, was a phenomenal success. Cornell played Elizabeth Moulton-Barrett to great acclaim; the role became a signature character for Cornell, and she played in successful revivals of the play throughout her career, including a frontline production for United States troops during World War II and a television performance in the 1950s.

Their considerable success in New York encouraged Cornell and McClintic to take their company on a tour of nearly one hundred cities. With a repertory that included the *The Barretts of Wimpole Street*, Shaw's *Candida*, and Shakespeare's *Romeo and Juliet*, the nationwide tour solidified Cornell's fame; she was thought to be one of the most talented actresses in the country. When the company performed *Romeo and Juliet* in New York City at the tour's end in 1934, Cornell's production

1 John Corbin, "Among the New Plays: A Brilliant, Discussable Sex Comedy from the Theatre Guild," *New York Times*, 9 Mar. 1924

2 Brooks Akinson, "Katharine Cornell, Edith Evans and Basil Rathbone in a Revival of 'Romeo and Juliet'," *New York Times*, 21 Dec. 1934

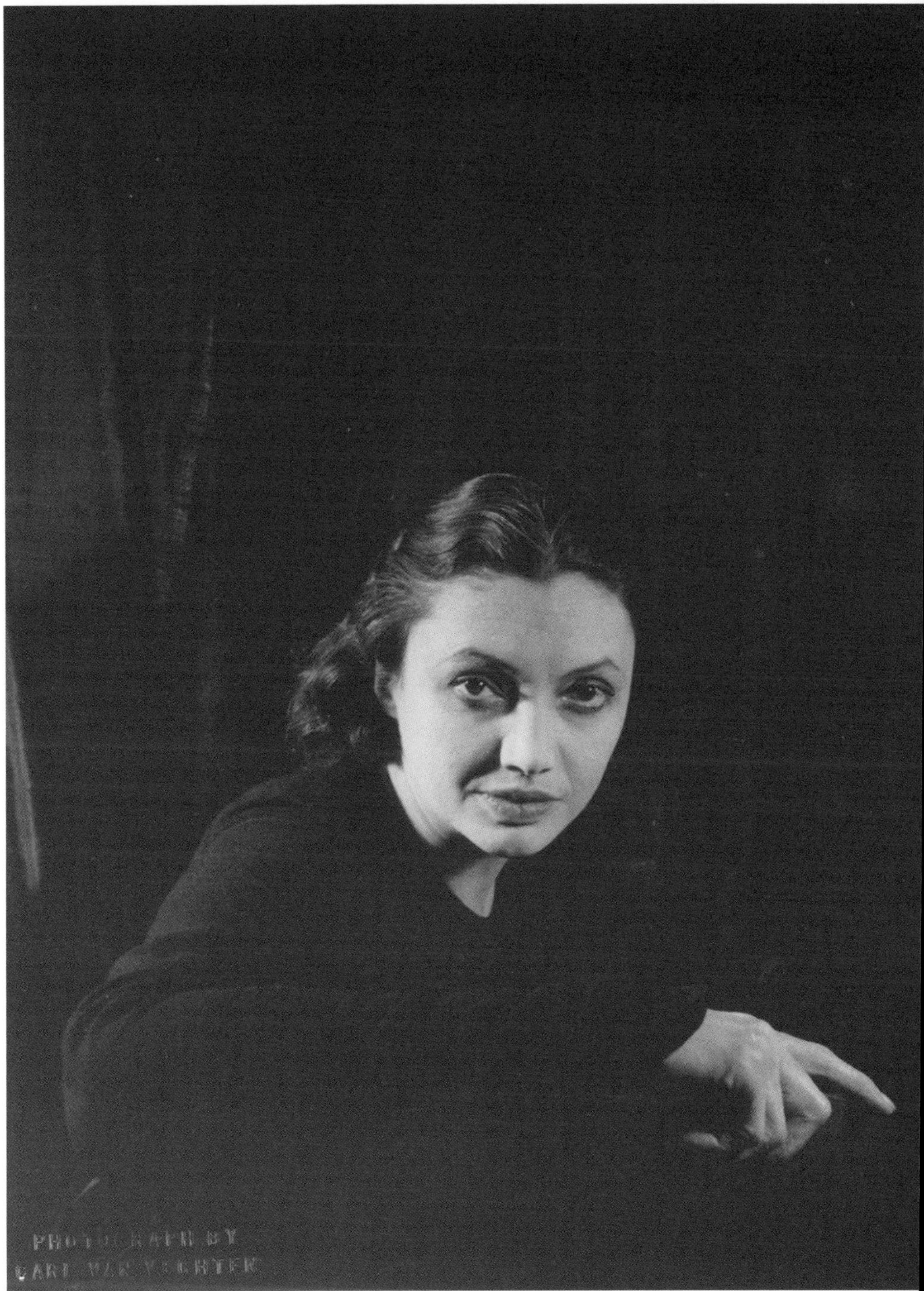


and her portrayal of Juliet earned her best reviews to date. "Miss Cornell has hung another jewel on the cheek of the theater's nights" Brooks Atkinson wrote of the production, "her *Romeo and Juliet* . . . is on the high plane of modern magnificence."[2]

Cornell continued to perform regularly until her husband died in 1961, after which she retired from her work as actress and producer and moved to her home on Martha's Vineyard. Throughout her career, Cornell's talent and drive earned her awards, honorary degrees, and other distinctions, including the dedication of the Katharine Cornell–Guthrie McClintic Room at the New York Public Library's Performing Arts research center at Lincoln Center.

PHOTOGRAPHED JANUARY 10, 1933

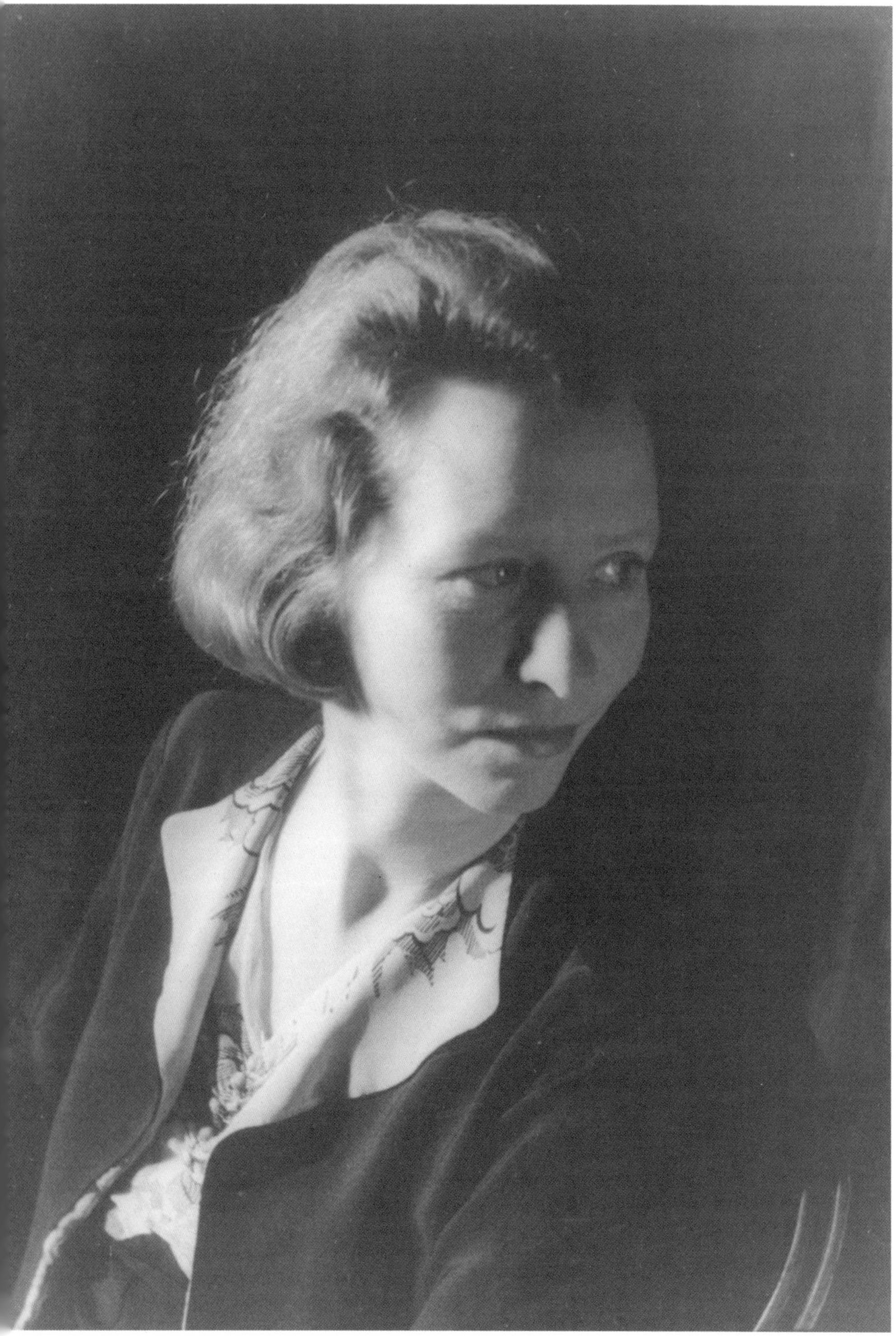

PHOTOGRAPHED ON JANUARY 14, 1933

Edna St. Vincent Millay achieved greater fame and wealth as a poet before her thirtieth birthday than most writers enjoy after a lifetime of achievement. Her poetry readings drew tremendous crowds and often listeners were moved to tears by her dramatic performances. As "the Madonna of her time,"[1] Millay and her success represented new possibilities for career, lifestyle, and creativity available to women early in the twentieth century.

Millay and her two sisters grew up in Maine, raised by their mother who worked as a nurse to support the family. They spent much time reading together, and Millay, called Vincent by her family, was supported in her pursuit of writing from an early age. It was her mother, in fact, who encouraged the nineteen-year-old poet to enter one of her early poems, "Renascence," in a poetry contest sponsored by *The Lyric Year*. The poem, still considered to be one of Millay's most successful and accomplished works, was awarded an honorable mention and was printed in the magazine. This early publication won Millay the attention of many influential readers; one, a Miss Caroline Dow, was so impressed she offered to help with Millay's college expenses. She attended Vassar on a scholarship and with the support of Dow and other sponsors.

After graduation, Millay moved to Greenwich Village in New York City. Her fame as a poet increased with the publication of *Renascence, and Other Poems,* and other early collections,

# EDNA ST. VINCENT MILLAY

## POET

including *A Few Figs from Thistles,* and *Second April*. During her time at Vassar and her first years in New York, Millay had a number of love affairs with both men and women. These relationships often provided material for her work, especially her romantic and passionate sonnets. Millay wrote openly about female desire and sexuality, subjects that were not commonly considered by other women writers. During this period, she wrote magazine fiction using the pen name Nancy Boyd. Many of these stories were about young women living in New York and struggling for self-determination.

In 1923, Millay's *The Harp Weaver, and Other Poems* was awarded the Pulitzer Prize for poetry, making her the first woman to receive that honor. In the same year, she married Eugen Jan Bossevain. Theirs was an open marriage and Millay continued to pursue other relationships. Bossevain was completely dedicated to Millay and her poetry; he gave up his own work and devoted himself to developing Millay's career. The couple bought a country home in Austerlitz, New York, which they named Steepletop. Millay lived there for the rest of her life.

After a car accident in 1936, Millay began using morphine and developed an addiction to it. Her writing suffered; her work became more politically motivated and was generally criticized as mere propaganda. Her reputation faded. When her husband died in 1949, Millay suffered a nervous breakdown and was briefly hospitalized. She died the following year after falling down the stairs at Steepletop; it is unclear whether the fall was an accident or a successful suicide. She was fifty-eight years old.

Millay's traditionally formal poems contrasted sharply with the literary experimentation of many of her contemporaries, including modernist writers such as Gertrude Stein, T. S. Elliot, H. D. and Ezra Pound. Many have maligned her work, calling it sentimental and arch; she is often dismissed as a very minor poet whose work is not worthy of serious consideration. Others, however, maintain that much of Millay's subject matter, especially her investigations of desire, sexuality, and female independence, represent a break with the simple and popular "women's poetry" with which she is often associated.

1 Danitia Smith
"Romantic Rebel of the Jazz Age"
*New York Times*
30 Aug. 2001

# ALINE BERNSTEIN

## SET & COSTUME DESIGNER



Aline Bernstein was the first woman in the United States to gain prominence in the male-dominated field of set and costume design. The industry's reluctance to accept women into its ranks was certainly evident when, in 1926, as the first woman to be granted membership in the United Scenic Artists Union she was sworn in as "Brother Bernstein."

The daughter of an actor, Bernstein spent her childhood surrounded by members of the New York theater community. Though she had an obvious talent for drawing, she hoped to pursue a career as an actress. Both of her parents died by the time she was in her late teens, and she spent a difficult time in the care of her drug-addicted aunt. Soon, however, a family friend intervened, helping Bernstein get a scholarship to Hunter College's School of Fine Art. There she began a course of study that would include work with painter Robert Henri. She developed considerable skill as a portrait painter.

After she married a successful stockbroker, Bernstein began to volunteer backstage at a friend's small theater group. As the group grew into a prominent "off-Broadway" company, Bernstein had many opportunities to design and create sets and costumes. By the mid 1920s, Bernstein had developed a reputation as an imaginative designer whose subtly suggestive sets and costumes complemented perfectly the scripts and characters they supported. She began to work with prominent companies such as the Theatre Guild and the Civic Repertory Theatre. Her most significant design projects of this period were for productions of the classical Indian play, *The Little Clay Cart*, and the Jewish folktale, *The Dybbuk*. As her work received greater notice by critics and audiences, fellow designers began to copy her style.

In 1925, Bernstein began an affair with a young playwright, Thomas Wolfe. Though she and her husband remained married, Bernstein and Wolfe had a volatile love affair that lasted a number of years. Wolfe, who was some twenty years younger than Bernstein, counted on his lover for financial support and artistic inspiration. It was after she encouraged him to attempt writing novels that he produced *Look Homeward Angel*. Under the writer's influence, Bernstein wrote and published a collection of short stories and two novels, including the best seller *Miss Condon*.

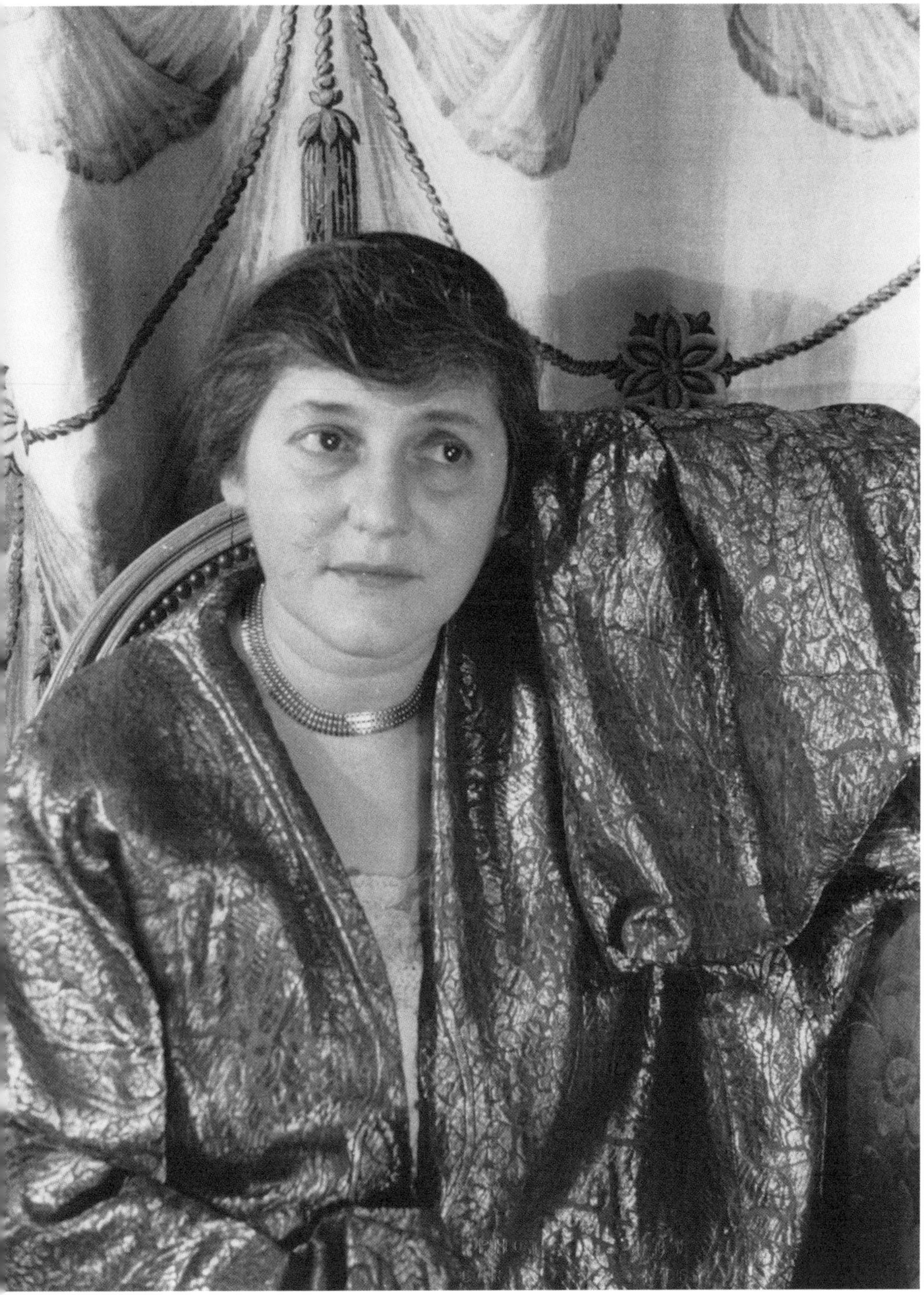

Wolfe and Bernstein both wrote fictionalized accounts of their relationship, Wolfe in "The Web and the Rock," and Bernstein in "The Journey Down." When the affair ended badly, Bernstein attempted suicide. 

During the course of her remarkable career, Bernstein designed sets and costumes for more than one hundred plays. After decades of work in the theater, she embarked on a successful academic career. During the last fifteen years of her life, Bernstein taught and served as a consultant in theater programs at Yale University, Harvard University, and Vassar College.

PHOTOGRAPHED ON FEBRUARY 26, 1933

PHOTOGRAPHED ON MARCH 23, 1933

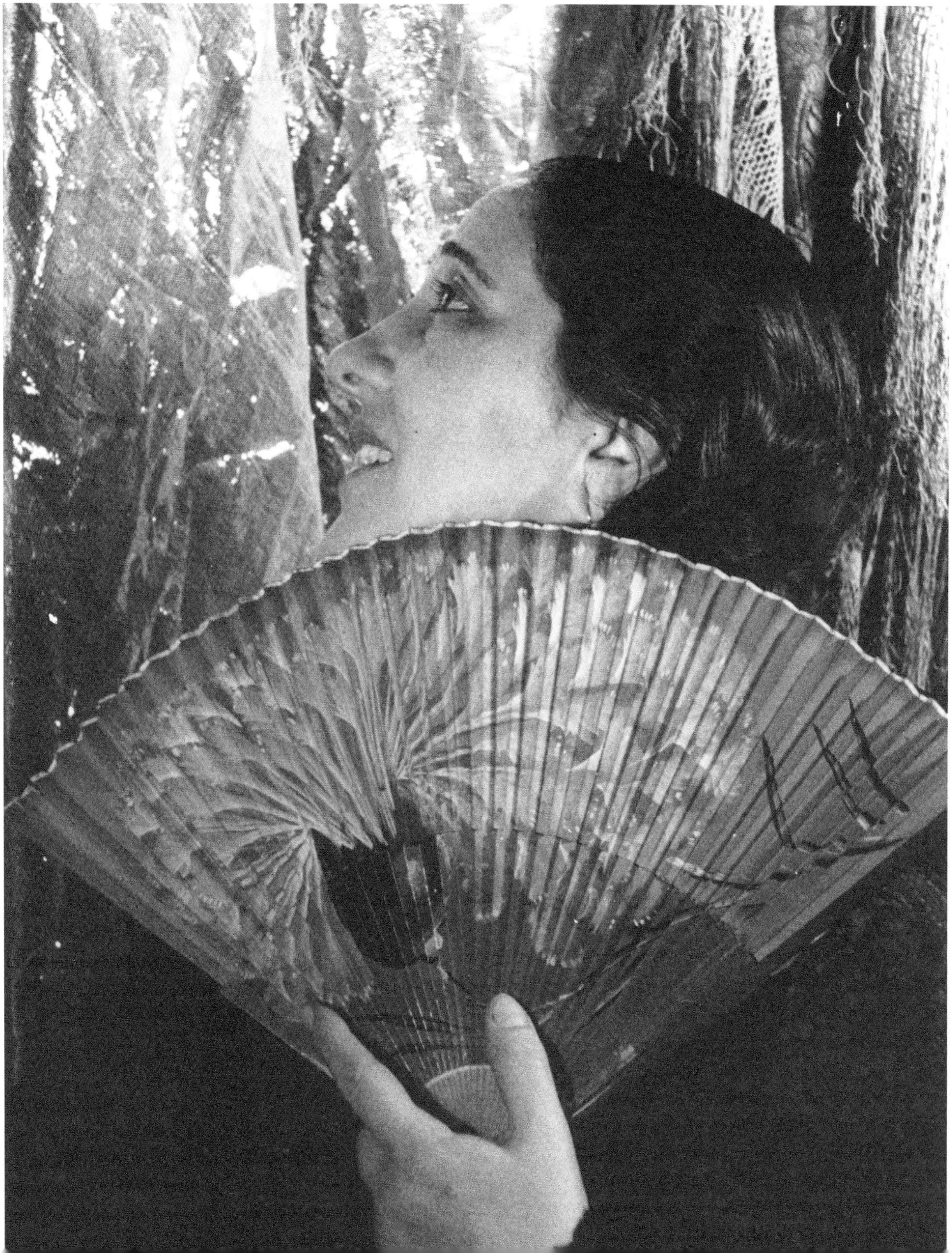

# MARGUERITE D'ALVAREZ

## CONTRALTO

Born in Liverpool, England, to Peruvian parents, Marguerite d'Alvarez began her stage career when she was still a teenager. She made her first public performance, at a diplomatic affair in London, when she was just sixteen. Two years later, in 1904, d'Alverez made her operatic debut at the Rouen Opera House as Dalila in *Samson et Dalila*. Before the end of the decade, she was performing with Oscar Hammerstein's Manhattan Opera Company.

For her debut performance with the company, d'Alvarez sang the part of the mother in *The Prophet*. While rehearsing for the show, she met a young critic for the *Times* as she was leaving the opera house. "I found him very intelligent, with a wisdom beyond his years," d'Alvarez wrote of the meeting, "and when we parted I said I would like to see him again and asked him his name. It was Carl Van Vechten."[1]

A life-long opera lover and a leading opera critic of the 1910s, Carl Van Vechten admired Marguerite d'Alvarez's rich voice and powerful performance style. In an April 22, 1920 advertisement for an d'Alvarez performance, he wrote:

> Marguerite d'Alvarez may be regarded as one of the most unique singers before the public. God, the good fairies, and the Fates have united to endow her with ten or a dozen qualities, any one of which would be sufficient to give her a notable position. . . . She is gifted with a most extraordinary contralto voice of great range and flexibility, and of a mellow and luscious quality.[2]

D'Alvarez was quite fond of Carl Van Vechten, too, and of his wife Fania Marinoff. Of meeting d'Alvarez, Anna May Wong wrote to Marinoff, "one person I simply adore and have only met this trip is Marguerite d'Alvarez. She is so fond of you and talks of you and Carl incessantly. Even if I had not had an instantaneous affection for her, I would have loved her for her devotion to you both."[3]

During the early years of her career, d'Alvarez performed in operas at the London Opera House, Covent Garden, and with companies all over the world. Later, she primarily sang in concerts. She also made a number of recordings, the best known being *Samson et Dalila*. In 1939, she retired from performing after an impressive career, singing her last concert in London.

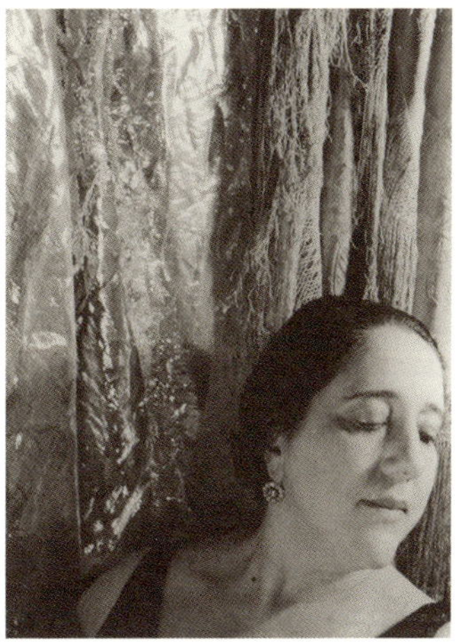

1 Marguerite d'Alvarez
*Forsaken Altars*
London: Rupert Hart-Davis
1954
p. 228

2 Van Vecthen
Advertisement for Marguerite d'Alvarez Concert
Musical Courier
22 Apr. 1920

3 Anna May Wong to Fania Marinoff
19 Apr. 1937
Van Vechten Papers
Beinecke Library
Yale University

# FREDI WASHINGTON



1 Donald Bogle
*Toms, Coons, Mulattoes, Mammies, & Bucks: An Interpretive History of Blacks in American Films*
NY: Viking, 1973
p. 62

2 *Toms, Coons, Mulattoes, Mammies, & Bucks*
p. 62

A fair-skinned, green-eyed African-American actress, Fredi Washington was well respected for her talent as a film and theater performer. Nevertheless, she consistently faced difficulties because of the conflict between her light complexion and her social identity as an African American. She was cast in very limited roles, playing stereotypical mulatto characters—tragically beautiful girls doomed because of their mixed race. As a result of Hollywood's merciless typecasting, Washington was never able to achieve her full potential as an actress.

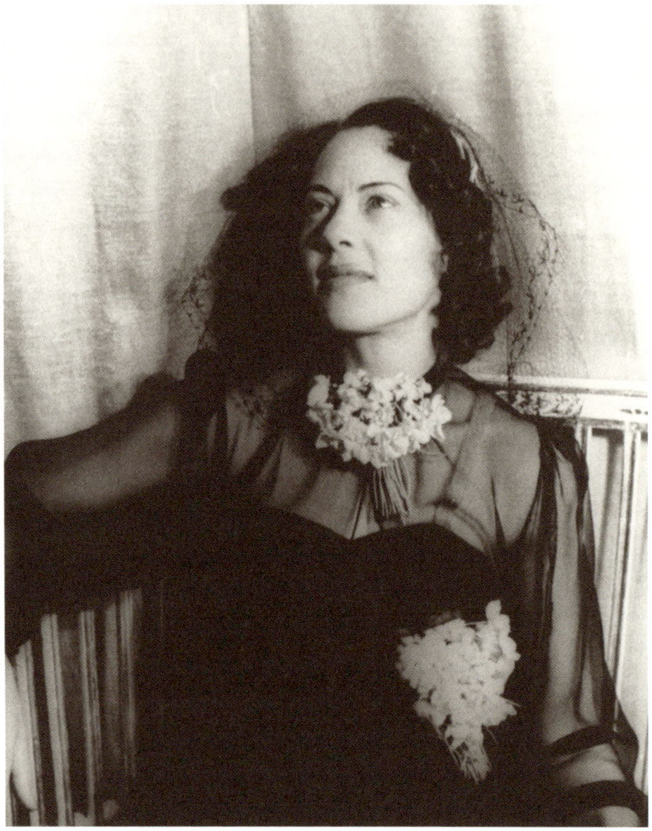

In *Black Boy*, one of her early theater successes, Washington starred with Paul Robeson, playing a black girl who passed for white. Audiences were interested in the play in large part because Washington was viewed as a curiosity, a black girl who looked white. Her part in *Black Boy* was Washington's first in a long line of mulatto characters who suffered terribly as a result of their mixed racial heritage. In her most famous role of this type, Peola in *Imitation of Life*, Washington "emerged as the archetypal tragic mulatto for the Depression era."[1] *Imitation of Life* starred Claudette Colbert as a widow and Louise Beavers as her servant; the two become friends and business partners and share the challenges of raising their daughters alone. Washington's character, Peola, the maid's mulatto daughter, figures in a subplot that is so affecting it nearly eclipses the primary story. Peola leaves home, passes for white, and marries a white man. In spite of her outstanding performance, Washington received no offers for lead roles in other films. Of Hollywood's typecasting of Washington and other African-American actresses, Donald Bogel suggests, "the movies were not ready for idealized tragic black heroines. Audiences preferred mammies and jemimas who could be laughed at or enjoyed or pitied but who would not strike at their consciences."[2]

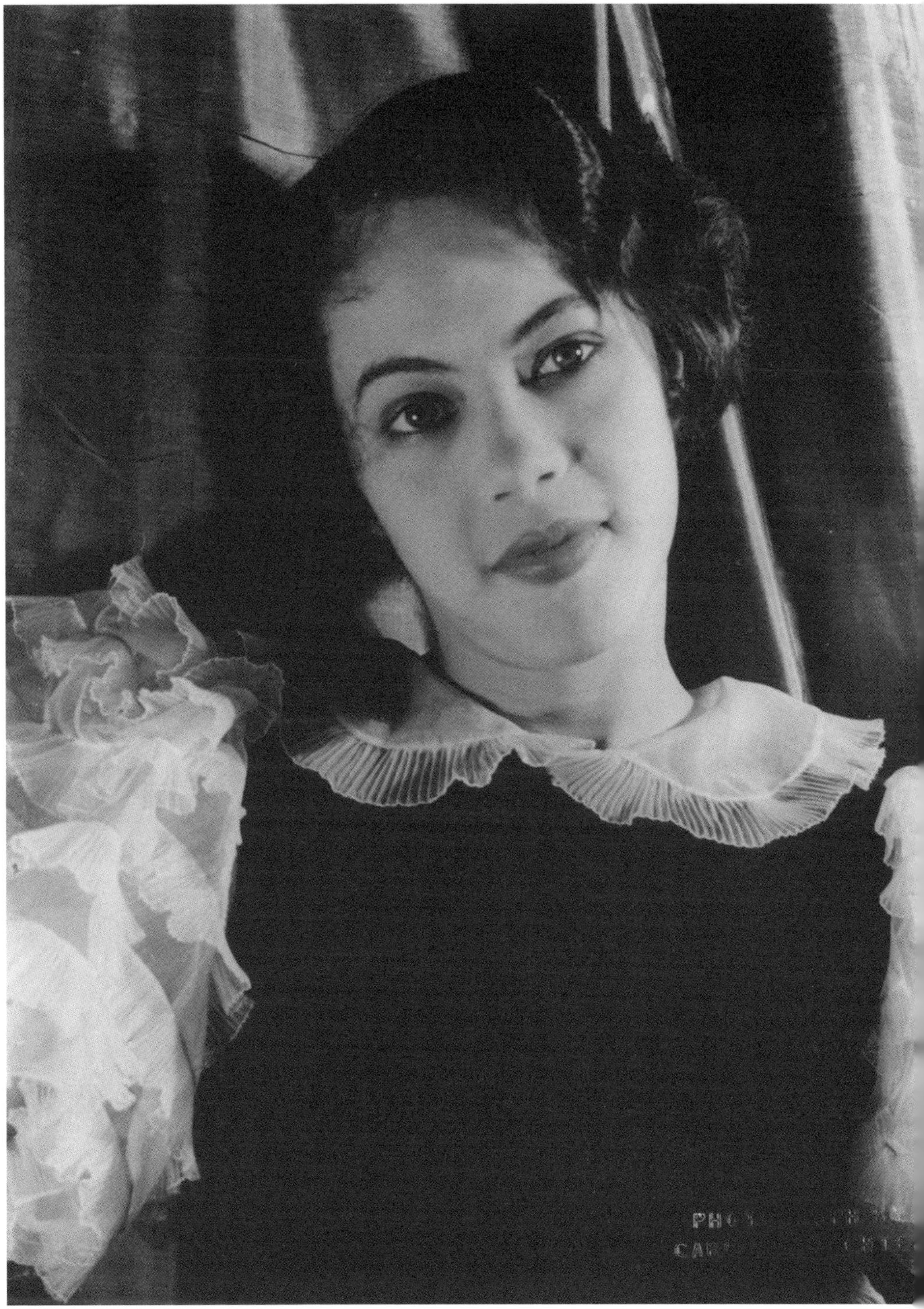

Hollywood's discomfort with Washington was evident not only in the limited roles she was offered, but also in her treatment at the hands of the industry. When she appeared in *The Emperor Jones* with Paul Robeson, for example, Will Hays, the then powerful head of Hollywood's censoring agency, insisted that Washington wear dark makeup to conceal her light complexion, insuring that the audience would not mistake her for a white woman in her love scenes with Robeson. Frustrated by the racist treatment she faced in Hollywood, Washington eventually gave up her film career.

Though she received more diverse roles in the theater, she was still frustrated by the entertainment industry's limited view of African Americans and its insistence on promoting racial stereotypes. As a result, Washington founded the Negro Actors Guild of America, an organization devoted to challenging the entertainment industry's narrow representations of African Americans. Through this organization she worked to encourage the creation of better, more realistic roles for people of color and the elimination of stereotypical characters and scenes from the film and theater marketplace. In addition, Washington worked with the NAACP on behalf of actors, hoping to secure greater participation in the arts for African Americans. She also developed a reputation in New York as a theater critic for the popular Harlem paper, *The People's Voice.*

PHOTOGRAPHED ON MARCH 28, 1933

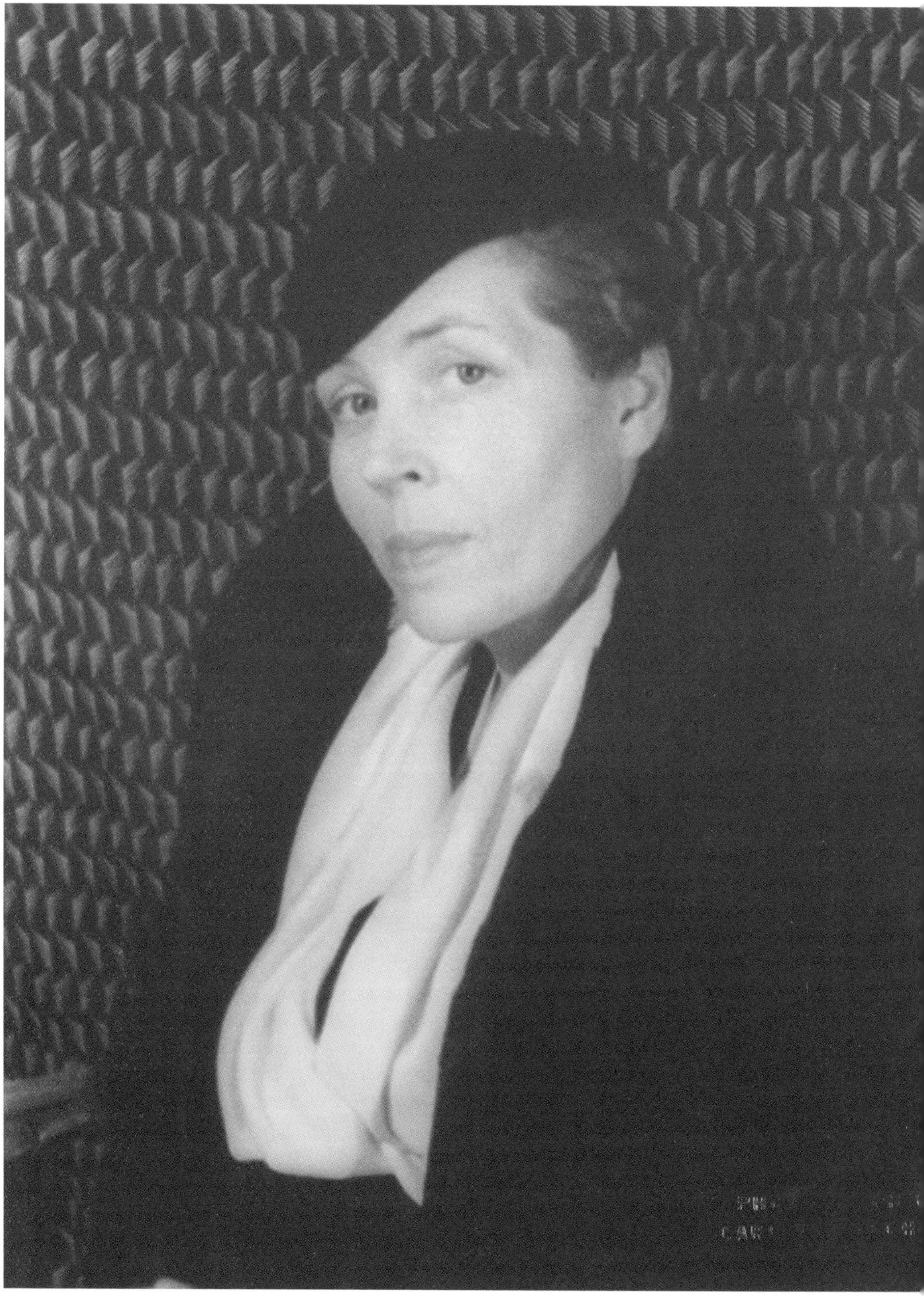

48 Though she wrote only one major book, Djuna Barnes's *Nightwood* was one of the most influential novels of the modernist period and of the twentieth century; it has remained in print since its publication in 1936 and is more widely read today than it was at the time of its publication. Barnes was a central figure in the American expatriate community in Paris in the 1920s, but in her later years she separated herself from other writers and became something of a recluse. She refused to allow much of her work to be reprinted; as a result, she has never enjoyed the reputation her literary work deserves.

Before she left New York for Paris, Barnes was a regular contributor to popular magazines such as *Smart Set* and *Vanity Fair*. Her first major publication, a chapbook entitled *The Book of Repulsive Women: 8 Rhythms and 5 Drawings*, was published in 1915. She also had some success as a playwright in 1919 when Eugene O'Neill and the Provincetown Players produced three of her one-act plays. These plays, and a collection of Barnes's poems, short prose pieces, and drawings were later published as *A Book*. Though these early books received little public attention, other writers began to notice Barnes's work.

PHOTOGRAPHED ON NOVEMBER 29, 1933

# DJUNA BARNES



In the early 1920s, Barnes moved to Paris where she joined a group of literary and artistic women on the Left Bank, which included, among others, Gertrude Stein and Alice B. Toklas, Janet Flanner, and Sylvia Beach and Adrienne Monnier. Some critics claim that Barnes's novel, *Nightwood*, is largely autobiographical and that the novel's characters are based on Barnes and her Paris circle.

*Nightwood* does, in fact, recount the story a woman in 1920s Paris, Robin Vote, and her various love affairs. Robin first marries Felix Volkbein, but she soon falls in love with a woman named Nora Flood—the character many believe is based on Barnes. Later, Robin leaves Nora for another woman. The novel is often praised for its musical and imagistic prose, and its structural complexity. *Nightwood* is emotionally complex as well, at once comic and painful, powerful and horrific. Some contemporary critics misunderstood the novel, but other praised its fluidity and its resistance of fictional realism. "In her novel," one reviewer wrote of *Nightwood*, "poetry is the bloodstream of the universal organism, a poetry that derives its coherence from the meeting of kindred spirits."[1] "Her work," Barnes's friend Sylvia Beach wrote, "with its strangeness and its melancholy note—which contrasted with her delightful smile—did not resemble that of any other writer of her time."[2]

After the publication of *Nightwood*, Barnes virtually stopped writing. She left Paris and returned to New York where she lived in seclusion in a Greenwich Village apartment. The entire literary output of the last forty years of her life was a handful of poems and a short play. It wasn't until after her death that some of her early works were reprinted.

1 Alfred Kazin
"An Experiment in the Novel"
*New York Times*
7 Mar. 1937

2 Sylvia Beach
*Shakespeare and Company*
NY: Harcourt, 1956
p. 112

# EMMA GOLDMAN

## ANARCHIST & SOCIAL CRITIC



One of the twentieth century's most famous advocates of anarchism, Emma Goldman earned the nickname Red Emma for her controversial political activism. Her eloquent and compelling public speeches won considerable support for her radical ideas. Often, her work also caught the attention of the United States government and she was jailed more than once.

Goldman was born in Lithuania in 1869. She lived alternately with her parents and her grandmother, and after just a few years of formal education, she went to work in a St. Petersburg factory to help support the family. As a teenager, she moved with her sister to Rochester, New York. Goldman took work in a clothing factory where she became acquainted with members of a German socialist group and began to develop an interest in their political agenda. She soon moved to New Haven, Connecticut, where she met a community of Russian socialists and anarchists. She grew increasing committed to the idea of anarchy and decided to move to New York to work actively as an anarchist.

In New York, Goldman joined a radical community surrounding the anarchist newspaper, *Die Freiheit*, edited by Johann Most. She became involved with another Russian anarchist, Alexander Berkman. Though the relationship was cut short when Berkman was sent to prison for his attempted murder of Henry C. Frick (Goldman admitted to helping plan this crime), they resumed contact after his release and continued to work together. In the meantime, Goldman developed a talent for public speaking. In 1893, she was arrested for inciting a riot when she told workers to demand bread and to take it if it wasn't given to them. She was sentenced to a year in prison.

After her release, Goldman gave lecture tours in the United States and throughout Europe. She founded and edited *Mother Earth*, an anarchist magazine in which she called for the complete abolishment of government. Her speeches and writings influenced many, including Leon Czolgosz, who assassinated President McKinley in Buffalo, New York, in 1901. Czolgosz claimed that Goldman inspired him to take action against the government. Though she was never connected to the crime, Goldman defended Czolgosz's actions, which led to significant police harassment and public scorn.

As World War I approached, Goldman and Alexander Berkman coordinated an anti-conscription campaign. They were arrested for conspiracy to obstruct selective service and imprisoned for two years. Upon her release late in 1919, a federal court stripped Goldman of her United States citizenship. She, along with Berkman and other political dissidents, was deported. Goldman spent many years traveling throughout Europe seeking refuge. During this time, she wrote two books, *My Disillusionment in Russia* (1923) and *Living My Life* (1931).

1 Van Vechten "Some Literary Ladies I Have Known" *Yale University Library Gazette* 26:3 (1952) p. 106

2 Goldman to Van Vechten 26 Aug. 1934 Van Vechten Papers Beinecke Library Yale University

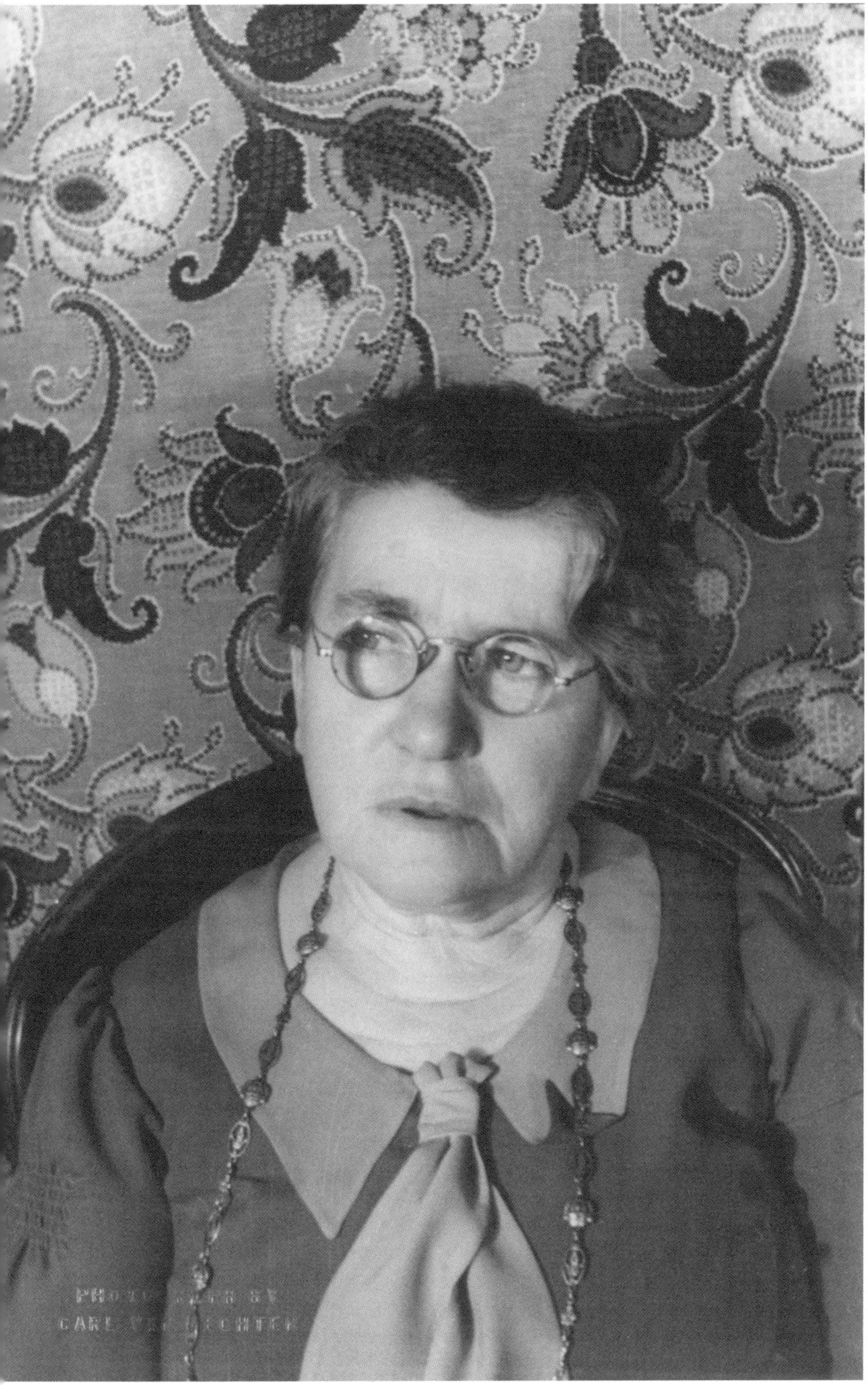


After her deportation, Emma Goldman returned to the United States only once, on a ninety-day visa. It was during this visit that Carl Van Vechten photographed her. The two had known one another since the days of Mable Dodge Luhan's New York City salon in the 1910s. "Though she was referred to disrespectfully by the press of the day as 'that Goldman woman,'" Van Vechten wrote, "I found her about as radical as a Presbyterian in good standing. The anarchist, of course, believed in complete individualism but when one of her group was tarred and feathered . . . she sent for the police."[1]



Van Vechten's photos of Goldman are some of the most famous images of the woman who has been called the mother of anarchism in America. Goldman liked the photographs, which, in a letter to Van Vechten, she referred to as "the splendid work you have done with my mug."[2]

PHOTOGRAPHED MARCH 6, 1934

# GERTRUDE STEIN & ALICE B. TOKLAS

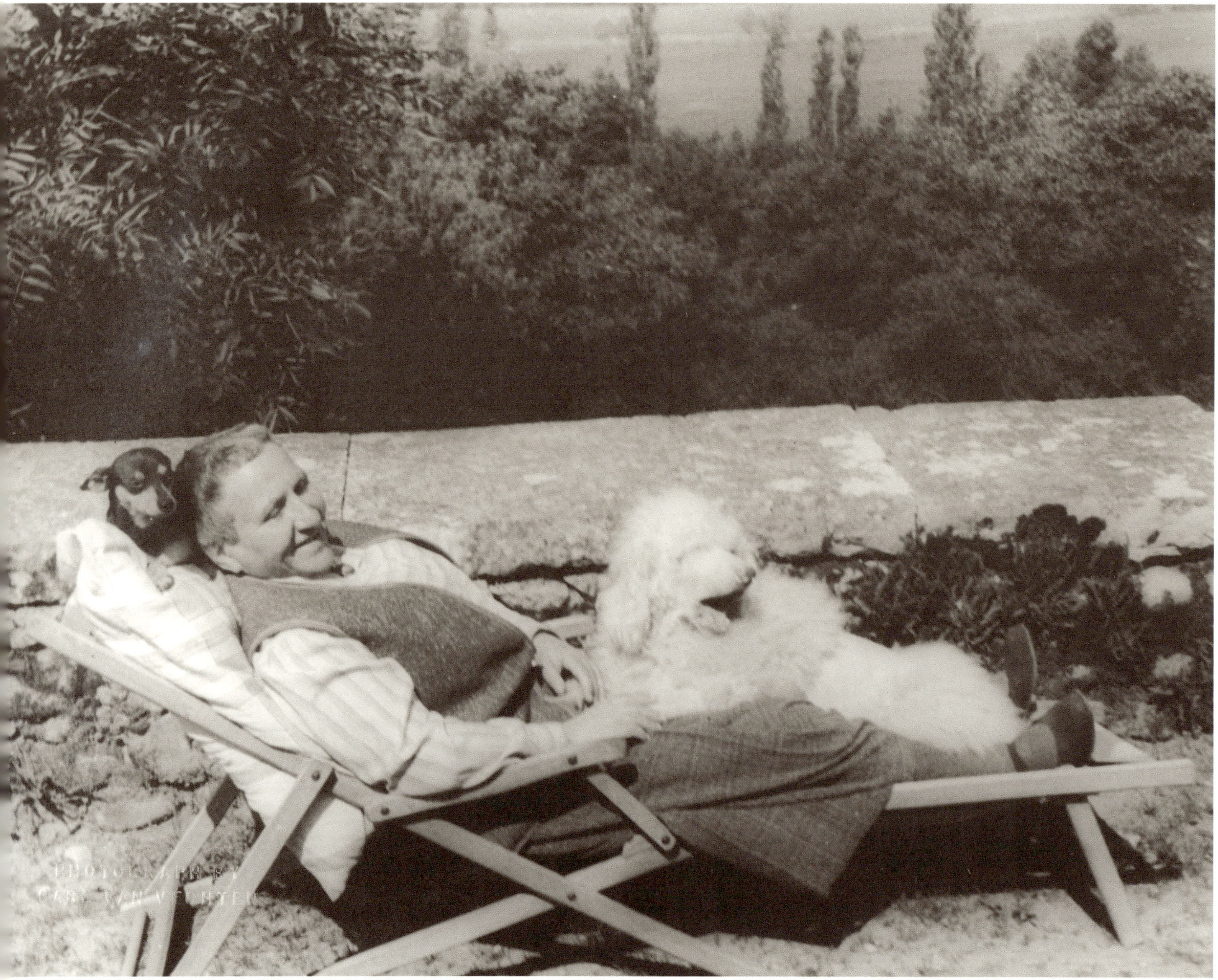

GERTRUDE STEIN PHOTOGRAPHED ON THE TERRACE AT HER VILLA AT BILIGNIN WITH HER DOGS, PEPE AND BASKET I, ON JUNE 13, 1934

# WRITERS

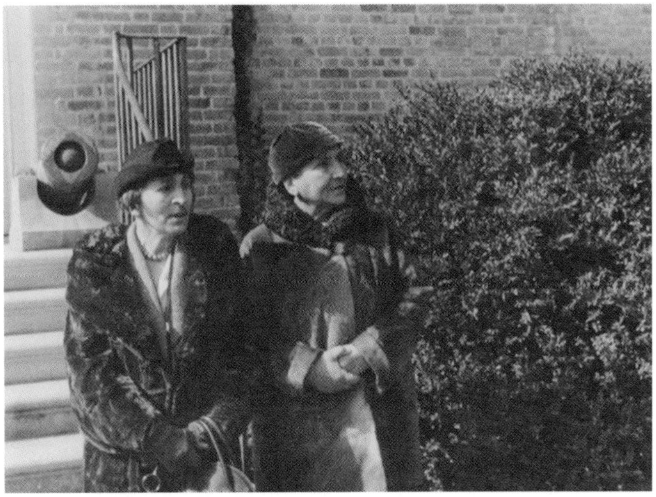

Gertrude Stein is a famed and formidable icon of modernism. As novelist, poet, theorist, playwright, and even librettist, Stein produced some of the most provocative—and difficult—texts of her time. *Three Lives, Tender Buttons,* and *The Making of Americans* to name just a few of her more famous books, are notorious for their disjunctive syntax, their repetitions, their surprising humor, and their overall subversion of linear thinking and experience. Stein above all was a modernist who treated linguistic play as a serious business.

Taken on the strength of her body of work alone, Stein would be counted as a significant figure; however, the salon she hosted with her partner Alice B. Toklas in their Paris home brought together confluences of talent and thinking that would help define modernism in literature and art. Regular guests included Pablo Picasso, Ernest Hemingway, F. Scott Fitzgerald, Sinclair Lewis, James Joyce, Henri Matisse, and many others. These writers and artists knew Stein's writing, which was often called a literary equivalent to cubist painting techniques, and the degree to which it influenced their work is a topic of much debate among scholars. Stein's interest in perception and the rhythms of language, as well as her abandonment of traditional narrative structures certainly played a part in shaping the course of modernist writing and thinking.

For her part, Alice B. Toklas provided support and assistance to Stein by running the household, typing and editing her work, and correcting proofs of her books. She also asserted her ambitions for Stein and worked as a kind of manager, publicist, and agent for her and her work. Toklas founded her own small press, The Plain Edition, to publish Stein's work, and after Stein's death, Toklas devoted the rest of her life to promoting her partner's work. She also wrote books of her own after Stein's death—two cookbooks, and a memoir of the couple's life together.

As important as Stein's and Toklas's Paris salon was, it should not overshadow the significance of their relationship with Carl Van Vechten. As a friend, supporter, critic, and advocate, Van Vechten played a major role in the promotion and reception of Stein's work in the United States. In fact without his efforts, it is possible that Stein's work would never have gained a serious audience outside of Paris. Van Vechten, before he and Stein actually met, had written articles about her work, praising its formal innovation, wit, and intelligence, but it was after they met in Paris in 1913 and became friends, that Van Vechten became her informal, stateside literary agent. After the incomparable success of Stein's *The Autobiography of Alice B. Toklas*, Van Vechten played no small part in orchestrating their lecture tour of the United States.

Before the lecture tour in 1934, Stein hadn't set foot in the United Sates in many years. Though she grew up in California, she moved to Paris to live with her brother Leo in 1903. Stein had followed her brother from California to Cambridge, Massachusetts, a few years earlier when he entered Harvard

PHOTOGRAPHED ON THE CAMPUS OF THE COLLEGE OF WILLIAM & MARY IN WILLIAMSBURG, VIRGINIA, ON FEBRUARY 8, 1935

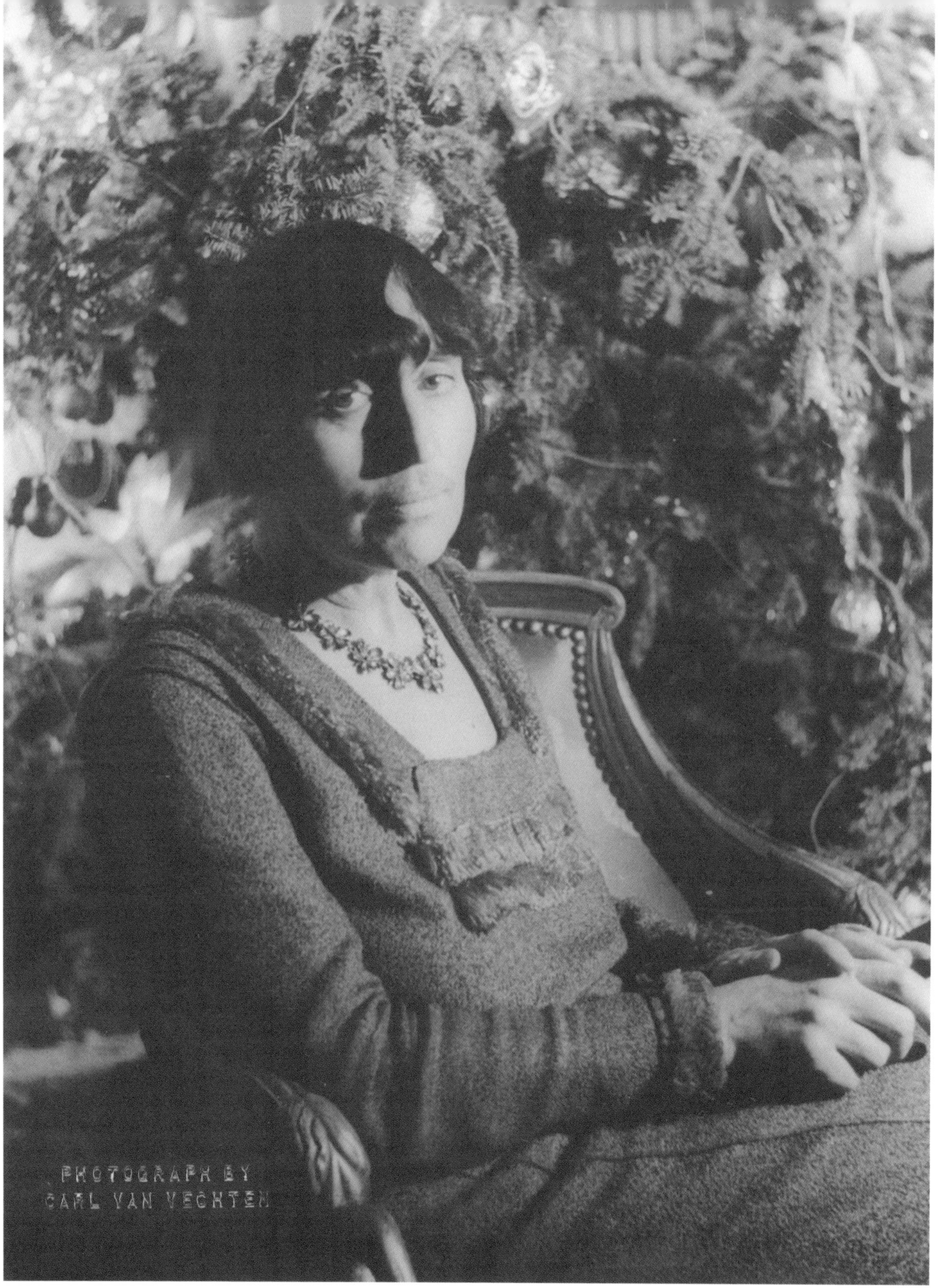


ALICE B. TOKLAS PHOTOGRAPHED ON JANUARY 4, 1935

University. She enrolled in the Harvard Annex, the women's college that would become Radcliffe, where, among other things, she studied psychology with the philosopher William James, who profoundly influenced his pupil's ideas about literature and art.

After arriving in Paris, Gertrude and Leo Stein quickly became members of the Parisian art scene. They began collecting the work of artists they admired, beginning what would become one of the most remarkable private collections of modern art ever assembled, including the work of Picasso, Matisse, Gris, Cezanne, and others. It was in Paris that Stein began writing seriously, determined to make writing her life's work. It is also where she met Alice B. Toklas.

Toklas, who was also raised in California, was the daughter of an upper middle class Jewish family from San Francisco. For a time she studied piano in hopes of becoming a concert pianist. Her plans changed, however, after her mother's death when she moved with her father to his parents' home, where she would spend several years keeping house for her father, brothers, uncles, and grandparents. In 1907 Toklas took a trip to Paris and met Stein the very night she arrived. Within months of their meeting, Stein and Toklas agreed to live as husband and wife, a relationship that would last until Stein's death.

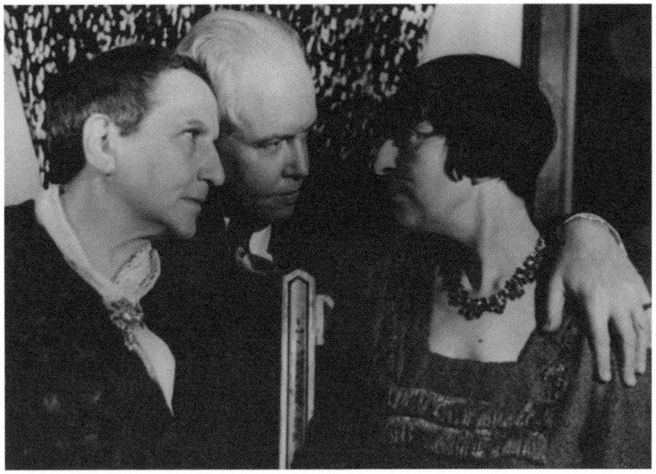

Well known in her adopted home as a powerful intellectual and artistic force, Stein was otherwise a coterie author. That was to change when *The Autobiography of Alice B. Toklas* was published in the early 1930s. The book, thanks in large part to Van Vechten's shrewd promoting, became an immediate sensation, making both Stein and Toklas literary celebrities. By this time, Van Vechten had become one of the couple's closest friends. They had adopted pet names for each other that implied the familial intimacy of their relationship: Van Vechten was known as Papa Woojums, Toklas as Mama Woojums, and Stein as Baby Woojums. Van Vechten acted as host for much of their trip, arranging visits with many of his friends, including a party with some of Harlem's finest writers and a tea with actress Katharine Cornell, who served Stein and Toklas lemon pie.

The relationship of these three is an intersection that would shape the early and middle part of the twentieth century's artistic production. The sheer strength of influences and number of cross-continental connections they both provided and represented stands as a central factor in the dialogue between American and European Modernism.

SELF PORTRAIT WITH GERTRUDE STEIN AND ALICE B. TOKLAS PHOTOGRAPHED JANUARY 4, 1935

# BRICKTOP

## NIGHT CLUB OWNER & ENTERTAINER



1 Langston Hughes
*The Big Sea*
NY: Knopf, 1940
p. 177

2 *The Big Sea*
pp. 180-81

3 *The Big Sea*
p. 178

4 Bricktop with James Haskins
*Bricktop*
NY: Atheneum, 1983
p. 116

5 Van Vechten
"Portraits of the Artists"
*Esquire*
58:6(1962)
p. 257

6 Van Vechten to
Langston Hughes
29 Nov. 1939
*Remember Me to Harlem: The Letters of Langston Hughes and Carl Van Vechten 1925-1964*
Ed. Emily Bernard
NY: Knopf, 2001
pp. 156-57

7 "Portraits of the Artists"
p. 257

Throughout much of the twentieth century, Bricktop, otherwise known as Ada Smith Ducongé, was a popular and renowned performer and hostess. In the early 1920s while performing in a Harlem nightclub, Ducongé became known as Bricktop because of her bright red hair; she was to become so well known by this nickname that during her lifetime she owned and ran no fewer than three nightclubs known simply as "Bricktop's." Her Paris nightclubs were famous for their fine entertainment; on any given night one might hear Ethel Waters, Noel Coward, Helen Morgan, or Cole Porter. Her clubs were equally well known for their rich and glamorous clientele, including royals from across Europe, expatriate writers such as Scott and Zelda Fitzgerald and Ernest Hemingway, and famous artists and performers—from Pablo Picasso to Tallulah Bankhead.

Bricktop was born in West Virginia, and given the elaborate name Ada Beatrice Queen Victoria Louisa Virginia Smith. Her father died when she was a child and her mother, a former slave, moved the family north to Chicago. It was in Chicago that Ada Smith would make her stage debut in *Uncle Tom's Cabin* at the Haymarket Theater. She was five years old. After traveling with a vaudeville troupe in the earliest days of her career, Bricktop performed in the most popular clubs in Chicago, Los Angeles, San Francisco, Seattle, and of course, New York where she was the headliner at the fashionable Harlem club, Connie's Inn.

Bricktop moved to Paris in 1924, where she performed at Le Grand Duc. On her first night at the club Bricktop met the poet Langston Hughes who, then just twenty-two years old, was working in the club as a busboy. "You liked her right away," Hughes wrote of meeting Bricktop.[1] "She liked everybody and made everybody like her. . . . Bricktop was simply a good old girl of the kind folks call 'regular.'"[2] Before long, "Bricktop was the toast of Montmartre, with dukes and princes at her tables."[3]

Hughes's remark recalls Bricktop's friendship with the Prince of Wales, who held a party in her first club on its opening night. The Prince, who knew Bricktop as the woman who had introduced Paris to the Charleston, asked her if she would teach him the latest dance, the Black Bottom. "The Prince and I went out onto the floor," Bricktop wrote, "and I showed him some of the steps. It didn't take him long to catch on. He was a very good dancer."[4]

Carl Van Vechten met Bricktop in her club in Montmartre in the late 1920s. Of their first meeting, Van Vechten wrote:

> I became interested in her when it was reported to me that she had journeyed to Le Harve to meet the Negro Gold Star Mothers, after the Great War, when they were given the opportunity to visit the spots where their sons fought and died and were buried. Accompanying them to Paris, she spoke French for them and

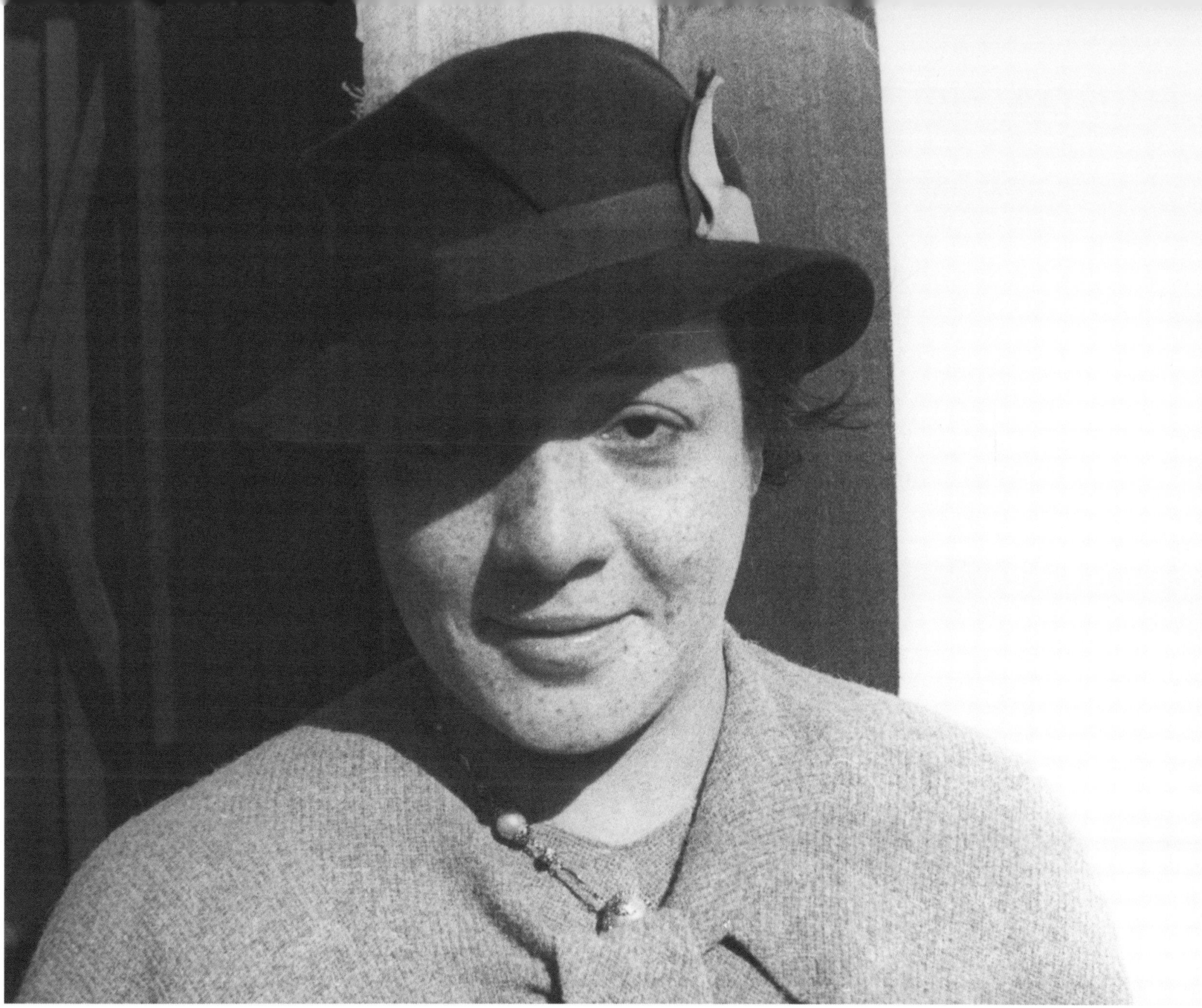



> found them places to sleep. This story endeared her to me so that when Fania and I were in Paris . . . we sought her out.[5]

Many years later, after seeing Bricktop in New York, Van Vechten wrote in a letter, "Brick was here for dinner last night in her most reserved and ladylike mood. But she was grand."[6]

Van Vechten photographed Bricktop on the streets of Paris, her adopted home. "We wandered pretty much all over Montmartre to discover appropriate locations," Van Vechten wrote.[7] He included images of Bricktop in one of his earliest photography exhibitions.

PHOTOGRAPHED IN PARIS ON JUNE 22, 1934

# HEDDA HOPPER

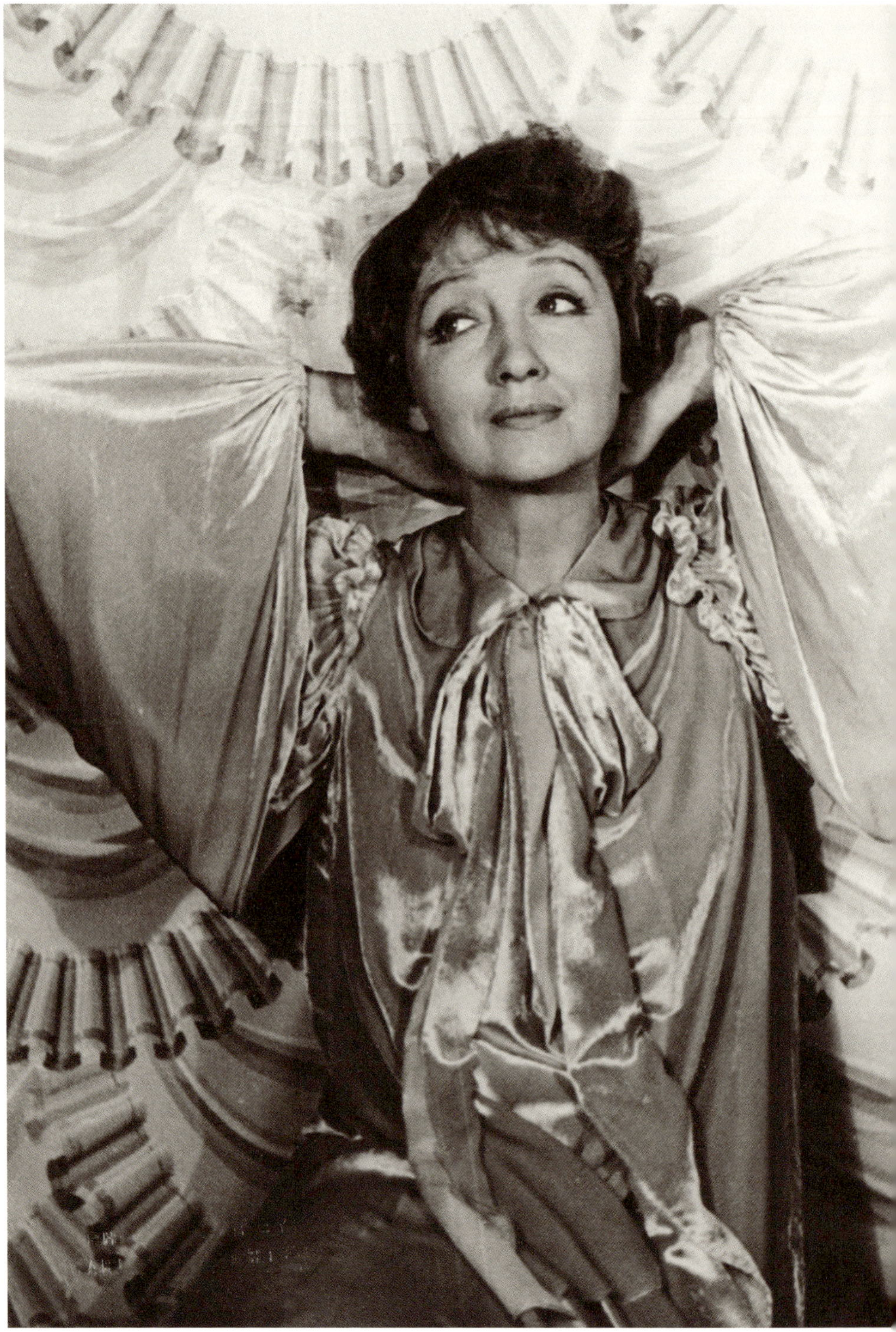

PHOTOGRAPHED ON OCTOBER 18, 1934



Hedda "The Hat" Hopper earned her nickname as a young actress because of her love of high fashion hats. After she gave up acting and gained popularity as a Hollywood gossip columnist, Hopper's fans often sent her ever more wild, outlandish, unusual hats and she was said to have spent many thousands of dollars a year on her trademark garment. Late in her life, Hopper said, "If you wear a crazy hat, no one notices the tired face beneath it."[1]

Born Elda Furry, the daughter of a Pennsylvania butcher, Hopper dropped out of the Carter Conservatory of Music in Pittsburgh as a teenager and headed for New York. She wasn't a particularly talented dancer or singer, but because of her height, handsome legs, and her striking green eyes, she soon found a place on a chorus line. In New York she met and fell in love with a popular comic actor named William DeWolf Hopper. Though he was nearly thirty years older than she was, Elda Furry married Hopper in 1913, becoming his fifth wife.

Hopper, who had changed her name several times already—she was known variously as Elda Furry, Elda Curry, Ella Furry, and Elda Millar—was happy to take her husband's last name, hoping the recognized name would help boost her career. She did not like, however, that her husband often referred to her by the names of his former wives: Edna, Ida, Ella, and Nella. Thus, in 1918, she sought help choosing a new name from a

## GOSSIP COLUMNIST & ACTRESS

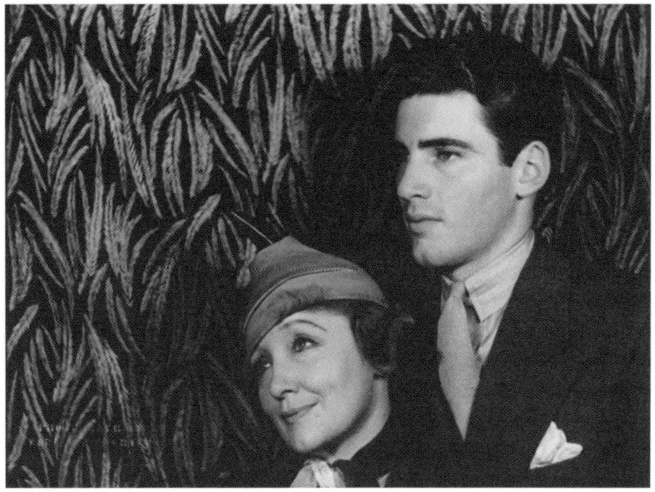

numerologist-astrologer. After the ten-dollar consultation, she became Hedda Hopper. She also changed her birth date to a more favorable day some five years after her actual birth.

During these years, Hopper enjoyed a moderately successful stage and film career. After her divorce from William DeWolf Hopper in 1922, she struggled financially and aggressively sought work. Hollywood was not yet the only site for serious film making, and Hopper worked for several East Coast studios, especially in New York and New Jersey. When she finally moved to California, it was at the urging of Louis B. Mayer, who cast Hopper in his first film, *Virtuous Wives* (1919). Though she played only bit parts and secondary characters, Hopper made more than one hundred movies.

As her acting career began to falter, a friend helped Hopper get a break as a columnist. Her brief reports on Hollywood did not initially take off, in part because columnist Luella Parsons had the gossip market cornered. Soon, in an effort to diffuse Parsons's considerable power in Hollywood, Louis B. Mayer arranged for Hopper, with the help of his studio's publicity office, to write a rival column. Her comparatively mild column began to appear regularly in a handful of papers; however it was "not until Hedda resorted to bare-nails bitchery was she able to put her career into orbit."[2]

Hedda Hopper became well known in Hollywood for her sharp wit and vicious tongue. She quickly developed a reputation for writing malicious stories and occasional false reports on the lives of the stars. Her ruthlessness and willingness to ignore her subjects' wishes made it possible for her to write the shocking and edgy stories her fans came to love.

In many ways, Hopper was an unsavory character who used her power to damage and destroy other's careers. She was a radical political conservative and, in the 1950s, she was a leading supporter of Senator Joseph McCarthy's assault on Hollywood; she served as the second vice president for the Motion Picture Alliance of the Preservation of American Ideals. Hopper was considered by many to be an anti-Semite.

Because it was often said that she could "make or break" a career, Hopper became one of Hollywood's most feared figures. When she used the proceeds from her column to buy a mansion in Beverly Hills, Hopper referred to it as "the house that fear built." She commonly offered unsolicited advice to movie stars in her column, and, on occasion, to others; "at the height of World War II, Hedda announced that Winston Churchill should hire a manager because he was 'making too many speeches and repeating himself.'"[3]

1 Eells, George
*Hedda and Louella*
NY: Putnam, 1972
p. 61

2 *Hedda and Louella*
p. 173

3 Lemon, Richard
"The Warrior Queens of Gossip"
*People Weekly*
13 May 1985
p. 132

PHOTOGRAPHED WITH HER SON, ACTOR WILLIAM DEWOLF HOPPER, JR., ON OCTOBER 18, 1934

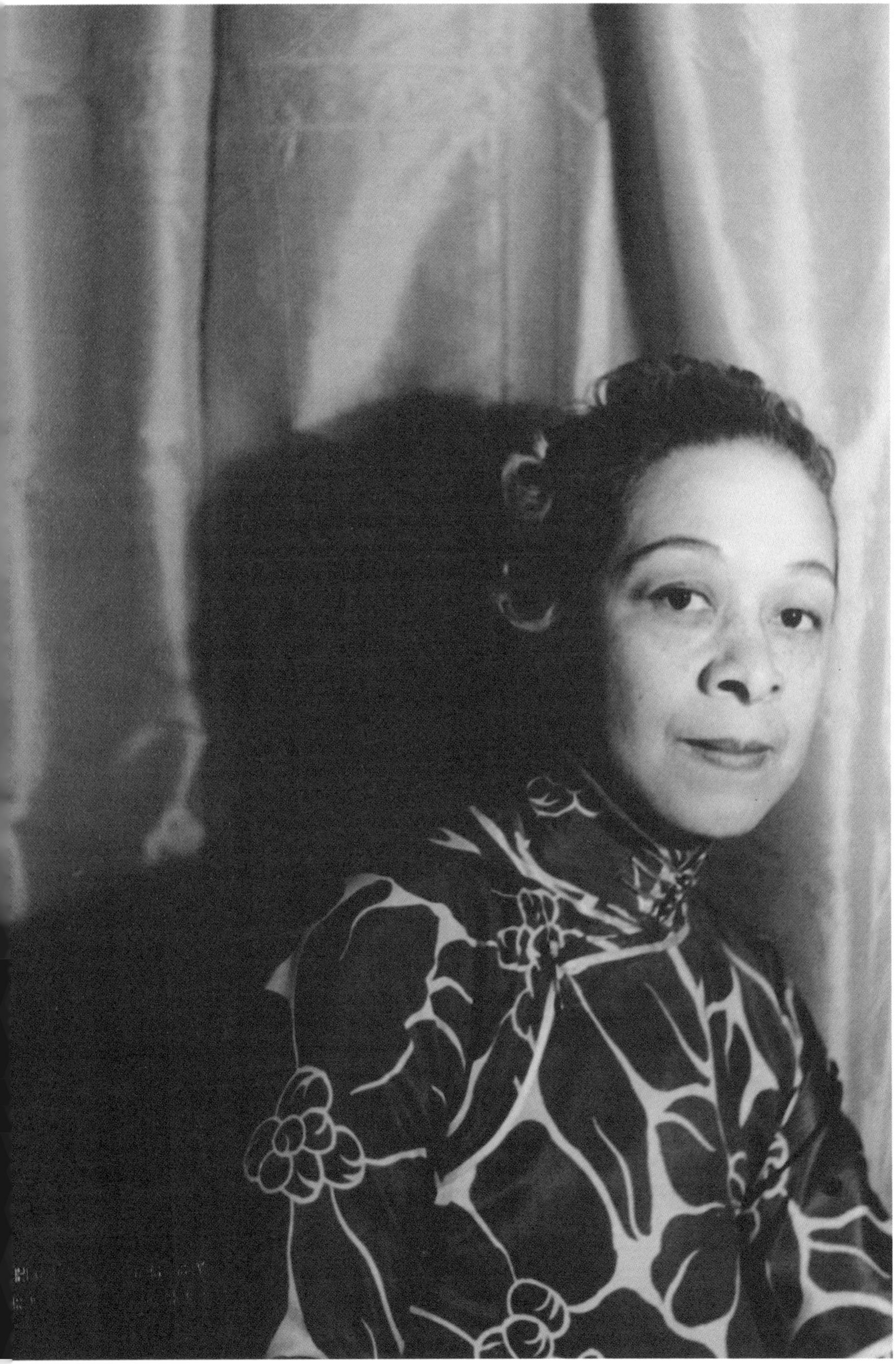

PHOTOGRAPHED ON OCTOBER 26, 1934

## SINGER & MUSIC CRITIC

Nora Holt and Carl Van Vechten met in a Harlem speakeasy in the early 1920s and remained close friends until the end of Van Vechten's life. During the 1920s and 1930s Holt often performed in New York and was a regular guest at Van Vechten's (and others') parties, where she sang bawdy songs and danced all night. She was known as well for her platinum blond hair as she was for her scandalous love life, which included a high profile divorce and a great many lovers.

Nora Holt's reputation is misleading; she was much more than just a rich party girl whose escapades were a staple of gossip columns. She was an accomplished singer and a serious scholar of music. By the time she met Van Vechten in Harlem, Holt had already become the first African American in the United States to earn a master of music degree (from Chicago Music College) and she had been the music critic for the *Chicago Defender* for several years. By the 1920s, she had also helped to found the National Association of Negro Musicians, and she had published a magazine entitled *Music and Poetry.*

In spite of these successes, around Harlem in the 1920s Holt was known as a wild socialite who lived high on her inherited fortune. Her many marriages—Holt was named in *Ebony* magazine's 1949 article "Most Married Negros"—were often

# NORA HOLT

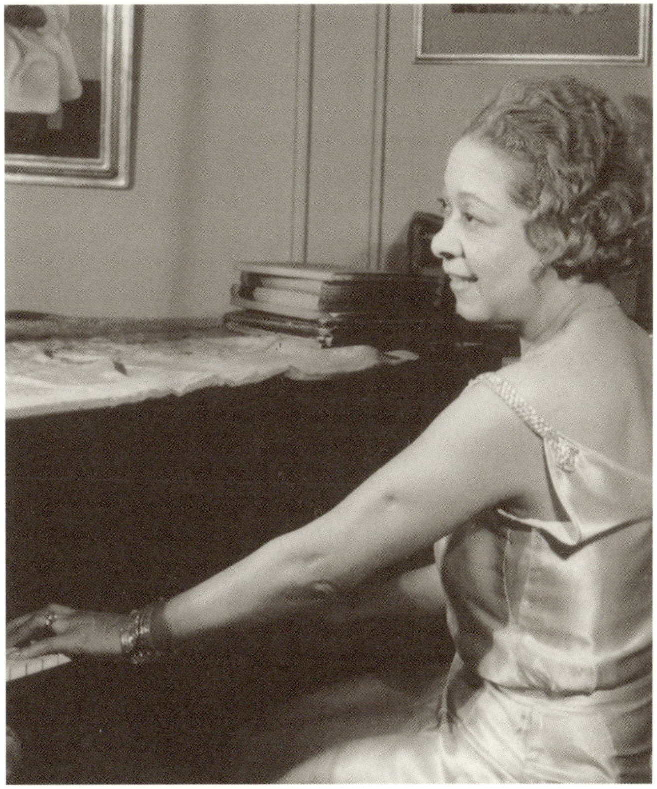

the subject of gossip, even among her friends. "Her trail is strewn with bones," Carl Van Vechten wrote of Holt in a letter to H.L. Mencken in 1925.[1] When she married Joseph L. Ray in 1923, the society papers described in detail Holt's diamond earrings (six carets in each ear) and her pearl-beaded dress. Even more interesting to the society papers, however, was the fact that Holt appeared at the wedding with a black eye, rumored to be the result of a fight with her lover, Gordon Jackson.

Holt and Ray remained married for only nineteen months; their separation and divorce generated even more gossip than their wedding. Charges of fraud, accusations of adultery, and a number of suits and counter suits kept the press busy for some time. Holt was savvy about the fact that her prominence in the press might enhance her opportunities. Of one of Ray's legal assaults, Holt wrote to Van Vechten "The whole thing is a flimsy suit, no weight and I can beat it hands down, but did not want the annoyance. However, the publicity should be of value."[2]

In the early years of their friendship, Carl Van Vechten was so taken with Holt that he used her as the model for Lasca Sartoris, a character in *Nigger Heaven*, his controversial 1926 novel. Like Holt, Lasca Sartoris was a beautiful and wild young woman, a constant subject of conversation: "It could hardly be said that Harlem, generally speaking, had received the tidings of Lasca's wayward adventures with approval, even equanimity, but those who knew her apparently liked her, and the rest . . . would be won over by her money, her beauty, her wit, and her charm."[3]

After years in Harlem, Holt moved to California, where she taught music in public high schools and owned a beauty parlor: "Nora Holt is opening a swanky beauty shop in Los Angeles," Van Vechten wrote to Langston Hughes in 1939. "Therein, no doubt, she'll turn colored brunettes by scores into blondes."[4] Holt returned to New York in the 1940s, where she became the music critic first for the *Amsterdam News*, and later for the *New York Courier*. Throughout the 1950s, and until her death in 1974, Holt was a highly influential music critic, producing and hosting radio programs highlighting the work of African-American artists.

PHOTOGRAPHED MARCH 18, 1932

1 Van Vechten to H.L. Mencken [1925] *Letters of Carl Van Vechten* Ed., Bruce Kellner New Haven: Yale, 1987 p. 87

2 Holt to Van Vechten 20 Sept. 1927 Van Vechten Papers Beinecke Library Yale University

3 Carl Van Vechten *Nigger Heaven* NY: Knopf, 1926 p. 82

4 Langston Hughes to Van Vechten 15 Dec. 1939 *Remember Me to Harlem: The Letters of Langston Hughes and Carl Van Vechten, 1925-1964* Ed., Emily Bernard NY: Knopf, 2001 p. 165

# ZORA NEALE HURSTON

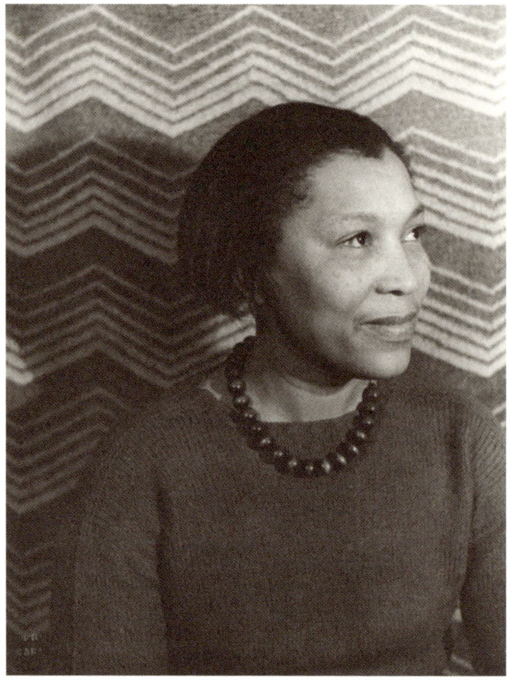



The author of novels, short stories, scholarly studies of African-American, Haitian, and Jamaican folklore, and autobiographical writing, Zora Neale Hurston is among the most celebrated writers of the Harlem Renaissance. Hurston's warmth and charm along with her vibrant personality made her one of the best-liked members of the 1920s Harlem literary elite, a group which included Langston Hughes, Countee Cullen, Dorothy West, and Nella Larsen. That Hurston gave this set the sobriquet "niggerati" is evidence of her considerable wit.

Hurston was raised in the all-black town of Eatonville, Florida, though she moved north at eighteen. She spent a year at Howard University studying with the influential African-American scholar Alain Locke; it was at Howard that Hurston's earliest stories were published, in the university's literary magazine and in *Opportunity*, from which she received an award for her story "Spunk" in 1925. From Howard she went on to New York to attend Barnard College on a scholarship. Though she continued writing at Barnard, Hurston also studied anthropology and folklore. After completing her bachelor's degree, Hurston received a grant to travel throughout the American south studying African-American folk traditions. This research led to numerous scholarly articles and the book *Mules and Men* (1935).

Hurston incorporated her research into her novels about southern African Americans, *Jonah's Gourd Vine* (1934) and *Their Eyes Were Watching God* (1937). She wrote dramatic pieces, too, and contributed work to African-American revues. She collaborated briefly with Langston Hughes on a play, *Mule Bone.* The project led to a deep conflict between the two writers and wasn't produced until the 1991, when it played at the Lincoln Center Theater in New York.

Carl Van Vechten met Zora Neale Hurston when she was working as a secretary for the writer Fannie Hurst. They liked each other instantly and shared a close friendship thereafter. "Zora is picturesque, witty, electric, indiscreet, and unreliable," Van Vechten wrote of his friend. "The later quality offers material for discussion; the former qualities induce her friends to forgive and love her. No engagement, no matter with whom, is sacred to Zora; nor does she find it important to advise you that she intends to break it."[1] He went on to remark on her unique

1. Van Vechten, "Some Literary Ladies I Have Known," *Yale University Library Gazette* 26.3 (1952) p. 113
2. "Some Literary Ladies I Have Known" p. 113
3. Fannie Hurst, "Zora Neale Hurston: A Personality Sketch" *Yale University Library Gazette* 35.1 (1960) p. 19
4. Zora Neale Hurston to Van Vechten in *Jonah's Gourd Vine* Philadelphia: Lippincott, 1934 Beinecke Library

PHOTOGRAPHED APRIL 3, 1935

sense of style, "she once appeared at a party we were giving attired in a wide Seminole Indian skirt, contrived of a thousand patches; still another time in a Norwegian skiing outfit, with a cap over her ears."[2]

For her part, Hurston was tremendously fond of Van Vechten. "If Carl was a people instead of a person," Hurston once said to Fannie Hurst, "I could then say, these are my people."[3] Van Vechten's copy of Hurston's novel *Jonah's Gourd Vine* bears the inscription, "For Carl Van Vechten who blows the slide trombone in the same band with Ol' Gabr'el."[4]

Hurston returned to Eatonville toward the end of her life. She withdrew from the literary scene and worked as a domestic in the home of a white family. She died in Eatonville in relative obscurity. Hurston's work returned to popularity in the 1970s in large part through the efforts of other African-American writers and scholars.

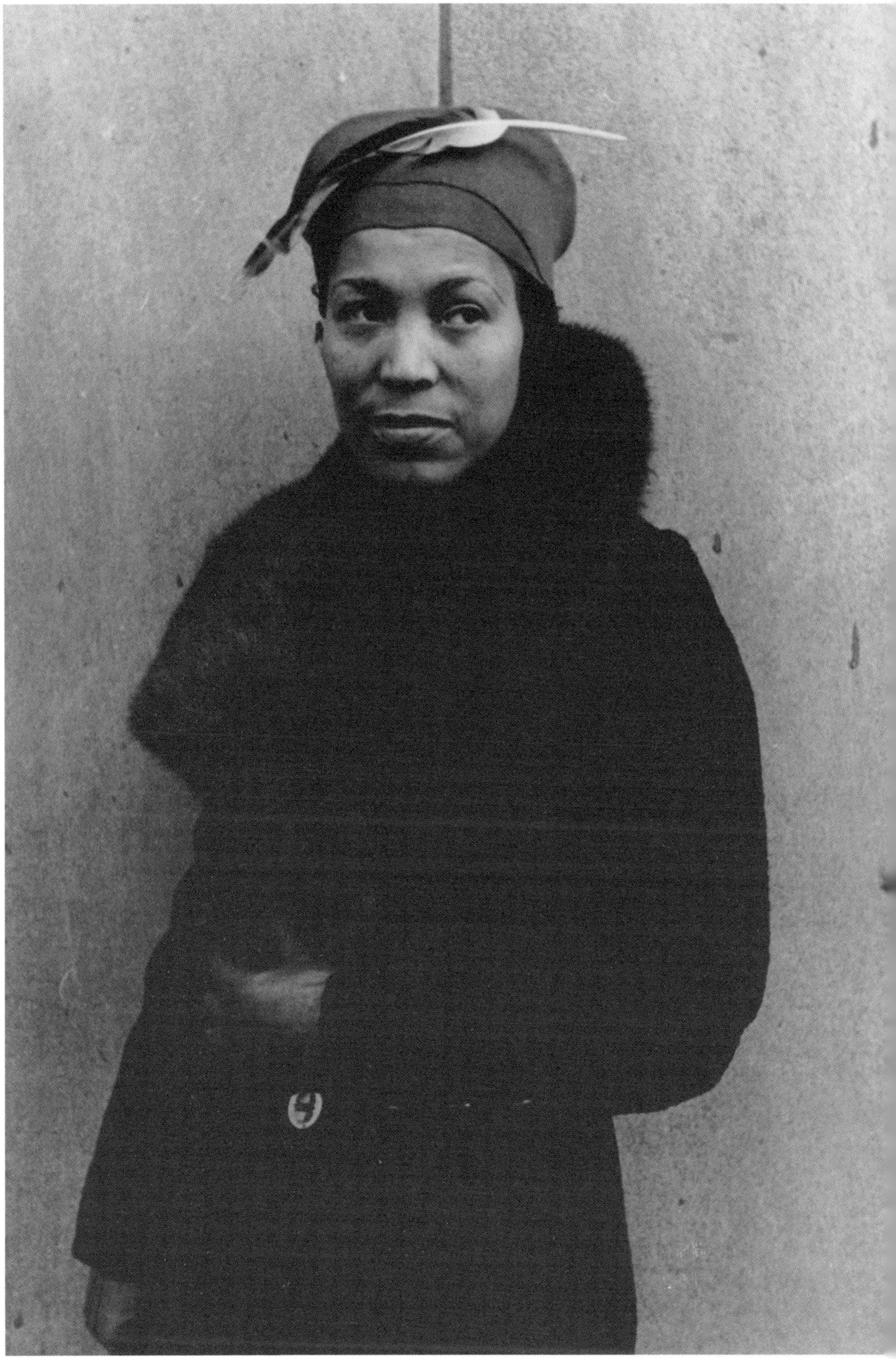

PHOTOGRAPHED IN CHICAGO ON NOVEMBER 9, 1934

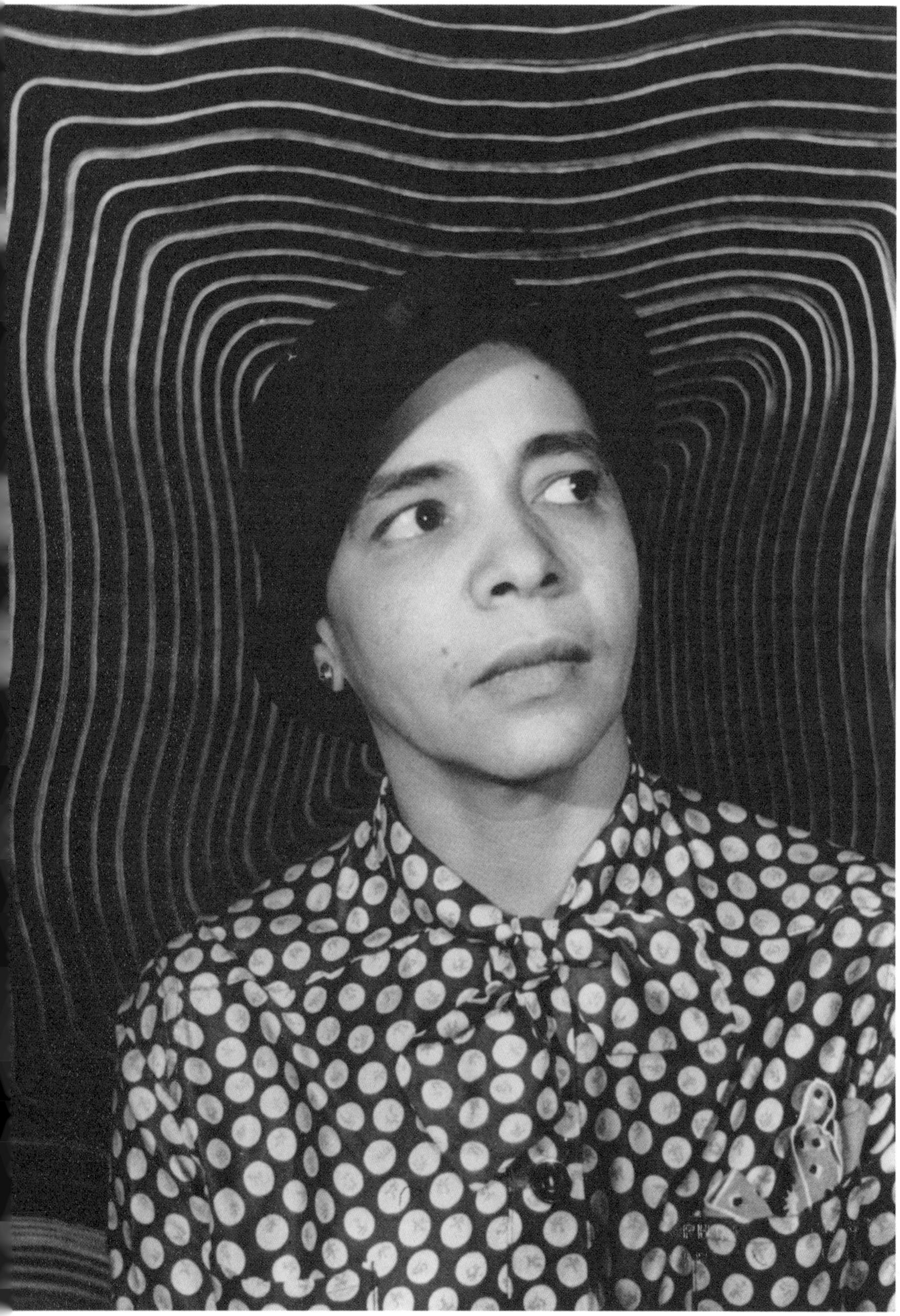

PHOTOGRAPHED ON NOVEMBER 23, 1934

## WRITER

The daughter of a white Danish mother and a black West Indian father, novelist Nella Larsen explores the complex issues of racial identity and identification in her fiction. Though critics remain conflicted about her novels, *Quicksand* (1928) and *Passing* (1929), there can be no question that they are significant, groundbreaking American literary texts. Larsen received a number of awards for her writing; in 1930, she was the first black woman to receive a Guggenheim Fellowship for creative writing. Along with her contemporary, novelist Zora Neale Hurston, Larsen is considered to be one of the most important female voices of the Harlem Renaissance.

Born in Chicago, Larsen lost her father when she was a child and her mother married a Dane. Though Larsen stated that she lived in Denmark as a teenager and that she returned to that country to attend the University of Copenhagen, some scholars argue that there is no documentary evidence to support these claims. She did, however study at Fisk University, the Lincoln Hospital Training Program where she studied nursing, and the New York Public Library's librarian training program. Through the height of her writing career Larsen worked as a nurse and as a children's librarian at the 135th Street Branch of the New York Public Library.

Carl Van Vechten was an early supporter of Larsen's work; "Who discovered this writer?" asked Thelma Berlack in the *Amsterdam News*, "Carl Van Vechten—and in her living room

# NELLA LARSEN



is an autographed photograph of him."[1] Van Vechten introduced Nella Larsen to his publishers, Blanche and Alfred Knopf, who later issued both her novels. Larsen and Van Vechten shared a warm friendship throughout the 1920s, when both were highly visible members of Harlem's literary community.

*Quicksand*, Larsen's first novel, was inspired in part by her experiences as a mixed-race woman in Harlem, the southern United States, and abroad. The novel's main character, Helga Crane, is the daughter of a white mother and black father. She faces hypocrisy and prejudice and her efforts to fit into various white and black communities are unsuccessful. The novel won the Harmon Foundation prize and the praise of contemporary critics and readers.

Larsen's second novel, *Passing*, is also concerned with the complexities of racial identity. *Passing* is the story of Clare Kendry, a mixed race woman who passes for white and marries a white man. Eventually, however, Clare risks her husband's discovery of her true identity because she feels compelled to go to Harlem and spend time with African Americans. Like Helga Crane, Clare is a woman who feels marginalized in both white and black communities. *Passing* was not as well received by critics as *Quicksand*; nevertheless, many agreed with one unsigned review which remarked that *Passing* was "an earnest and courageous attempt to deal with the whole theme, not just part of it selected as suitable for racial defense or propaganda."[2] Because of its subject matter, the novel was widely read, in spite of the mixed reviews it received. The controversy over the idea that some African Americans might pass for white is evident in an advertisement for the novel: "Every woman who 'passes' is a possible storm center. Nella Larsen knows her subject and around this sensational question she has written a fast-moving, action-filled story that will startle both Negroes and whites."[3]

Larsen began but never completed a third novel. In spite of her literary success, she went back to nursing and spent the next thirty years working at a Brooklyn hospital. The success of *Quicksand* and *Passing* speaks to Larsen's potential as a novelist and suggests that had she continued to write, she would likely have developed ever-greater skill. Though her books were out of print for some time, in recent years she has regained a reputation as a writer whose work reveals the complexity of her subject with both sensitivity and clarity.

1 Thelma E Berlack "Nella Larsen" *Amsterdam News* 23 Mar. 1928

2 *"Passing"* Unsigned review *New York Sun* 1 May 1929

3 Advertisement for *Passing* *New York World* 26 Apr. 1929

# MERCEDES DE ACOSTA

## WRITER



Though she was the author of books of prose, collections of poems, and scripts, Mercedes de Acosta is rarely remembered for her writing. She is, instead, celebrated as a passionate lover who had affairs with some of the most intriguing and beautiful women of her time. De Acosta is rumored to have boasted often of her prowess as a lover, even going so far as to declare "I can get any woman from any man."[1] Her list of lovers is long, including Eva Le Gallienne, Isadora Duncan, Marlene Dietrich, and, most famously, Greta Garbo.

De Acosta, the daughter of affluent Cuban immigrants, grew up in New York where, in the 1920s, she was a figure in both the city's "high society" and its drag clubs and speakeasies. "These were years guided by the spirit of the New," she wrote of this period; "We were on fire with fire, with a passion to create and a daring to achieve."[2] Equal to the times, de Acosta was a forward-thinking student of eastern religions and a strict vegetarian. An early feminist, de Acosta advocated, along with her friend and lover the dancer Isadora Duncan, the elimination of uncomfortable and restricting fashions for women; while other women were lacing themselves into corsets, de Acosta was often seen wearing trousers. When she convinced Garbo to visit her tailor and get a pair also, the two caused a great commotion on Hollywood Boulevard. "GARBO IN PANTS!" the headlines exclaimed. "Considering what walks down Hollywood Boulevard now," de Acosta wrote in 1960, "it seems strange that Greta and I should have caused such a sensation."[3]

After a life surrounded by fame, glamour, and wealth, Mercedes de Acosta spent her last years in loneliness and poverty. She suffered a variety of illnesses later in life, requiring several painful surgeries, and was forced to sell her diamonds to pay her medical bills. Her 1960 tell-all autobiography, *Here Lies the Heart,* alienated many of de Acosta's friends. Some claimed the book to be wildly exaggerated and even blatantly untrue.

An April 2000 exhibition entitled "Garbo Unsealed" at the Rosenbach Museum and Library in Philadelphia generated new interest in de Acosta. The controversial and eagerly anticipated exhibition displayed a group of the actress's letters to de Acosta, letters that had never before been available for public view. Finally, fans and scholars hoped, light would be shed on Garbo's long-rumored love affair with the writer and socialite. The letters, however, defy easy interpretation. Some say they carry no hint of a romantic relationship between the two women; others claim that the letters prove beyond a doubt that Garbo and de Acosta were lovers.

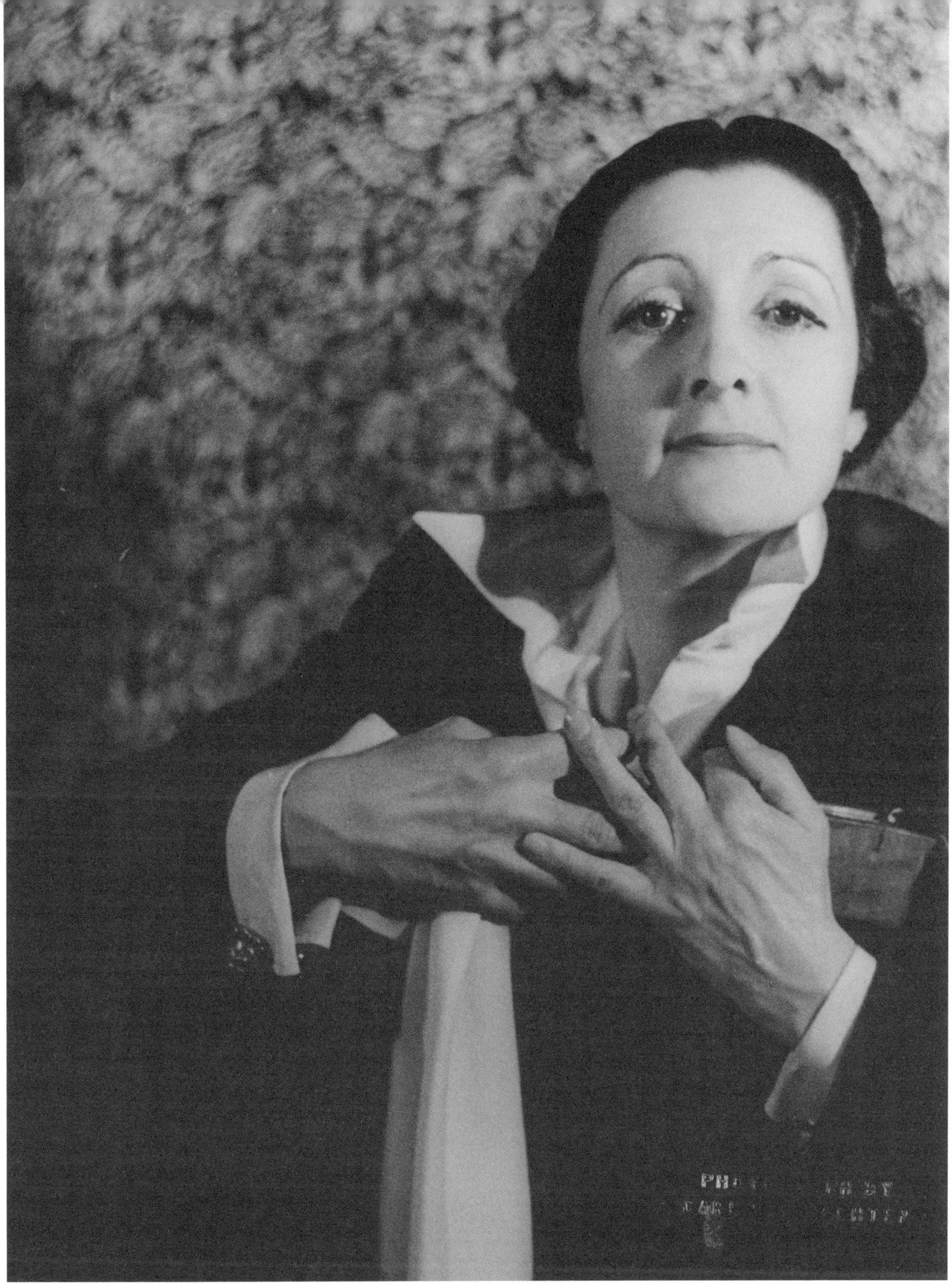


PHOTOGRAPHED ON MARCH 8, 1935

1 Hugo Vickers
*Loving Garbo: The Story of Greta Garbo, Cecil Beaton and Mercedes de Acosta*
London: Jonathan Cape
1994
p. 8

2 Mercedes De Acosta
*Here Lies the Heart: A Tale of My Life*
NY: Reynal and Company
1960
p. 67

3 *Here Lies the Heart: A Tale of My Life*
p. 229

SOPRANO



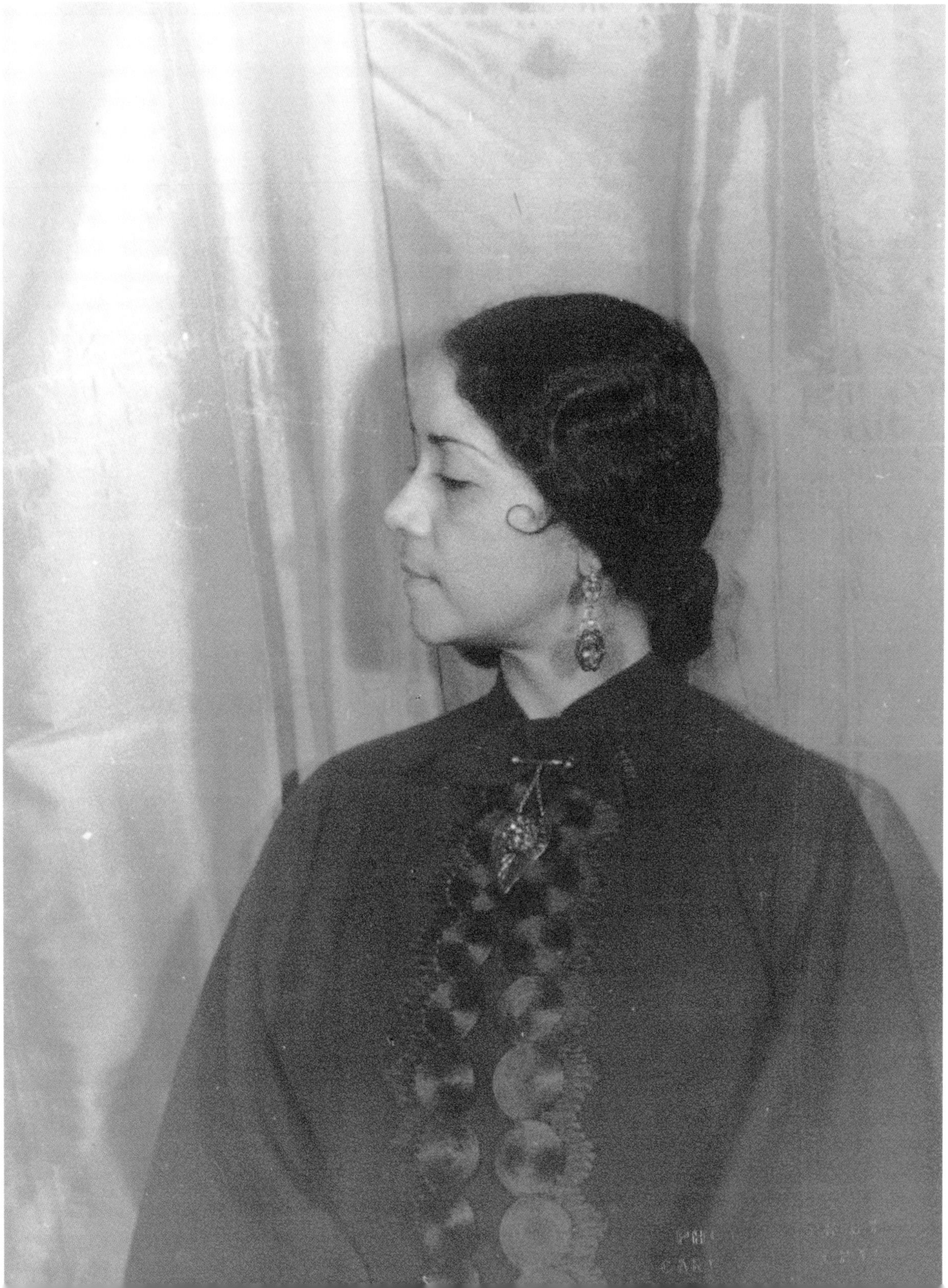

# LILLIAN EVANTI



Annie Lillian Evans, who would later become the famed classical singer Lillian Evanti, was by many accounts the first African American to sing grand opera professionally anywhere in the world. She was born in Washington, D.C. into a prominent, historically significant family. The Evans family claimed a Revolutionary War soldier, two abolitionists who took part in the Harper's Ferry Raid, and the first African-American United States Senator among their ancestors. Evanti's own parents were well educated and accomplished; both dedicated their lives to education, her mother as a music teacher, her father as founder and principal of Washington, D.C.'s Armstrong High School.

After graduating from her father's school, Evanti went to a teacher's college and briefly taught kindergarten. She gave up teaching to study music at Howard University. After completing a bachelor of music degree in 1917, Evanti married one of her professors, Roy W. Tibbs. At the suggestion of poet and editor Jessie Fauset, she combined Evans and Tibbs to form the more elegant "Evanti," the name she would use professionally thereafter.

In 1925, Evanti moved to France in hopes of breaking into the European opera scene. During the next few years she performed with the Nice and Paris opera companies throughout Europe. She remained in France until the outbreak of World War II, at which time she returned to the United States. She was well received by audiences in the United States, though she periodically faced racism in the opera community. In one instance, the director of the Metropolitan Opera invited Evanti to audition, but he was unable to convince racist board members to hire an African-American singer.

Evanti was one of the founders of the National Negro Opera Company, and one of its most popular performers. When she sang *La Traviata* with the company in New York, the interest was so great that additional shows had to be arranged to accommodate the demand for tickets. For this occasion, Evanti translated the opera, which she had performed many times in French and Italian, into English. When the company took the show to Evanti's hometown, her interpretation of Violetta was highly praised: "She is a coloratura whose vocal gifts and attainments include all the resources of the lyric soprano. Her interpretation was, in consequence, both brilliant and sympathetic."[1]

Evanti, who spoke (and sang) five languages, was a particularly versatile singer. She was known for her dynamic performances and her commanding presence on stage. Some time before African-American singers such as Leontyne Price and Adele Addison began to appear regularly in American operas, Lillian Evanti struggled to realize her tremendous potential as a performer in spite of the racism embedded in the opera world of her day.

1 Glenn Dillard Gunn "National Negro Opera Enchants 12,000 Here" *Washington Times Herald* 29 Aug. 1943

PHOTOGRAPHED ON OCTOBER 31, 1935

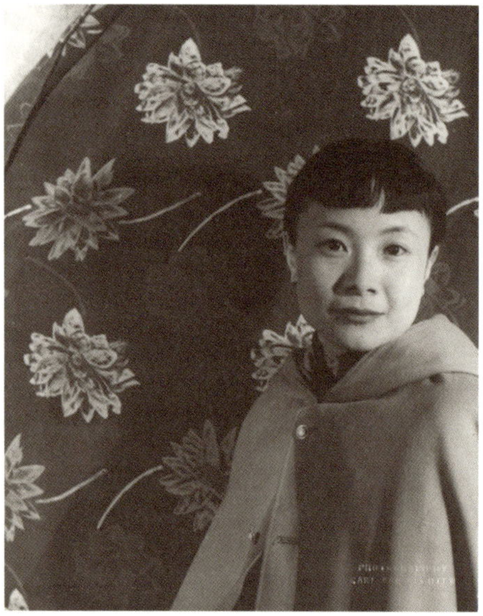

# MAI-MAI SZE

## ACTRESS, AUTHOR, PAINTER, & ADVOCATE



The daughter of a Chinese ambassador to England and the United States, Mai-Mai Sze achieved a significant level of accomplishment in literature and the fine and performing arts. Born in China, Sze spent her childhood in Great Britain and Washington, D.C. where she was educated at the National Cathedral School. She went on to study at Wellesley College, from which she graduated in 1931.

After finishing college, Sze's first career was as a landscape painter. Though her work was exhibited in New York, and in galleries in Paris and London, Sze's most notable work was her drawing of playwright Eugene O'Neill, which was reproduced on book jackets, theater programs, and in magazines. In 1946, Sze wrote a book about Chinese painting, *The Tao of Painting*, volume two of which was her translation of the *Mustard Seed Garden Manual of Painting*, a 15th-century Chinese text. Sze's translation is still used by painters and art students today.

Success in one field did not prevent Sze from pursuing other interests. In the mid 1930s, she appeared in a popular Broadway show, *Lady Precious Stream*, by S.I. Hsiung. In this "lovely and humorous"[1] story of a romance set in ancient China, Sze played the narrator, "Honorable Reader."

Around this time, Sze became an advocate for relief in her native China, often lecturing about the country and the needs of its people. She founded the Chinese War Relief Committee in New York and helped to raise support for the medical and other needs of the Chinese people. In the 1940s, Sze wrote *China*, a book about her ancestral home.

Perhaps Sze's greatest success was as a writer. The author of several books of fiction and non-fiction, she was a well-known columnist for the *New York Post* and a contributor to national magazines. Sze wrote an autobiography, *Echo of a Cry: A Story Which Began in China* (1945), and a novel, *Silent Children* (1948). Of *Silent Children*, the story of a group of young refugees trying to survive in a bleak, post-war landscape, John Bicknell wrote, "The theme is as poignant as any in our time, with its counterpart in every country touched by the war. [Sze's] picture of the children's community is vivid and compassionate without being sentimental."[2] Sze made additional contributions to the literary community as a frequent book reviewer for the *New York Times*.

In March of 1940, just a month after Van Vechten photographed Mai-Mai Sze in New York, she wrote a letter thanking him for sending her prints of the photos. "Thank you so much for sending the pictures—I especially like the profile," she wrote. "You are the only person who has ever made me feel I had one. [Plus] something of a nose!"[3]

PHOTOGRAPHED ON FEBRUARY 12, 1940

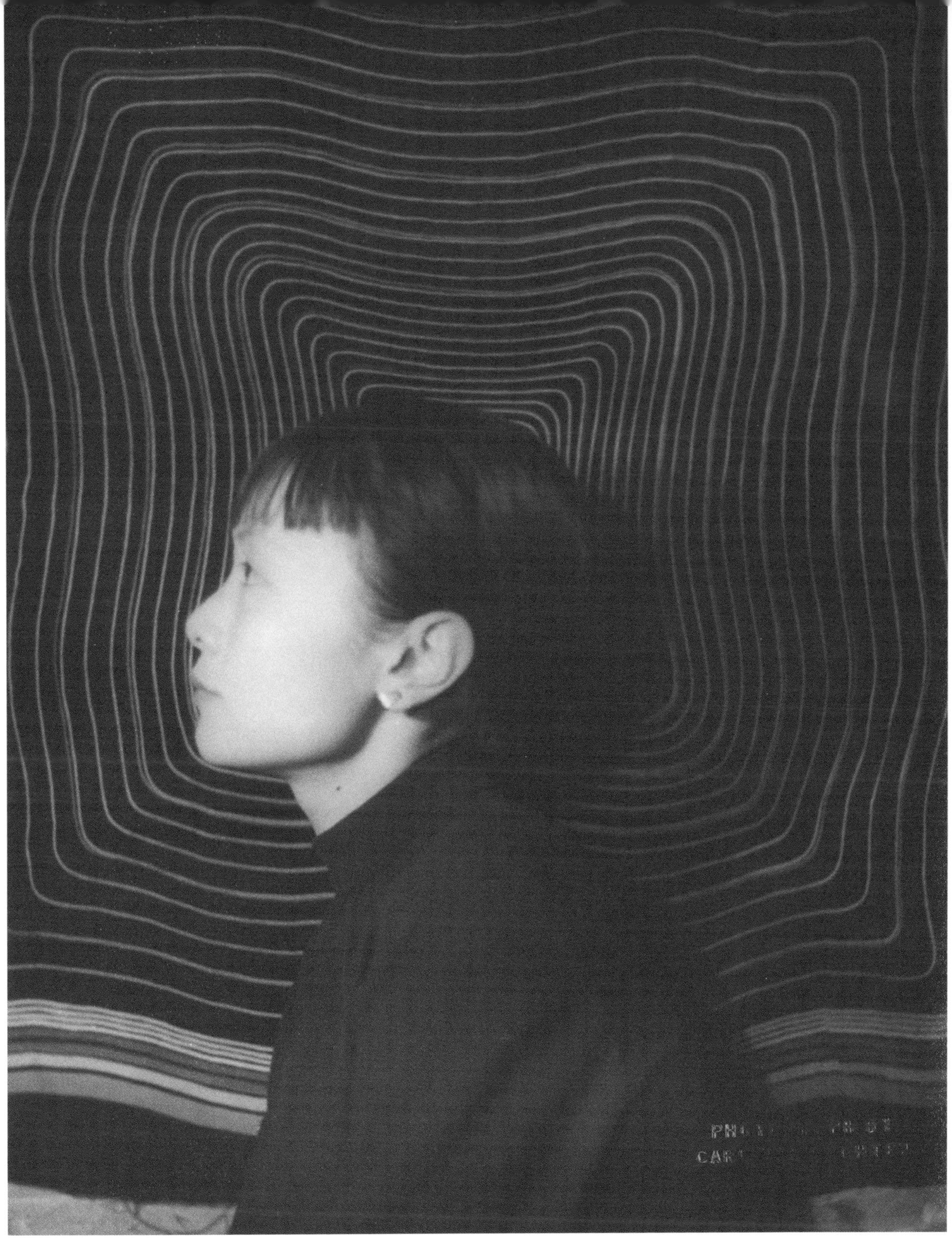

PHOTOGRAPHED ON DECEMBER 29, 1935

1 Brooks Atkinson
"Lady Precious Stream by Dr. S. I. Hsiung, or the Poor Gardener Who Made Good"
*New York Times*
28 Jan. 1936

2 John Bicknell
"China's Children (Review of *Silent Children* by Mai Mai Sze)"
*New York Times*
18 Apr. 1948

3 Sze to Van Vechten
24 Mar. 1940
Van Vechten Papers
Beinecke Library
Yale University

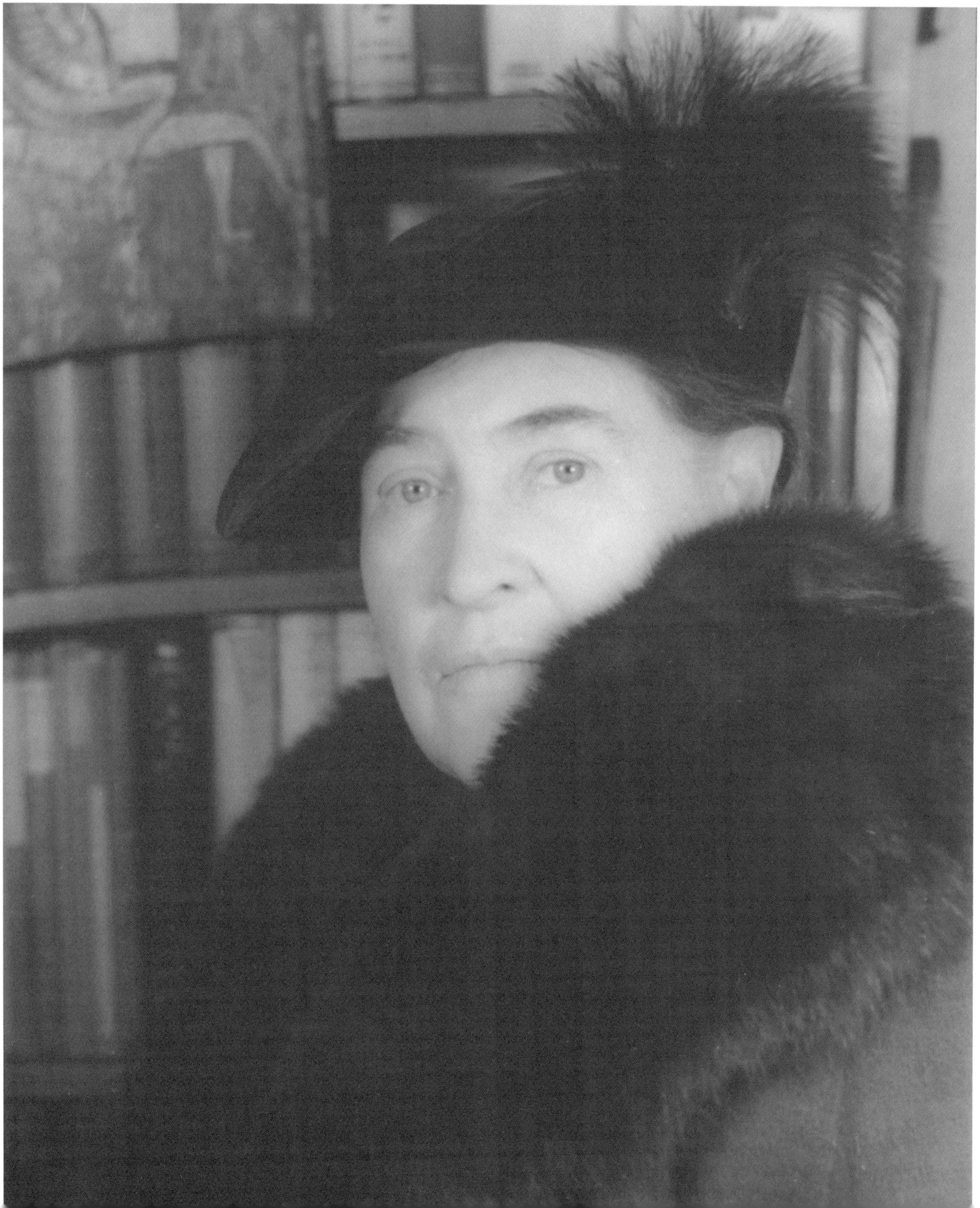

# WILLA CATHER

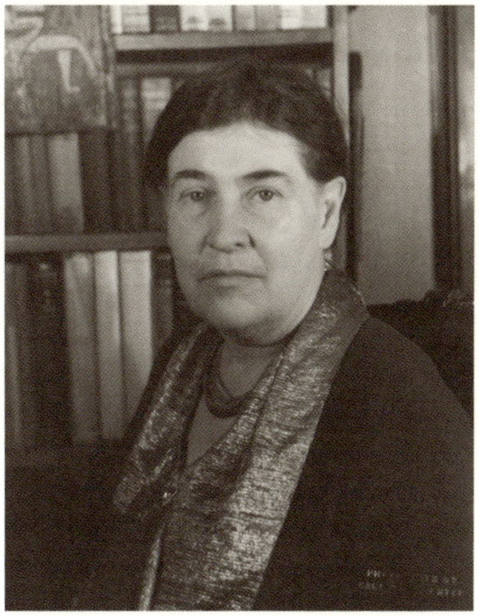



Willa Cather and Carl Van Vechten had little in common aside from their editor, Blanche Knopf, and a shared love of the opera. Though they were never close friends, they met from time to time at the Knopfs' table where they enjoyed discussing their favorite opera singers and recent performances. They talked at length about Olive Fremstad, a singer they both admired and on whose life Cather based her novel *The Song of the Lark*.

Willa Cather is one of American's finest novelists and perhaps the most influential to emerge from the central Plains states. She grew up in Red Cloud, Nebraska, and many of her most celebrated novels take place in the farming communities of the Nebraska prairie, portraying the difficult lives of pioneering families in this unforgiving landscape. The most famous of these books, *O Pioneers!* (1913), *My Antonia* (1918), and the Pulitzer Prize winning *One of Ours* (1926), demonstrate Cather's forceful and unadorned prose style. Though she has been criticized for her sometimes-nostalgic vision of the American prairie, her work is also praised for its unflinching depiction of the region. One contemporary critic wrote of Cather:

> Her gift is a vivid expositional narrative form that reveals the soul through remarkable characterization. Her psychology never goes deeper than it does when her characters are working arduously on their farms or battling their way through the terrible Nebraskan blizzards. Then a rich magic creeps into her pages. . . . There is no American author living who can better exploit her own region than Miss Cather.[1]

During her childhood, Cather was a classic tomboy, even referring to herself as William. In spite of her mother's opposition, she flouted convention by wearing trousers and cutting her hair short. As a young woman, she studied at the University of Nebraska before moving east to Pennsylvania to work as an editor. She wrote in her spare time for more than ten years before, at the urging of her mentor, writer Sarah Orne Jewett, she decided to devote herself to her literary ambitions full time.

Van Vechten tried for some time to persuade Cather to allow him to photograph her; he even enlisted the aid of their mutual friend, Blanche Knopf. "I have just been talking to Miss Cather," Knopf wrote in a letter to Van Vechten, "and I suggest to you that if you could have her come over in the daytime she would come to have her picture taken. I think the idea of her coming for dinner and then having her picture taken rather worried her."[2] After nearly a year, Cather finally consented to Van Vechten's request. In the end, she hated the photos that resulted from the sitting. In a letter, she voiced her displeasure and asked Van Vechten to destroy the prints and the negatives. Whether the subject thought the photographer would comply with her wishes is unclear. "At any rate," Van Vechten wrote, "I saw little of her after the photographs were made."[3]

1 Herbert S. Gorman
"Willa Cather, Novelist of the Middlewestern Farm"
*New York Times*
24 June 1923

2 Blanche Knopf to Van Vechten
14 Mar. 1935
Van Vechten Papers
Beinecke Library
Yale University

3 Van Vechten
"Some Literary Ladies I Have Known"
*Yale University Library Gazette*
26:3 (1952)
p. 106

PHOTOGRAPHED JANUARY 22, 1936

# BESSIE SMITH

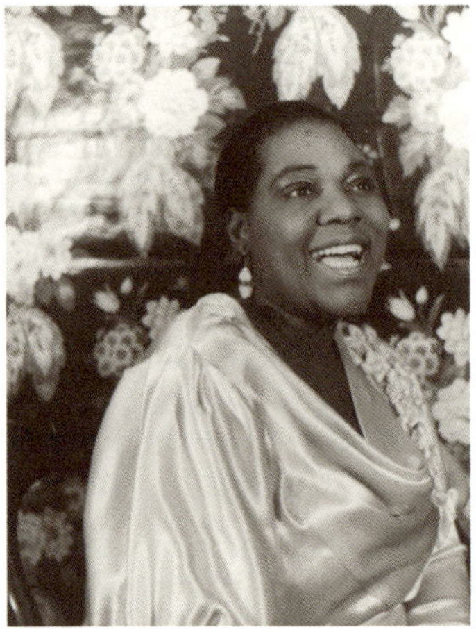

Orphaned as a little girl, Bessie Smith joined a vaudeville company when she was still a child. During a performance, legendary blues singer "Ma" Rainey discovered her. Intriguing rumors surround their meeting—"legend has it that Ma Rainey literally kidnapped Bessie, that she and her husband forced the girl to tour with their show, teaching her in the process how to sing the blues."[1] In this version of the story, the women became lovers. There is little evidence to support the kidnapping or love affair, but Rainey did invite Smith to join her show; she taught Smith the music business and helped develop her voice and performance style. In this way the "Mother of the Blues" launched the career of the "Empress of the Blues." The two women remained lifelong friends.

For the next decade, Smith traveled all over the south, singing and dancing in the tent shows that were a major venue for African-American performers—most southern theaters were closed to African-American audiences and entertainers alike. Smith's distinct southern blues style became popular and as a result of her relentless touring, she developed a following in the south, Philadelphia and New York, and the Midwest. Smith made her first record in 1923. It sold almost 800,000 copies in a year. She made nearly eighty more records before 1930. Her most popular songs included "Nobody Knows You When You're Down and Out," "St. Louis Blues," and "Gulf Coast Blues."

Smith rode high through the 1920s, earning more money than any other African-American entertainer. When Carl Van Vechten wrote an article for *Vanity Fair* about Smith in 1926, he introduced many in the magazine's largely white audience to the blues. When Van Vechten's friend, the poet Langston Hughes, told Smith about the article, she was not impressed:

> I went back stage to meet Bessie Smith. . . . [She] says she has got herself a tent and is going back down to Bam this summer and make a few more thousands. She remembered you and your wife but didn't seem at all concerned as to whether articles were written about her or not. And her only comment on the art of the blues was that they had put her "in de money."[2]

Smith was a woman with a large personality, a raunchy sense of humor, and complex relationships with those closest to her. Her first marriage, to a Philadelphia police officer named Jack Gee, was volatile and often violent. In response, Smith turned to alcohol, and to various lovers, both men and women. Gee sometimes knew of her infidelities, but Smith concealed her relationships with women, fearing that Gee might seek revenge on her female lovers. The couple split when Smith learned that Gee was funding his lover's show with Smith's money.

Smith's career slowed down in the 1930s; she struggled to update her style in light of the new jazz and swing craze. She became involved with an old friend, Richard Morgan, a quiet man who had loved her for years. Carl Van Vechten photographed Smith during this time; she arrived at his apartment between

1 Chris Albertson, *Bessie*, NY: Stein and Day, 1972, p. 27

2 Langston Hughes to Van Vechten, 20 Jan. 1926, *Remember Me to Harlem: The Letters of Langston Hughes and Carl Van Vechten 1925-1964*, Ed., Emily Bernard, NY: Knopf, 2001, p. 35

3 Van Vechten, "Memories of Bessie Smith" *Jazz Record*, Sept. 1947, p. 29

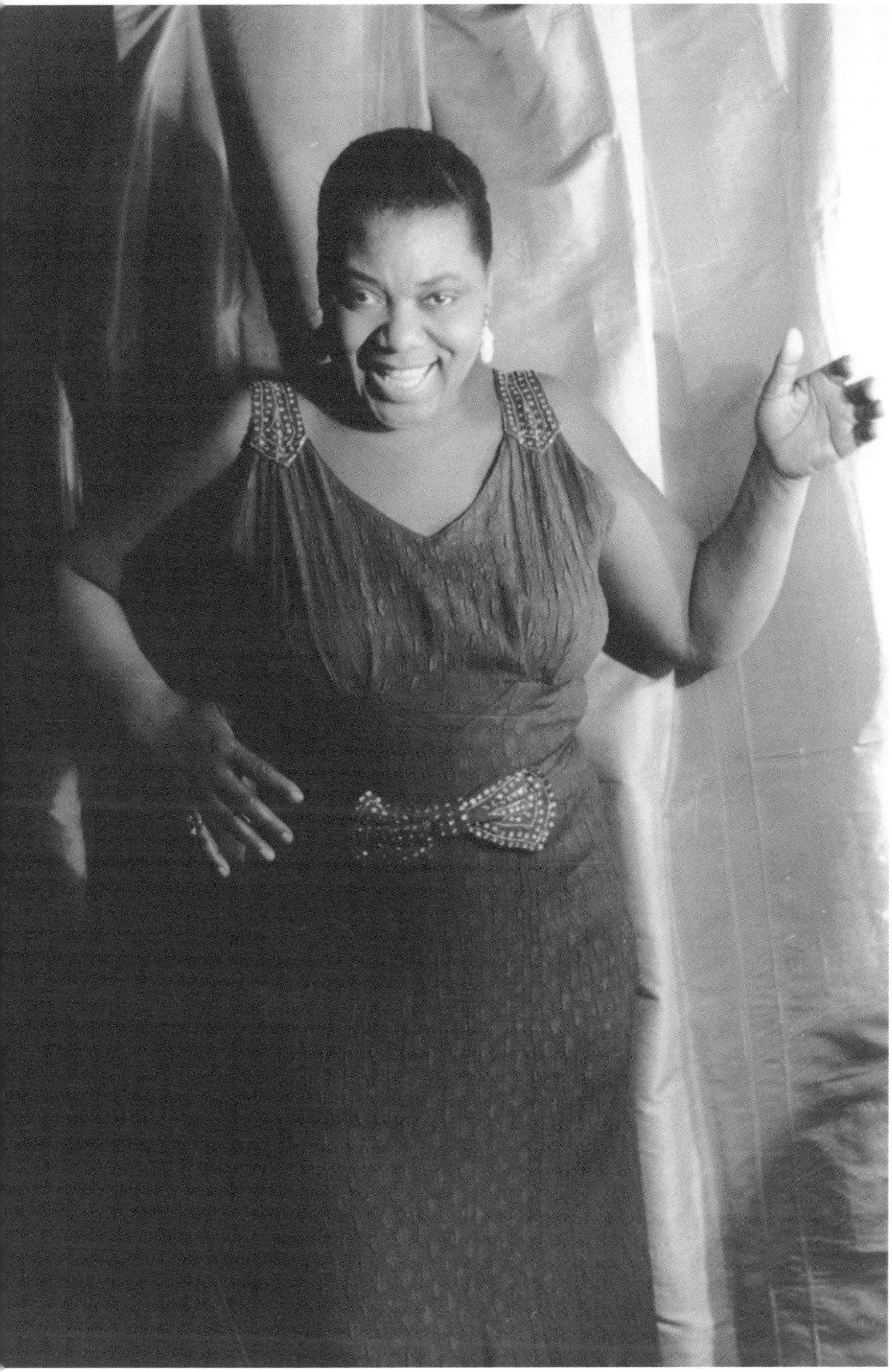

## SINGER

shows at a nightclub, sober and contemplative. With these photographs, Van Vechten felt he had come "closer to her real personality than I ever had before and these photographs, perhaps, are the only adequate record of her true appearance and manner that exist."[3]



Bessie Smith died after a late night car accident two years after Van Vechten photographed her; she was fifty years old. Contradictory reports surround Smith's death, which, like much of her life, remains shrouded in rumor. Some say a doctor at the scene abandoned Smith to treat a white couple who had received minor injuries in the crash. Others suggest that Smith bled to death in the ambulance on the long drive in search a of hospital that treated African Americans. It has been suggested, too, that Smith was refused treatment at a nearby white hospital. This scenario is the subject of Edward Albee's play *The Death of Bessie Smith*.

PHOTOGRAPHED ON FEBRUARY 3, 1936

# ACTRESS

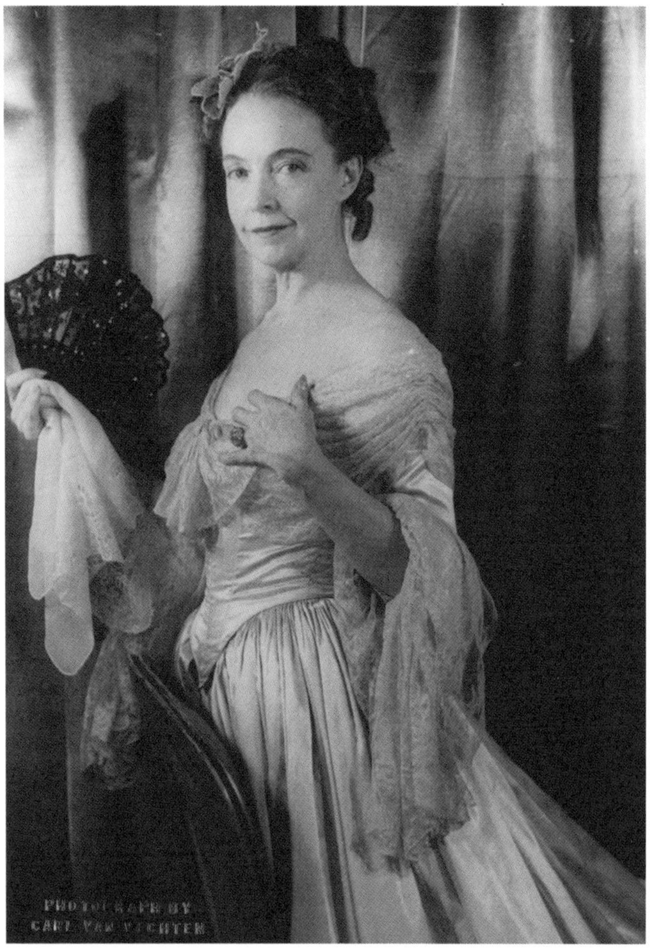


PHOTOGRAPHED OCTOBER 28, 1947

In the very earliest days of her career, Gish, then known as "Baby Lillian," began performing with the tenants of the theatrical boarding house her mother operated in New York City. Her father had abandoned the family when Gish and her sister, fellow actress Dorothy Gish, were very small, and their mother continually struggled to support them. She allowed Gish to travel with a number of vaudeville shows and companies as a young child, often without a guardian. During these difficult times, Gish developed the determination and commitment that would become her professional trademarks.

Lillian and Dorothy Gish arrived in Hollywood during the early days of the silent film industry. There, the Gish sisters encountered Gladys Smith, an old friend from New York. Smith—better known by then as Mary Pickford, the silent film star—introduced Gish to the already prominent director D.W. Griffith. In the years that followed, Gish worked closely with Griffith on a great many films, sometimes making as many as twelve movies in a year. He helped to polish and improve her skills in acting and dancing, and it was as the star of Griffith's films that Gish became a leading film actress, developing a reputation as the "Bernhardt of the screen." With Griffith, she made more than fifty short and feature-length films, including the notorious and still controversial *Birth of a Nation.* In film appearances she was often thought to be "fragile and misty;"[1] a quality of innocence and frailty emerged from her forceful and deliberate performances, and was at the center of Gish's distinctive acting style.

When "talkies" arrived ending the silent film era, Gish left Hollywood after nearly twenty years and returned to New York to pursue work in the theater. In spite of the incredible success Gish achieved as a silent film actress, many doubted she could perform as well on stage. Her early stage appearances proved that Gish was a talented actress on the boards as well on the silver screen. Her 1930 portrayal of Helena in Chekhov's *Uncle Vanya* earned her critical praise and the enthusiastic response of audiences. When she appeared as a character based on Lizzie Borden in John Colton's *Nine Pine Street*, one critic wrote: "[Miss Gish] gives a fine performance in all its varied details, and they are many, ranging as they do from love

1 "Who's Who in Pictures" *New York Times* 10 Dec. 1933

2 "Miss Lillian Gish, as a Reincarnation of Lizzie Borden, Appears in 'Nine Pine Street'" *New York Times* 28 Apri. 1933

3 Gish to Van Vechten 16 July 1940 Van Vechten Papers Beinecke Library Yale University

# LILLIAN GISH

to murder. She injects into the whole play a feeling of sincerity and those parts of it that seem most real are due to her."[2] Of her roles throughout the thirties and of Carl Van Vechten's photographs of her during the period, Gish wrote to the photographer, "The subject looks a little more world-weary than she feels at the moment—no doubt due to the fact that she was playing sad, sad parts and has now turned into a happy comedienne."[3]

Later in her life, Gish returned to film and began making television appearances. She made films well in the 1980s, staring in her last film, *The Whales of August* in 1987 with Bette Davis. Gish died in 1993 at the age of ninety-nine. She worked in theater and film for more that seventy-five years.

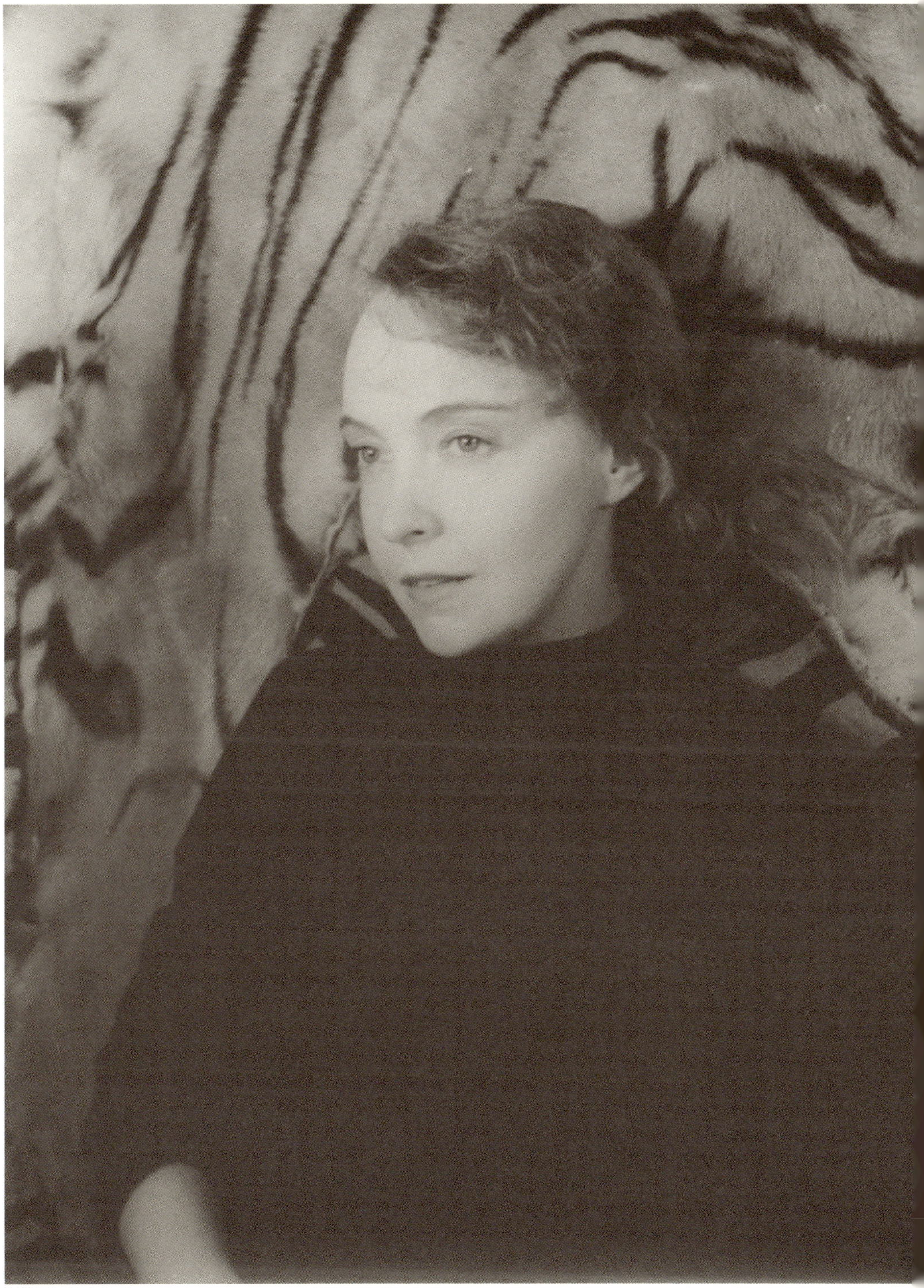

PHOTOGRAPHED APRIL 12, 1937

# ACTRESS



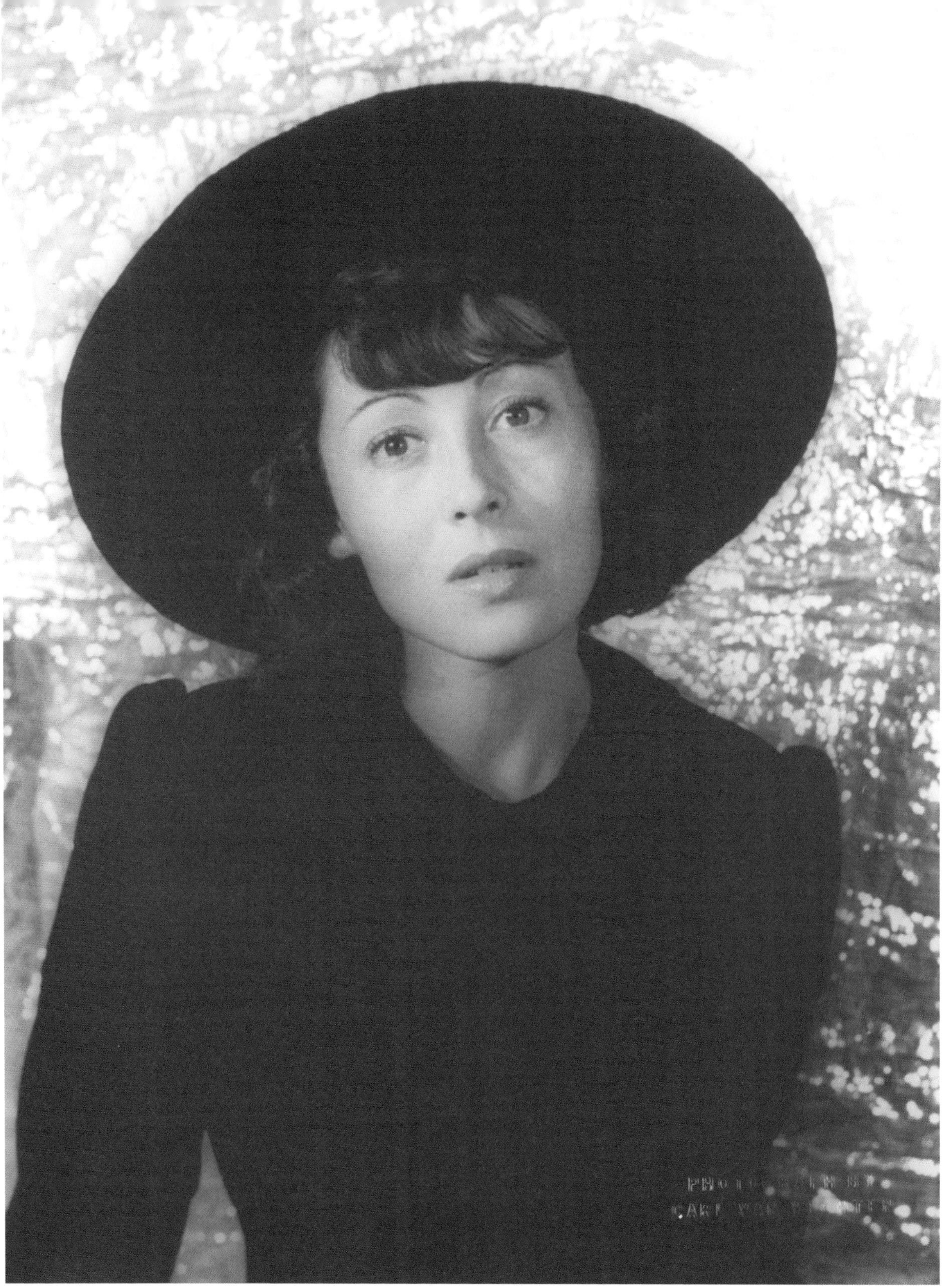

# LUISE RAINER

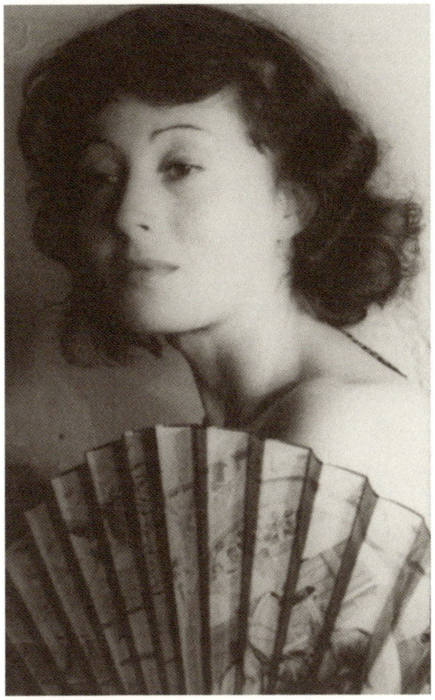



The first actress to win two consecutive Academy Awards for Best Actress, Luise Rainer was admired for her extremely vivid and emotional acting style. She was known for her expressive physical gestures, her sensitive eyes, and her demonstrative hand movements. After a handful of successful performances, Rainer fell out of fashion with movie studios and virtually vanished from Hollywood films.

After making a few films in Germany in 1935, Rainer made her first Hollywood film, *Escapade,* starring William Powell. Because of her accent and European demeanor, she was compared to Greta Garbo, who was then one of the most popular stars in Hollywood. In 1936 she appeared opposite Powell again in *The Great Ziegfeld*. Her skillful and flamboyant portrayal of Ziegfeld's first wife, French actress Anna Held, earned her the first of her two Best Actress Oscars. She was just twenty-six years old.

The very next year, Rainer beat out Anna May Wong for the role of O-lan, the Chinese peasant at the center of *The Good Earth*, a film adapted from Pearl S. Buck's novel. In contrast to the part of Anna Held, O-lan was defined by her humility and her silent submission to her husband's will. Rainer had few lines in the film, and she rarely looked directly at the camera. Because of its difference from her earlier roles, Rainer's O-lan was widely praised as evidence of her strength and range as a dramatic actress. In 1937 she was chosen over Greta Garbo to receive the Academy Award for Best Actress.

Rainer made a few more films, all of which were unremarkable. After a few years, she broke her studio contract and retired from Hollywood film. Though she later made guest appearances on popular television shows and in made-for-TV movies, she was largely forgotten by Hollywood and the general public.

According to Hollywood superstition, Rainer was a victim of the so-called Oscar Curse; it was with Rainer, in fact, that the myth that Oscar success might actually signal the end of one's career originated. "The Oscar is not a curse," Rainer has said, "the curse is that once you have an Oscar they think you can do anything."[1] Her film career ended, Rainer speculates, not because she was no longer offered parts but because Hollywood thought she could salvage otherwise bad scripts and studios no longer offered her quality roles.

She remained the only winner of back-to-back Oscars until Katherine Hepburn won the award in 1967 and 1968.

1 "Oscar Jinx" *People Weekly* 11 Apr. 1988 p. 85

PHOTOGRAPHED ON SEPTEMBER 2, 1937

# BERENICE ABBOTT



From an early age, Ohio native Berenice Abbott felt restricted by the societal expectations placed on girls and women during her time. She resisted the traditional and pursued independence and personal satisfaction over social acceptance. A rebellious and unconventional woman, Berenice Abbott changed her name to signify her break with cultural norms, adding an "e" to the common spelling of her name, "Bernice."

Abbott left Ohio as a young woman, moving to New York where she intended to study journalism. She soon tired of that work and took up drawing and sculpture. After a few years in New York, Abbott headed to Paris, seeking additional training in the arts. It was in Paris that Abbott was first introduced to photography, when she became an assistant to the influential photographer and surrealist painter, Man Ray. She gave up sculpture completely to pursue photography. Abbott worked under Ray for three years, developing her skills as a photographer; she then opened her own portrait studio in Paris. Her studio was immediately successful and Abbott became well known among Paris's artistic and expatriate communities.

Like Van Vechten, Abbott is well known for her portraits of famous, fashionable people. Her style, however, differs significantly from his; "Abbott's cool and restrained portraits, made in her Paris studio in the late 1920s, stress silhouette and neutral, uncluttered backgrounds."[1] Abbott's famous subjects for this period include James Joyce, Janet Flanner, Djuna Barnes, Edna St. Vincent Millay, Jean Cocteau, and André Gide. Portraits she made during these early years remain among her most famous images; her portraits of Joyce, for example, are among the most widely reproduced photographs of the novelist.

In Paris, Abbott became interested in the work of an unknown photographer, Eugene Atget. She promoted his work, and when he died in 1927 she purchased his prints, negatives, and slides. Throughout her life, Abbott arranged exhibitions and publication of Atget's photographs. Because of her commitment to his art, Atget's photographs of Paris are well known today and he is considered an important French photographer.

Atget's photographs of Paris had a profound influence on Abbott. When she returned to New York, she undertook a major photographic project documenting New York City and its changing landscape. She worked for years, as old buildings were torn down and replaced by skyscrapers. Abbott "looked upon the urban scene as a challenge to the camera artist who must extract an aesthetically compelling statement from a chaotic field and still capture the city's distinctive character."[2] *Changing New York*, a book of photographs from the project, was published in 1939.

In contrast to *Changing New York*, in her next project Abbott attempted to photograph scientific processes and to illustrate basic principles of physics and chemistry. That some of this work was intended for textbooks did not undermine Abbott's

1 Naomi Rosenblum, *A History of Women Photographers*, NY: Abbeville Press, 1994, p. 127

2 *A History of Women Photographers*, p. 176

3 Charles Hagen, "Berenice Abbott, 93, Dies; Her Photographs Captured New York in Transition," *New York Times*, 11 Dec. 1991

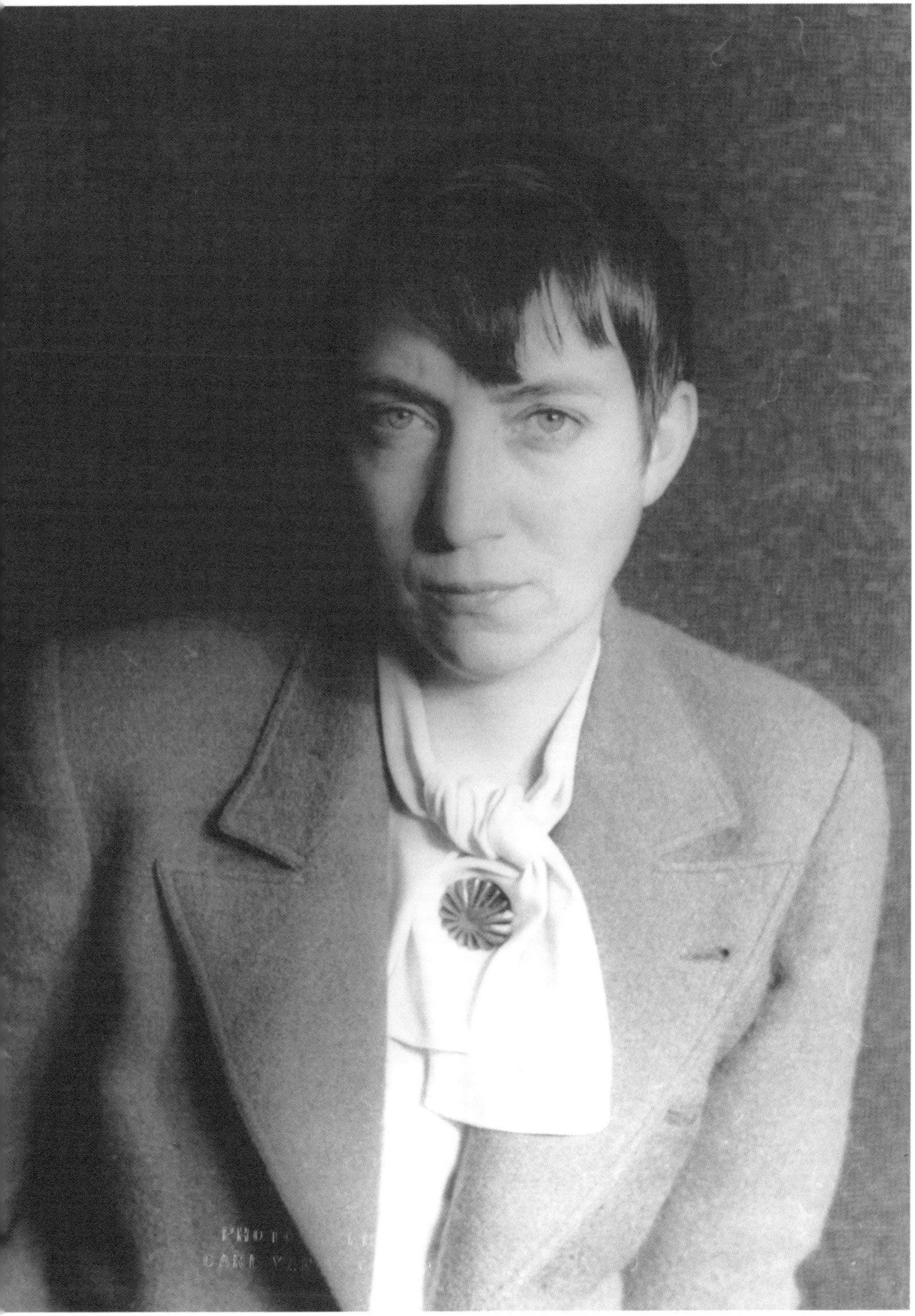

PHOTOGRAPHED ON NOVEMBER 8, 1937

## PHOTOGRAPHER

aesthetics, and some believe the work from this period is her most accomplished. Abbott's scientific photography was made difficult by a general mistrust among scientists that photography could be used as a scientific tool. Furthermore, the near total lack of women in science and a common feeling that women could not participate meaningfully in such fields presented many roadblocks to Abbott's ambitious projects. 

Throughout her career, Abbott committed time and energy to promoting the still-new art of photography. A proponent of documentary photography, Abbott "argued that photography was uniquely a descriptive medium, and should not be used to simulate effects that could be better achieved by other arts."[3] She also helped to develop the photography program at the New School for Social Research. Abbott did not shy away from discussing the political implications of her work, especially with regard to the ways her photographs documented the changing social and economical conditions in 1930s New York.

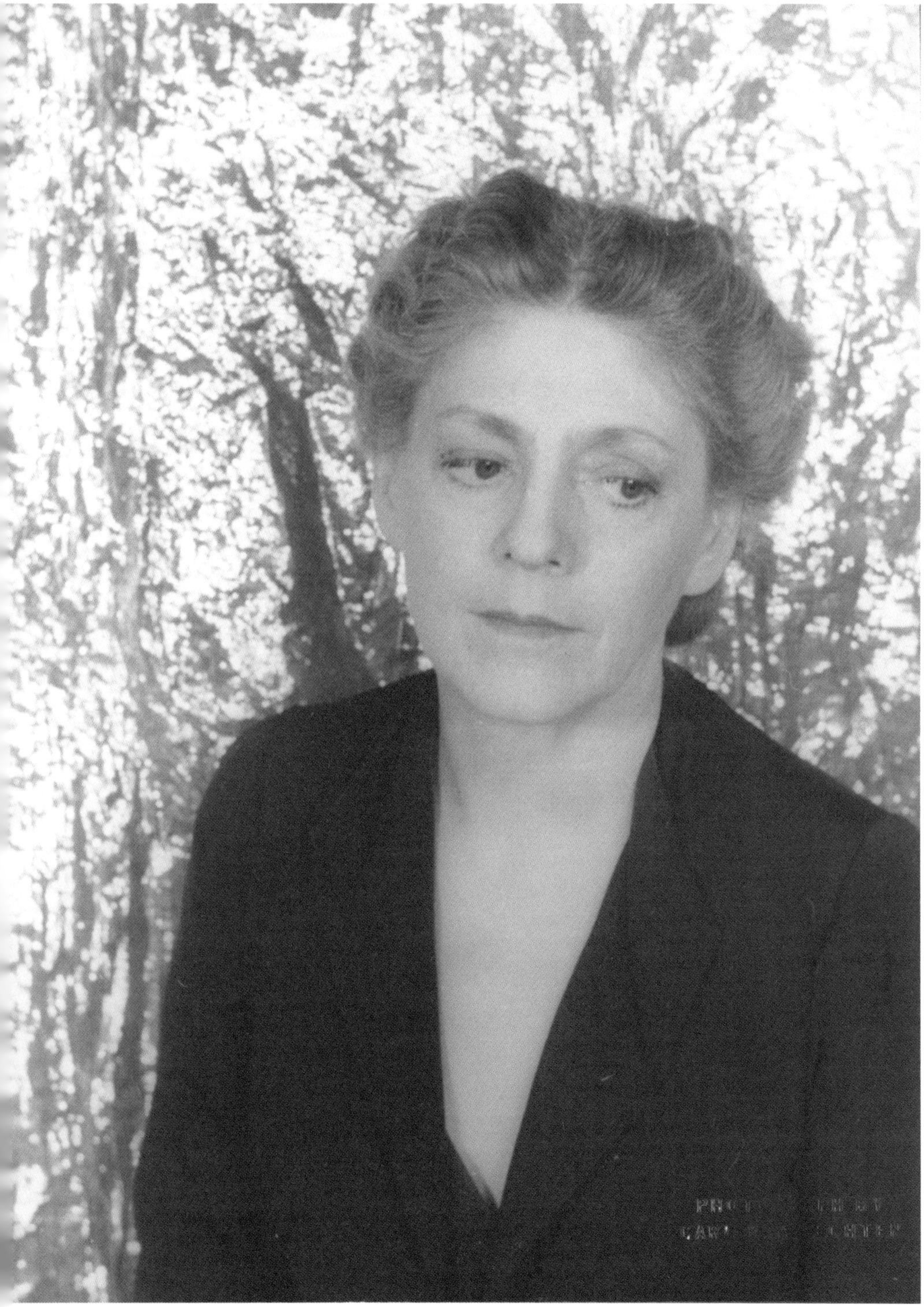

PHOTOGRAPHED ON DECEMBER 12, 1937

## ACTRESS

Often called "the first lady of the American stage," Ethel Barrymore came from an historic theater family. Her grandmother, an actress and theater manager in Philadelphia, had several children who also became successful actors, including Ethel Barrymore's mother, Georgiana. Georgiana married a British actor, Herbert Blythe, who, using the stage name Maurice Barrymore, became a popular leading man. Maurice and Georgiana had three children: Ethel, Lionel, and John. All three had celebrated acting careers, earning them the nickname, "The Fabulous Barrymores."

In her youth, Ethel Barrymore was strikingly beautiful and graceful. The term "glamour girl," some say, was coined to describe her. Talented as well as attractive, she began appearing in significant roles on stage before she was twenty and soon earned a reputation as an actress capable of intelligent as well as charming performances. Her first major success, a 1901 appearance in *Captain Jinks of the Horse Marines* by Clyde Fitch, led to additional lead roles, generally in light and romantic works.

Though some were skeptical of her ability to play serious, difficult parts, Barrymore sought out challenging characters and performed them beautifully. In 1905, she took the part of Nora in Ibsen's *A Doll's House*, in spite of the fact that among many in the

# ETHEL BARRYMORE



theater community, "any thought of her ability to realize the deeper notes of Nora's development was regarded as little short of folly."[1] Barrymore proved her talent and skill by giving an outstanding performance; one reviewer wrote, "it is difficult to see how any one . . . can fail to admit that she has fully justified her claims to be considered seriously."[2] Nevertheless, Barrymore continued to pursue diverse roles. Of her appearance in Somerset Maugham's social comedy *Lady Frederick*, a *New York Times* critic wrote:

> The character of a young widow . . . departs sufficiently from the familiar lines of the typical Miss Barrymore role, but she adapts herself to it so snugly, with such genuine suggestion of good humor, and such admirably facile method, that it might have been written to her order, so well does it take her measure.[3]

During these early years of her career, Barrymore was the subject of much romantic attention; one of the many marriage proposals she declined was from a young man named Winston Churchill. When Barrymore finally married Russell Colt in 1909, it was a troubled match. Colt beat her regularly, often brutally. They separated on several occasions and finally divorced in 1923.

In spite of her personal difficulties, Barrymore's career soared. She appeared in one Broadway success after another. As she aged, she moved effortlessly from the enchanting youthful roles for which she was well known to more mature characters. Among her most impressive parts, in fact, was that of Miss Moffat in a 1940 production of Emlyn Williams's *The Corn is Green*. Barrymore thought that the schoolteacher Miss Moffat was her greatest part, "I like it better than anything I've ever had," she said. "It has everything in it that I care about."[4]

Barrymore devoted herself to a stage career, but she did make occasional films. It was in a 1932 film, *Rasputin and the Empress*, that the three "Fabulous Barrymores" made their only appearance together. Though most of Ethel Barrymore's films were forgettable, she received a Best Supporting Actress Academy Award in 1944 for her performance with Cary Grant in *None but the Lonely Heart.*

1 "Miss Barrymore's Nora A Fine Achievement" *New York Times* 3 May 1905

2 *New York Times* 3 May 1905

3 "Miss Barrymore in 'Lady Frederick'" *New York Times* 10 Nov. 1908

4 Sidney M. Shallet "Miss Ethel Barrymore Moffat" *New York Times* 22 Dec. 1940

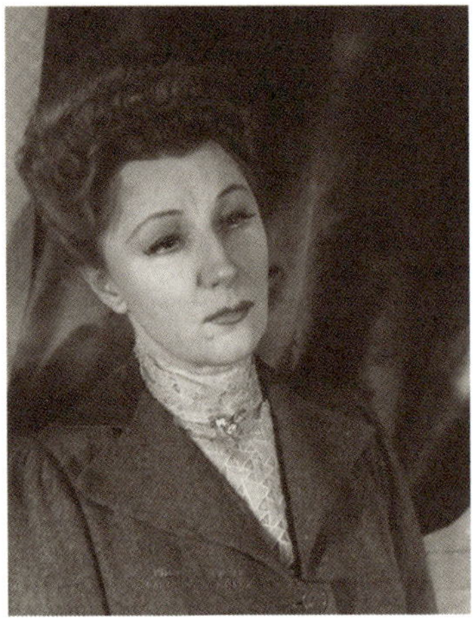

# JUDITH ANDERSON



Brooks Atkinson 1
"Medea for Moderns"
*New York Times*
26 Oct. 1947

Australian actress Judith Anderson made her professional debut in Sydney at the age of seventeen. Early success in Australia encouraged Anderson to travel to the United States in 1917 in hopes of landing parts in Hollywood movies. She was unsuccessful, however, owing in part to the fact that the American film industry then favored tall actresses (Anderson was only five feet four inches tall). From this uncertain beginning, Judith Anderson would go on to become a leading actress throughout the 1930s and 1940s, and a well-known figure in theater, movies, and television until her death in 1992.

Undeterred by her disappointing experiences in the young movie industry, Anderson moved to New York to pursue work in the theater. She struggled at first, working irregularly, but she soon made her Broadway debut in Martin Brown's *Cobra*. By the late 1920s, her performances in dramas such as Eugene O'Neill's *Strange Interlude* and *Mourning Becomes Electra* earned Anderson a reputation as an actress whose performances displayed emotional depth and intensity.

Anderson achieved fame as a classical actress with roles including *Hamlet's* Gertrude, in a production with John Gielgud playing the title role and Lillian Gish as Ophelia, and Lady MacBeth opposite Sir Laurence Olivier in a London production in 1937 and Maurice Evans's production on Broadway in 1941. Anderson won a Tony award in 1948 for her performance of *Medea* in a version written by the poet Robinson Jeffers.

Jeffers, Anderson's long-time friend, wrote his adaptation of the play specifically for her, and her performance of the dark and ruthless character was highly praised by critics. In his review of her performance (which he said would "[make] your scalp tingle"), Brooks Atkinson wrote:

> Hell hath no fury like Judith Anderson as Medea. For Medea is a woman who has been spurned and Miss Anderson, always a superb actress, is now crowning her career with an inspired performance of rage and revenge. . . . The performance is a fluid pattern of minor impulses—anger, guile, cunning, tenderness, malice, doubt, and resolution.[1]

Despite her early failure in Hollywood, later in her career Judith Anderson appeared in a number of movies, often to great acclaim from reviewers and audiences. Anderson was, in fact, nominated for an Oscar for her performance as Mrs. Danvers, the creepy and cold housekeeper in Alfred Hitchcock's *Rebecca*. Perhaps her most famous film performance, however, is her portrayal of Big Mama in the 1958 adaptation

PHOTOGRAPHED FEBRUARY 3, 1943, AS OLGA IN THE "THREE SISTERS"

## ACTRESS

of Tennessee Williams's *Cat on a Hot Tin Roof,* in which she appeared with Paul Newman, Elizabeth Taylor, and Burl Ives. Later, Anderson played Minx Lockridge on NBC's popular soap opera *Santa Barbara* and she appeared in *Star Trek III: The Search for Spock* as a Vulcan High Priestess. Though these projects diverged from her earlier classical theater work, they were among her most popular roles.

In 1960, Queen Elizabeth II knighted Judith Anderson, conferring upon her the title Dame Commander of the British Empire for her contributions to the theater. Anderson was the first Australian-born actress to receive such an honor.

Carl Van Vechten photographed Judith Anderson on several occasions. He documented a great many of her theatrical roles, often photographing her in costume. Van Vechten included images of Judith Anderson in the first exhibition of his photographs in 1933 at Bergdorf-Goodman's in New York.

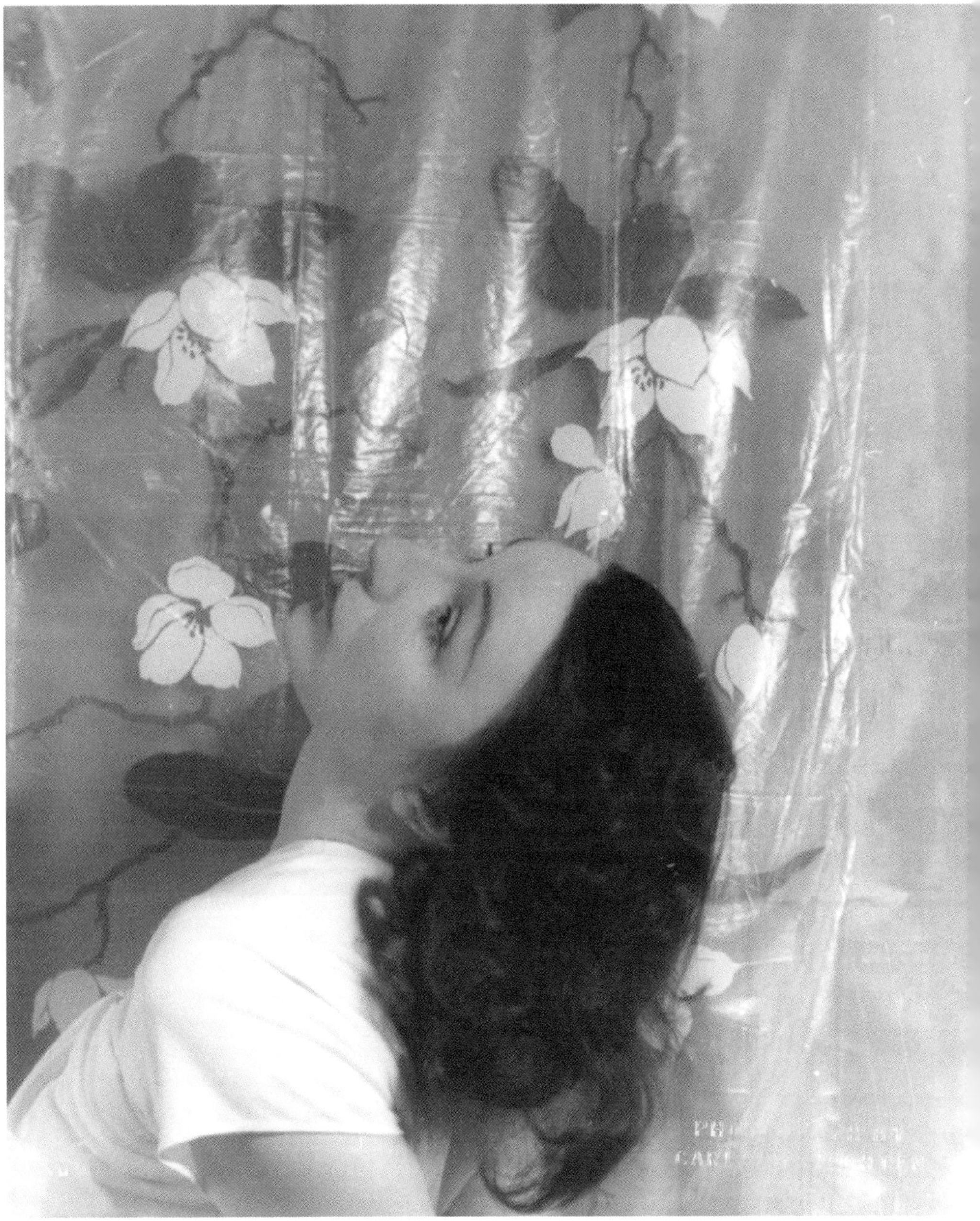

PHOTOGRAPHED ON FEBRUARY 2, 1938

# MARGARET BOURKE-WHITE

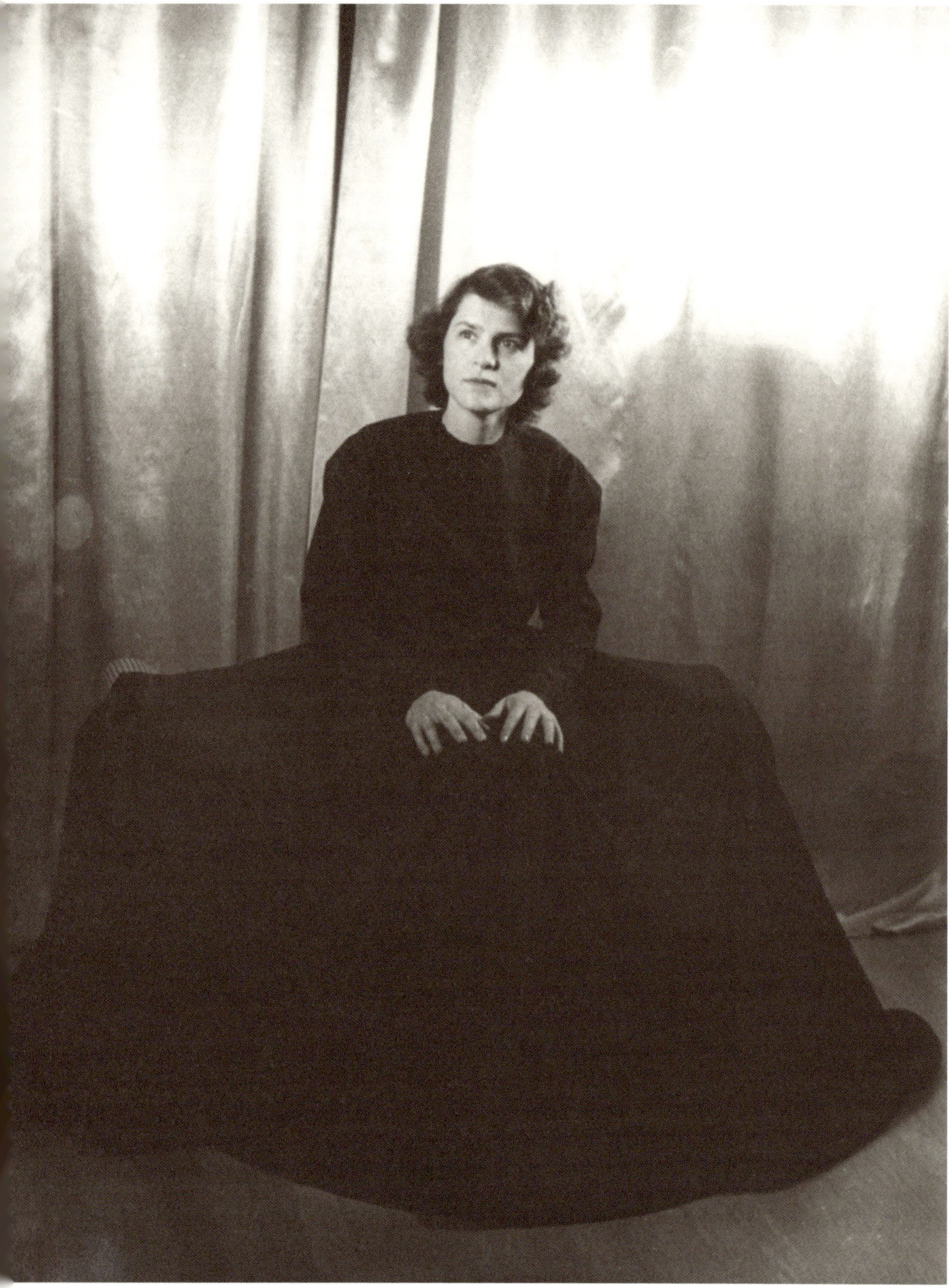

Among the best-known photographers of her time, Margaret Bourke-White recorded the physical and social landscape of the first half of the twentieth century, exploring the mechanical as well as the humanistic in American culture. Industrial and architectural subjects dominate her early work, though she would later become interested in photographing people as well as machines. Bourke-White also became a leading photojournalist in Europe during World War II.

Though she set out to concentrate on the biological sciences, as a student at Columbia University Bourke-White studied photography under Clarence H. White, a photographer associated with Alfred Stieglitz and his circle. In spite of her increasing interest in pursuing photography, Bourke-White left Columbia after just one year. She attended a number of schools before earning a degree in biology from Cornell University in 1927. To support herself at Cornell, Bourke-White began taking photographs of the campus and selling them to other students and to alumni. During this time, she became a skilled architectural photographer and decided to pursue a career in the field.

By 1929, Margaret Bourke-White had moved to New York City and taken a photographer's position with a new business magazine, *Fortune*. In 1930, *Fortune* sent her to the Soviet Union where she was to do a story on Russian industrialization.

PHOTOGRAPHED ON MARCH 24, 1938

## PHOTOGRAPHER

Bourke-White's photographs from this trip presented a more wide-ranging and thorough photographic record of the Soviet Union than Americans had seen before. These photos of Soviet Russia were collected as Bourke-White's first book, *Eyes on Russia* (1931).

By the mid-1930s, Bourke-White's photographs focused less on the industrialization of America and she began to use her camera to document other, more human aspects of modern life. In 1934, she covered the Dust Bowl, the severe drought and dust storms, or "black blizzards," that crippled the Plains states for the first half of the decade.

Her interest in documenting human experience led to Bourke-White's first collaboration with Erskine Caldwell, the 1937 book *Have You Seen Their Faces*, which used both text and photographic images to detail the lives of sharecroppers in the American south. Though Bourke-White and Caldwell married in 1939, they remained together for only three years. Despite their failed union, they collaborated on two additional projects: *North of the Danube* (1939) and *Say, Is This the USA* (1941). Her collaborations with Caldwell were very well received, and *Have You Seen Their Faces* is still considered one of her most important works.

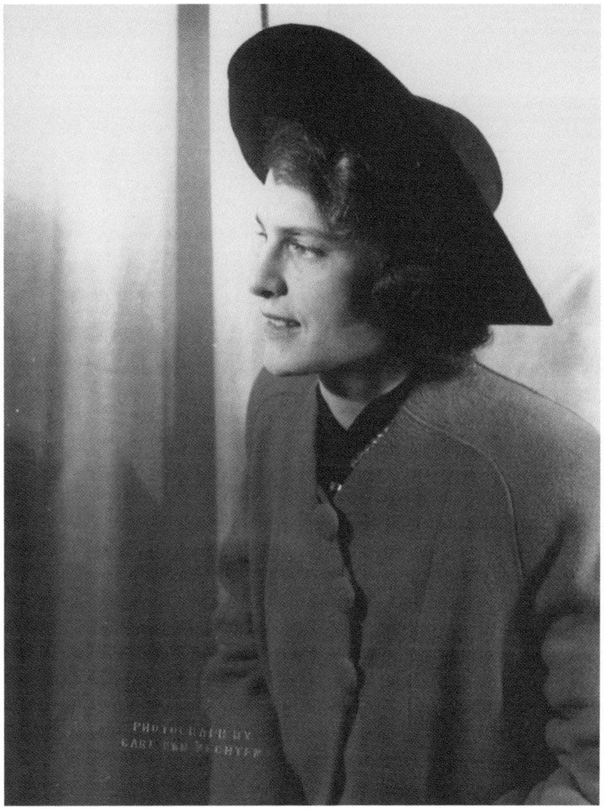

During World War II, Bourke-White returned to the Soviet Union to cover the war there for *Life* Magazine. When the Germans invaded in January 1941, Bourke-White was the only American photographer in the country and so was able to provide exclusive photos of the Soviet War for the magazine. As a war correspondent, Bourke-White did not yield to discriminatory practices that often held women reporters back; as a result of her determination she became the first woman to accompany a United States Air Force bombing mission.

Margaret Bourke-White is known equally as an artist (Alfred Stieglitz is said to have called her "one of the world's great artists") and as a journalist who documented the social and industrial landscape of her day.

# ANN ANDREWS

## ACTRESS



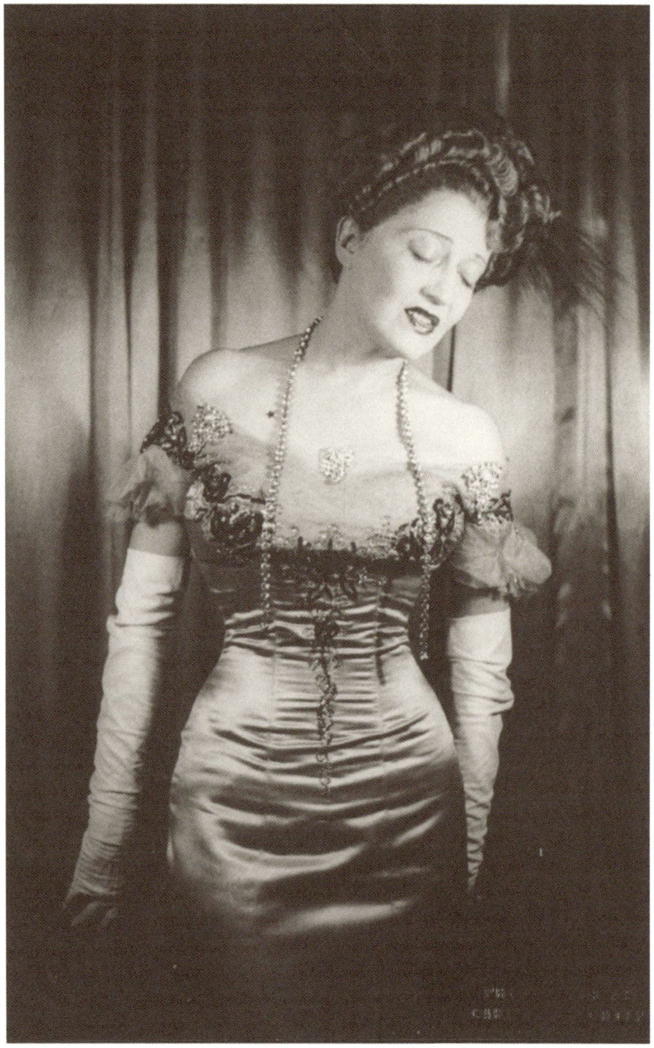

Actress Ann Andrews was born in Los Angeles in 1895. Though she studied acting for just three months, her theater career in California and New York spanned more than three decades. Andrews made her first stage performance in Los Angeles in 1916 in a production of the Russian play *Nju* by Ossip Dymow, in which she played the title role. She continued in the part when the production traveled to New York City. Her productions were well received; the audience met her performance in Edward A. Paulton's farce *Her Temporary Husband* with "shouts and laughter, . . . the comely Ann Andrews . . . seems to be growing in grace and skill as the season jogs along."[1]

Carl Van Vechten and Ann Andrews exchanged letters for many years, gossiping about theater successes and failures and sharing their love of cats. Andrews often enclosed newspaper and magazine comics about cats and their owners in her letters to Van Vechten, who wrote a book about cats called *The Tiger in the House* in 1920 and who donated the Pollock Collection of Books about Cats to the Yale University Library. Andrews peppered her letters with exclamations like "Cats in the Belfry!" and referred to Van Vechten as a "cat angel."

In her letters to Van Vechten, Ann Andrews often used quirky greetings and endearments specific to their friendship. Van Vechten, who was known among his friends for the unique and clever ways he signed letters—such as "Pats and purrs to you!"[2] or "Hearts and flowers and gold and pearls to you"[3]—must have enjoyed being referred to as "Fabulous Carlo" and "Carlo da Vinci." Other salutations reflected their mutual affection for cats: "Cool Cat Carlo," "Carlo King of the Cool Cats," and "My sainted cat of God" were favorites.

In response to a book about cats that Van Vechten sent her in 1964, Andrews wrote a brief telegram: "Another one of your gifts is to discover jewels."[4]

PHOTOGRAPHED ON OCTOBER 29, 1932

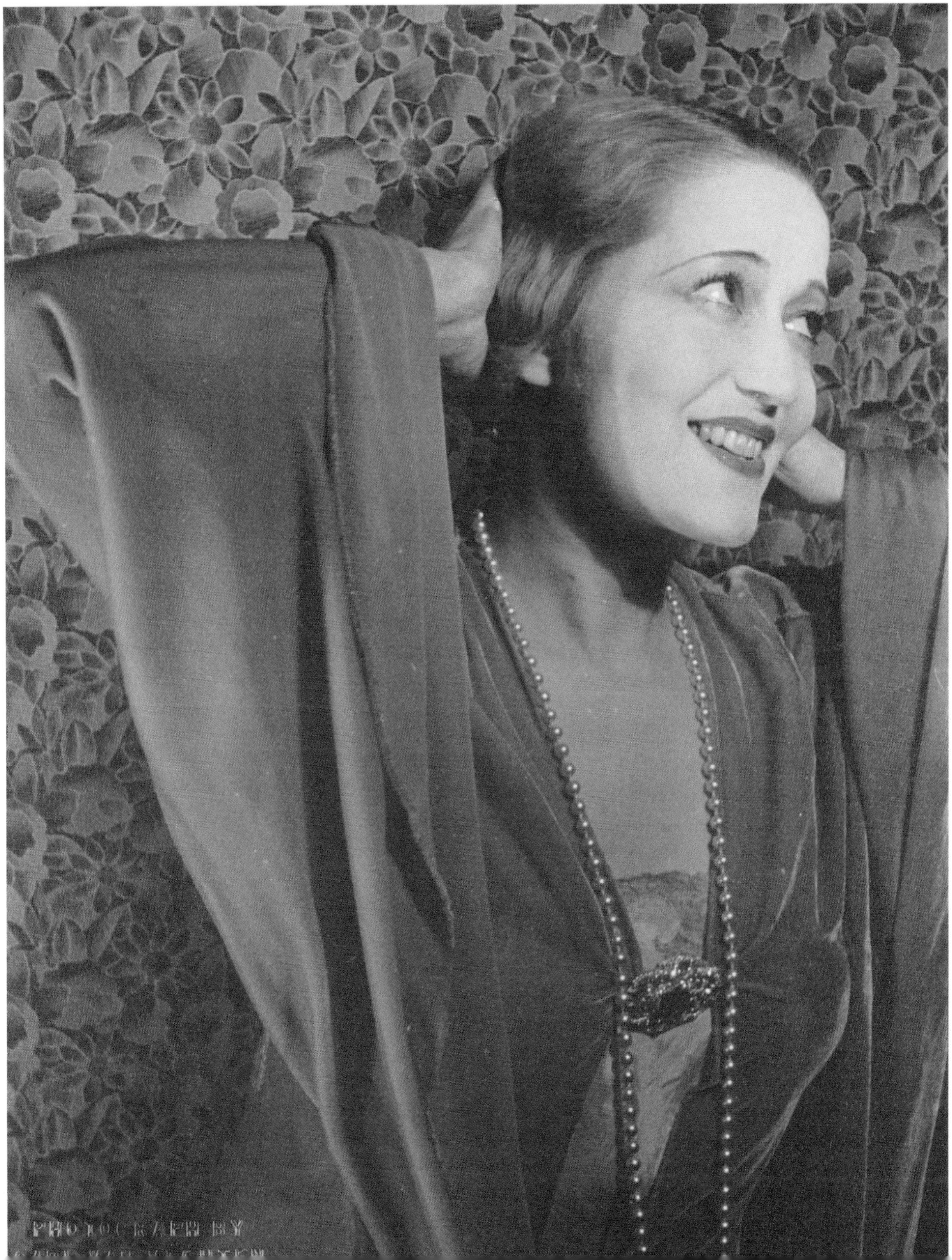




1 Alexander Woollcott
"The Play: Old Time Farce at the Frazee"
*New York Times*
1 Sept. 1922

2 Van Vechten to Fannie Hurst
23 Aug. 1932
*Letters of Carl Van Vechten*
Ed., Bruce Kellner
New Haven: Yale, 1987
p. 127

3 Van Vechten to Ethel Waters
6 Nov. 1944
*Letters of Carl Van Vechten*
p. 206

4 Andrews telegram to Van Vechten
21 Oct. 1964
Van Vechten Papers
Beinecke Library
Yale University

PHOTOGRAPHED ON JUNE 2, 1938

# ACTRESS



Brooks Atkinson 1
"The Drama: Noting the Return of John Barrymore; 'Juno and the Paycock'"
*New York Times*
28 Jan. 1940

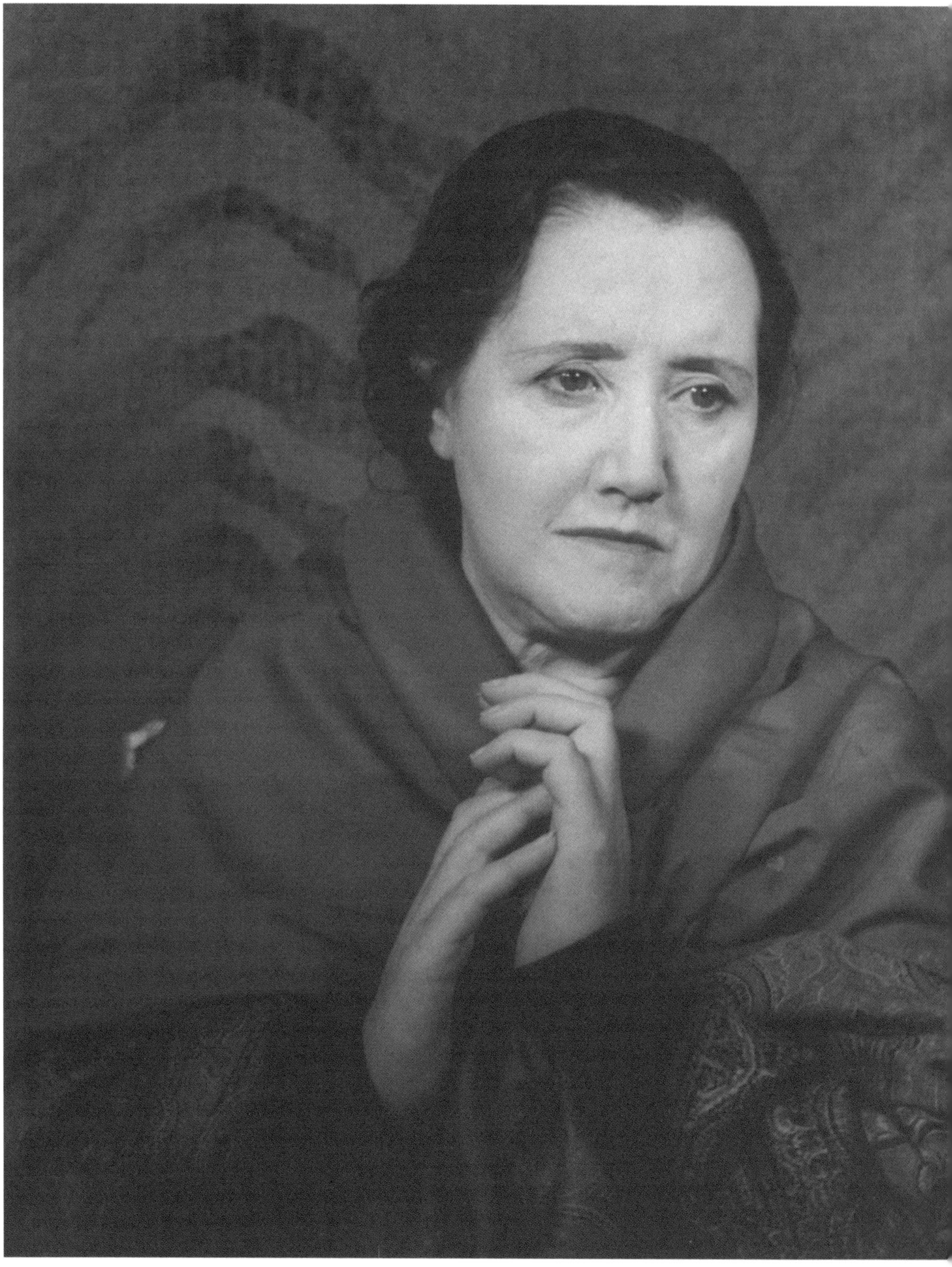

PHOTOGRAPHED ON SEPTEMBER 13, 1938, IN "RIDERS TO THE SEA"

# SARA ALLGOOD

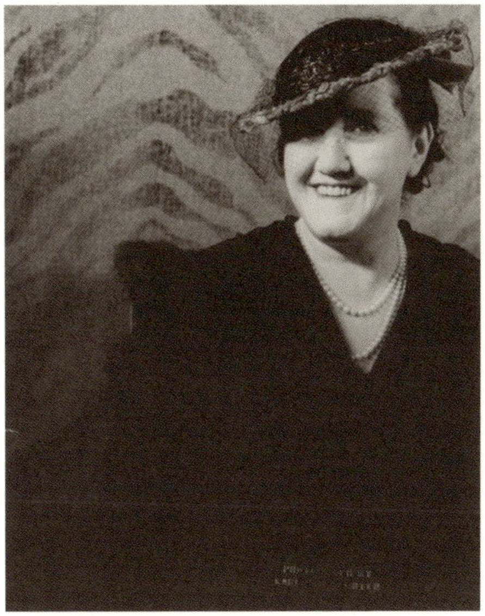

Irish theater luminary Sara Allgood began her acting career in 1904 as a member of the renowned Abbey Theatre Company of Dublin when she appeared in the company's production of Lady Augusta Gregory's *Spreading the News*. Her triumph in this performance led to other major roles and to work with the Liverpool Repertory Theatre, including appearances in W.B. Yeats's *Cathleen ni Houlihan* and J.M. Synge's *Riders to the Sea*. Because of the European success of many of these productions, Allgood had the opportunity to perform in a number of well-received tours of the United States, England, Australia, and New Zealand.

While touring Australia with a production of J. Hartly Manner's *Peg o' My Heart*, Allgood married actor Gerald Henson in 1916. Shortly afterward, Allgood suffered two major tragedies: in November 1917 her husband died, a victim of the influenza epidemic, and then, in January of 1918, Allgood gave birth to a daughter who survived for only an hour.

Allgood performed in London for several seasons before returning to Dublin and the Abbey Theatre Company. It was during this time that she delivered some of her most successful performances. The role of Juno in Sean O'Casey's *Juno and the Paycock* in 1924, for instance, was so influential it has become a legendary part of Irish theater history. When Allgood performed in a revival of the play in New York City in 1940, Brooks Atkinson wrote, "Some day, somewhere, some young people will be thinking enviously of the time when Sean O'Casey was writing mighty plays and Barry Fitzgerald and Sara Allgood were around to act them. . . . [This] will seem like a golden age."[1]

In 1940, Allgood gave up theatrical work to pursue a film career in Hollywood. She moved to California and, in 1945, became a United States citizen. Unfortunately, Allgood never achieved the success she hoped for in the film industry. In spite of her reputation and talent, she was offered only minor parts in movies, playing stereotypical Irish characters. Allgood died in Hollywood, alone and penniless, in 1950.

# BRYHER



Though her work is not widely read today, Bryher was the author of many well-respected historical novels; her books explore a variety of periods in human history, from the last days of the Roman Empire to the Norman Conquest. Today Bryher is, perhaps, better known as a central figure in an international community of modernist writers and intellectuals that included James Joyce, Marianne Moore, Gertrude Stein, Sylvia Beach, and Ernest Hemingway, among others. Another member of this group, Hilda Doolittle, the celebrated imagist poet known as H.D., was Bryher's lifelong partner.

Bryher's novels were popular and critically successful at the time of their publication. In her review of Bryher's *Fourteenth of October*, the poet Marianne Moore wrote, "The author's undeceived eye for beauty and her passion for moral beauty have produced a Bayeux tapestry."[1] Readers of historical novels admired Bryher's "instinctive art in storytelling; economy of phrasing in a paragraph, an unforced union of atmosphere, action, and meaningful imagery."[2]

The daughter of Sir John Ellerman, a wealthy and powerful British shipping magnate, Bryher was born Annie Winifred Ellerman and throughout her life she was known to her family as Winifred. Her resistance to traditional female roles complicated her early relationship with her family; as one scholar has noted, "Bryher grew up intelligent, rebellious, and furious she was not a boy."[3] Bryher renamed herself after one of the Scilly Isles off the coast of England where her family spent summers when she was a child. The Ellermans traveled extensively when Bryher was growing up; early visits to Egypt, the Middle East, the Mediterranean, and elsewhere led to her interest in archeology and history and were influential in shaping her writing.

As a young woman, Bryher traveled to the United States with H.D. While visiting New York City, she met Robert McAlmon, a writer. Soon after they met, Bryher and McAlmon were married. Marriage freed Bryher from her family's control, allowing her to live as she pleased without her parents' interference. Together the couple founded Contact Editions, which published avant-garde literature. Bryher and McAlmon were quite different—she preferred to stay at home and meet quietly with friends while he liked to go out to cafés and bars with other writers and intellectuals. He was popular with Paris's bohemian artists in no small part because of his openhandedness at these gatherings. "The drinks were always on him," Sylvia Beach wrote of McAlmon, "and alas! often in him."[4] Bryher's marriage to McAlmon lasted fewer than ten years.

Bryher was a generous and courageous woman who aided many in the arts in a variety of ways. Her commitment to artists is evident in her founding of the Bryher Foundation, an organization that made monetary grants to writers and artists. More significantly, however, Bryher used her wealth and influence to rescue innocent people, including many writers and intellectuals, from the Nazis during World War II. She was very private about her efforts to assist her friends in their flight from Nazi-occupied areas and so she is not commonly recognized for this remarkable effort.

1 Marianne Moore, "In Herald's Service (Review of *Fourteenth of October* by Bryher)" *New York Times* 27 Apr. 1952

2 Horace Gregory, "The Adventures Of Running Water (Review of *Ruan* by Bryher)" *New York Times* 6 Nov. 1960

3 Barbara Guest, *Herself Defined: The Poet H.D. and Her World* NY: Doubleday, 1984 p. 113

4 Sylvia Beach, *Shakespeare and Company* NY: Harcourt, 1956 p. 102

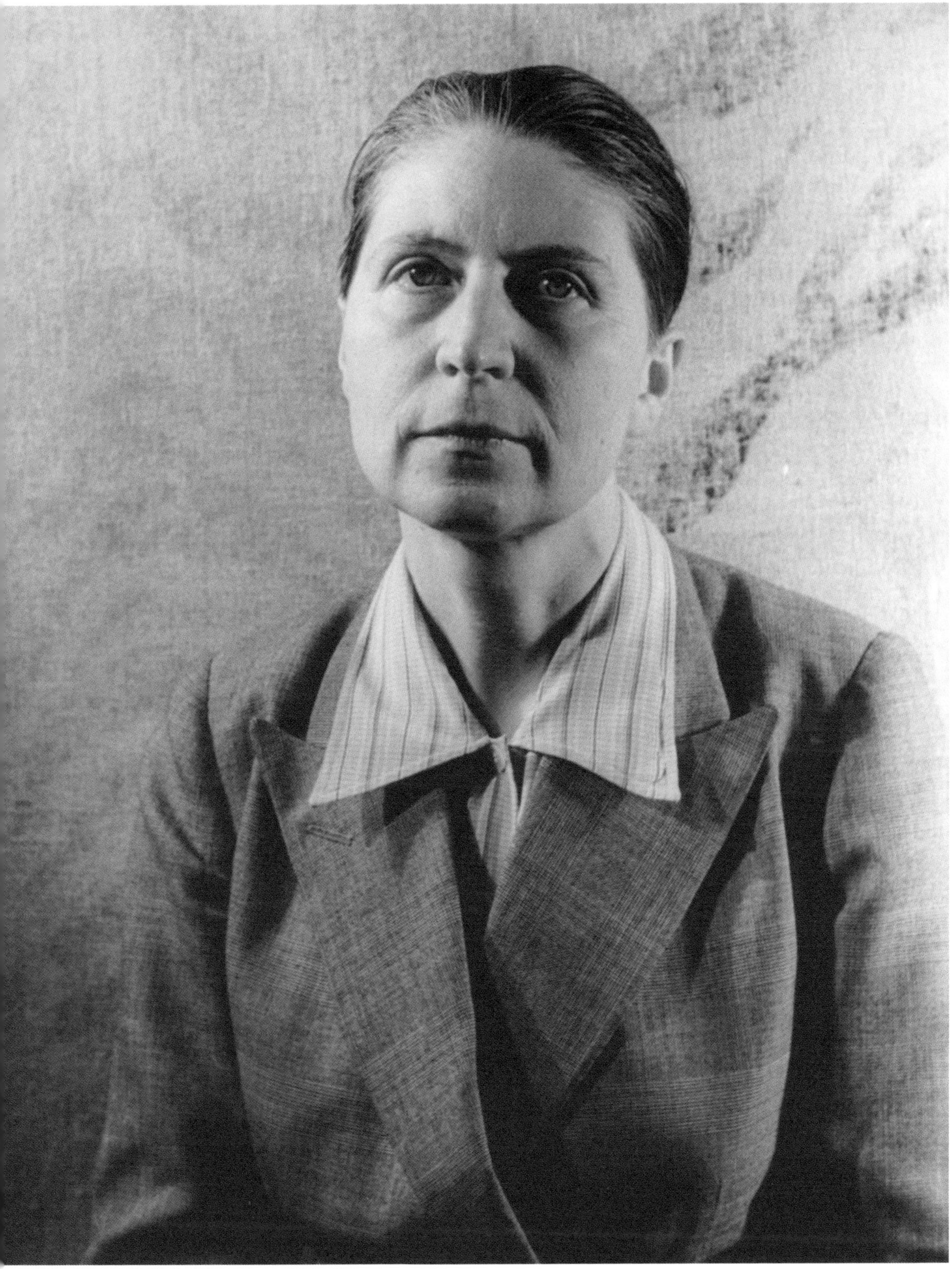

WRITER

PHOTOGRAPHED ON DECEMBER 21, 1938

# FANIA MARINOFF



Fania Marinoff spent much of her life in the shadow of her husband, Carl Van Vechten. Though she had an extraordinary sense of drama and a great deal of flair, she was sometimes eclipsed by Van Vechten's larger-than-life personality, so that even during her lifetime Marinoff was known to many mainly as "Carlo's wife." In spite of this, Marinoff was a woman of achievement in her own right.

An actress from the time she was a child, Marinoff began her stage career when she was eight. She enjoyed considerable success during the 1910s and the 1920s, performing in New York City and on nation-wide tours. She appeared in a variety of shows, from classical plays to theatrical experiments. Though she preferred more challenging roles, she occasionally appeared in light, popular productions as well.

Fania Marinoff, called Fanny as a child, was born in Odessa to Russian Jews, the thirteenth child in her family. Her mother died when she was a child. Soon after, her father remarried and moved his family to Boston. As a girl, Fanny Marinoff was spirited and wild. When her older brother decided to move west to join another Marinoff brother and his wife in Denver, the aging father encouraged him to take his sister along, hoping the young couple would be better able to care for her.

By the time she was twelve, Marinoff had joined a small traveling theatrical company. When the company folded, leaving her stranded in Nebraska, Marinoff had the good fortune to find a

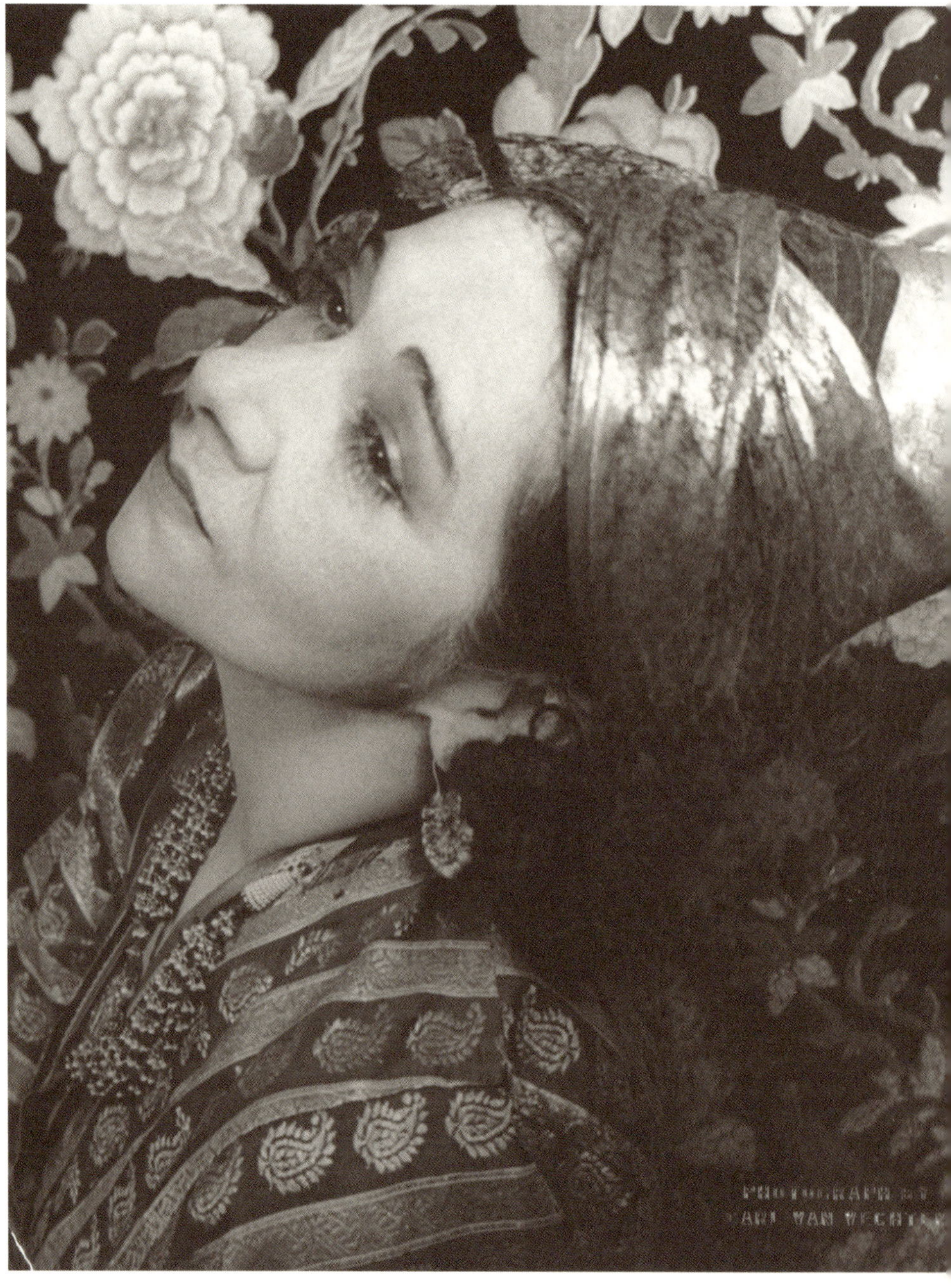

PHOTOGRAPHED ON JANUARY 9, 1939

part in a show being performed by a well-known actress named Blanche Walsh. When Walsh went on to New York, she took the young actress with her. In New York, Marinoff earned increasingly important roles with notable theater companies. She soon changed her first name to the more Russian-sounding, Fania.

It was in New York that Marinoff met a young theater critic named Carl Van Vechten. Their attraction was mutual and immediate. After a passionate courtship that included a trip to Europe, they married in 1914. Fania Marinoff continued to perform on stage and screen. In the years just after her marriage, she performed some of the roles she felt were her best, including an appearance as Ariel in a very successful production of *The Tempest* in 1916. Her next show was a controversial, sexually explicit play by Frank Wedekind, entitled *Spring's Awakening*. The cast performed just once before the police closed the show.

Fania Marinoff and Carl Van Vechten shared a singular partnership; though Van Vechten had a number of male lovers throughout his life, husband and wife remained emotionally committed to one another for more than forty years. Each drew considerable strength from the love and devotion of the other. In spite of this, "no one would ever refer to the Marinoff-Van Vechten alliance as serene."[1] Van Vechten and Marinoff were prone to public scenes and volatile discussions, though often these would dissolve into affectionate exchanges of pet names.

Because they were apart periodically during their marriage while Marinoff toured or traveled, they exchanged a great many letters; "the list of their private nicknames and terms of endearment in letters to each other was as long as it was ridiculous."[2] When Marinoff was traveling with a production of *Call the Doctor* in 1921, her husband wrote "Dearest Baby Marinoff, I was so blue yesterday that I nearly died; it seems so silly to be *here* and you *there*; I missed you so much and everything went wrong."[3] Many of Van Vechten's letters to his wife read like the letters of a newlywed who can't bare to be separated from his bride, even those written after decades of marriage.

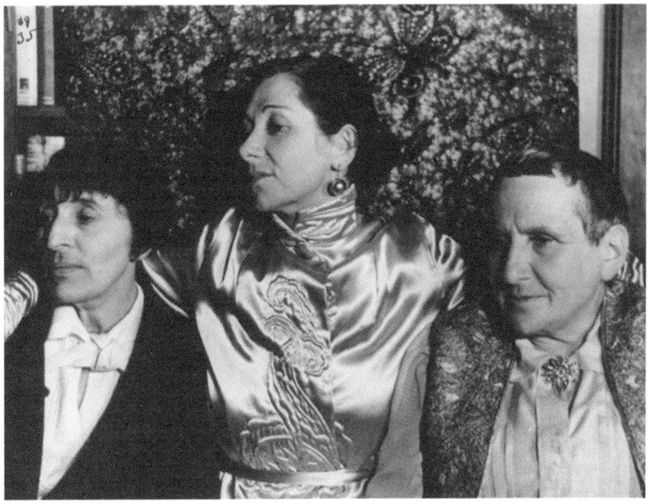

1 Bruce Kellner
*Kiss Me Again: An Invitation to a Group of Nobel Dames*
NY: Turtle Point Press
2002
p. 169

2 *Kiss Me Again: An Invitation to a Group of Nobel Dames*
p. 169

3 Van Vechten to Marinoff
3 Mar. 1921
*Letters of Carl Vechten*
Ed., Bruce Kellner
New Haven: Yale, 1987
p. 35

PHOTOGRAPHED WITH GERTRUDE STEIN AND ALICE B. TOKLAS ON MAY 2, 1935

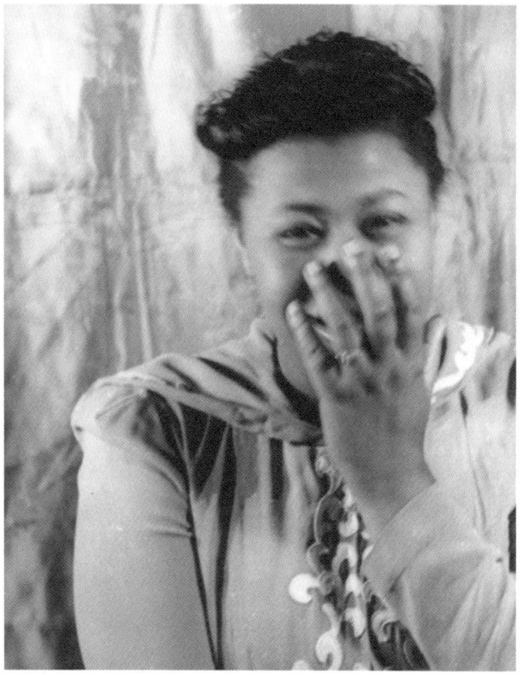

## SINGER



Known to her fans simply as Ella, Ella Fitzgerald was one of the single most influential American singers of the twentieth century. Through the course of her more than sixty-year-long career, Fitzgerald made hundreds of recordings and won no less than fourteen Grammy awards. Her simple and direct singing style was popular with audiences all over the world, and Fitzgerald is often credited with gaining countless new fans for jazz music with her performances and recordings of standards from the 1930s and 1940s.

Though she was born in Newport News, Virginia, Fitzgerald's family moved to New York when she was a child and it was there that she began her career. In 1935, when she was sixteen, Fitzgerald won a talent contest at Harlem's famous Apollo Theater. She gained the attention of New York jazz musicians in the audience, including bandleader Chick Webb. He invited Fitzgerald to audition with his band when they played a show in New Haven, Connecticut. She sang with Webb's band as the featured singer for several years and, when he died in 1939, she took over as bandleader.

After years of performing and recording, Fitzgerald made her famous "songbook" recordings. These albums remain among the most influential popular records in American music. Accompanied by the best orchestras of the period, Fitzgerald sang many of the great compositions of George and Ira Gershwin, Cole Porter, Duke Ellington, Richard Rodgers and Lorenzo Hart, Irving Berlin, Johnny Mercer, and others. These records earned Fitzgerald a larger popular audience and, as they are regularly reissued, they continue to win new fans for her music.

Fitzgerald was known for her clarity of voice and her perfect pitch. According to many, it was perfect pitch that enabled her to successfully perform the "scat" singing—the singing of nonsense words and syllables to embellish a melody—for which she became famous. Fitzgerald was also known as a singer who could convey rhythm as well as meaning through song lyrics. She generally preferred to sing more upbeat songs, and this preference suited her performance style. Her audiences were charmed by her tendency to forget song lyrics and replace them with made up, comic substitutions.

# ELLA FITZGERALD

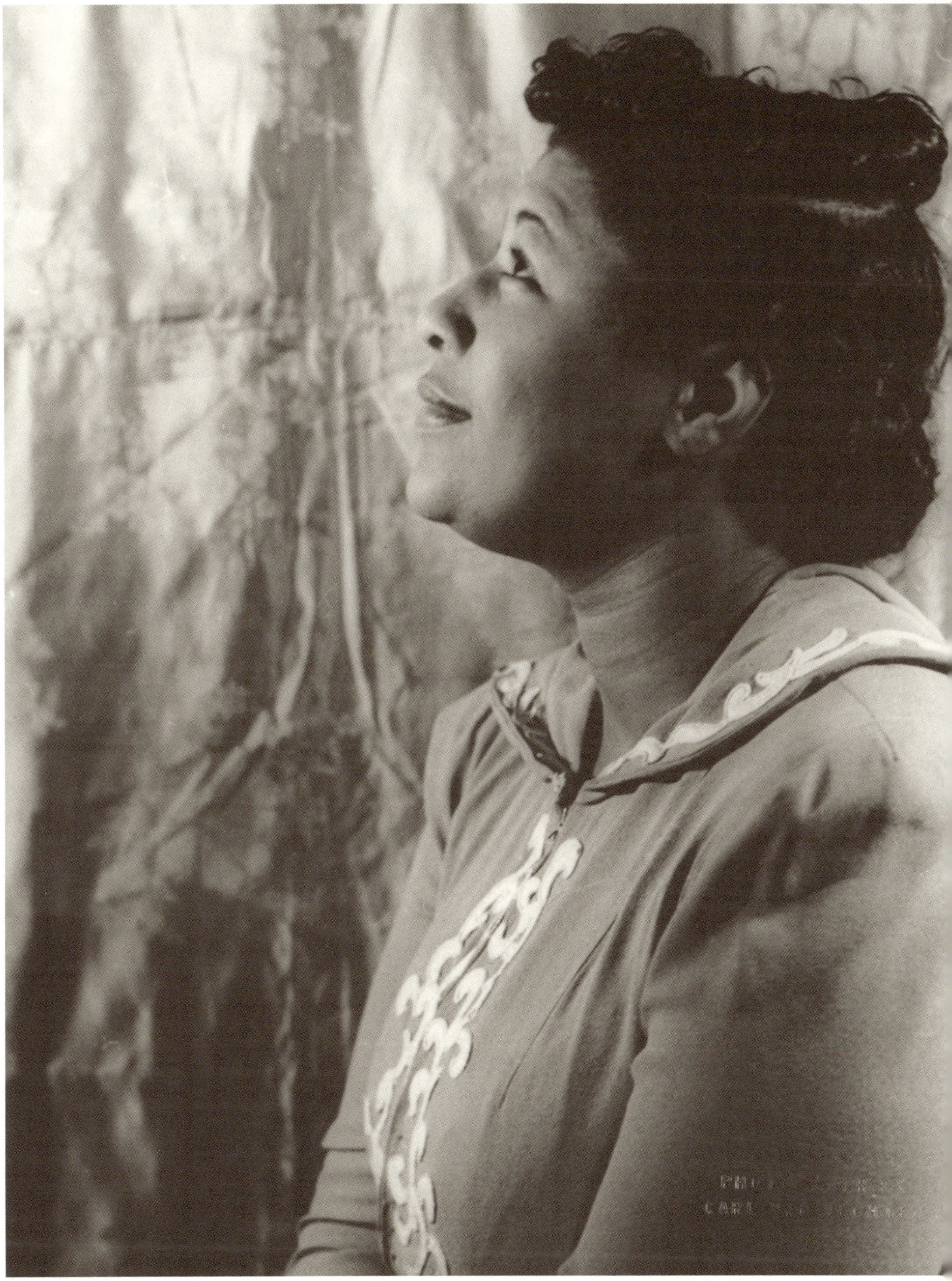

In contrast to the high life of many of her fellow singers, Fitzgerald was deeply shy and she lived a quiet life. She was plagued by self-doubt, and in spite of her great achievements, she never took her success for granted. As she aged, her voice lost some of its former clarity and resonance; nevertheless, Fitzgerald continued to tour until poor health prevented her from performing. A few years before her death in the 1990s, Fitzgerald had both legs amputated below the knee as a result of complications from diabetes.

Often called The First Lady of Song, Ella Fitzgerald performed and recorded with the finest jazz performers of all time, including Benny Goodman, Count Bassie, Dizzy Gillespie, and Teddy Wilson. Many of her most famous recordings, including "Lady Be Good," "How High the Moon," and "A Tisket A Tasket," remain popular today, decades after she first recorded them. She was the recipient of many awards, honorary degrees, and the National Medal of Arts. The Ella Fitzgerald School of the Performing Arts at the University of Maryland was named in honor of her tremendous contribution to American popular music.

PHOTOGRAPHED ON JANUARY 19, 1940

# AGNES DE MILLE



Agnes de Mille was born in 1905 into a prominent family. Her grandfather was political economist Henry George, her father William de Mille was a successful playwright, and her uncle was film director Cecil B. de Mille. In her childhood autograph album, de Mille's father encouraged her: "My first-born child you are / But that's nothing. / I'd rather love you / For what you do / Than because you're mine. / So go to it."[1] Agnes de Mille revolutionized the American musical comedy; "After Isadora Duncan and Martha Graham," the *New York Times*'s Jay Carr wrote in 1979, "Miss de Mille has done more than anybody to give dance a foothold in this country."[2]

In 1942, de Mille enjoyed her first major success with the ballet, *Rodeo*. With a score composed by Aaron Copland, the ballet was one of the first to focus on American themes, as well as to combine classical ballet with folk dancing, modern dance, and mime. The ballet was a huge success, receiving twenty-two curtain calls at its premiere.[3]

De Mille's success with *Rodeo* led her to choreograph Rodgers and Hammerstein's *Oklahoma!*, and as Jay Carr stated, "Hoping for freshness, they got genius."[4] The dance sequences in *Oklahoma!* altered the face of the American Broadway musical forever after. Previously, dance numbers had had little or no connection to a musical's storyline, but were tacked on merely as a divertissement. In *Oklahoma!*, however,

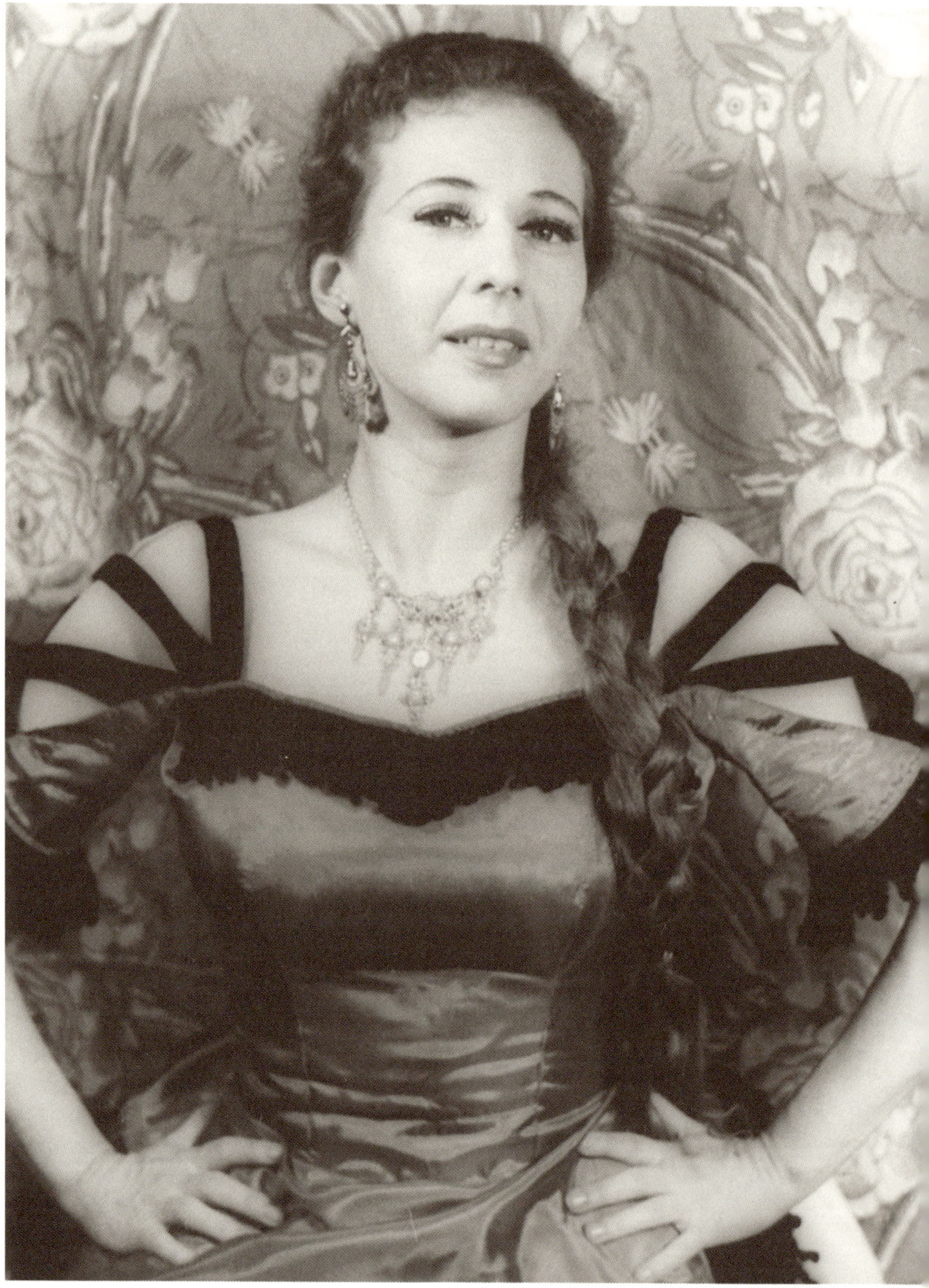

PHOTOGRAPHED ON APRIL 8, 1940, IN "HELL ON WHEELS"

dance was integrated into the plot and used to further the action. The famous dream sequence in *Oklahoma!* that explored the main character's psychology and inner turmoil was so groundbreaking that within a few months every new musical on Broadway contained a similar dream scene. Van Vechten described *Oklahoma!* in his article "Terpsichore and the U.S. Army" as "a work—still alive nine years after its creation—which completely changed the role of dancing in subsequent musicals and which elevated Agnes de Mille to an important position in the theatre world."[5]

Subsequently, de Mille choreographed other musicals, including *Carousel* (1945), *Brigadoon* (1947), and *Paint Your Wagon* (1951). In 1944-45, with three hit musicals on Broadway, "she became the first woman to equal the accomplishments of Berlin, Gershwin, and Porter."[6] With *Allegro* in 1947, de Mille became the first woman to both choreograph and direct a major Broadway musical.

In 1940 and 1941, Van Vechten photographed de Mille in a number of her roles, including in costume for *Hell on Wheels*, as Venus in Antony Tudor's *The Judgment of Paris*, and as a virgin ("The Priggish One") in *Three Virgins and a Devil.*

De Mille wrote over a dozen books on dance, and she has been called "one of the finest and most eloquent writers on dance the world has known."[7] In a review of her autobiography *Dance to the Piper*, Van Vechten wrote, "nobody can read this history of courage and belief in an ideal without understanding both dancing and human nature a little better. Indeed, I believe nobody can read this book without following it up with a salutation, 'Bravo, Agnes de Mille!'"[8]

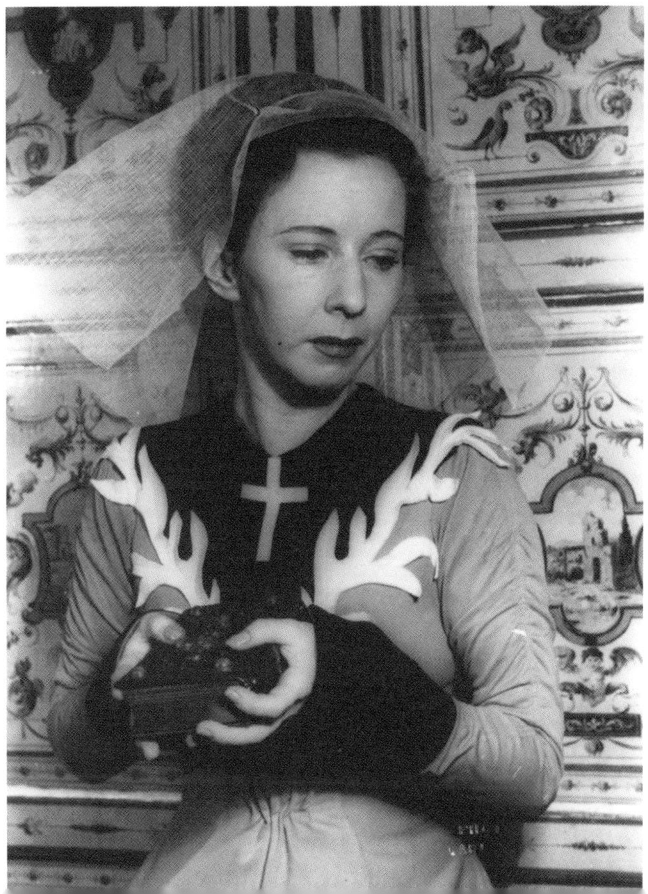

PHOTOGRAPHED ON MARCH 18, 1941, IN "THREE VIRGINS AND A DEVIL"

1 Agnes de Mille
*Speak to Me, Dance with Me*
Boston: Atlantic Monthly Press, 1973
p. 9

2 Jay Carr
"Agnes de Mille Steps Out With an Old Friend–'Oklahoma!'"
*New York Times*
9 Dec. 1979

3 Jack Anderson
"Gala Evening of Dance Honors Agnes de Mille"
*New York Times*
18 May 1983

4 "Agnes de Mille Steps Out With an Old Friend–'Oklahoma!'"

5 Van Vechten
*The Dance Writings of Carl Van Vechten*
Ed., Paul Padgette
NY: Dance Horizons, 1974
p. 53

6 Carol Easton
*No Intermissions: The Life of Agnes de Mille*
Boston: Little, Brown 1996
p. 4

7 Clive Barnes
"The De Mille Legacy"
*Dance Magazine* 68:1 (1994)
p. 66

8 *The Dance Writings of Carl Van Vechten*
p. 52

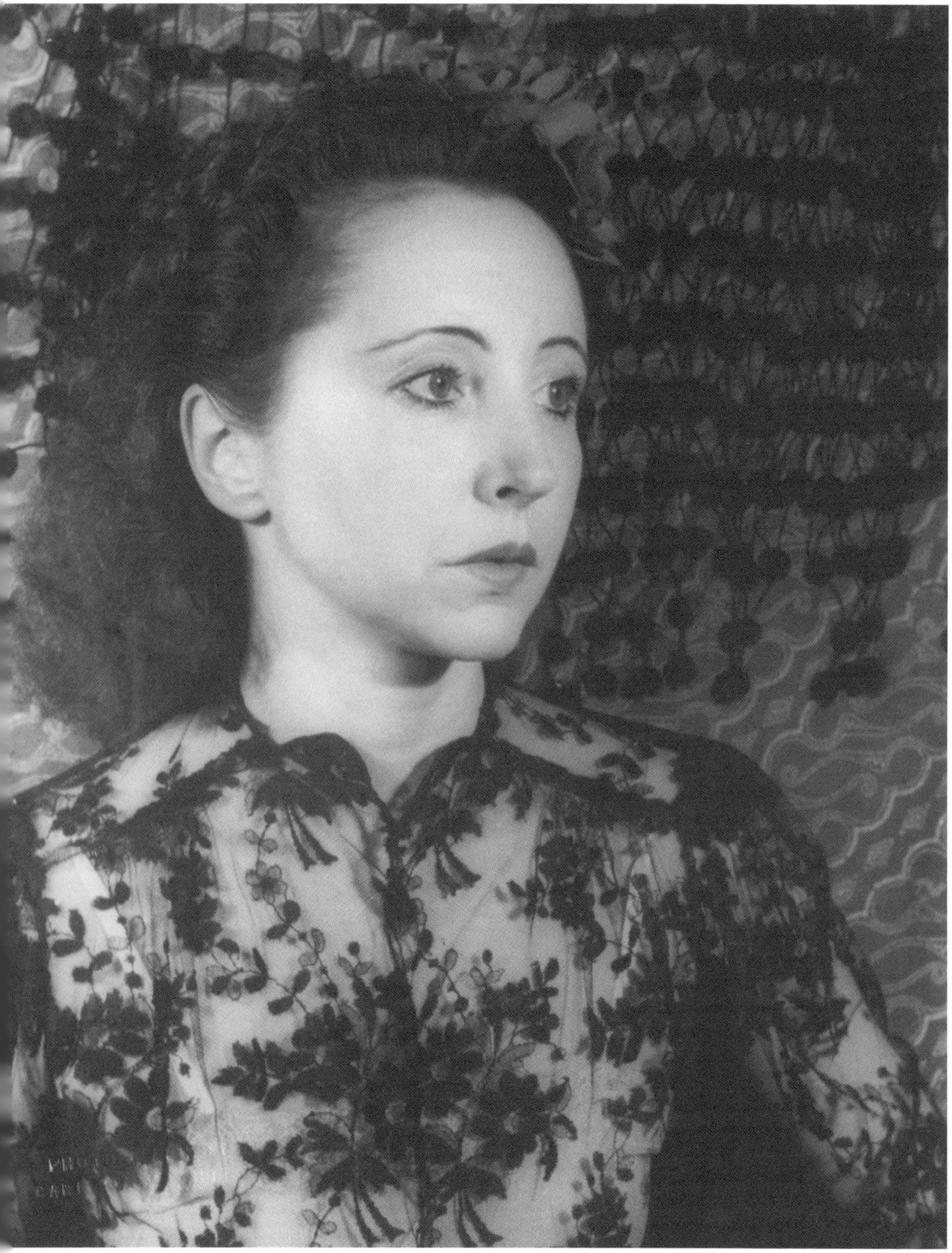

## DIARIST

Anaïs Nin began her famous diary when she was just eleven years old. The diary, which she kept for the rest of her life, eventually filled more than two hundred manuscript volumes, nearly forty thousand pages. Because of her frank writing about sexuality and her sometime promotion of antiquated feminine roles and values, Nin's diaries and other writings have remained controversial. At one time a source of much debate among feminist writers and scholars, Nin's work has fallen from favor in recent years. Nevertheless, her contribution to the art and study of autobiography is undeniable.

The daughter of an esteemed Spanish composer and a French classical singer, as a child Nin met some of the finest artists and performers in Europe. When her father abandoned the family, Nin's mother moved with her daughter and two sons from Barcelona to New York City. To earn money during this time, Nin worked as a model for artists and clothing designers. When she was twenty, she married a banker named Hugh Guiler and moved with him to Paris.

In Paris, Nin continued her diary, but she also began writing work she hoped would be published. She sought contact with other writers and artists, becoming acquainted with Henry Miller and his wife, June. The Millers introduced Nin to other artists and, as some of their associates were drug addicts and prostitutes, to the city's seamier side. Henry Miller and Nin became very close and he had a significant influence on her

# ANAÏS NIN

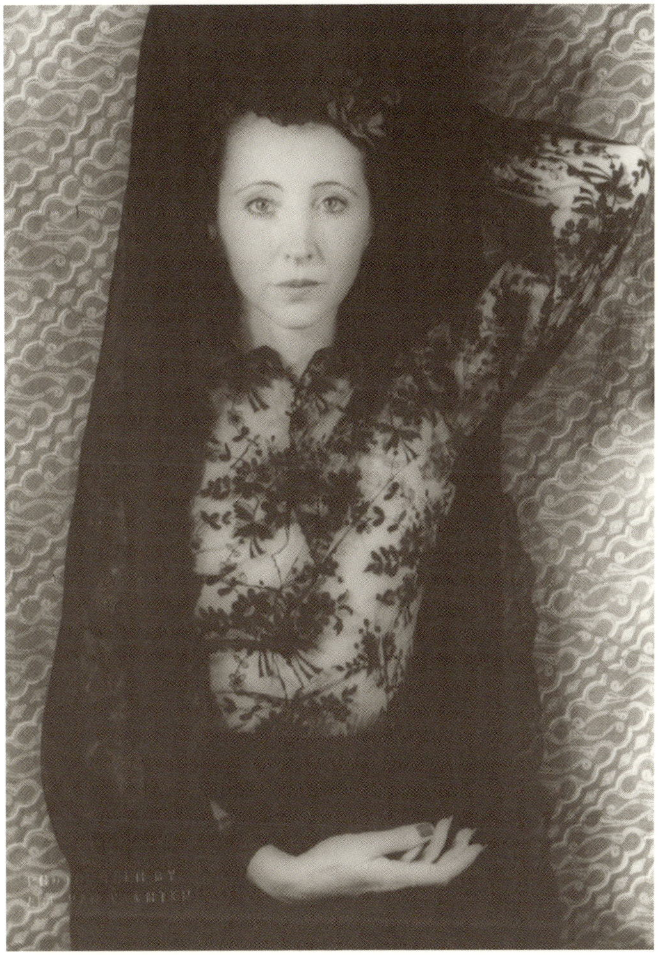



life and work. During this period, Nin wrote her first major works, *The House of Incest* (1936), and a group of novellas, *The Winter of Artifice* (1939).

Nin became interested in psychoanalysis in the 1930s and sought treatment from several well-known analysts. She incorporated her experiences in analysis into both her diary and her public writing. Her novels were to become very introspective, taking self-exploration and awareness as important themes. Much of Nin's work is replete with the surreal, dreamlike, private images often associated with personal and psychological investigation. Though some have dismissed this writing as overly abstract and self-absorbed, others have championed it as poetic and groundbreaking.

In Paris, Nin moved between the artists' world and her more conventional life as a banker's wife. Her many illicit love affairs, with, among others, both Henry and June Miller, her analysts, and her father, provided material for Nin's erotic fiction, much of which remained unpublished until her death in 1977. In addition, the sexually explicit writing in her diaries was left out of the heavily edited editions published during her lifetime. Later editions restore the diaries, including material Nin feared would hurt her husband and other loved ones.

Nin, Miller, and several other writers founded Siana Editions in Paris, to publish their own work and that of other avant-garde writers. When Nin returned to New York to escape World War II, she again had trouble finding a publisher for her work. Ultimately, she used her own printing press to set and print her books. She asked friends to buy copies to support her publishing endeavors. "I would love to give you a copy of this new book I am bringing out as it includes the story inspired by your home's great beauty," Nin wrote to Carl Van Vechten of *Under a Glass Bell*, "but I do need subscriptions to pay the bookbinder as that is the only part of the work I cannot do with my own hands."[1]

1 Nin to Van Vechten
No date but probably Nov. 1943
Van Vechten Papers
Beinecke Library
Yale University

PHOTOGRAPHED ON OCTOBER 6, 1940

# ARGENTINITA

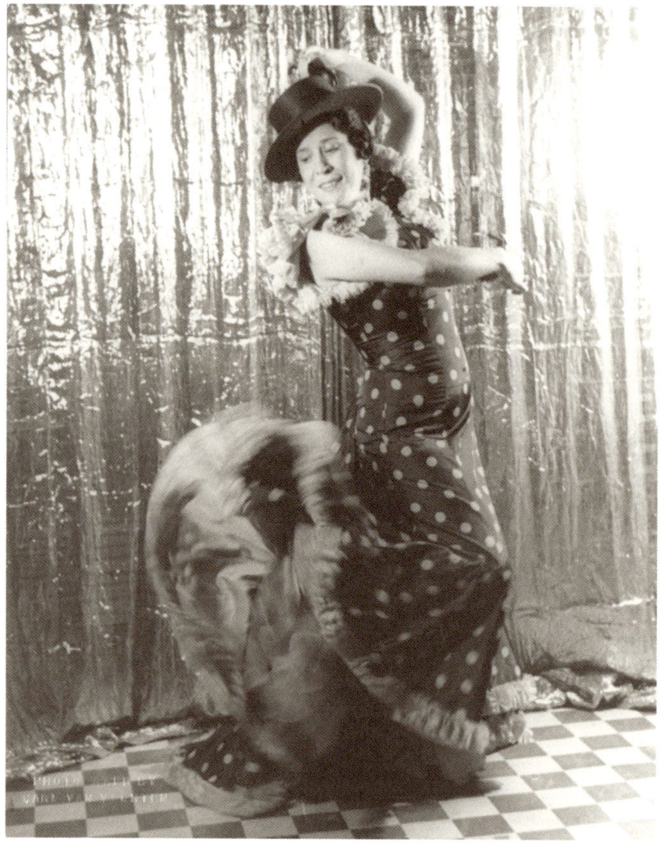



The dancer La Argentinita was born López Encarnación in Buenos Aires, Argentina. She grew up in Spain, where she started dancing while still a child, soon mastering both the classical and regional dances of Spain. She eventually became so well known that she was dubbed "the queen of the dance."

In 1927 Argentinita formed her own gypsy dance troupe, which toured France and Latin America performing flamenco and traditional gypsy dances. Around the same time, she and the poet Federico García Lorca recorded Spanish folk songs, with Lorca playing the piano and Argentinita singing. In 1932 she and Lorca established the Madrid Ballet, which was intended to preserve old-style gypsy dancing. With the onset of the Spanish Civil War and the execution of Lorca, Argentinita left Spain in 1937.

She made a disastrous U.S. debut in 1930 when she performed in Lew Leslie's *International Revue*. The presentation of Argentinita's piece was conditioned by stereotypes about Spain, as well as by contemporary theatrical tastes. Set against a flashy backdrop and chorus girls wearing Broadway-style Spanish dresses, Argentinita's authentic dress and intimate, understated dancing style failed to impress the New York theater public.

By the 1920s, Carl Van Vechten had emerged as the country's foremost dance critic; by many accounts, in fact, he was America's first dance critic, as well as a prominent critic of music and other performing arts. In this capacity, one of Van Vechten's most noteworthy contributions was his writings on the arts and culture of Spain. His volume *The Music of Spain* (1918) filled an important gap in America's musical knowledge, championing the passion and skill of Spanish dancing to his readers. In his essay "The Land of Joy" written in November 1917, Van Vechten laments the difficulty American audiences had in understanding the intricacies of Spanish dance. Van Vechten discusses the revue *The Land of Joy* performed by "a Spanish company, unheralded, unsung, indeed unwelcomed"[1] by the city, and exclaims, "Fancy the average New York first-night

1 Van Vechten
*The Music of Spain*
NY: Knopf, 1918
p. 94

2 *The Music of Spain*
p. 95

3 *The Music of Spain*
p. 96

4 Sol Hurok and Ruth Goode
*Impresario*
NY: Random House, 1946
p. 282

5 *Impresario*
p. 282

## DANCER

audience, stiff and unbending, sceptical and sardonic, welcoming this exhibition!"[2] Eventually, the infectious performances, "inflamed with life," began to affect audiences. Van Vechten wrote, "Fortunately the Spaniards in the first-night audience gave the cue, unlocked the lips and loosened the hands of us cold Americans. For my part, I was soon yelling *Olé!* louder than anybody else."[3]

After her unsuccessful debut, Argentinita was reluctant to dance in America again, but impresario Sol Hurok finally persuaded her to perform at the Majestic Theatre in 1938. This time, the critics warmed to her immediately, and "Manhattanites thronged the theatre," and "stamped and yelled."[4] By bringing the folk dances she had observed first-hand in the native villages of Spain and South America to United States and European audiences, Argentinita increased awareness of and appreciation for these dance forms. It was Argentinita "who translated so perfectly to the theatre the pure dance of Spain that she brought with it the atmosphere of dancing for the joy of dancing itself."[5]

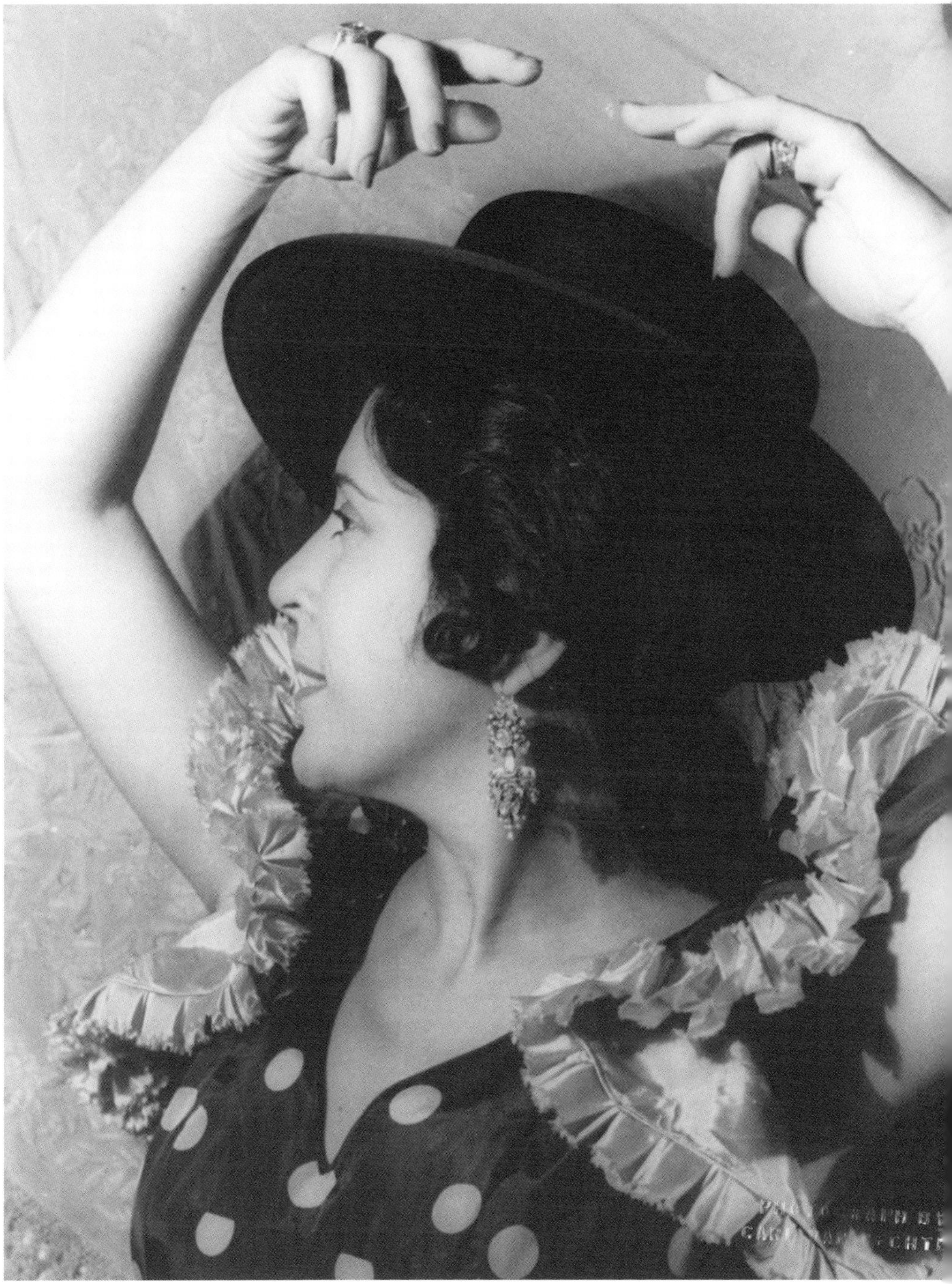

PHOTOGRAPHED ON OCTOBER 17, 1940

# TALLULAH BANKHEAD

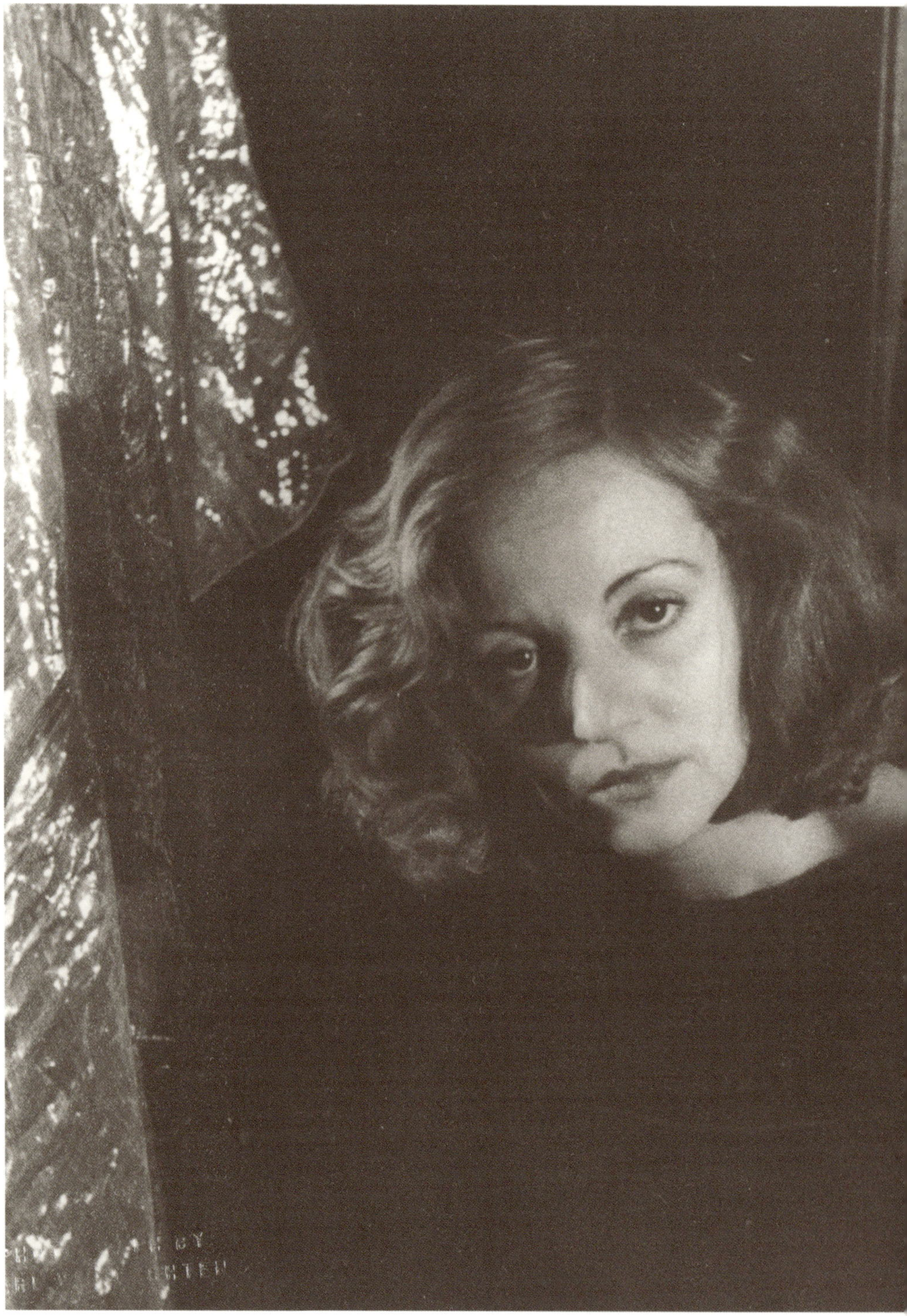



"The Wham from Alabam'," as Tallulah Bankhead was called, is one of entertainment's most colorful personalities. She is now known mainly for her wild antics: she was said to have smoked over one hundred cigarettes and consumed two bottles of bourbon a day, and had over five hundred love affairs. Marlene Dietrich called her "the most immoral woman who ever lived," and Bankhead herself wrote, "Apostates have hinted that I'm the ill-begotten daughter of Medusa and the Marquis de Sade."[1] But she was also dubbed "one of the great wits of an entire era"[2] and "perhaps the greatest actress this country has ever produced."[3]

At fifteen, Bankhead won first prize in a *Picture Play* magazine contest—a trip to New York and a part in a film. Upon arriving in New York, she moved into the Algonquin Hotel and soon charmed her way into its famous literary and artistic circles. She befriended Ethel Barrymore, who tried to convince her to change her name to Barbara. However, Joseph Hergesheimer and Carl Van Vechten threatened her with, "If you change your name, we'll neither of us ever write another word." Van Vechten added, "Keep it. It is very odd; also it is very easy to remember."[4] She agreed, and *Vanity Fair* later wrote, "she's the only actress on both sides of the Atlantic to be recognized by her first name only."[5]

## ACTRESS

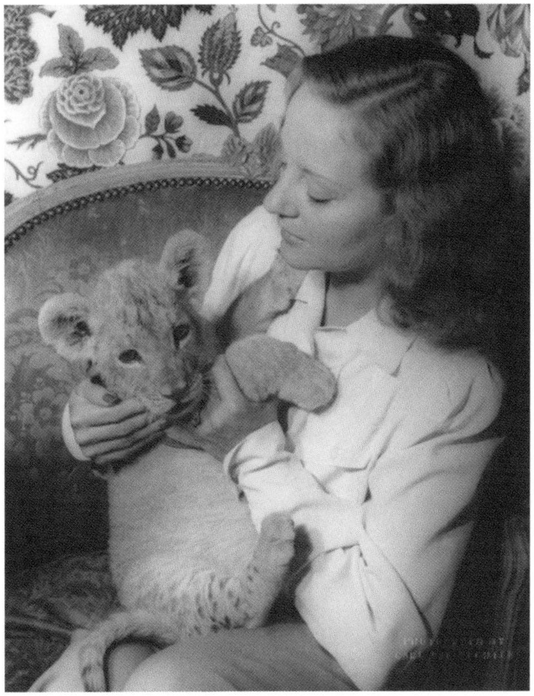

Bankhead's stage and film roles at this time were minor. Frustrated, she went to London; her first appearance there, in *The Dancers*, created a sensation. A Tallulah craze was born, and young women began to dress, talk, and wear their hair like her. Her fans were dubbed the "gallery girls" by the press, and whenever she came onstage they became ecstatic, chanting "Tallulah, Tallulah" or "Tallulah Hallelujah."

After her success in London, Bankhead went to Hollywood under contract with Paramount Pictures. They billed her as "the next Marlene Dietrich," but all her films were mediocre. In 1936, convinced that she could "play the pants off Scarlett," she campaigned for the role of Scarlett O'Hara in *Gone with the Wind*, but was denied the part. Film success came only in 1944 with Alfred Hitchcock's *Lifeboat*. Her performance earned her a New York Film Critics Award.

Bankhead also had mixed success on the stage. In 1937, she and then-husband John Emery staged *Anthony and Cleopatra*, with Carl Van Vechten's wife Fania Marinoff playing the role of Charmian. The play garnered Bankhead her worst reviews ever, including, "Tallulah Bankhead barged down the Nile last night as Cleopatra—and sank." In true Bankhead fashion, she was undaunted, claiming, "As far as I'm concerned Shakespeare should have left Anthony and Cleopatra in Plutarch, where he found them." In 1939, however, she had a hit as Regina Giddens in Lillian Helman's *The Little Foxes*. Her performance has been called "a theatrical milestone." In 1942, she had her second great success in Thornton Wilder's *The Skin of Our Teeth*. Production was often difficult as there was considerable tension between Bankhead, her producers, and her fellow actors.

From 1943 to 1956, Bankhead lived on her sixteen-acre estate, named Windows, with her numerous pets, including several dogs, a mynah bird, and a pet lion named Winston Churchill. Van Vechten's photograph of Bankhead includes Winston as a cub; Bankhead gave Winston to the Bronx Zoo when he became too big and "started gnawing on people's ankles."

Bankhead died in 1968, but she did not disappear. Several plays based on her life have played on and off-Broadway. Tovah Feldshuh, star and co-author of *Tallulah Hallelujah!* and star of *Tallulah's Party*, said, "She was a groundbreaker for women. She was a self-created woman. She didn't take no for an answer. And she would not give up her youth."[6]

1 Tallulah Bankhead
*Tallulah: My Autobiography*
NY: Harper, 1952
p. 1

2 Anita Loos
"Tallulah"
*Playbill* for the Helen Hayes Theatre
Feb. 1969

3 Michael Myerberg to Thornton Wilder
23 Oct. 1942
Thornton Wilder Papers
Beinecke Library
Yale University

4 Bruce Kellner
*Carl Van Vechten and the Irreverent Decades*
Norman: Oklahoma, 1968
p. 150

5 Cleveland Amory and Frederic Bradlee
*Vanity Fair: A Cavalcade of the 1920s and 1930s*
NY: Viking, 1960
p. 149

6 Richard Zoglin
"Tallulah Times Three"
*Time*
27 Nov. 2000
p. 86



PHOTOGRAPHED ON JULY 15, 1941

# LENA HORNE

## SINGER & ACTRESS



Lena Horne 1
"Believing in Oneself"
In *Many Shades of Black*
Eds., Stanton L. Wormley and Lewis H. Fenderson
NY: William Morrow, 1969
p. 96

Lena Horne 2
*In Person: Lena Horne as Told to Helen Arstein and Carlton Moss*
NY: Greenberg, 1950
p. 85

"Believing in Oneself" 3
pp. 99-100

John McDonough 4
Review of *Being Myself*
*Down Beat*
65:9 (1998)
p. 42

Now considered a jazz icon, Lena Horne was one of the top African-American entertainers during the 1940s and 1950s, and in 1981 her *Lena Horne: The Lady and Her Music* became the longest-running one-woman show on Broadway. However, her career has been marked by the discrimination she faced as an African American, and in 1969 she wrote, "When I look back over my life, my sharpest impressions are of the many ways in which I have been segregated, the many kinds of prejudice I have experienced."[1]

As a child, Horne was abandoned by her parents and was raised by her grandmother, a civil rights activist who enrolled her granddaughter in the NAACP at age two. Horne's first professional job was at Harlem's famous Cotton Club; she was hired less for her singing ability than because her youth, beauty, light skin, and "good hair" were appealing to the club's white clientele. Nevertheless, she landed a job with Noble Sissle in 1935. Touring with Sissle's all-black orchestra opened her eyes to racial prejudice, and in her autobiography she wrote, "I didn't like sleeping in the bus at night because there were cities in which we couldn't get rooms in a white hotel, and there were no hotels for colored."[2] Five years later, traveling with Charlie Barnet's all-white band, she faced equal discrimination. Restaurants often refused to serve the band if Horne was with them, and audiences sometimes objected to her singing onstage with the white musicians.

In 1941, Horne began to sing at Café Society Downtown in New York. The club catered to an intellectual and integrated clientele, and for the first time, she was allowed to sing as herself and not according to a stereotype. She also became close to Paul Robeson, who shared her interest in the Civil Rights movement. In 1963, she participated in the March on Washington, and in 1969 she wrote, "The Civil Rights movement, more than any other one thing, has given me the urge to find out who I am and what I'm doing here."[3]

In 1942, MGM Studios offered Horne a film contract. Familiar with the discrimination prevalent in Hollywood, she considered refusing it, but friends such as Duke Ellington convinced her to accept it and work to improve the Hollywood image of African Americans. Horne's seven-year contract was only the second term contract signed by an African-American woman, and the first since 1915. Once she started making films, however, the studio considered her too light-skinned to play opposite black actors, but was unwilling to feature her with white actors. Her film appearances were therefore limited mainly to "specialty sequences," in which she sang, elegantly dressed and leaning provocatively against a pillar, which could be cut when the films were shown in the South. Her major films were the 1943 all-black musicals *Cabin in the Sky* and *Stormy Weather*. The song *Stormy Weather* became her trademark.

Although Horne sometimes claimed that she did not like her singing voice, John McDonough wrote of her 1998 album *Being Myself*, "Her voice is an aristocratic combination of mature luster and fine grain, and the phrasing is soaked in the honey-combed drawl and still crackles with open vowels that have always been her signature."[4] Now recognized as an accomplished performer and singer on her own terms, Horne is said to have claimed, "In my early days I was a sepia Hedy Lamarr. Now I'm black and a woman, singing my own way."

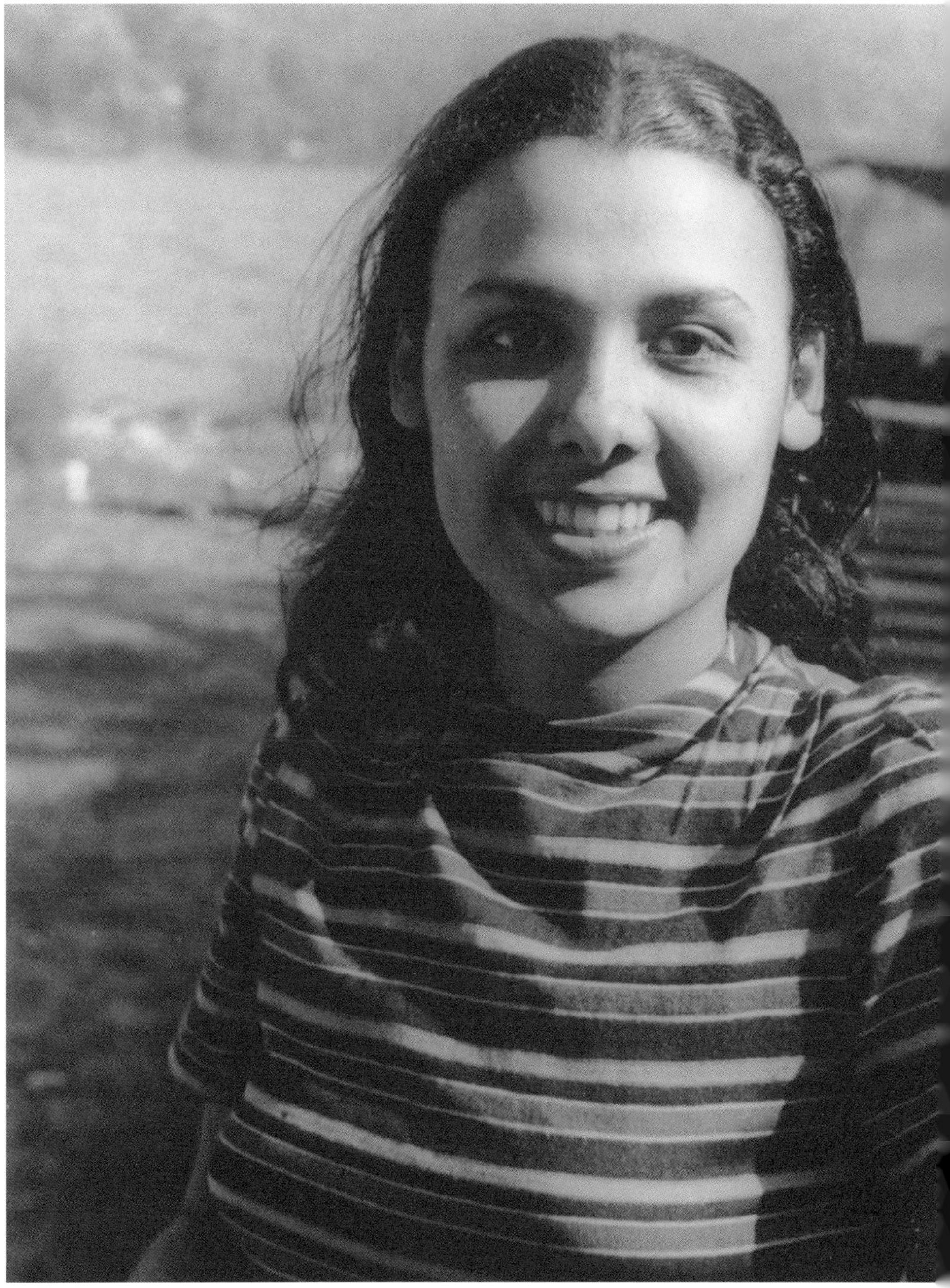

PHOTOGRAPHED ON SEPTEMBER 15, 1941

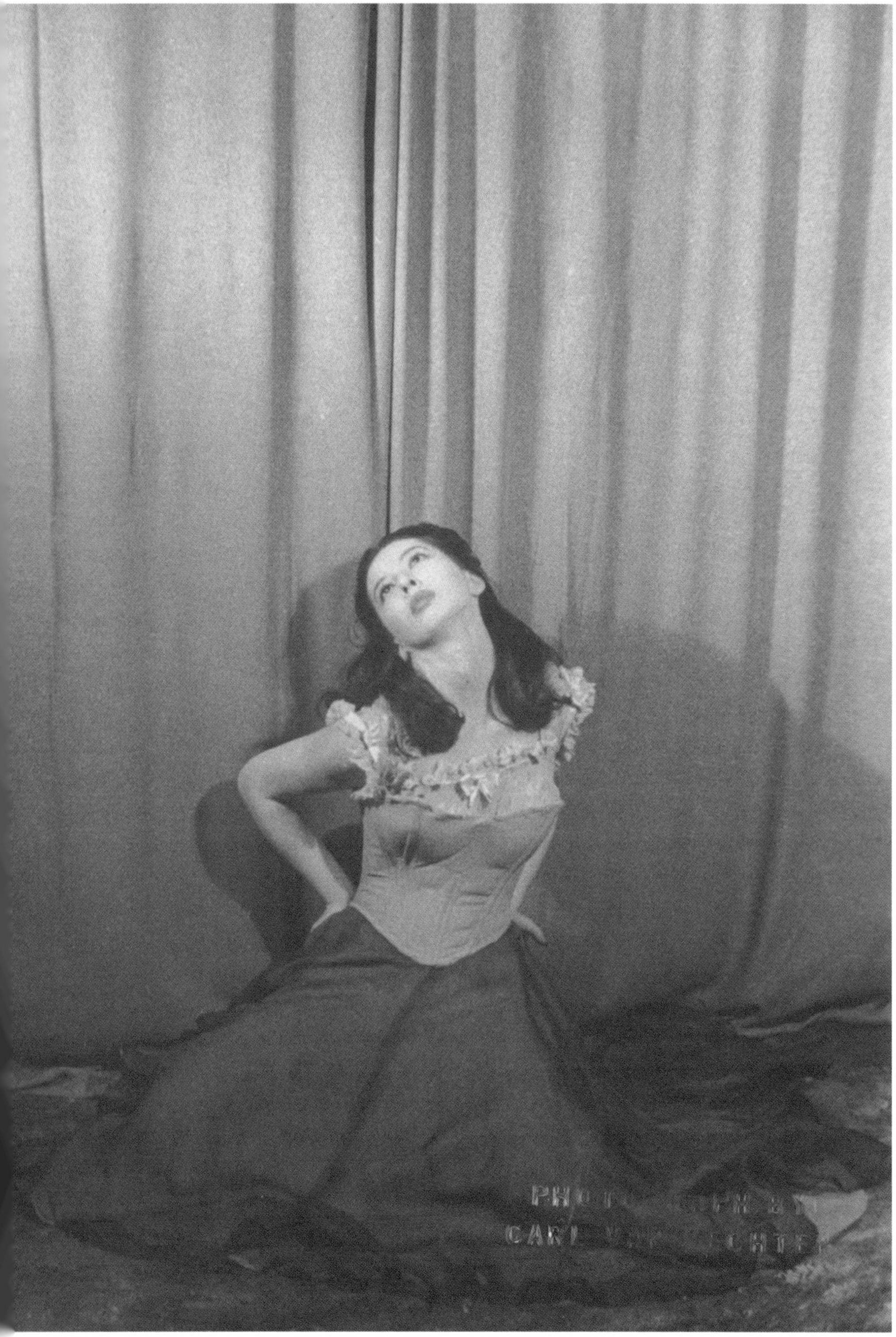

PHOTOGRAPHED ON APRIL 16, 1942, IN "PILLAR OF FIRE"

Sono Osato attended her first ballet performance at the age of eight, when her mother took her to see Diaghilev's Ballets Russes; Osato was mesmerized by Léonide Massine in Fokine's *Cléopâtre*. Soon after, she saw Tamara Toumanova dance and was inspired to become a dancer herself. She began to study ballet at age ten, and four years later, in 1934, a friend of her teacher arranged an impromptu audition with Wassily de Basil's Ballet Russe de Monte Carlo. She was accepted into the company, and soon found herself dancing alongside both Toumanova and Massine.

Osato was the Ballet Russe's youngest and first American, as well as its first Japanese, member. Born of a Japanese father and an Irish-French Canadian mother, Osato grew up in the United States and France, constantly feeling like an outsider. Although dance was a means for her to escape this feeling of difference, she often had to disguise her Oriental features with heavy make-up. Unlike the other non-Russians, however, Osato refused to adopt a Russian name. She wrote, "The colonel suggested that I take a Russian name. I refused. . . . My name remained my own."[1]

Osato left the Ballet Russe in 1940, tired of appearing in the chorus with few solo roles. She soon joined Ballet Theater,

# SONO OSATO

## DANCER

dancing under her mother's maiden name, Fitzpatrick, due to anti-Japanese sentiments. One of Osato's most memorable performances with Ballet Theater was her creation of Rosaline in Antony Tudor's *Romeo and Juliet*, developed specifically for her. Another was her creation of a Lover-in-Experience in Tudor's *Pillar of Fire*. Osato wrote, "I always felt he [Tudor] wanted the body to sing, rapturously, languorously, and longingly in turn. . . . When I was finally able to move as he wished, I felt a new sense of satisfaction in my dancing."[2]

In 1942, Osato left Ballet Theater to marry, but the couple's financial situation forced her to resume her career. Nora Kaye, a former colleague, told Osato to write to Agnes de Mille, who was choreographing the Mary Martin vehicle, *One Touch of Venus* (1943). The comic solo that de Mille eventually created for Osato established her popularity. The morning after her smash debut, Osato received a call from Paramount Pictures. At the time, she refused to make any films for them, telling her husband, "As long as the war lasts . . . what on earth could I do in Hollywood with my looks? Sit around the back lot waiting to play a Japanese spy?"[3] She would, however, eventually make one film, *The Kissing Bandit* (1947), starring Frank Sinatra and Kathryn Grayson. Her main task in the film was "to be sexy and to entice Frank, the Kissing Bandit."[4]

Summarizing her career, Osato stated that "any strong endeavor that gives you a sense of joy is the greatest thing in life. . . . If I could point to the most powerful experience of my ballet career, it would be the rehearsals of Antony Tudor's *Pillar of Fire*. That was the greatest artistic and emotional experience I've ever had. What I got out of it was immense."[5]



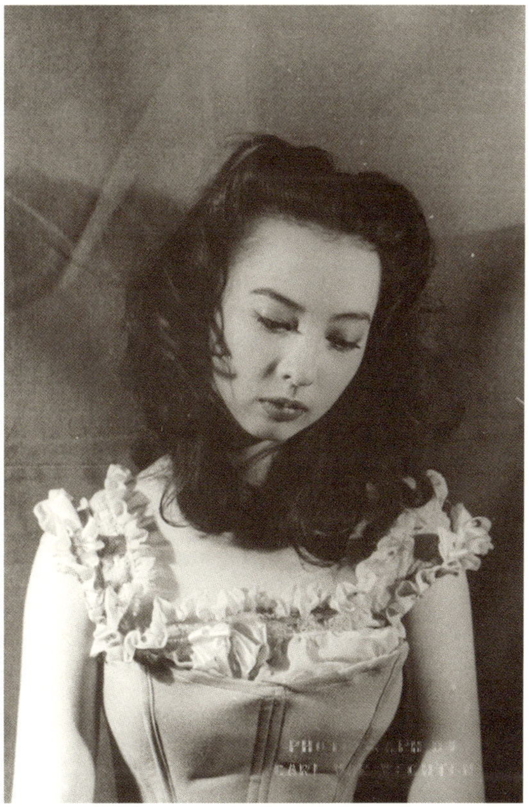

1 Sono Osato
*Distant Dances*
NY: Knopf, 1980
p. 30

2 *Distant Dances*
p. 194

3 *Distant Dances*
p. 221

4 *Distant Dances*
p. 254

5 John Gruen
*The Private World of Ballet*
NY: Viking, 1970
p. 74

# TATIANA RIABOUCHINSKA

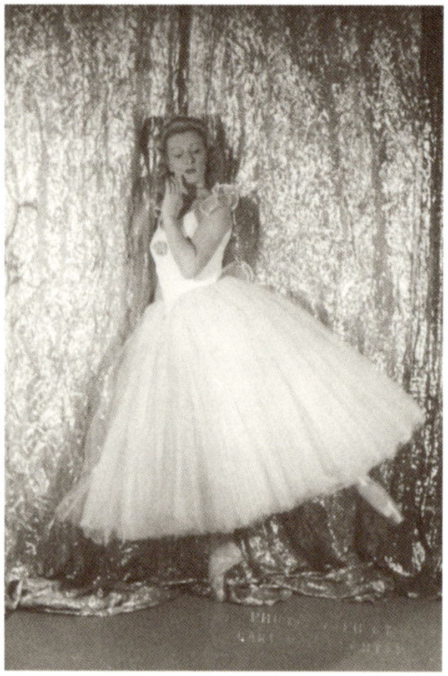

By the age of fifteen, Tatiana Riabouchinska had achieved worldwide renown as one of the celebrated trio of "Baby Ballerinas" of the newly formed Ballet Russe de Monte Carlo. After the death of Serge Diaghilev in 1929, Europe was left without a major ballet troupe, and interest in the ballet had declined. Hoping to fill this gap, Colonel Wassily de Basil established his Ballet Russe, pinning all his hopes on the Baby Ballerinas, so called because none of them was over fifteen.

The Baby Ballerinas were a sensation. Crowds flocked to see them, and audiences discovered that they were not just lovely novelties, but truly fine dancers. Of their 1933 London debut Agnes de Mille wrote, "London was knocked into a heap. Nothing so fresh and hopeful in ballet had happened since the war."[1] Clive Barnes credits the Baby Ballerinas with reviving interest in the ballet, stating, "The year of the Baby Ballerinas was 1933, and they aroused the interest of nations, and in a very real sense started the cult of balletomania in the Western world."[2]

Riabouchinska reached artistic maturity between 1937 and 1939 working with the great choreographer Michel Fokine. Critics and audiences were impressed with her quick footwork, the height of her jumps, her expressive arms, and her ethereally light movements. Fokine created several roles for Riabouchinska, including those that would become her most famous: the Golden Cockerel in *Le Coq d'Or*, the title role in *Cinderella*, and the Florentine Beauty in *Paganini*. Some consider the last of these to be her finest work, due to a nearly impossible set of whirling pirouettes that she executed before collapsing at the feet of Paganini. Dance critic Arnold Haskell called her performance, "among the most moving I have seen on the ballet stage."[3]

After leaving the Ballet Russe in 1942, Riabouchinska continued to make guest appearances with her husband, choreographer David Lichine. They also made two Walt Disney films, first serving as the models for the dancing hippopotamus and her alligator partner in *Fantasia*, and later dancing in silhouette in *Make Mine Music*. In 1953, the couple founded the first Los Angeles ballet company.

Riabouchinska will be remembered for her highly individualized style, a quality that made it difficult for other dancers to attempt her roles. Haskell commented that when Riabouchinska was replaced by another dancer, "something positive was missing. The feeling of spontaneity that Riabouchinska had, a lightness of mind equal to her lightness of dancing. The understudy acted, Riabouchinska lived."[4]

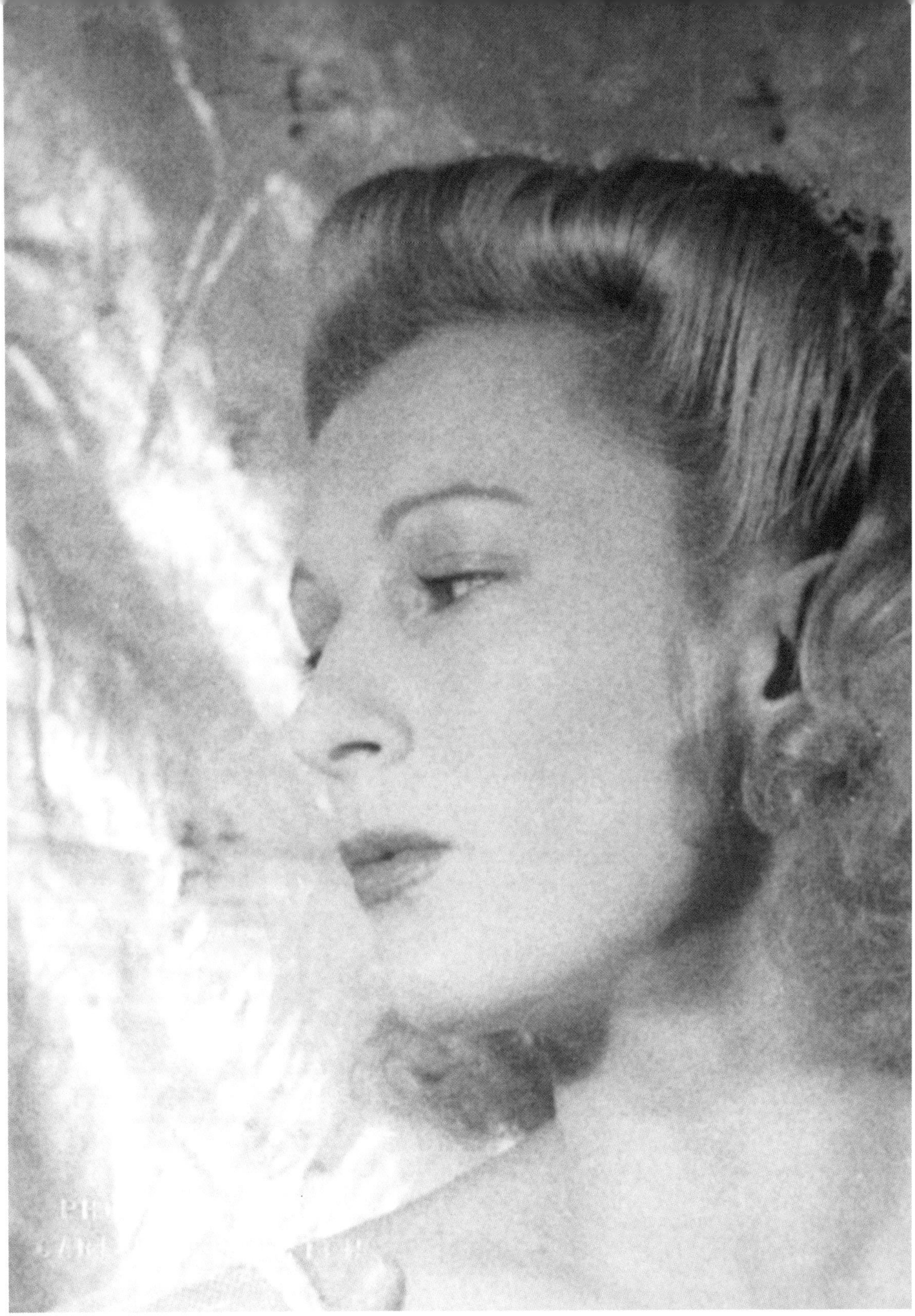

PHOTOGRAPHED ON NOVEMBER 5, 1942

## DANCER



1 Agnes de Mille
*Speak to Me, Dance with Me*
Boston: Atlantic Monthly
1973
p. 196

2 Clive Barnes
"Barnes on . . . the legend of the 'Baby Ballerinas'"
*Ballet News*
3:7 (1982)
p. 46

3 Arnold L. Haskell
*Ballet Vignettes*
Edinburgh: The Albyn Press
1948
p. 26

4 *Ballet Vignettes*
p. 25

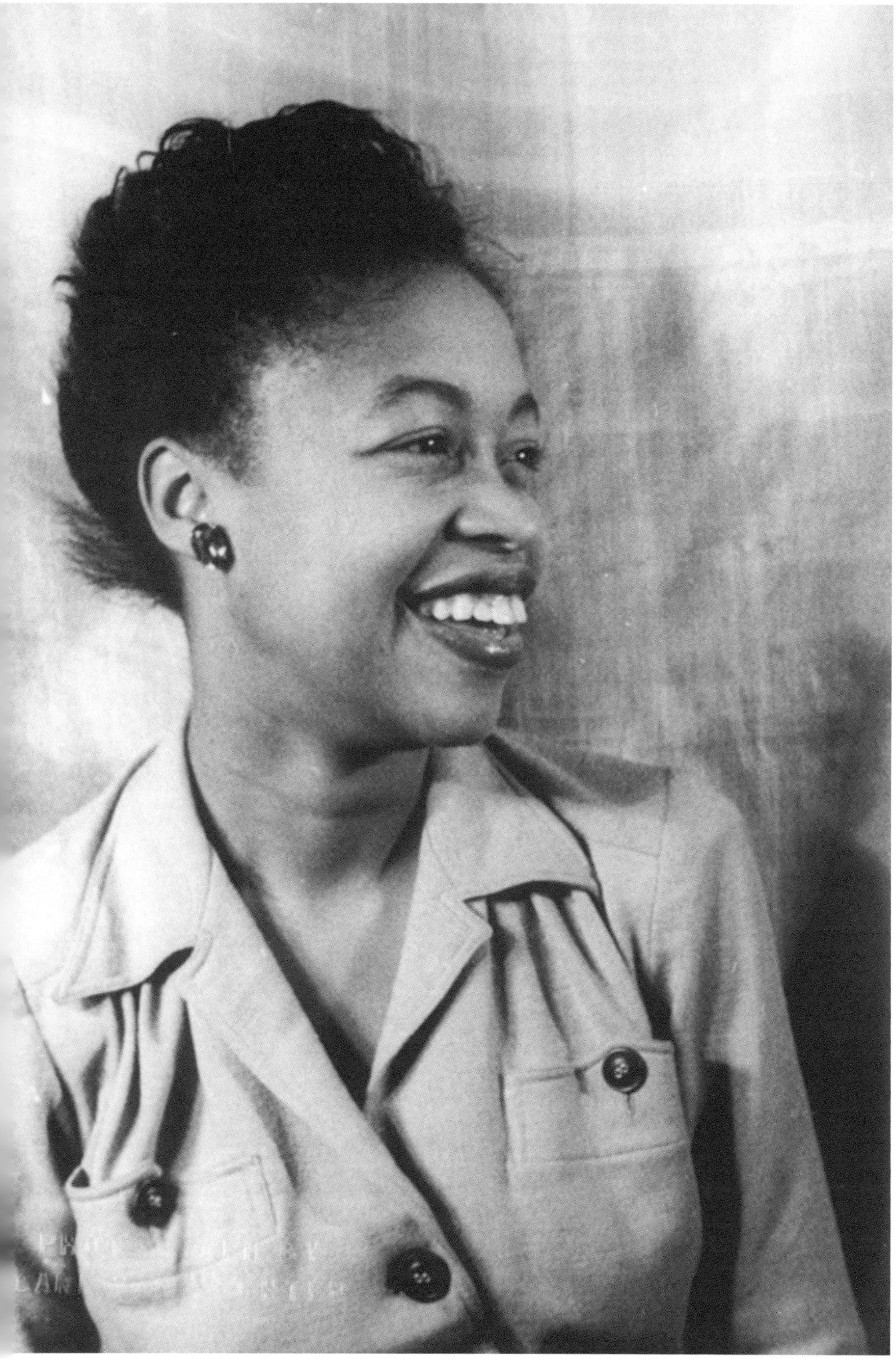

PHOTOGRAPHED ON NOVEMBER 27, 1942

A writer whose accomplishments exceed her reputation, Margaret Walker made significant contributions to American literature and to the study of African-American culture and history. Throughout her long career as a writer, educator, and scholar, Walker received many awards and accolades for her creative and critical writing, including the Yale Series of Younger Poets Award, a Fulbright Fellowship, a Senior Fellowship from the National Endowment for the Humanities, and numerous honorary degrees. Her poetry and fiction influenced and inspired such writers as Alice Walker and Nikki Giovanni.

Walker was born in Birmingham, Alabama, the daughter of a Methodist minister and a music teacher. The family moved to New Orleans, Louisiana, when both her parents joined the faculty of New Orleans University, now known as Dillard University. Walker's mother and father encouraged her to keep a journal and to read widely in both European literary classics and contemporary American literature. Her reading included the work of Langston Hughes, Zora Neale Hurston, and other Harlem Renaissance writers flourishing at the time.

# MARGARET WALKER

## WRITER



As a young woman, Walker had the opportunity to meet Langston Hughes when he visited New Orleans on a reading tour. Hughes recognized her talent and encouraged Walker, who was enrolled at the time in New Orleans University, to seek greater educational opportunities at a northern university. On his advice, Walker went to Chicago to study at Northwestern University. After graduation, she worked with the Works Progress Administration Writer's Project where she met other Chicago writers, including Richard Wright, who would later write *Native Son*.

In the 1930s, Walker went to graduate school at the University of Iowa where she completed her first collection of poems. After entering the manuscript in the Yale Younger Poets competition twice, she submitted the collection a third time and won; Stephen Vincent Benét selected her book, *For My People* (1942), for publication by Yale University Press. Though some were surprised that the prestigious award should go to a young, African-American woman (the *New York Times* headline announcing the award read "Negro Girl Wins Yale Poetry Prize"[1]), Benét praised the poems. "They are set for voice and the blues," he wrote, "they could be sung as easily as spoken, and first and last, they are a part of the earth."[2]

In addition to poetry, Walker wrote a novel, *Jubilee*. Called "The reverse side of *Gone with the Wind*,"[3] *Jubilee* is based on Walker's great grandmother's life. The story follows a slave girl from her childhood on a southern plantation, through the Civil War, to her life as a free woman during Reconstruction. *Jubilee* was praised for its historical accuracy as well as its high literary quality. Walker presents such a carefully researched and historically accurate picture of the lives of southern slaves that the novel has been taught in American history classes.

Because of her commitment to the understanding and study of African-American history and culture, Walker founded the Institute for the Study of Black History, Life and Culture of Black People. The institute is located at Jackson State College in Jackson, Mississippi, where Walker was on the faculty from 1949 until her retirement in the 1970s. Walker served as director of the Institute and donated her own archive there to create the Margaret Walker Alexander National Resource Center.

1 "Negro Girl Wins Yale Poetry Prize"
*New York Times*
4 Nov 1942

2 "Negro Girl Wins Yale Poetry Prize"

3 Wilma Dykeman
"A Talent for Survival (Review of *Jubilee*)"
*New York Times*
25 Sept. 1966

# PEARL PRIMUS

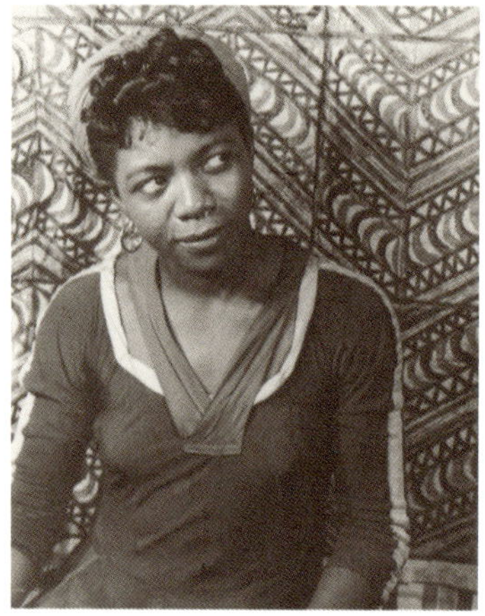



Performer and scholar Pearl Primus has been called "the grandmother of African-American dance." An innovative dancer and choreographer, her work is characterized by speed, intense rhythms, high jumps, and graceful leaps. A Ph.D. in anthropology and sociology, Primus studied African and African-American culture and incorporated her considerable knowledge into her dance programs. Throughout her career, Primus married the art of dance to social commentary, historical study and interpretation, and community action.

Born in Trinidad and raised in New York City, Primus developed a serious interest in dance only after she had graduated from Hunter College with a bachelor's degree in biology. Unable to find work in her field because few scientific jobs were available to African Americans, Primus began studying with the National Youth Administration's New Dance Group. She took to dance immediately.

Primus began performing in public with dance groups and in solo appearances at New York's Café Society Downtown. In an early show, Primus's performance was so compelling, she "literally stopped the show."[1] She formed her own company and choreographed both group and solo pieces. Primus developed dances that incorporated elements of social protest, such as "Strange Fruit" and "The Negro Speaks of Rivers." These dramatic and moving pieces affected audiences profoundly. John Martin described a 1945 performance: "Miss Primus is always engrossing to watch, for she moves superbly and with a great inward strength."[2]

A 1948 Rosenwald grant allowed Primus to visit Africa to study African dance. She traveled throughout the continent, learning traditional dances and rituals; her work was deeply influenced by her experiences in Nigeria, Zaire, Rwanda, and Ghana. Returning to the United States, Primus introduced American audiences to African dance. "Everything I do is consistent with what I saw in Africa," Primus said, "except for wearing a bra. I have to make that concession to modern standards."[3]

Primus also introduced many American dancers to African dance traditions. Primus ran her own dance schools for children and adults, and she taught dance, dance education, and ethnic studies at New York University, the Five College Consortium in Amherst, Massachusetts, and other colleges and universities.

Carl Van Vechten aptly described Pearl Primus as a dancer who had "developed a fine style all of her own, moving expertly, with great precision to Negro folk tunes, and who later became adept in authentic African gyrations."[4] But his statement fails to acknowledge the depth of Primus's contributions as choreographer, activist, and educator.

PHOTOGRAPHED OCTOBER 11, 1943

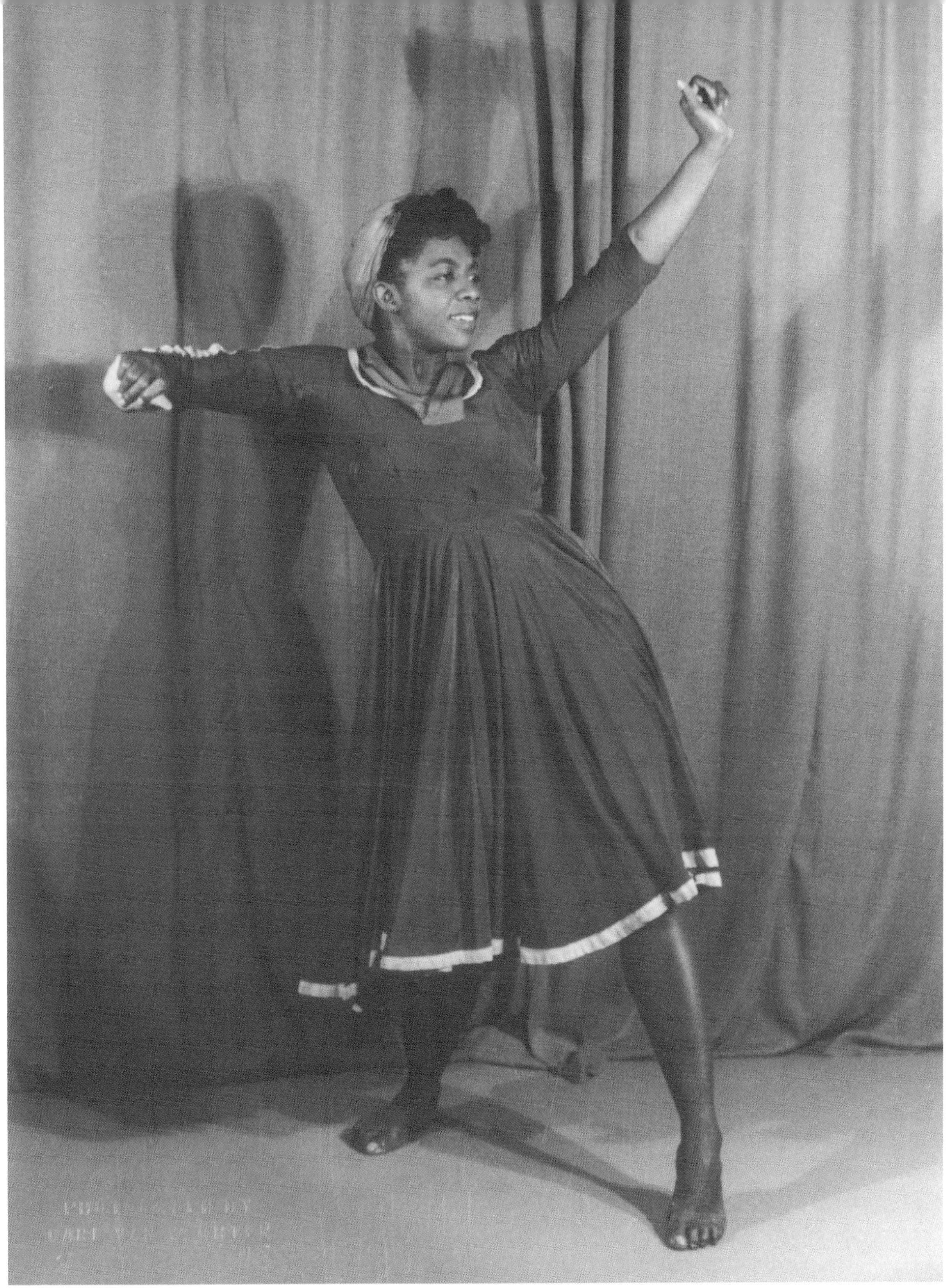

## DANCER & EDUCATOR



1 John Martin
"African Dancers in Festival Here"
*New York Times*
14 Dec. 1943

2 John Martin
"4 Dancers Appear in New Group Fete"
*New York Times*
16 June 1945

3 *Time*
21 May 1951

4 Van Vechten
*The Dance Writings of Carl Van Vechten*
Ed., Paul Padgett
NY: Dance Horizons, 1974
p. 43

# MURIEL RAHN

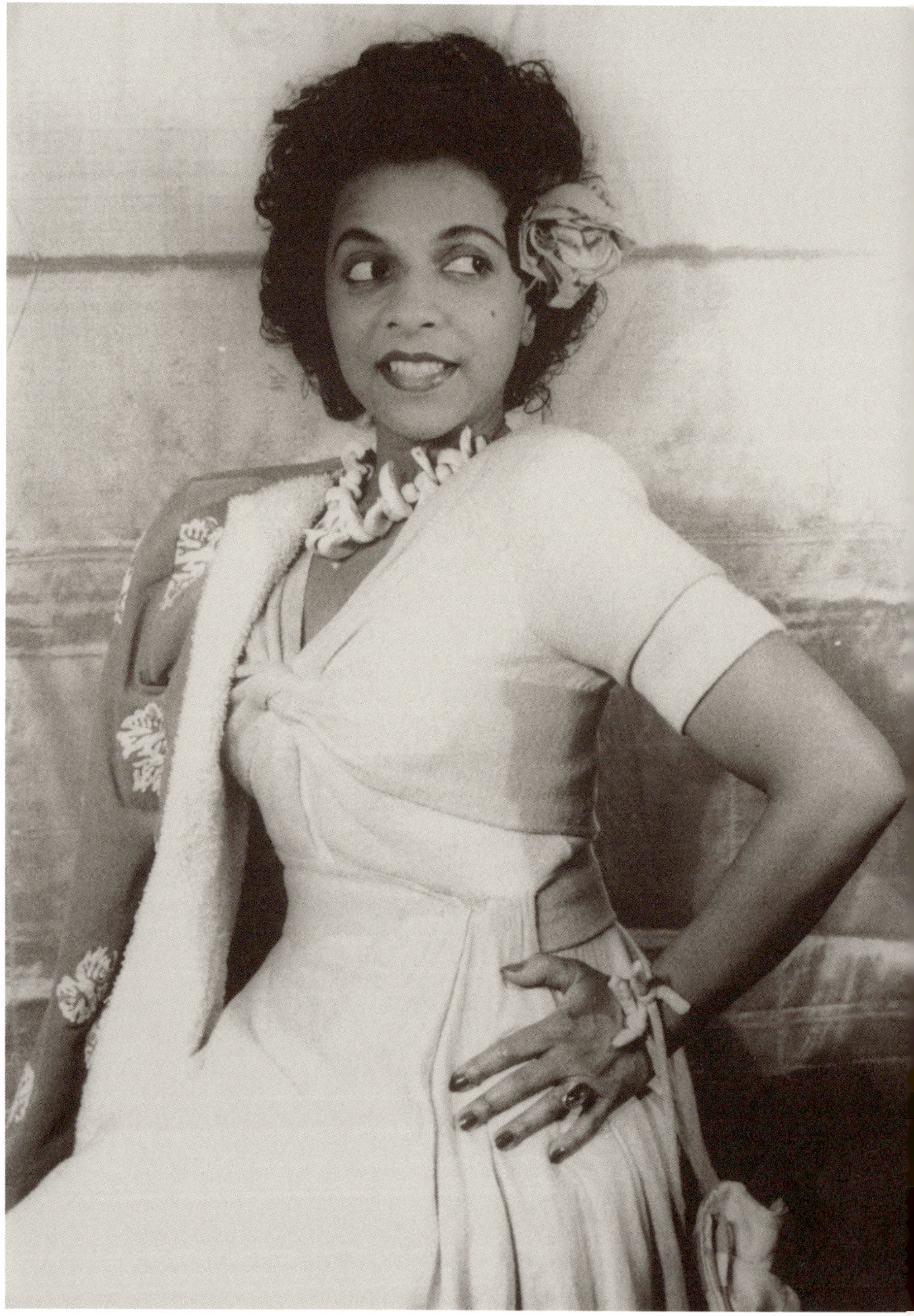

PHOTOGRAPHED ON FEBRUARY 29, 1944, AS CARMEN JONES



Best known for her performance in the title role of the Broadway play *Carmen Jones*, singer and actress Muriel Rahn was born in Boston and raised in Tuskegee, Alabama. In college at Atlanta University and the University of Nebraska at Lincoln, Rahn studied music and education. She spent a short time as a public school teacher before devoting herself completely to her career in show business.

Through the course of her career, Rahn developed a reputation as the kind of rare performer who is equally talented as a singer and as an actress. Many of her major operatic roles, including Salome and Aida, allowed her to exercise these dual strengths. Muriel Rahn became the first African-American singer to perform in an opera at Carnegie Hall when, in 1942, she appeared in Mozart's *Abduction from the Seraglio*. In spite of her great success in operatic performances, Rahn was best known for her concerts and for her performances in many Broadway and off-Broadway shows.

Rahn's last Broadway appearance was as Cora Lewis in *The Barrier*, the American opera based on Langston Hughes's play *The Mulatto*. Her performance in this role received excellent notices by critics who called her an "admirable singer and actress" and described her performance as "superb."[1] To the role of Cora, Howard Taubman wrote, Rahn brought "a personal dignity and sincerity to the part and her singing is not only accurate and full-blooded, but charged with dramatic cogency."[2]

*The Barrier*'s New York success led to the scheduling of performances in a number of cities. When it was discovered that *The Barrier* was to play in Baltimore at the Ford Theatre, a theater that insisted on segregated seating of white and black audience members (restricting black viewers to the worst seats in the house), "Muriel Rahn declared that she would sing (honoring her contract) and, when not on stage, would picket the production."[3] Others associated with the production, including Langston Hughes, announced that they would join Rahn's picket line. Rather than endure the publicity the protest would cause, the theater cancelled the performance.

Rahn's willingness to fight racial prejudice and injustices was not limited to this occasion. Among her colleagues in show business, Rahn was well known as an advocate for the fair treatment of African-American performers. She often stood up to theater producers and owners, calling attention to their unjust treatment of black performers and, on several occasions, forcing them to honor contracts with black performers and pay promised wages.

On January 7, 1950, Muriel Rahn sang spirituals and an aria from *The Barrier* at the formal opening of the James Weldon Johnson Memorial Collection of American Negro Arts and Letters founded by Carl Van Vechten at Yale University.

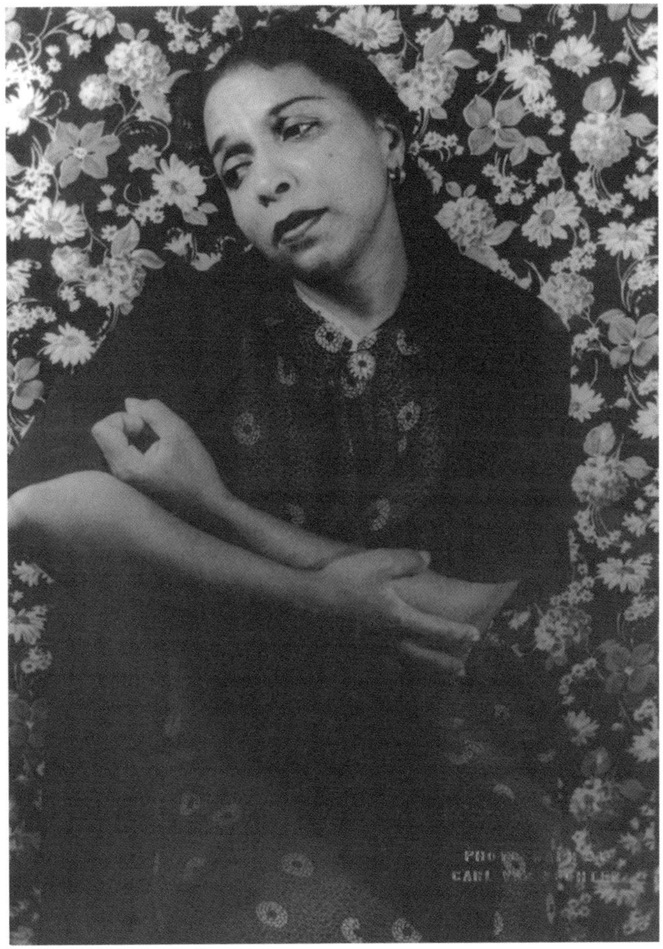

PHOTOGRAPHED ON JANUARY 29, 1950, AS CORA IN "THE BARRIER"

1 Brooks Atkinson
"At The Theatre"
*New York Times*
3 Nov. 1950

2 "Muriel Rahn, Soprano, Is Dead"
*New York Times*
9 Aug. 1963

3 Arnold Rampersad
*The Life of Langston Hughes*
*Volume II: 1941-1967*
*I Dream A World*
NY: Oxford, 1988
p. 183

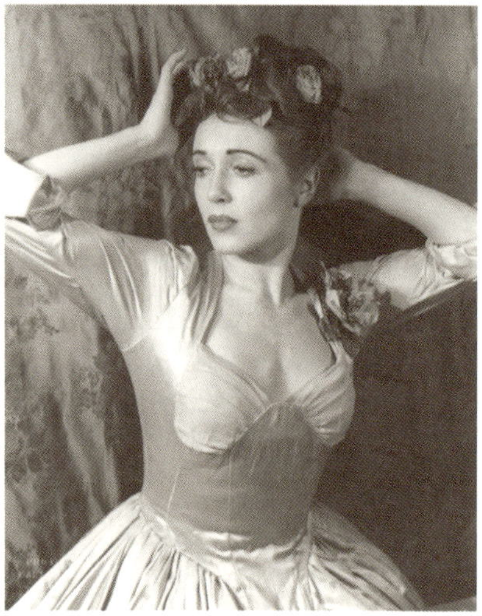

# JANET REED

## DANCER



Dancer Janet Reed was born in Tolo, Oregon, a town with a population of fifteen families. She began performing with the San Francisco Opera Ballet in 1937. Although the fashion at that time was for Russian themes and styles, and ballet companies were featuring glamorous, European-looking ballerinas, San Francisco audiences were enchanted with Reed, a petite, red-haired, blue-eyed dancer who embodied the American girl next door. After her first big role as Swanhilda in *Coppélia*, Reed became the star of the Opera Ballet, and while with them danced the roles of Swanhilda, Juliet in *Romeo and Juliet*, and the Swan Queen Odile in the first American full-length production of *Swan Lake*. When she performed this role for the first time, "San Francisco ballet-goers fairly burst with pride."[1]

In 1941, Reed went to New York to join the Dance Players, an experimental dance group focusing on American themes. Although Dance Players was financially unsuccessful and closed the following year, it was an artistic success that allowed Reed to try new styles and discover her love for modern ballet. After the closing of the Dance Players, Reed danced first with Ballet Theater and then with the New York City Ballet.

Reed's first major success in New York City came in 1944 playing a passer-by picked up by a sailor in Ballet Theater's production of *Fancy Free*. The ballet featured music by Leonard Bernstein and choreography by Jerome Robbins; John Martin declared it "a smash hit" in the April 19, 1944, *New York Times*. After the sensational opening numbers, "everyone on both sides of the footlights was aware that a success was being born—a most exhilarating experience in the theater."[2]

While with Ballet Theater, Reed also danced in *Pillar of Fire* and *On Stage* with Nora Kaye, replaced Tatiana Riabouchinska in *Graduation Ball*, and danced the roles of Juno and, after Agnes de Mille, Venus in Antony Tudor's ballet *The Judgment of Paris*. Van Vechten's portrait of Reed shows her in her role as the wife in Agnes de Mille's ballet *Tally-Ho!*, a comedy of the morals and manners of old Versailles. De Mille had originally danced the part herself, but John Martin found Reed's interpretation to be more delicate, with a lighter touch and greater charm. In his essay "Choreography for Americans," Van Vechten stated that Reed had brought "something both distinguished and lusty" to the role.[3]

In summing up the ballet season in the March 21, 1954, issue of the *New York Times*, Martin praised Reed as being "just about as complete a theater dancer as the ballet possesses." Always popular with theater audiences, who found her "adorable," Reed was an accomplished artist, with a comic gift, "the talents of a first-rate actress," and the ability to make a role uniquely her own. "She has the ability to make you always believe her," Martin wrote, "and this with a work of fantasy makes the difference between success and failure."

PHOTOGRAPHED ON OCTOBER 27, 1944, IN "TALLY-HO!"

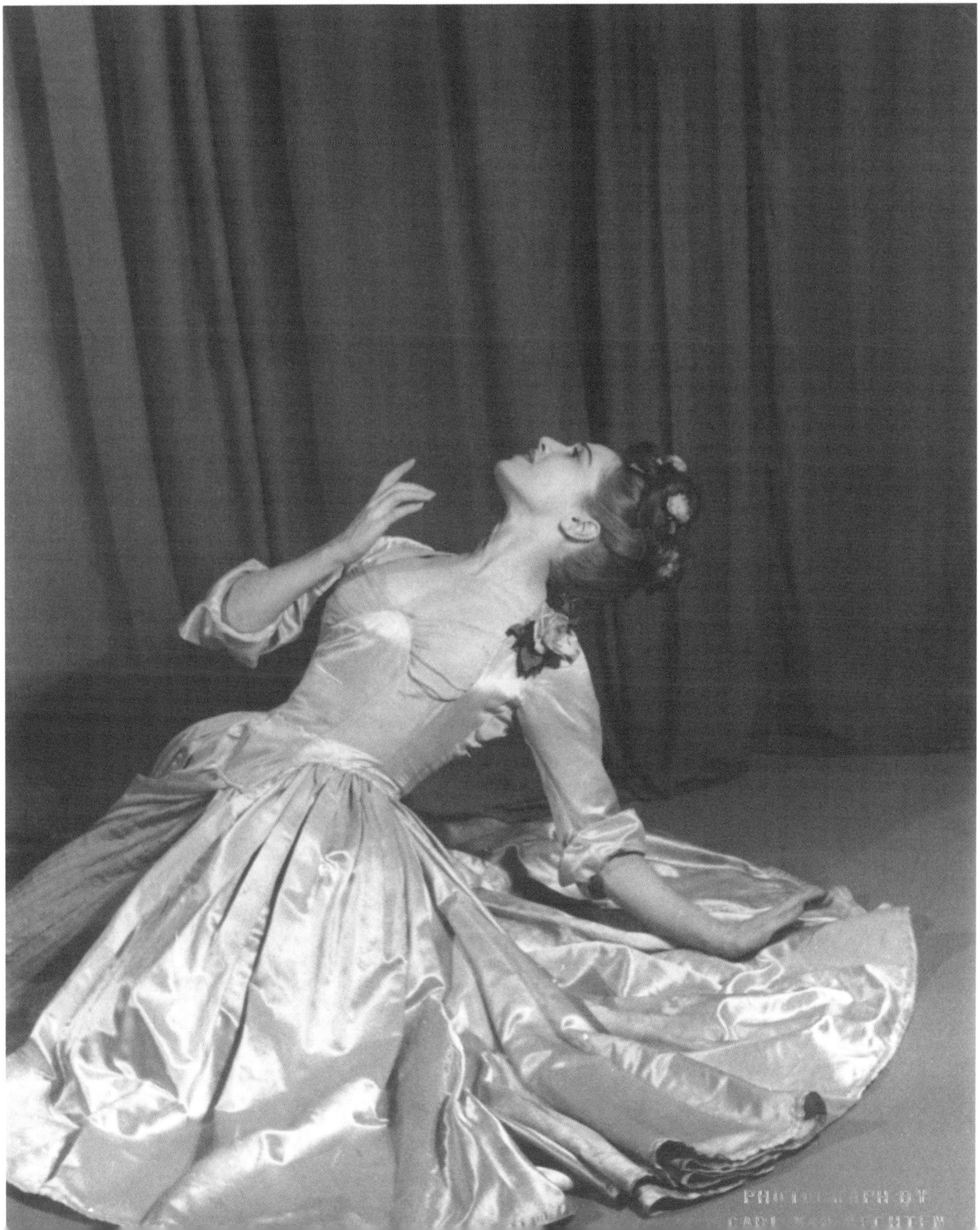



1 Margaret F Atkinson and May Hillman
*Dancers of the Ballet*
NY: Knopf, 1955
p. 128

2 Grace Robert
*The Borzoi Book of Ballets*
NY: Knopf, 1946
p. 128

3 Van Vechten
*The Dance Writings of Carl Van Vechten*
Ed., Paul Padgette
NY: Dance Horizons, 1974
p. 48

# DANCER & ACTRESS



The dancer known as Vera Zorina was born Eva Brigitta Hartwig. However, as she states in her autobiography, "Vera Zorina was born, aged seventeen, at Covent Garden, during a heated discussion with Colonel de Basil, general director of the Ballet Russe de Monte Carlo."[1] Before her debut, de Basil ordered Zorina to choose a Russian name. When questioned, he replied, "Because, my dear, if every member who is not Russian keeps their own name, the ballet is not Russian ballet anymore, you understand? . . . Here is a list of Russian names. You choose."[2] She chose the only names on the list that she could pronounce and was thus known throughout her career.

Zorina danced with the Ballet Russe from 1934 to 1936. During that time, she had a passionate affair with choreographer Léonide Massine, who was twenty-three years older and married. Zorina eventually left the Ballet Russe to star in Rodgers and Hart's *On Your Toes*. She received positive reviews and was invited to dance in Samuel Goldwyn's film, *The Goldwyn Follies*, featuring music by George and Ira Gershwin and choreography by George Balanchine. Zorina performed in the film's "water-nymph" ballet, where she emerged from a pool, clad in a gold lamé tunic, and danced on a glass surface. The ballet was considered an innovation and was highly praised by critics. Although the film sustained heavy financial losses, it was instrumental in popularizing ballet by introducing it to the movies.

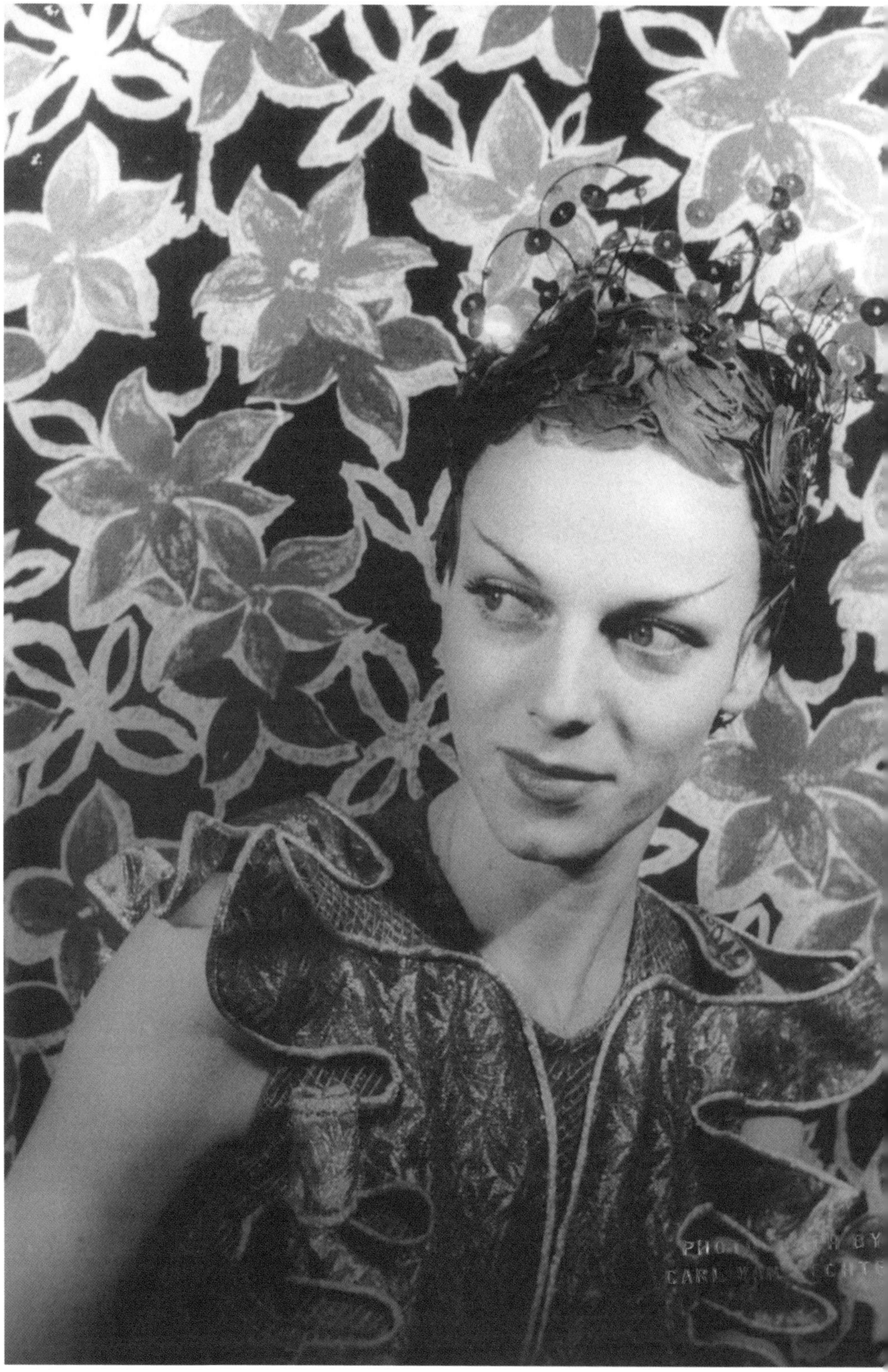

# VERA ZORINA



Soon after her appearance in *Follies*, Zorina starred in the 1938 musical *I Married an Angel*, also choreographed by Balanchine. The choreographer didn't think the costumes were appropriate for an abstract ballet, so he bought several colorful toothbrushes, strung them together, and Zorina wore them around her neck. After a Christmas Eve performance in New York, Zorina and Balanchine were married, although they eventually divorced in 1946.

After years of dancing in films and musicals, in 1942 Zorina auditioned for the more serious role of Maria in Hemingway's *For Whom the Bell Tolls*. Paramount gave her the part and she cut her hair to two inches in length, as the role required. However, after a day of shooting, the studio was unhappy with the results, so gave the role to Ingrid Bergman. In 1945, Zorina played Ariel in *The Tempest*. Because of her success in this role, the New York Philharmonic asked her to narrate several musical works. After her career as a narrator, Zorina began to direct operas, including Puccini's *La Bohème* and Stravinsky's *Perséphone* for the Santa Fe Opera, and *Pagliacci* for the New York City Opera. With regard to a career spanning almost fifty years, Zorina stated, "I've never been interested in standing still in one medium."[3]

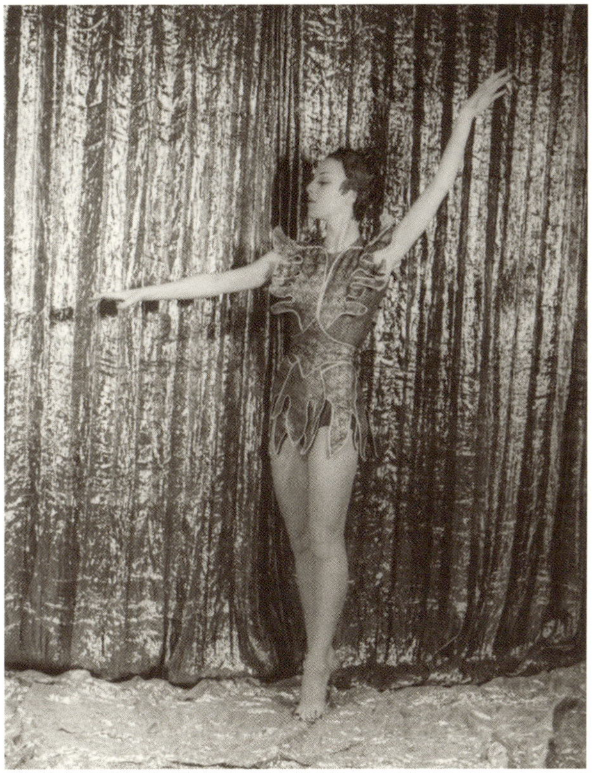

1 Vera Zorina
*Zorina*
NY: Farrar Straus & Giroux, 1986
p. 79

2 Zorina
p. 79

3 John Gruen
*The Private World of Ballet*
NY: Viking, 1970
p. 65

PHOTOGRAPHED ON APRIL 2, 1945, AS ARIEL IN "THE TEMPEST"

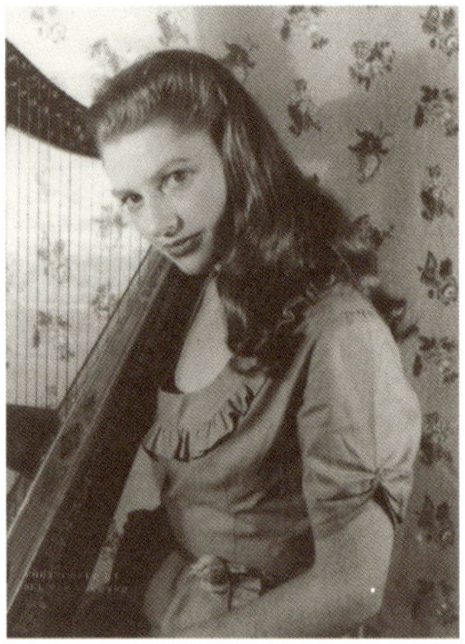

# SUSAN REED

## FOLK SINGER, IRISH HARP, & ZITHER PLAYER



The daughter of Daniel Reed, a successful entertainer, actor, director, and playwright, red-haired folk singer Susan Reed spent much of her childhood surrounded by entertainers. Though she was raised predominantly in South Carolina, she traveled frequently with her father and was exposed at a young age to the entertainment industry in New York, Los Angeles, and Hollywood. Guests in the Reed household often included accomplished singers, dancers, and musicians; it was her father's friends, the influential folk musicians Carl Sandburg and Huddie Ledbetter, who first introduced Susan Reed to American folk music. She received her earliest lessons in the tradition from some of its finest practitioners.

Members of the Abbey Theater Company of Dublin often visited the Reeds when the company toured in the United States. Actors and musicians from this company, including Ralph Cullinan and Farrell Pelly, introduced Reed to Irish folk music. She was so deeply influenced by these performers and their musical tradition that she began playing the Irish harp and learning Irish folk songs. In just a few years, Reed had mastered the instrument; she had also learned to play the zither and the Appalachian autoharp.

By the time Susan Reed was a teenager, her family had settled in New York City. She began performing in the City's popular nightclubs to much acclaim. After years of singing in church choirs and performing for wounded soldiers in VA hospitals, Reed had developed a beautiful singing voice that was perfectly matched to the music of her Irish harp. Soon she was traveling to clubs and music festivals all over the United States, playing traditional folk songs from many countries. Reed performed regularly on the radio and she appeared on a number of television programs, including major network specials.

Though Susan Reed enjoyed a great deal of success throughout her career, today her name and her music are not well known, even in folk music circles. Though few remember her, Susan Reed is among the pioneering musicians of the so-called "Hootenanny movement" responsible for exposing American audiences to traditional folk music from many cultures. In the 1950s, Reed made several albums of American and European folk songs; she recorded many folk standards, including "I Know My Love," "Jennie Jenkins," "Go Away From My Window," and "I'm Sad and I'm Lonely."

PHOTOGRAPHED ON SEPTEMBER 30, 1945

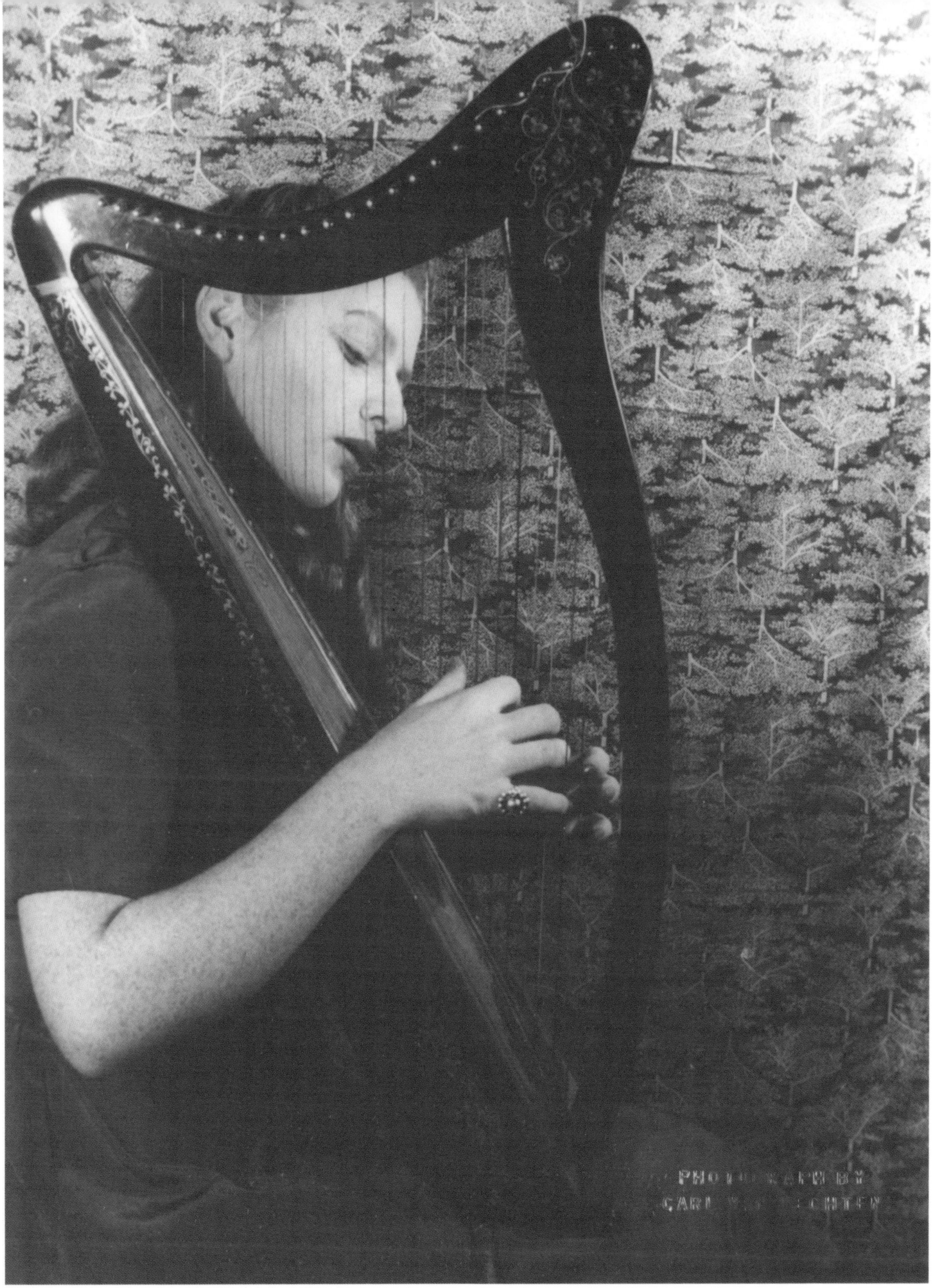

## SINGER



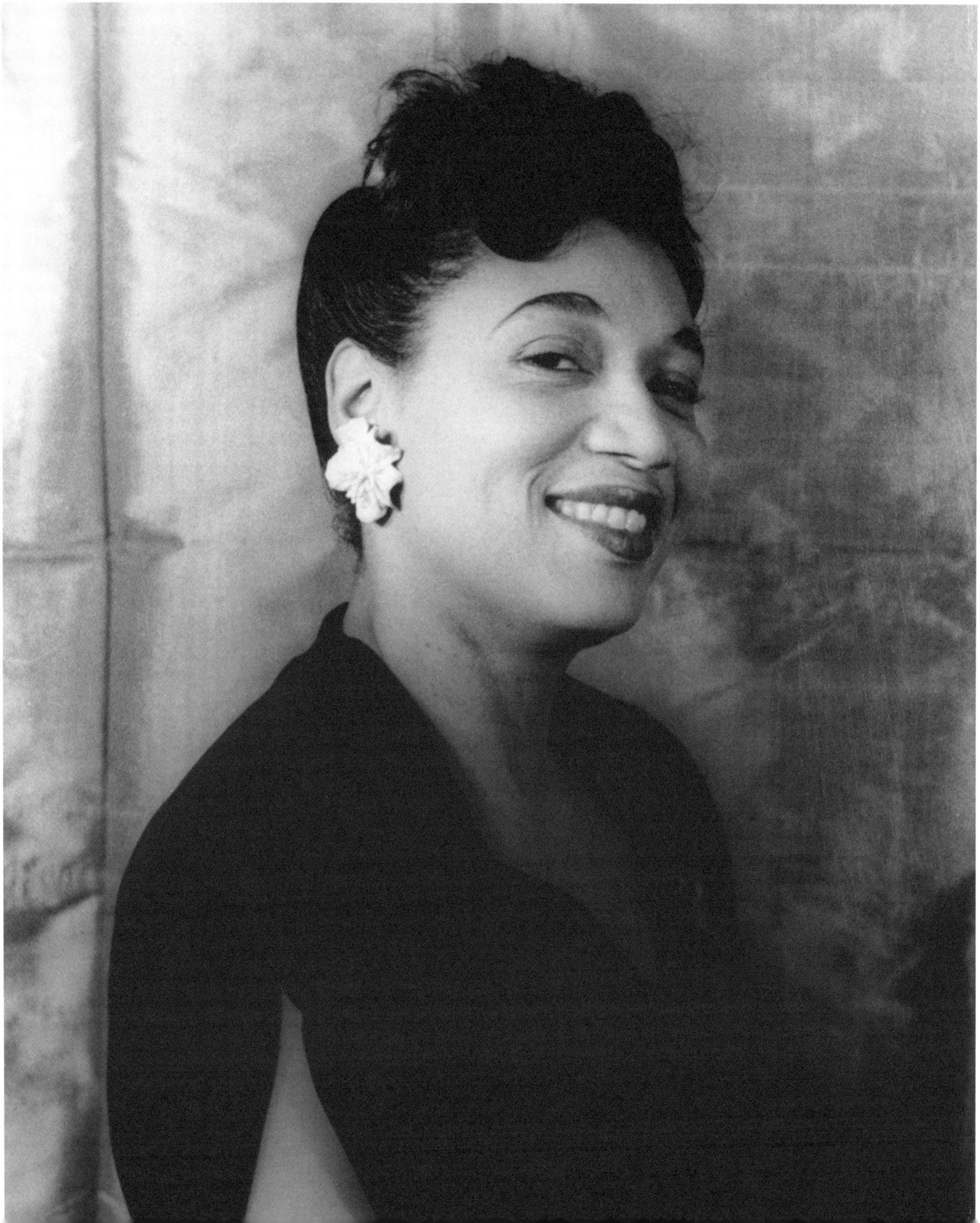

John S. Wilson 1
"Welcome Home, 'One-Song Welch'"
*New York Times*
16 May 1980

# ELISABETH WELCH

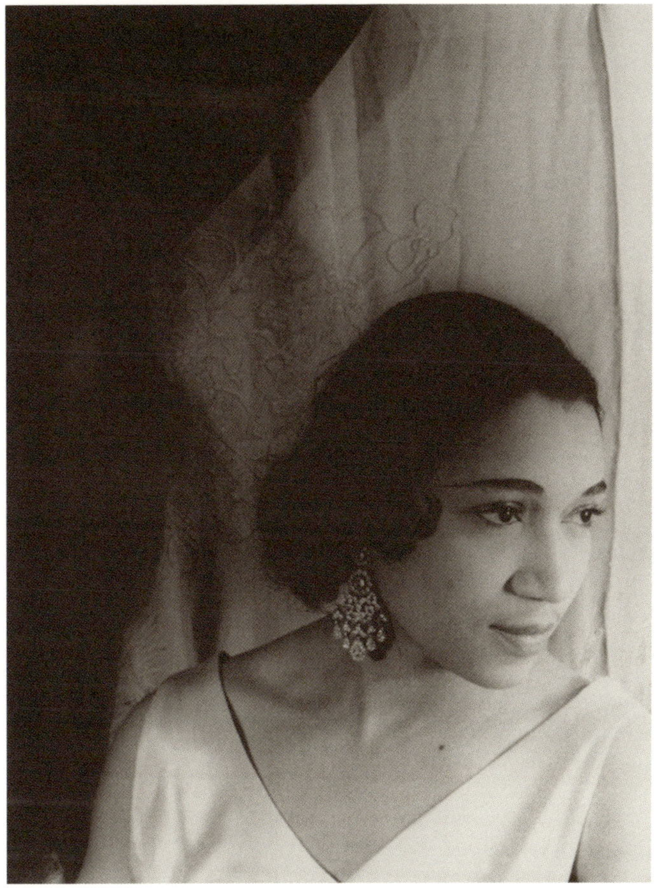

Like many African-American performers of her time, singer Elisabeth Welch found greater success in Europe than in the United States. After starting her career in New York, Welch performed in popular clubs in Paris and London, and, later, in British films. Before leaving New York, however, Welch made her Broadway debut in the 1923 musical *Runnin' Wild*, singing "Charleston" the "theme song of the jazz age."[1] Welch was still in high school at the time.

After singing for years in European clubs and shows, Welch returned to New York to a club called the Royal Box in 1930. While performing there, she sang Cole Porter's "Love for Sale," a song featured in *The New Yorkers,* which had just opened on Broadway to mixed reviews. A friend of Porter's heard Welch's performance and convinced *The New Yorker*'s producers to replace the white actress who sang the song in the show's opening with Welch. "Love for Sale" became one of Welch's most popular songs and her performance in the New York production of the musical was the first of many appearances she would make in Porter's productions. It also marked the beginning of a long friendship with Cole Porter.

Welch, who trained as a social worker before committing to a career in the theater, returned to England where she enjoyed a long and varied career including work in the theater, on the radio, and in films. During World War II, she performed for British troops as a member of Sir John Gielgud's company. Welch returned to New York in 1980 to appear in *Black Broadway*, a tribute to 20th century African-American theater in New York City.

PHOTOGRAPHED ON JUNE 12, 1946

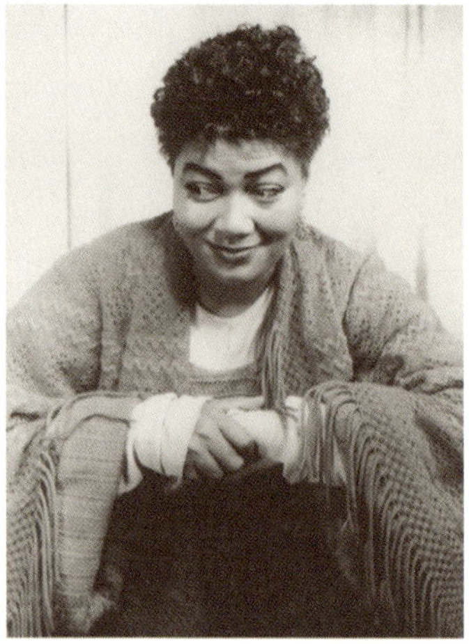

# PEARL BAILEY



Pearl Bailey 1
*The Raw Pearl*
NY: Harcourt
1968
p. 67

Pearl Bailey's remarkable career as a singer and stage and film actress lasted nearly sixty years. When she was twelve years old, Bailey won a five dollars first prize in a talent contest at the Pearl Theater in Washington, D.C. The contest management also promised a chance to perform several shows at the club, which for Bailey meant appearing alongside her brother, the well-known tap dancer Bill Bailey, who was performing there. After a few shows, the club closed and Pearl Bailey never received payment for her first professional theater job.

In spite of this, the little taste of success she experienced winning the contest convinced Bailey to give up her plans to become a teacher and pursue a career on the stage. She joined the chorus line of a vaudeville troupe and began a tour of Pennsylvania's vaudeville circuit. She soon graduated to solo performances in clubs from Washington D.C. to New York City. When she won another talent contest, this time at Harlem's Apollo Theater, the music and theater community began to notice Bailey. Audiences, too, were charmed by her trademark performance style, a casual and intimate presentation that made her skillful vocalization seem deceptively simple. Bailey began playing New York's finest clubs, becoming one of the city's favorite singers.

In the 1940s, in addition to her successful career as a singer, Pearl Bailey became a popular theater performer. She made her Broadway debut in 1946 in *St. Louis Woman*, an all-black musical by Johnny Mercer and Harold Arlen. Bailey sang two songs in the show: "A Woman's Prerogative," and "Legalize My Name." Audiences were thrilled by her performance and critics singled out her numbers for praise. That year, Bailey won the Donaldson Award for Best Newcomer on Broadway.

Her next Broadway appearance was a little less auspicious. The show, *Arms and the Girl*, in which one of her co-stars was a horse, received mixed reviews and wasn't popular with audiences. Though it was a disappointing way to follow up her first theatrical success, Bailey had a good sense of humor about it. "There was another star in the show, a horse. I mustn't forget him," she wrote in her autobiography, *The Raw Pearl*. "From the beginning there were misgivings about that horse, because they are show stealers, like children. Then, too, you can't pin down what they might do onstage."[1]

After that early misstep, Bailey made many memorable and successful Broadway appearances. Among her most famous roles were Madame Fleur, the West-Indian bordello owner in

PHOTOGRAPHED ON MARCH 12, 1950, AS CONNECTICUT IN "ARMS AND THE GIRL "

## SINGER & ACTRESS

*House of Flowers*, a musical written by Truman Capote and Harold Arlen, which also starred a young Diahann Carroll. Her biggest success came in 1967, however, when Bailey played Dolly Levi in the all-black version of *Hello, Dolly!* Bailey won a Tony award for her performance. The show played for two years and toured nationwide in the 1970s.

Bailey's popularity as a singer and stage actress led to many offers to appear in Hollywood films. Bailey played Frankie in the 1954 hit film adaptation of *Carmen Jones* which also starred Harry Belafonte and Dorothy Dandridge. In 1959, Bailey performed with Dandridge again in *Porgy and Bess*. The all-star cast also included Sydney Poitier and Sammy Davis Jr. During the 1970s, she appeared on several television programs, including her own brief series, *The Pearly Bailey Show*.

Though she had dropped out of school to become a performer, Bailey didn't give up on getting a formal education. When she was in her sixties, she went back to school, earning a bachelor's degree in theology from Georgetown University. She completed her studies at the age of sixty-seven.

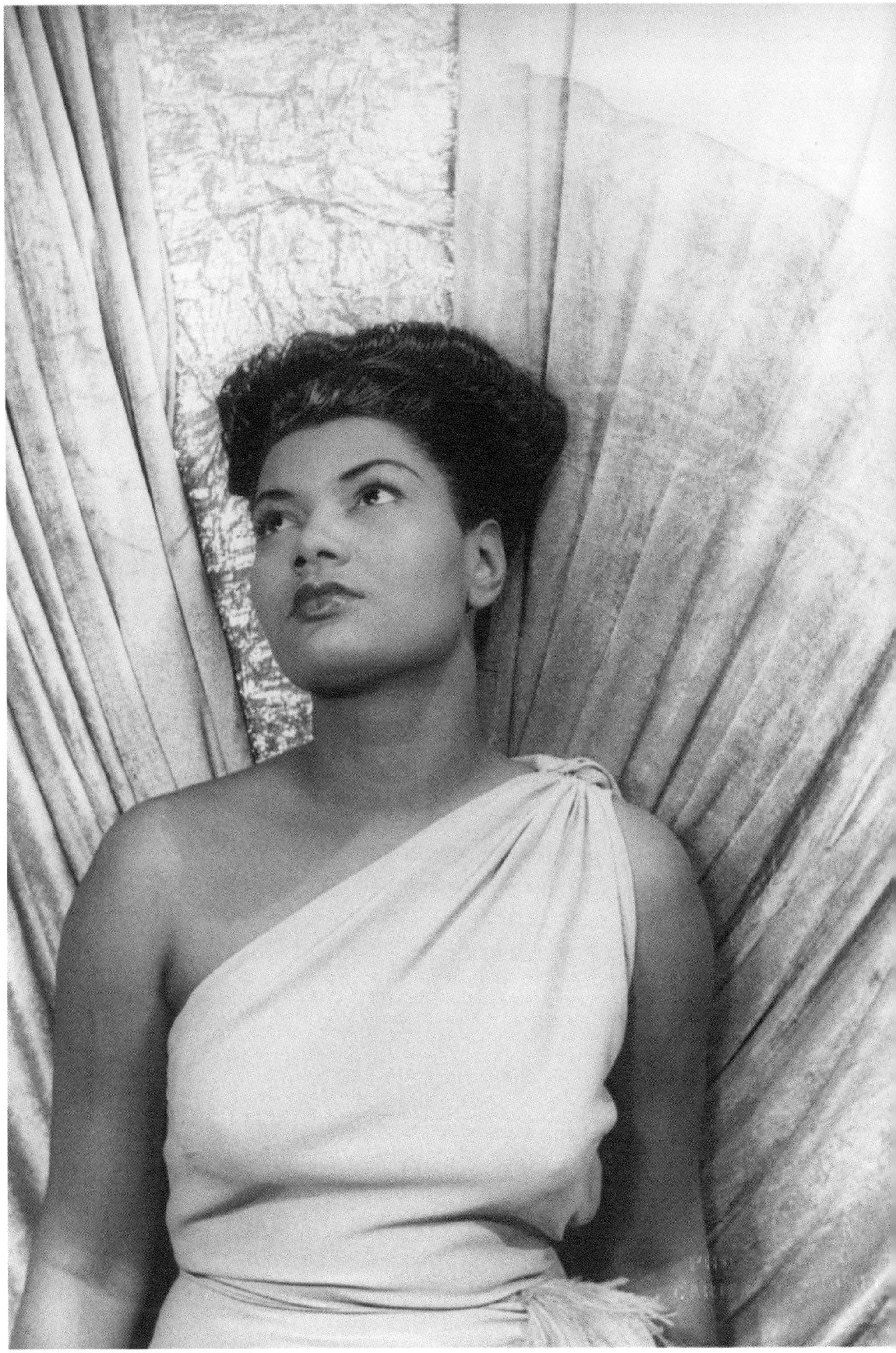

PHOTOGRAPHED ON JULY 5, 1946

# NORA KAYE

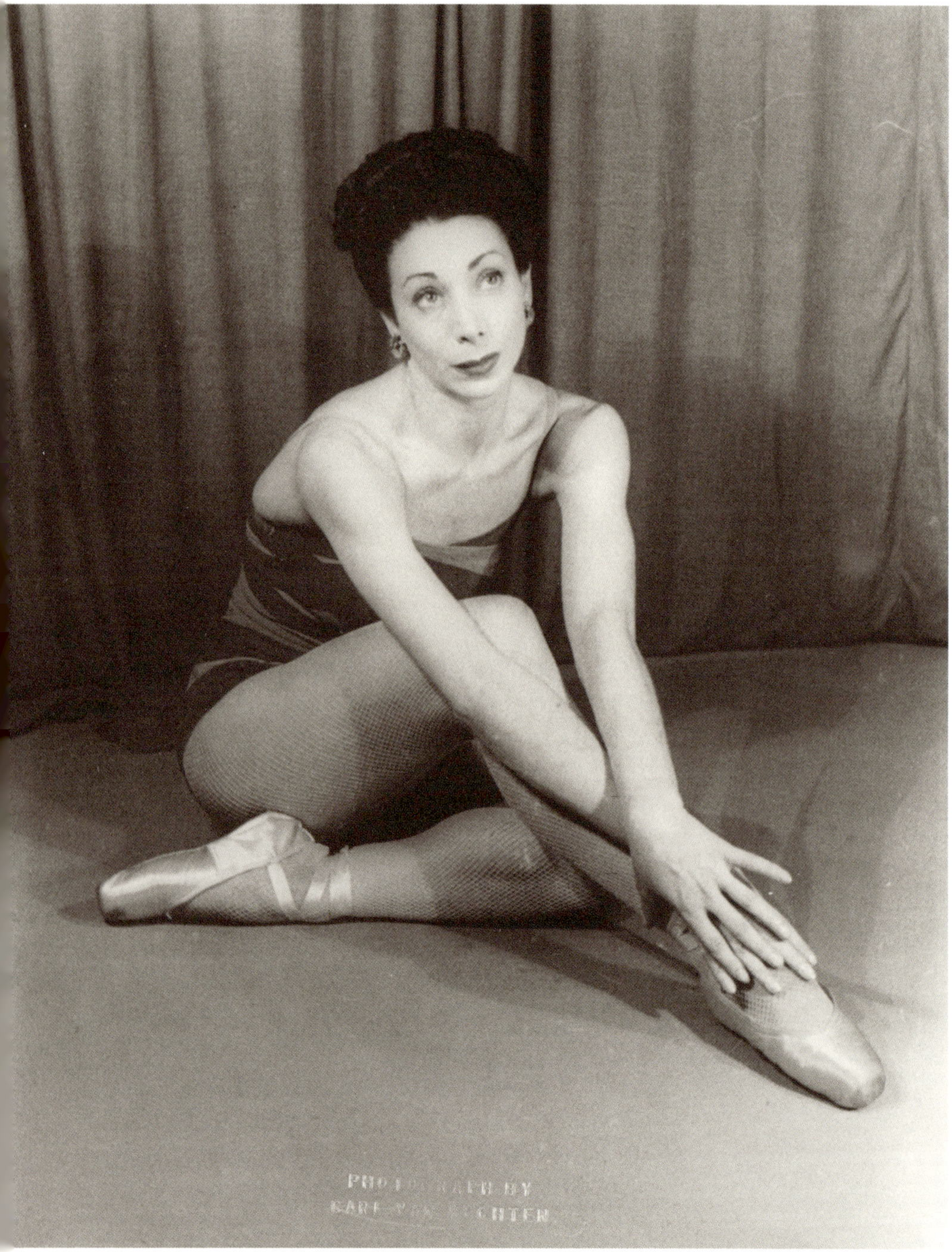

## BALLET DANCER

Before Nora Kaye quit dancing in 1961 and literally threw her ballet shoes out of a car window, she was, according to John Martin, "an artist of unique gifts and virtually limitless powers."[1] In establishing herself as a new type of dancer, the "dramatic ballerina," Kaye was the first American ballerina to be internationally acclaimed and to have a profound affect on ballet history.

Born Nora Koreff in New York City to Russian immigrant parents, Kaye changed her name because she felt that an American dancer should have an American name. After dancing with the Metropolitan Opera Ballet, she appeared in several Broadway musicals, including *Stars in Your Eyes* with Ethel Merman and Jimmy Durante in 1939. Kaye planned to pursue a theatrical career and only auditioned for Ballet Theater at a friend's urging.

After dancing with Ballet Theater for several years, Kaye was chosen for the lead in Antony Tudor's new ballet *Pillar of Fire*. Sometimes called a "play without words," it was a psychological exploration of Hagar, a sexually frustrated young woman who fears she will lose her lover to her attractive and enticing younger sister. Kaye's father had been an actor at the Moscow Art Theatre with Stanislavsky, so she was familiar with method acting and immediately understood its application to dance:

PHOTOGRAPHED ON OCTOBER 31, 1946, IN "FACSIMILE"

each of the dancer's movements was made to express Hagar's mental state. At its premiere in 1942, *Pillar of Fire* was recognized as an artistic phenomenon, setting the standard and establishing Kaye as a major artist. Sono Osato, who danced in *Pillar of Fire*, wrote, "After years of effort, years of classes and corps work and tiny solo roles, Nora Kaye's incomparable artistry made her a ballerina in thirty minutes. Her sublime acting in *Pillar of Fire* enlarged the possibilities of balletic expression for all time."[2]

Kaye danced particularly well in dramatic roles such as Hagar in *Pillar of Fire* or Lizzie Borden in Agnes de Mille's *Fall River Legend* (1948). However, she also showed her wide range as the light-hearted sophisticate in *Dim Lustre* (1944) and the overbearing prima ballerina in *On Stage!* (1946) with Janet Reed. Van Vechten captured Kaye in these and several other roles, photographing her from her earliest appearances in *Peter and the Wolf* (1941) and *Gala Performance* (1941). In 1946, Kaye wrote to Van Vechten that a portrait he had taken of her in profile was one of her best ever.

After she stopped dancing, Kaye produced several films, including *The Turning Point* (1977), *Pennies from Heaven* (1981), and *The Secret of My Success* (1987). However, her enduring legacy remains with dance. In 1950, she wrote,

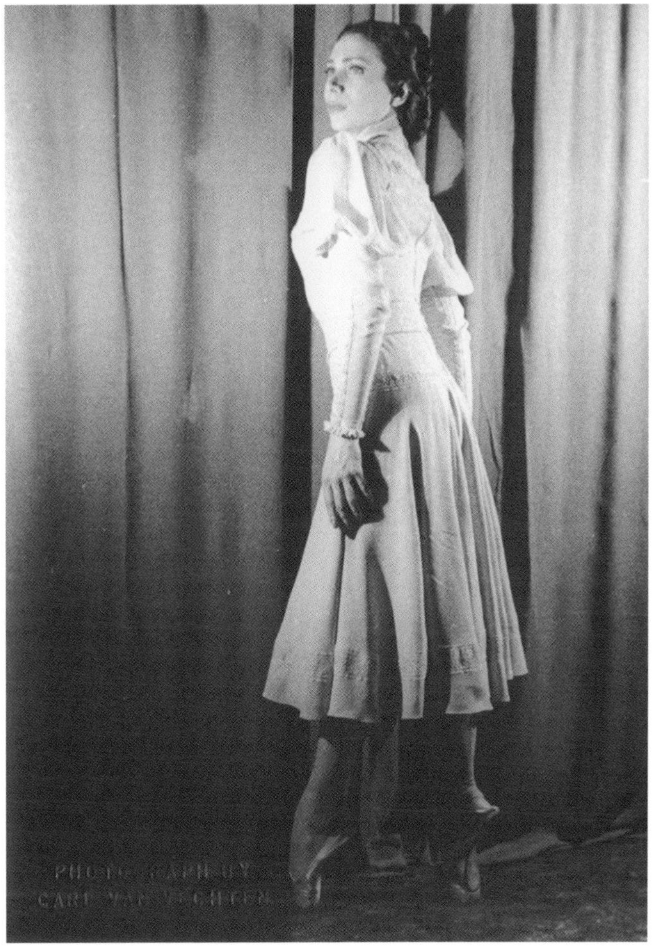

As an American ballerina, then, I never take anything for granted. I question each tradition, each interpretation, each movement. The answers I have found, sometimes right and sometimes wrong, constitute my contribution to the young American dancer of ballet: not to accept until you understand (at least to your own satisfaction), and not to dance any role, ancient or new, until you do understand. This urge to question and to discover is, I think, the trademark of American ballet.[3]



1 John Martin
"The Dance: Nora Kaye. Distinguished Artist, Joins New York City Ballet"
*New York Times*
11 Feb. 1951

2 Sono Osato
*Distant Dances*
NY: Knopf, 1980
p. 195

3 Nora Kaye
"The American Ballerina"
In *The Dance Experience: Readings in Dance Appreciation*
Eds., Myron Howard Nadel and Constance Nadel Miller
NY: Universe Books, 1978
pp. 249-50

PHOTOGRAPHED ON APRIL 16, 1942, AS HAGAR IN "PILLAR OF FIRE"

# DOROTHY WEST

## WRITER



Dorothy West was born and raised in Boston, where her father, a former slave, was a fruit merchant known as The Black Banana King. An avid writer from her early childhood, West published her first work in *The Boston Post*; she received a number of literary prizes from this paper and her work appeared there often. West stayed in Boston to study at Boston University; she later studied at the Columbia School of Journalism. Though she moved to Harlem as a young woman, West remained connected to Boston and was a frequent contributor to a prominent African-American magazine there, *The Saturday Evening Quill*.

When she was eighteen, West won a literary prize from *Opportunity* for her story, "The Typewriter." She shared the prize with Zora Neale Hurston. After attending the awards dinner in New York City, West decided to move to Harlem. She found her way into the Harlem literary scene by default when she moved into Hurston's old apartment. Because she was younger than most of the other writers, she was given the nickname "The Kid."

In 1931, West joined a large group of African-American writers and artists who traveled to the Soviet Union to make a film about race in different cultures. Though the film was never made, West remained in the Soviet Union for a year. She spent some of that time traveling with another member of the film group, the poet Langston Hughes. Hughes and West shared a close relationship, though it is unclear whether or not they were romantically involved. That West proposed marriage to Hughes in a letter, noting that her motivation was primarily to have a child, does little to clarify their relationship. West, who never married, declined a proposal from Countee Cullen, another Harlem Renaissance poet.

After her return to the United States, West became the founding editor of *The Challenge*, a magazine devoted to publishing the best writing by African Americans. When the publication failed, West founded and edited *The New Challenge*, maintaining her commitment to publishing new writing by African Americans. Both publishing efforts suffered from financial trouble and were eventually abandoned. West ultimately left Harlem and moved to Martha's Vineyard, where she lived until her death in 1998.

In much of West's writing, "white racism finds echoes in black society's obsession of gradations of skin color and the possibility of 'passing.'"[1] Her 1948 semi-autobiographical novel, *The Living Is Easy*, explores racism and class-consciousness among the African-American bourgeoisie in Boston. Though some critics have argued that West ignores many problems African Americans face as a result of racism, some suggest that she incorporates an element of social commentary in the

1 Elizabeth Benedict, "A Matter of Color," *Washington Post*, 8 Jan. 1995

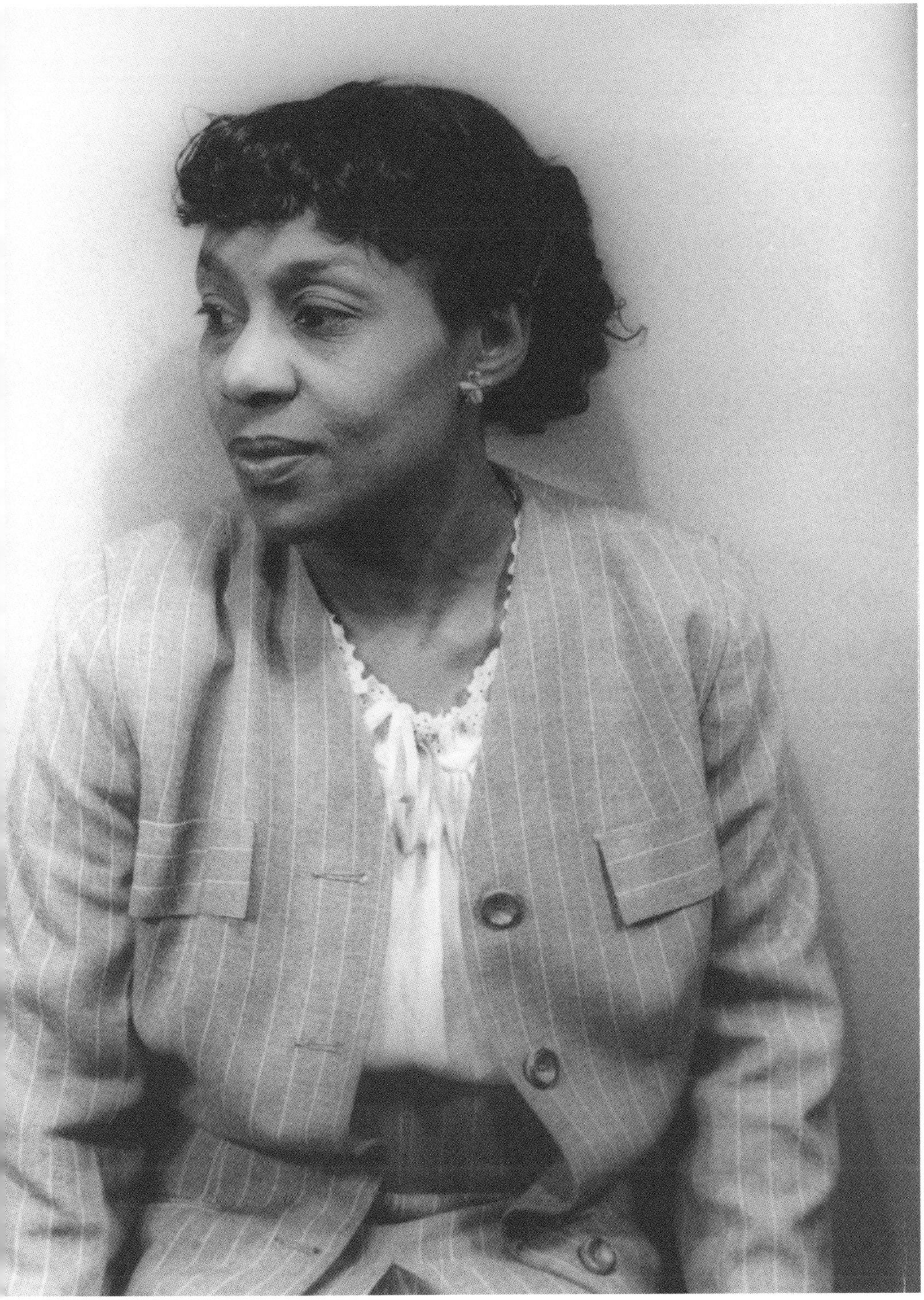

PHOTOGRAPHED ON MAY 17, 1948



book through her criticism of the values and ethics of the African-American middle class. A second novel, *The Wedding*, was started in the 1960s but West didn't complete it until the 1990s. Her editor for this book, her Martha's Vineyard neighbor Jacqueline Kennedy Onassis, read West's work in the island's local paper and encouraged her to complete the novel. Similar to her earlier novel and to many of her short stories, *The Wedding* examines issues of race and class among upper-middle class African Americans, this time in the Martha's Vineyard community, Oak Bluffs. After its publication, the novel was adapted for television by Oprah Winfrey; it starred Halle Berry.

# MARIANNE MOORE

## POET



One of the most innovative poets of the twentieth century, Marianne Moore is often placed on par with contemporaries such as Wallace Stevens, Ezra Pound, T.S. Eliot, and William Carlos Williams, all of whom admired her greatly. In his introduction to Moore's *Selected Poems* (1935), Eliot stated, "My conviction, for what it is worth, has remained unchanged for the last fourteen years: that Miss Moore's poems form part of the small body of durable poetry written in our time," and he credited her with one of the poet's greatest accomplishments, that of "maintaining the life of the English language."[1]

In 1915, Moore's poems began to appear in little magazines in the United States and Europe. Several of her poems were published in the *Egoist*, a bimonthly magazine based in London and edited by the writer H.D., Moore's Bryn Mawr classmate. Six years later, Moore's first book publication, *Poems* (1921), appeared without her knowledge when H.D. collected and printed twenty-four of Moore's poems as a surprise for her.

In 1918, Moore moved with her mother to Greenwich Village. From that point on, she would be indissolubly linked to New York City—first to Greenwich Village, and then to Brooklyn, where she lived for over thirty-five years. While living in Greenwich Village during the height of American modernism, Moore became involved in avant-garde literary circles and met poets such as William Carlos Williams and Wallace Stevens. She also began publishing in the *Dial*, the major American modernist journal of the time. In 1925, when Scofield Thayer stepped down as editor of the *Dial*, Moore took over until the journal closed four years later.

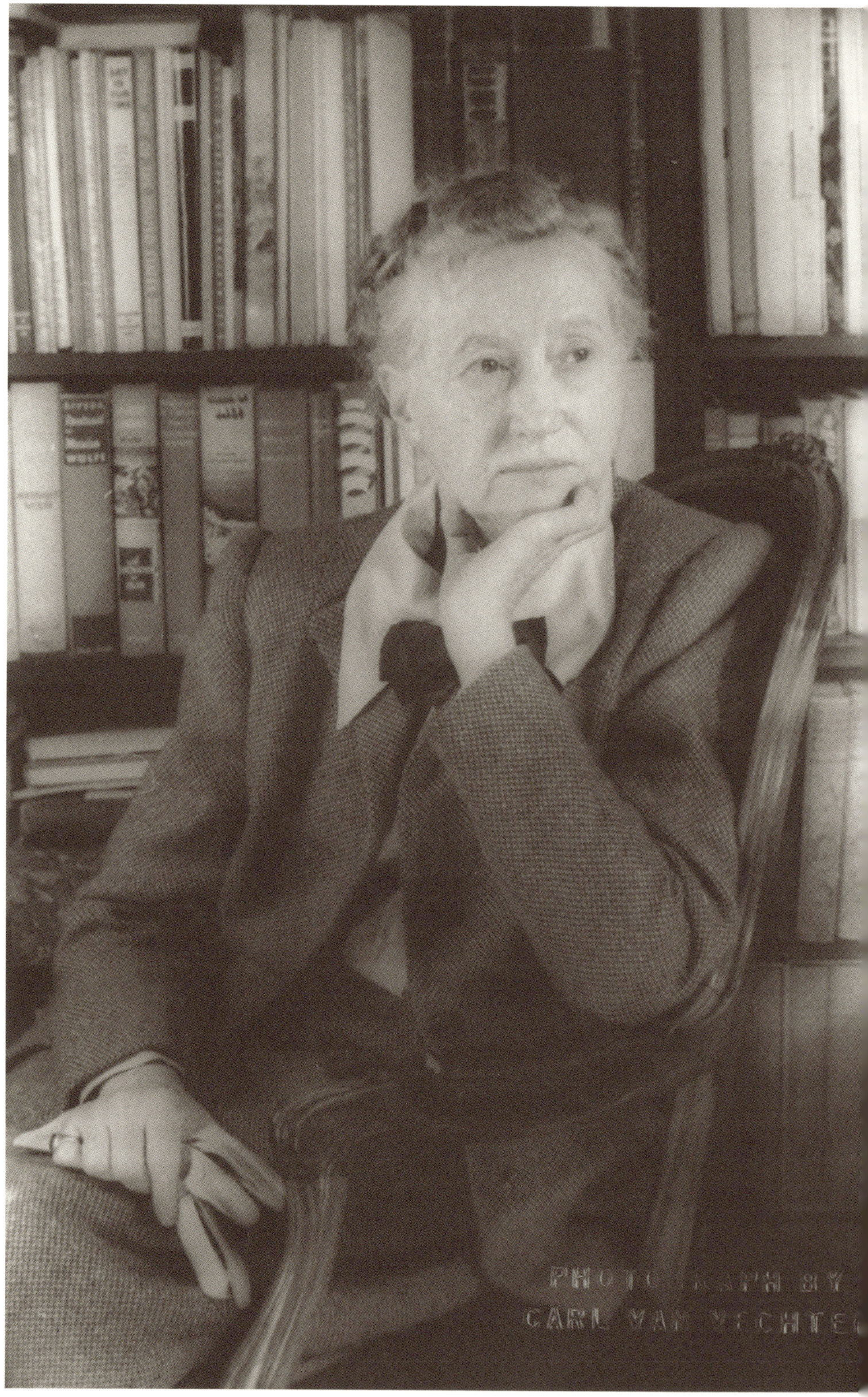

During the 1950s, Moore began to receive widespread public recognition that grew until she reached the level of a cultural icon. In the fall of 1956, Moore became famous overnight when her poem "Hometown Piece for Messrs. Alston and Reese," about the Brooklyn Dodgers, appeared on the front page of the *Herald-Tribune* on the first day of the World Series. From that point on, Moore became known as the poet who wrote about baseball, and as Charles Molesworth points out:

> Virtually every newspaper article and interview with Moore printed after the publication of "Hometown Piece" mentioned the poet's interest in baseball. These two elements—Brooklyn and baseball—would be linked with her name every time her audience extended beyond those who read her primarily as a modernist poet.[2]

Although she was mainly associated with the Dodgers and therefore Brooklyn, Moore also celebrated the New York Yankees in verse. Her 1961 poem "Baseball and Writing" compares the craft of writing to the excitement of a Yankees game, and in this it exhibits Moore's tendency to juxtapose two seemingly unrelated things in order to enhance a poem's emotional and visual effect. For example, in "An Octopus," she creates a metaphor between an octopus and Washington's Mt. Rainier, while in "The Pangolin," she compares the mammal with Leonardo da Vinci, a spruce cone, an artichoke, and Westminster Abbey.

During her later years, Moore developed a personal, and somewhat dramatic, sense of fashion, and often went out dressed in a tricorn hat and a long black cape, which became her trademark insignia. However, it was her originality of thought and sentiment that gave rise to her marked originality as a poet. As Carl Van Vechten stated, "There is nobody in the least like her. She speaks her own tongue in her own way and rapidly becomes almost a figure in fiction, out of Jane Austen perhaps. . . . Her mere presence has charm and fragrance."[3]

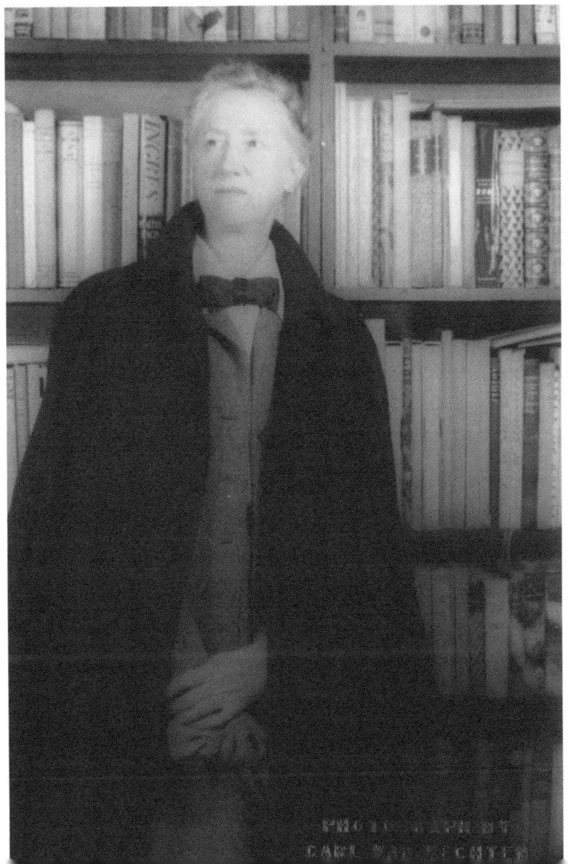

PHOTOGRAPHED ON NOVEMBER 13, 1948

1 T. S. Eliot
Introduction
In Moore, Marianne
*Selected Poems*
London: Faber, 1935
p. 12

2 Charles Molesworth
*Marianne Moore: A Literary Life*
NY: Atheneum, 1990
p. 433

3 Carl Van Vechten
"Some Literary Ladies I Have Known"
*The Yale University Library Gazette*
26:3 (1952)
p. 112

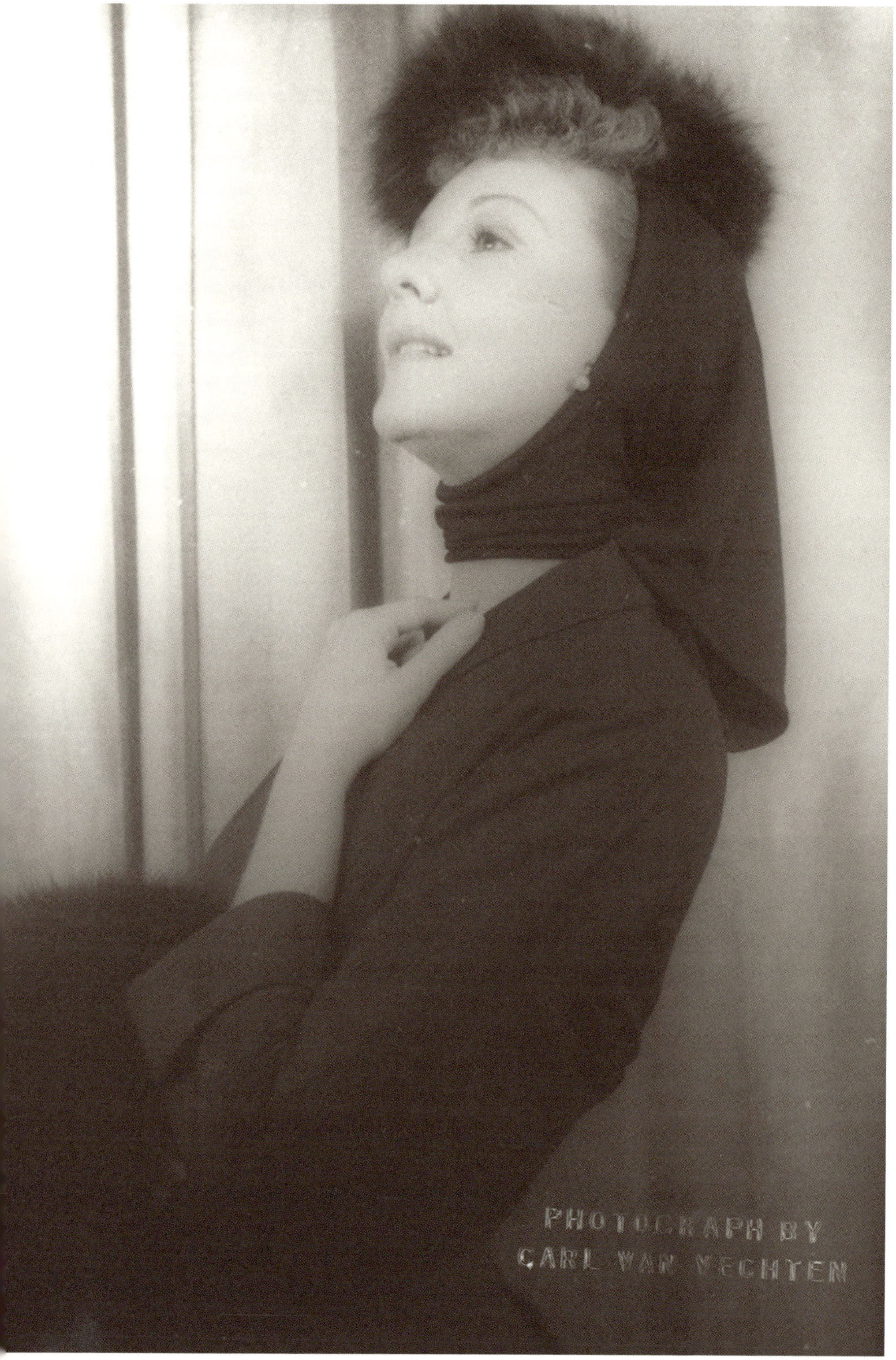


PHOTOGRAPHED ON JANUARY 12, 1949

# MARY MARTIN

A stage star of the 1940s and 1950s, Mary Martin created some of the best-loved characters of the American theater. She was the first actress to perform the role of Maria Von Trapp in the now-classic Rodgers and Hammerstein play *The Sound of Music*. In the first production of *South Pacific*, another Rodgers and Hammerstein play, Martin played Nellie Forbush. She sang the now-famous song "I'm Gonna Wash That Man Right Out-a My Hair" while shampooing her hair in more than 1,000 shows.

Martin was born and raised in Texas. She sang in public for the first time at a local fireman's ball; she was five years old. When she was fourteen, she fell in love with an older boy named Benjamin Hagman. Though her parents didn't approve of the relationship, Martin and Hagman married a few years later. Ultimately the marriage didn't last; it did, however, produce one child, a son named Larry. Larry Hagman eventually followed in his mother's footsteps and had a successful television career, starring in the popular shows *I Dream Of Genie* and *Dallas*.

When her marriage failed, Martin moved to Hollywood. Determined to become a star, she auditioned regularly but was

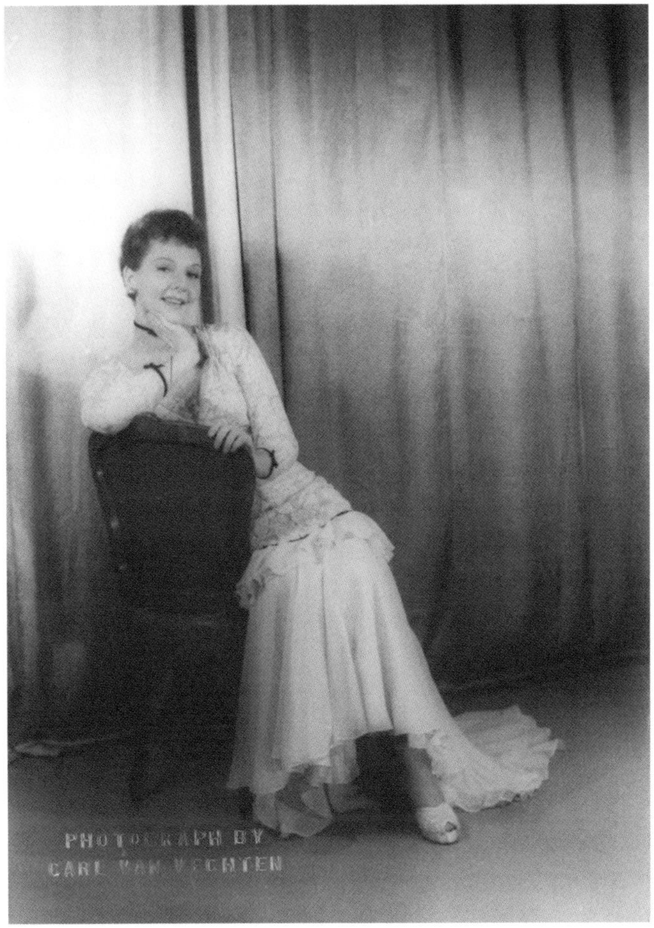




only hired to sing on radio shows. Finally, she got a job singing at the popular club, the Cinegrille Room. It was there that a New York producer discovered her and offered her a part in a Broadway show. She left Hollywood to perform on Broadway in Cole Porter's *Leave It to Me*. Audiences were immediately taken with Martin; after performing for just a week on Broadway, Martin appeared on the cover of *Life* magazine. Soon, Paramount Pictures offered her a contract.

After her return to Hollywood, Martin married for a second time, to a Paramount story editor named Richard Halliday. Halliday soon became Martin's manager and agent, committing himself to developing her career. It was Halliday who recognized that Martin's talents were better suited to the stage than to the screen and encouraged her to concentrate on her theater career. Though she turned down parts in some of the period's most important musicals—including *Kiss Me Kate*, *Oklahoma!*, and *My Fair Lady*—Martin met with great success in New York and on national tour in *One Touch of Venus* by Kurt Weill, Ogden Nash, and S. J. Perelman, and in England in a production of Noel Coward's *Pacific 1860*. When she wasn't on stage, she often appeared on the small screen on television variety shows and popular specials.

Martin and Halliday retired to Brazil, but after her husband's death, Martin returned to Hollywood. She appeared occasionally on television shows and, during the early 1980s, co-hosted her own talk show. In 1986, Martin made her final return to the stage, appearing with her friend Carol Channing in a touring production of James Kirkwood's *Legends*, a play about two aging actresses.

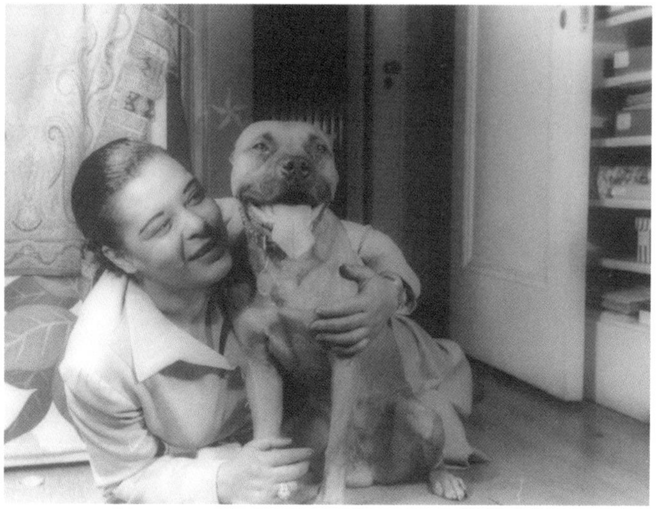

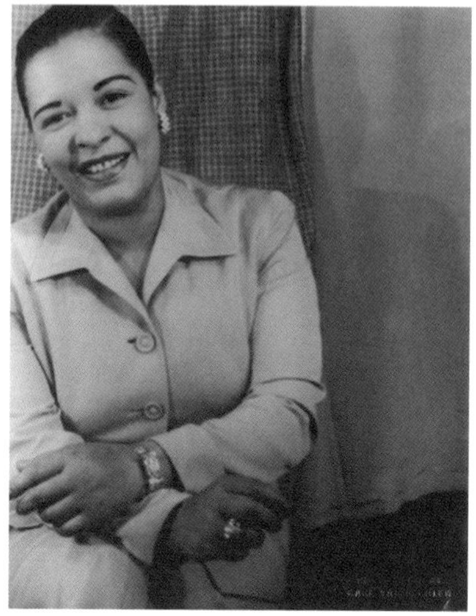



One of the most influential jazz singers of all time, Billie Holiday was born Eleanora Fagan, in Baltimore in 1915. Her father was a guitarist during the earliest days of jazz; his frequent absences led to her parents' separation. As a girl, Holiday ran errands for a neighborhood whorehouse; there, she heard jazz recordings of Louis Armstrong, and the blues music of Bessie Smith and other great singers of the period. She was still a child when she started calling herself Billie Holiday.

Her mother opened a boarding house when Holiday was ten. When a boarder raped Holiday, she was accused of causing the attack and was sent to a Catholic home for children. A few years later, Holiday's mother reclaimed her daughter and moved with her to New York City. They struggled to survive; when she was fifteen, Holiday was arrested for prostitution and sent to jail. After her release, she chanced into a singing job at a club.

Holiday was an immediate sensation and was soon performing with the best musicians in the city. Her sophistication and style earned her the sobriquet Lady Day. With an incomparable sense of phrasing and tonality, Holiday reinvented familiar tunes, revealing hidden depths in even the slightest compositions. She began to make successful records, increasing her considerable popularity. Eventually she would make numerous influential records such as "Strange Fruit," a song about southern lynching that she made famous in her shows at New York's Café Society Downtown. She became one of the most popular singers in the Harlem clubs and she also traveled to Chicago and California. She toured with the Count Bassie orchestra, but she became bitter about the discrimination she faced on the road, and eventually gave up touring.

Through much of her career, Holiday struggled with drug addiction. In 1947 she was arrested for possession of drugs and sent to a reformatory for a year. After being released, she was denied the cabaret license necessary to perform in most New York clubs. She was forced to travel to perform, though she hated life on the road. When she was forty-four years old, Holiday died of cirrhosis of the liver, kidney failure, and cardiac arrest.

Of the many famous and fashionable people Carl Van Vechten photographed, his session with Billie Holiday was among the most memorable. "I spent only one night photographing Billie Holiday," he wrote, "but it was the whole of one night and it seemed like a whole career."[1] The session began badly. Gerry Major had arranged the meeting, and had asked Holiday to wear a gown for the sitting. Holiday, however, arrived "at the appointed hour in a plain gray suit and facial expression equally depressing."[2]

In spite of his disappointment, Van Vechten began photographing Holiday. It wasn't going well and he was considering giving up when he thought to show Holiday his photographs of Bessie

Carl Van Vechten 1
"Portraits of the Artists"
*Esquire*
58:6 (1962)
p. 256

"Portraits of the Artists" 2
p. 256

"Portraits of the Artists" 3
p. 256

"Portraits of the Artists" 4
p. 256

# BILLIE HOLIDAY

## SINGER

Smith. The photographs brought Holiday to tears; she explained that Smith had been an inspiration to her in the early days of her career. Their discussion of Smith softened the mood, and Holiday agreed to wearing a drape fashioned to look like an evening dress instead of her suit for some of the photographs.

At midnight, Holiday announced that she had to go home; she promised to come back shortly. Van Vechten, afraid she might go in search of drugs, sent his assistant Saul Mauriber to Harlem with her to insure her return. Holiday and Mauriber reappeared with Mister, Holiday's boxer. She was in a different mood entirely, more lively and relaxed. Van Vechten continued to photograph her for some time.

Afterward, "she related in great detail the sad, bittersweet story of her tempestuous life."[3] Van Vechten's wife Fania soon joined the group, and "in a short time Fania, like the rest of us, was in tears, and suddenly, also like the rest of us, found herself attached to Billie as if she had known her intimately for years." Holiday didn't leave the apartment until shortly before dawn. "We never saw her again," Van Vechten wrote, "but not one of us will ever forget her."[4]

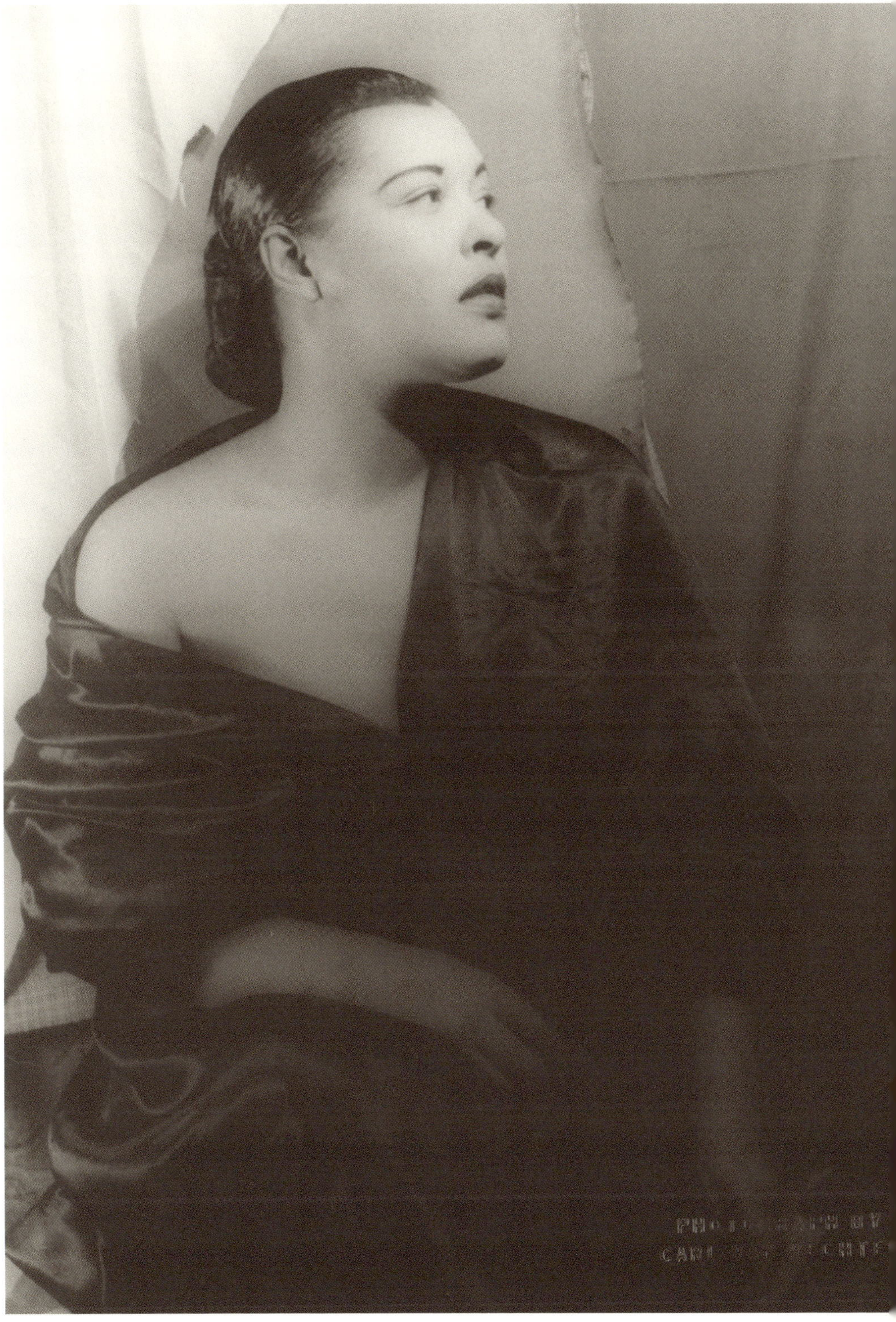

PHOTOGRAPHED ON MARCH 23, 1949

In 1931, Mary McLeod Bethune helped to arrange a reading tour for Carl Van Vechten's good friend, the poet Langston Hughes. The tour would take Hughes to many black colleges and universities throughout the south. In a letter to Van Vechten describing Bethune's appearance at one such reading, Hughes wrote, "Mrs. Bethune is marvelous as mistress of ceremonies—a sort of black Texas Guinan joyfully clothed in African dignity, presenting myself, with a full orchestra and a hundred student voices singing Negro music as a setting for my poems."[1]

Bethune was, perhaps, uniquely qualified to introduce Hughes to audiences for she had inspired his work "The Negro Mother." Once, when Hughes closed a reading with this poem, Bethune was so moved that she jumped up from her chair and ran to the stage to embrace him.

By the time she arranged Langston Hughes's visits to southern black colleges and universities, Bethune had worked as an educator for many years. She had, in 1904, founded the Dayton Normal and Industrial Institute, a school offering elementary and secondary courses for African-American children. Though the school started with only six students, and with so few resources that students sat on crates and used charcoal

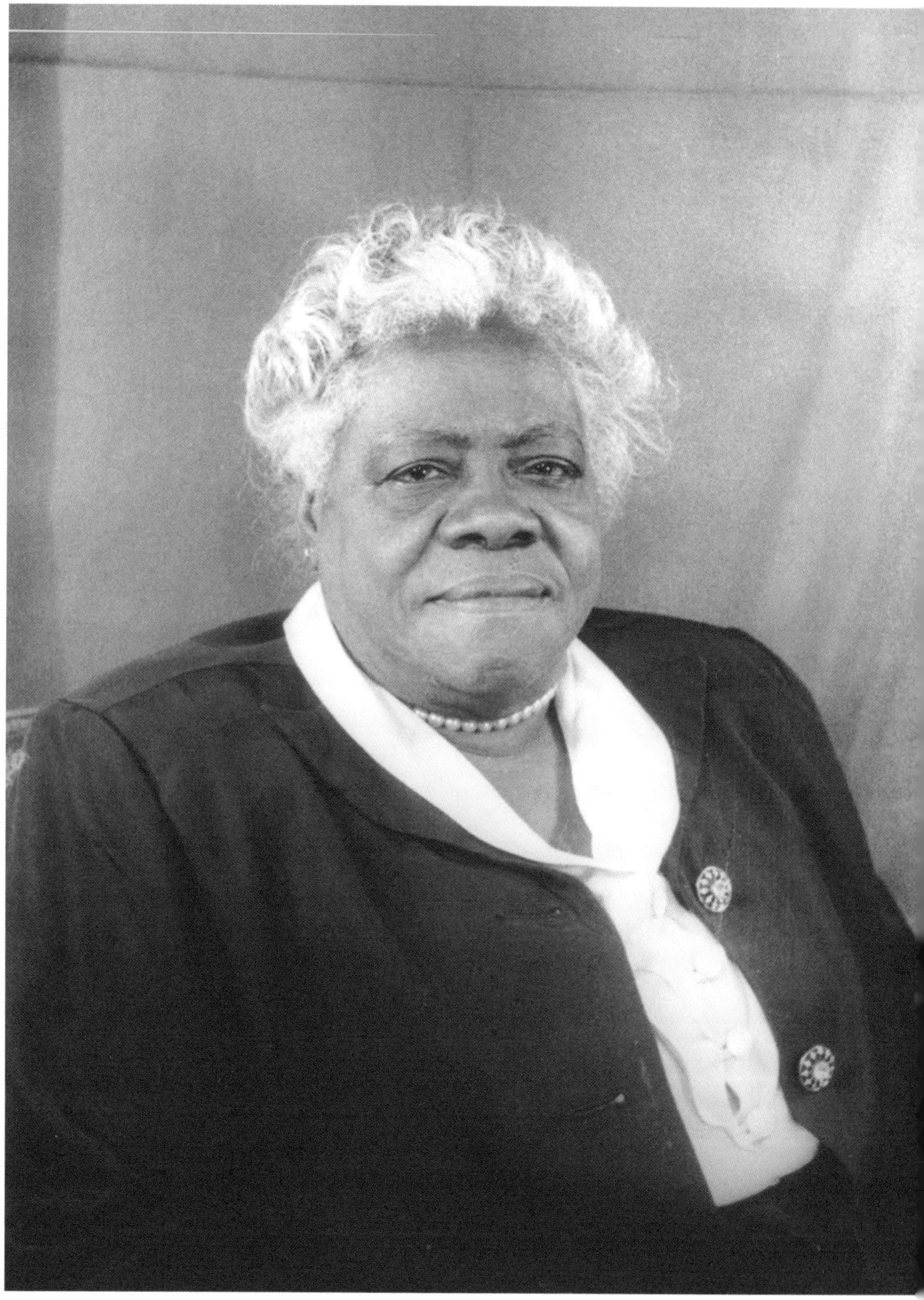

PHOTOGRAPHED APRIL 6, 1949

# MARY MCLEOD BETHUNE

## EDUCATOR & COLLEGE PRESIDENT



instead of pencils, Bethune's efforts to raise funds and increase the student body enabled the school to thrive. Bethune designed the curriculum to focus particularly on educating black girls and providing them with practical training that would enable them to secure jobs after graduation.

Some twenty years after the school opened its doors, it merged with the Cookman Institute to form Bethune-Cookman College. Bethune was named president of the college, a position she held until 1942. Under her leadership and direction the school became first an accredited junior college, and later a four-year liberal arts college. Today, Bethune-Cookman College is among the largest of the United Negro College Fund colleges.

Though she is remembered primarily as an educator, Bethune's influence extended far beyond the walls of her college. As an active advocate for the education of African Americans and for civil rights in general, Bethune was well known in political as well as educational spheres. She served two terms as president of the National Association of Colored Women and was founder and president of the National Council of Negro Women. She served also as vice-president of both the NAACP and the National Union League.

A woman of considerable political influence, Bethune served on presidential commissions under Calvin Coolidge, Herbert Hoover, and Franklin D. Roosevelt; she was a personal friend of Eleanor Roosevelt, and she met with President Roosevelt regularly throughout his presidency to discuss the needs of African Americans.

Mary McLeod Bethune was a commanding and important promoter of civil rights for African Americans, and the effects of her advocacy, especially in the area of education, cannot be overstated. "She is a power down here," Langston Hughes wrote to Carl Van Vechten of her influence among the southerners he met on his reading tour; that she was also "a power" among her friends is evident in Hughes's next sentence: "She sends her greetings to you; and commands that you visit her."[2]

1 Hughes to Van Vechten
29 Dec. 1931
*Remember Me to Harlem: The Letters of Langston Hughes and Carl Van Vechten, 1925-1964*
Ed., Emily Bernard
NY: Knopf, 2001
p. 90

2 Hughes to Van Vechten
10 Feb. 1932
*Remember Me to Harlem*
p. 93

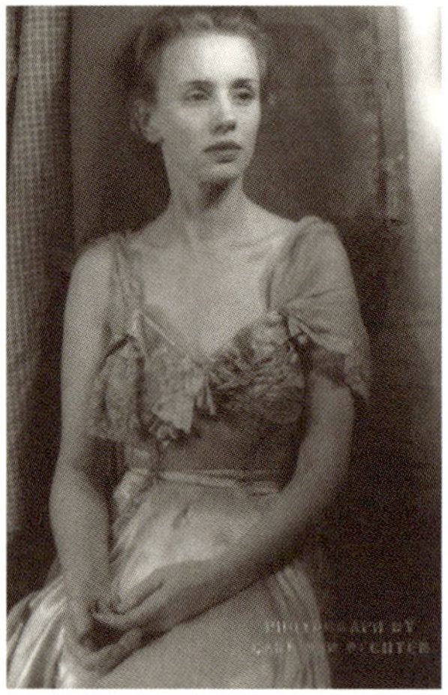

# JESSICA TANDY



In 1990, when London native Jessica Tandy became the oldest actress to date to win an Academy Award, she had been performing on stage and screen for more than sixty years. By the time of her award-winning performance in the 1989 film *Driving Miss Daisy*, Tandy was a well-respected actress who had appeared in more than one hundred films and theater productions.

After making her stage debut at the age of eighteen, Tandy played a wide range of characters in diverse plays, including comedies and dramas, classical plays and avant-garde theater experiments. Her willingness to take on vastly different kinds of roles made her one of the most versatile performers of her time. Though it challenged her talents and helped her develop as an actress, the diversity of Tandy's projects may have prevented her from achieving a significant measure of popularity with general audiences.

Tandy left England in 1940, moving to the United States where she had performed in several successful tours with British companies. She soon met and married director and actor Hume Cronyn. Throughout their lives, the couple worked together on a number of projects, including appearing together in productions of *The Fourposter* and *The Gin Game*. Of their 1977 production of D.L. Coburn's two-character play, *The Gin Game*, Jack Kroll wrote, "Jessica Tandy is . . . probably a saint: she gets more beautiful every year. . . . [She] turns from a frumpy wraith to a silvery coquette, a last flare-up of the warmth and danger of woman."[1] In 1979, Tandy won a Tony Award for her performance in *The Gin Game.*

Carl Van Vechten photographed Tandy as Blanche DuBois in Tennessee Williams's *A Streetcar Named Desire*—she was the first actress to play the role. Though Williams's own first choice to play the complicated, intense, and vulnerable Blanche was Lillian Gish, director Elia Kazan insisted the role go to Jessica Tandy. In his review of the production, Brooks Atkinson praised Tandy's performance:

> As Blanche DuBois, Jessica Tandy has one of the longest and most exacting parts on record. She plays it with an insight as vibrant and pitiless as Mr. Williams's writing, for she catches on the wing the terror, the bogus refinement, the intellectual alertness and the madness that can hardly be distinguished from logic. Miss Tandy acts a magnificent part magnificently.[2]

Tandy appeared in *A Streetcar Named Desire* with Marlon Brando in the role of Stanley. Brando, then a virtually unknown actor, was an erratic performer with a tendency to upstage other actors. Though he presented wildly different interpretations of his character from one show to the next, Tandy was able to

PHOTOGRAPHED APRIL 24, 1949, AS BLANCHE DUBOIS IN "A STREETCAR NAMED DESIRE"

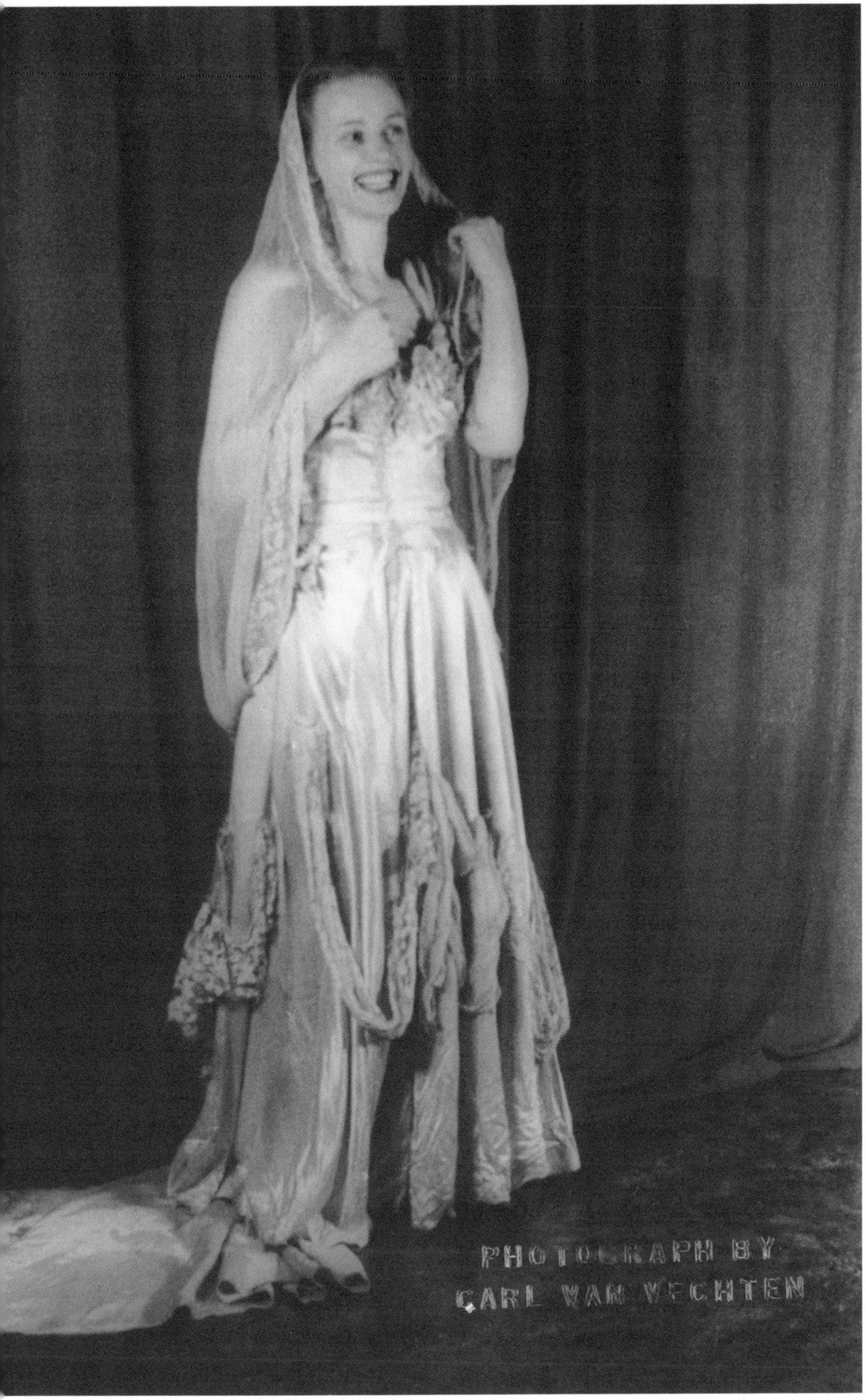






work against Brando's unpredictable performance to make Blanche DuBois one of the most successful roles of her career, earning her a Tony award in 1948.

In spite of her success in the theatrical production of *A Streetcar Named Desire*, Tandy was replaced in the film version by Vivien Leigh, a more conventionally good-looking and popular actress. Tandy didn't achieve major success in Hollywood until the end of her career, appearing in films such as the 1985 hit *Cocoon*, *Fried Green Tomatoes at the Whistle Stop Café* in 1991, and, of course, her Oscar winning performance in *Driving Miss Daisy.*

*Driving Miss Daisy*, in which Tandy plays a elderly Jewish woman in the south and African-American actor Morgan Freeman plays her chauffeur, was popular with both audiences and critics. Nevertheless, some criticized the film as sentimental at best, and racist at worst, arguing that "*Driving Miss Daisy* [sentimentalizes] the canned types of the lovable racist and the adoring servant. This is the same old 'song of the south,' with slightly new lyrics for the 1990s."[3] In spite of such criticisms, many believe that Tandy's performance resisted sentimentalism and revealed layers of complexity in the more than twenty-year relationship between the employer and her chauffeur. Of her character, Tandy said, "She was the product of her time and she had the prejudices of her time. But she does grow. She learns. By the end of the film she's really changed."[4]

Paul F. Driscoll 1
"Il Barbiere di Siviglia: Another View"
*Opera News*
60:6 (1996)
p. 28

Howard Taubman 2
"'Anya,' a Sentimental Muscial"
*New York Times*
30 Nov. 1965

"Il Barbiere di Siviglia: Another View" 3
p. 28

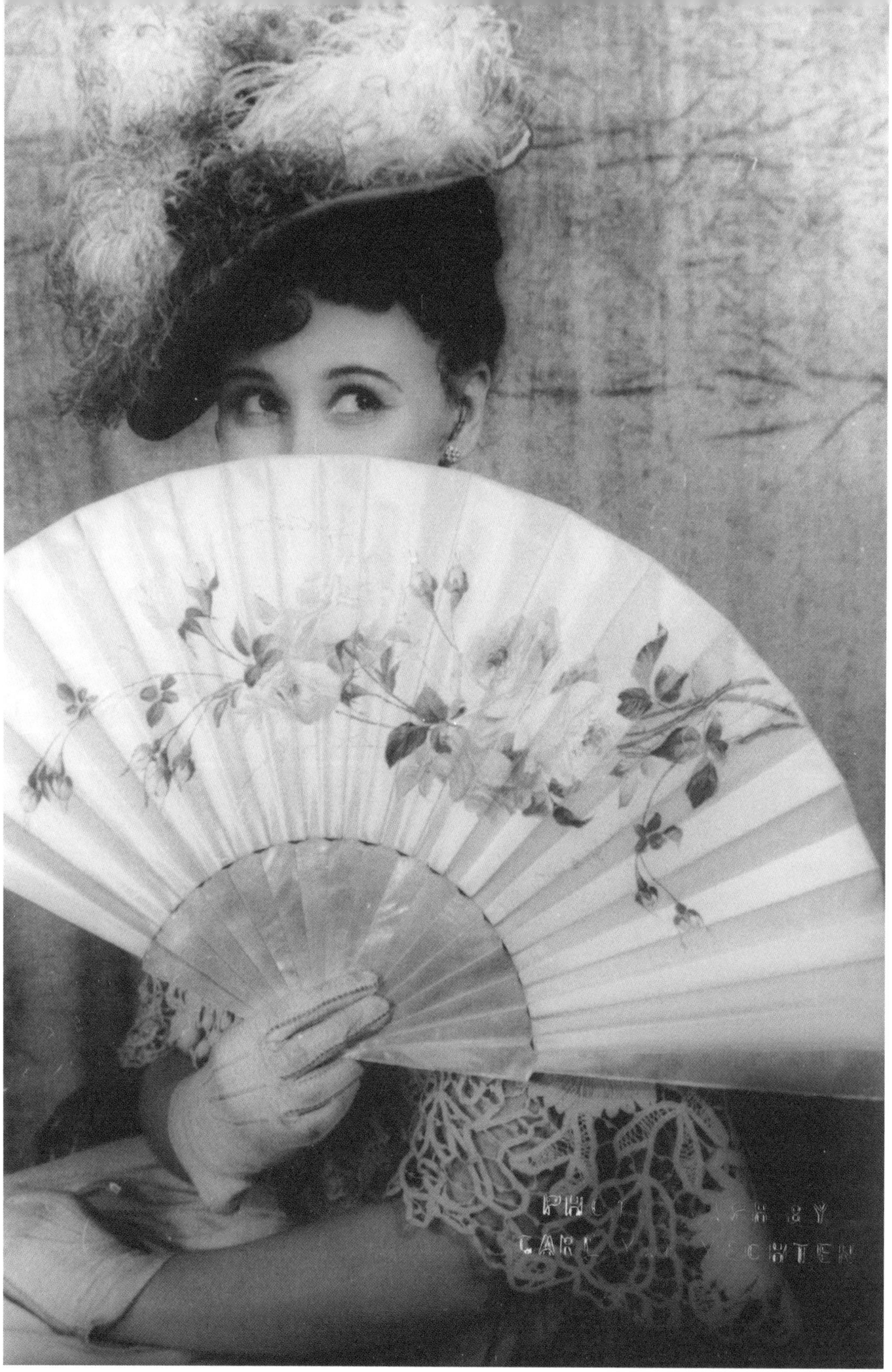

# IRRA PETINA

## MEZZO-SOPRANO



Though she was a minor performer, Russian-born operetta star Irra Petina sang in 444 performances in her nearly twenty years with the Metropolitan Opera. She is famous among opera lovers as the originator of the Old Lady in Leonard Bernstein's *Candide*, "in which Petina's gleeful performance as the uni-buttocked Old Lady has never been equaled."[1]

A vibrant comic performer and accomplished singer, Petina came from an important Russian family. Her father, General Stephen Petina, was a personal escort to Tsar Nicholas II during World War I. At the onset of the Russian Revolution, Petina's family left Russia, moving to China, where she received her earliest musical training. Later, she studied at the Curtis Institute of Music in Philadelphia.

Coincidental to her own background, in 1965 Petina appeared on Broadway with Lillian Gish in *Anya*, the story of a young woman discovered after the war and thought to be Princess Anastasia, the daughter of Tsar Nicholas II. Petina, who played Katrina, was credited with giving the play its comic element—in this show, she lived up to her reputation as "no slouch as singer or comedienne."[2]

Irra Petina was a valued member of the Metropolitan Opera and the international opera community for the length of her career. "Petina's intelligence, vivacity and wit, allied with her accomplished vocalism and imaginative acting," Paul F. Driscoll wrote in *Opera News*, "made her a unique and important personality, a worthy colleague of the great singers of her age."[3]

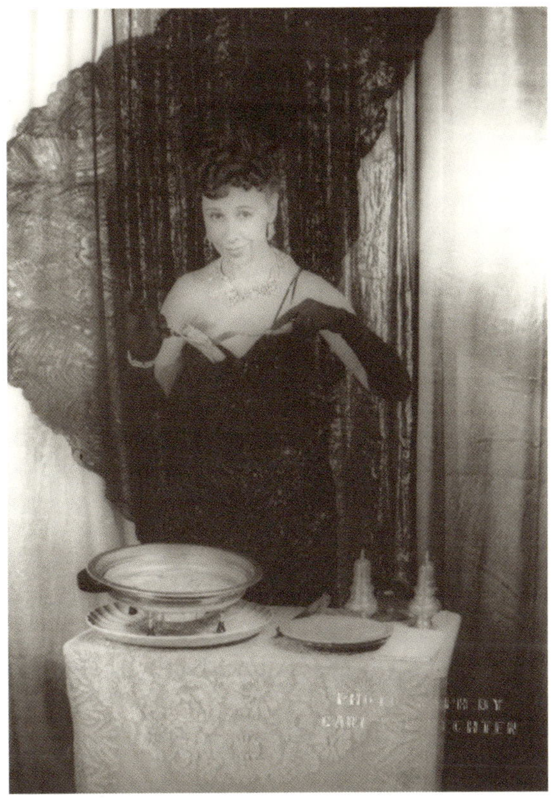

PHOTOGRAPHED ON DECEMBER 8, 1949, IN "MAGDELENA"

# JANE BOWLES

## WRITER

Though she wrote only one novel, one play, and a few short stories, Jane Bowles has long been admired as a "writer's writer;" her work has never received significant popular attention, but Bowles has often been cited as a major influence by other writers, including Truman Capote and Tennessee Williams. Her work, the whole of which fills only one slender volume, is often described as strange and surprising. In Bowles's writing there is an "extraordinary tension between the sturdy, supernormal physical world she describes and the gloriously unpredictable, fantastic movements of the eccentric personages who inhabit it."[1] Her work wasn't always well received by critics; in a review of *Two Serious Ladies*, one critic complained that the novel "strains too hard to startle and to shock and that it all too often is merely silly."[2] Because her work was witty and peopled with charming characters, some critics compared it to the novels of Carl Van Vechten.

Bowles's play, *In the Summer House*, was produced on Broadway in 1953, starring Judith Anderson. The play investigates the complexities of the mother-daughter relationship, reflecting, many believe, Bowles's complicated relationship with her mother. Like *Two Serious Ladies*, the play received mixed reviews. Though it did not appeal to audiences, some critics included it on their "best of the year" lists. Tennessee Williams is said to have called *In the Summer House* "one of the most original plays I have ever read."[3] In recent years, the play has been revived in several American theaters, receiving enthusiastic reviews. "Bowles uses interior monologue spoken aloud, like O'Neill and metaphoric, disoriented dialogue, like Tennessee Williams," William A. Henry III wrote in 1993. He continued, "her lurching narrative would suit Ionesco; her shackled hysteria echoes Lorca."[4]

In New York City during the 1930s, Bowles was a peculiar character; she dyed her hair bright red, dressed in men's clothes, and walked with an obvious limp (the result of a childhood injury). A regular at the city's lesbian bars, Bowles carried on a number of affairs; at one time she had a passionate crush on the famous torch singer, Helen Morgan. In 1938, she married Paul Bowles, an openly gay musician. The couple traveled in the city's gay literary and artistic circles with writers Tennessee Williams, Allen Ginsberg, and Gregory Corso. At one time, the couple lived in a New York boarding house where the other tenants included Carson McCullers and W.H. Auden. Though they spent time in New York, the couple lived a largely expatriate lifestyle; they traveled extensively in Europe, Central America, and Mexico. Eventually, they settled in Tangiers.

1 Francine DuPlessix Gray, "Jane Bowles Reconsidered," *New York Times*, 19 May 1978

2 Edith H. Walton, "Fantastic Duo (Review of *Two Serious Ladies*)," *New York Times*, 9 May 1943

3 Michelle Pearce, "Don't Tell Mother," *American Theater*, 10:9 (1993), p. 11

4 William A. Henry III, Review of *In the Summer House*, *Time*, 16 Aug. 1993, p. 61

PHOTOGRAPHED JANUARY 31, 1951

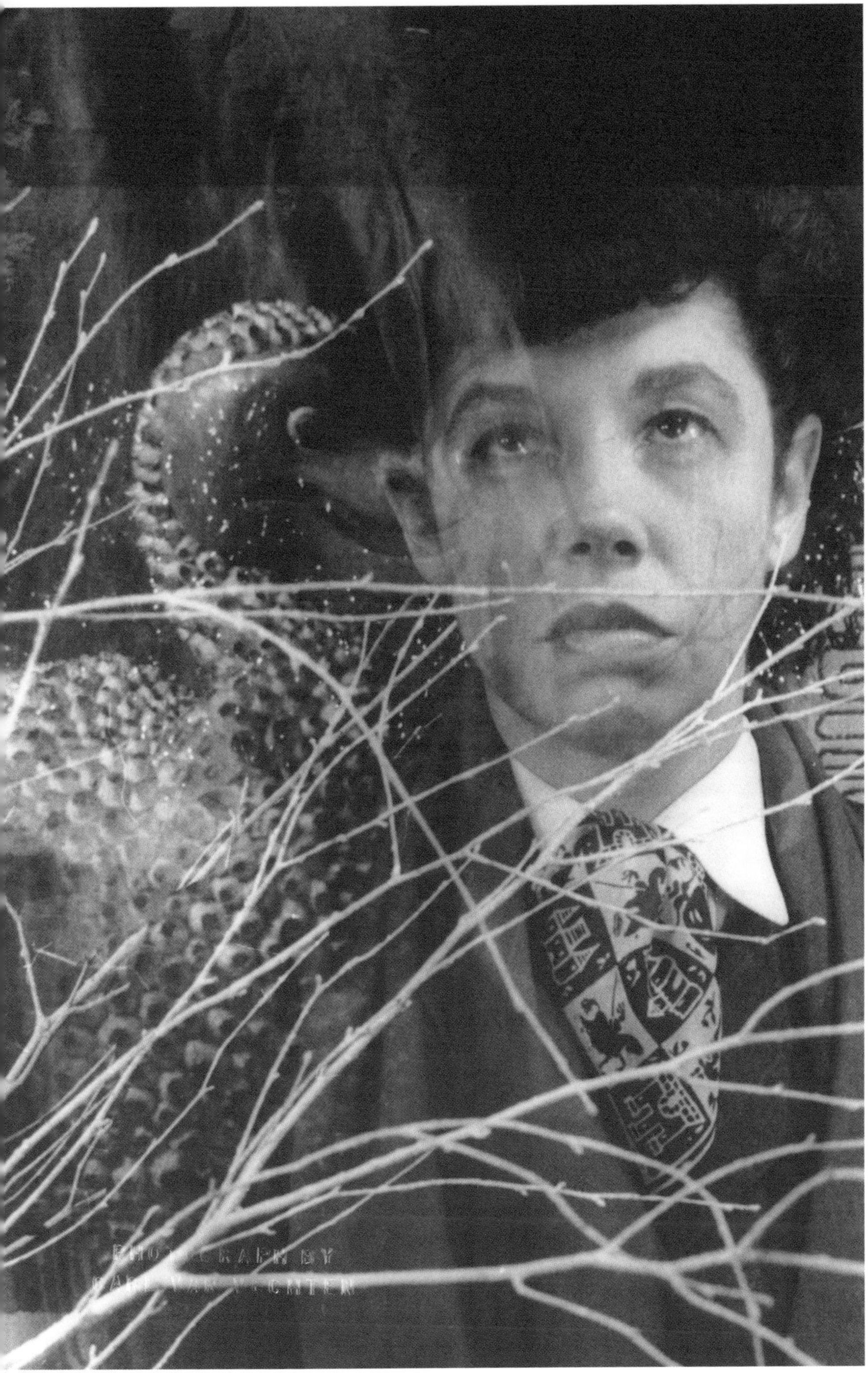



Bowles was highly dramatic (some might say melodramatic) and her love affairs were often complicated, passionate, and ultimately painful. One such affair led her to leave her husband and, when the relationship began to fail, to attempt suicide. In Tangiers, her love affair with a Moroccan servant caused her various problems, including financial difficulties, and eventually led to a permanent split with her husband. If Paul Bowles's suspicion that her lover was feeding her exotic Moroccan poisons was true, that relationship may also have contributed to Bowles's poor health. After a stroke in 1957, Bowles was no longer able to write. She began to drink excessively and to abuse prescription medications. She ended up living in the streets of Tangiers, harassing people and starting fights in bars. Unable to care for her himself, Paul Bowles was forced to have her admitted to a hospital, where she died in 1973.

# GERALDYN DISMOND (GERRY MAJOR)

GOSSIP COLUMNIST & PUBLICIST

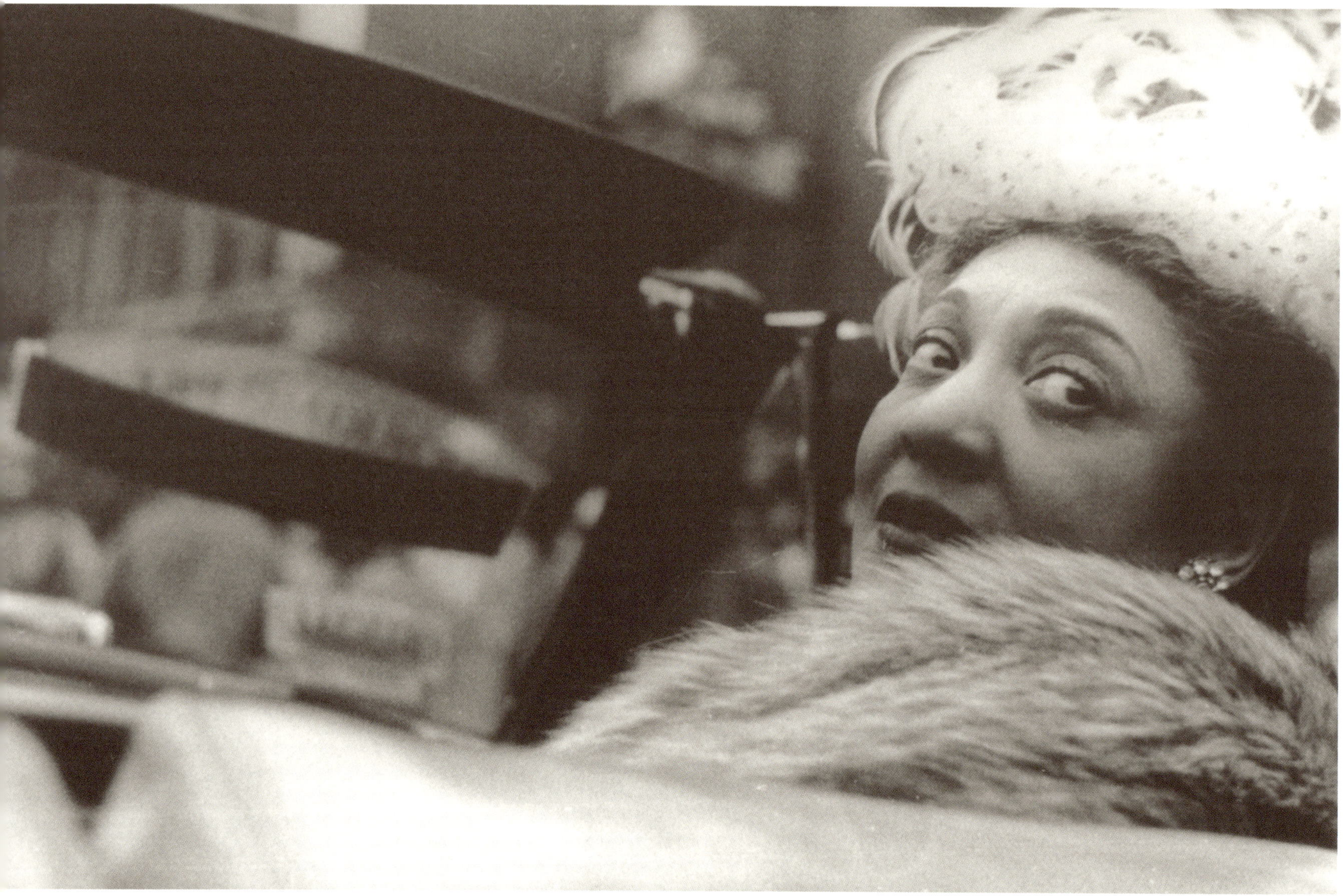

PHOTOGRAPHED IN NEW YORK CITY ON JOSEPHINE BAKER DAY, MAY 5, 1951

A familiar and visible figure in the Harlem Renaissance, gossip columnist Geraldyn Dismond reported on the Harlem social scene in *The Inter-State Tattler, The Amsterdam News, The Pittsburgh Courier,* and other African-American papers. She spent several years as managing editor of the *Tattler*, a New York City newspaper that gave accounts of African-American high society in Harlem, Chicago, and other cities.

Known to many as "Gerry Major," Dismond graduated from the University of Chicago, married a doctor, and worked briefly as a teacher. During World War I, she was a major in the Red Cross. Eventually, Dismond left her husband, moved from Chicago to Harlem, and found her "true vocation, . . . delineating the social scene in a series of columns."[1]

Dismond was a regular at A'Lelia Walker's salon, known as The Dark Tower, and her accounts of the comings and goings of Harlem's artistic and intellectual set at these affairs were read widely. Glamorous and lovely, Dismond held many parties of her own and was sometimes referred to as "Harlem's Hostess." In 1928, Geraldyn Dismond opened the Geraldyn Dismond Bureau of Specialized Publicity, on 135th Street. She gave herself the title "Publicity Agent."

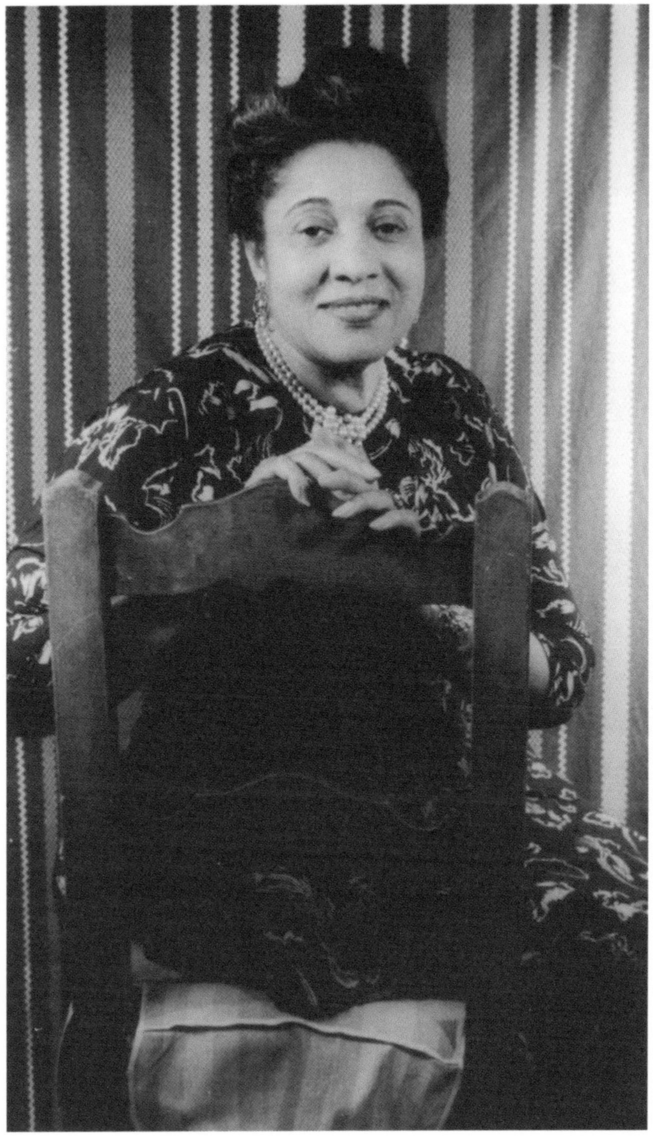

In addition to her society journalism and work as a publicity specialist, Dismond was also a radio announcer. She became the first African-American woman to host a regular show. Her program, "The Negro Achievement Hour," aired first on WABC and later appeared on other area stations.

1 Bruce Kellner
*The Harlem Renaissance*
Westport: Greenwood, 1984
p. 101

PHOTOGRAPHED ON JULY 20, 1951

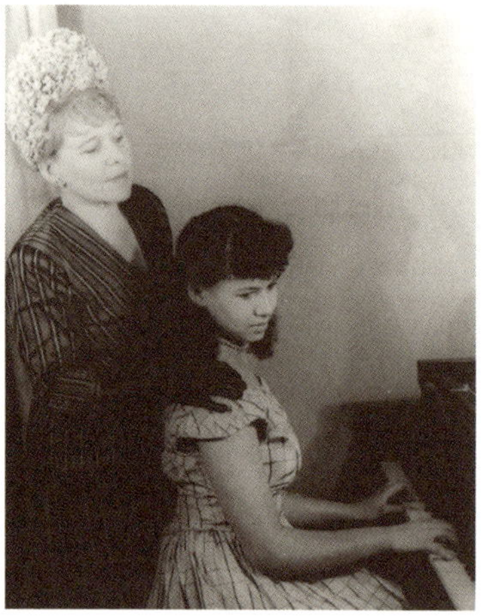

# PHILIPPA DUKE SCHUYLER



Known as "the baby genius of the Harlem Renaissance," Philippa Duke Schuyler was a child prodigy who became quite famous for her youthful accomplishments as a composer and pianist. By the time she was four years old, Schuyler was a skilled pianist; by five she was performing Mozart before audiences in concert halls. When she was six, she was touring to perform her own compositions; in 1940, at the age of eight, she performed for thousands of visitors at the New York World's Fair. She was ten when she became the youngest member of the National Association of American Composers and Conductors. To satisfy popular interest, magazines and newspapers including the *New Yorker*, *Time Magazine*, and the *New York Times*, included lengthy features outlining her achievements.

Schuyler's parents, too, were well-known figures in the Harlem Renaissance. Her father, George Schuyler, was a prominent and controversial African-American journalist. Her mother, Josephine Cogdell, a white woman, was a painter and writer. Both believed strongly in the theory of hybrid vigor and felt that children produced by interracial unions would inherit the strengths of both races and that ultimately mixed-race Americans would resolve the country's racial tensions. Schuyler's parents dedicated themselves to her success: Josephine Cogdell coached her daughter, pushed her to work hard, and acted as her agent; George Schuyler promoted Philippa Duke Schuyler in his newspaper columns and actively sought recognition for her successes in the white press. In an effort to keep her from becoming self-conscious, Schuyler's parents didn't allow her to see any of the considerable media attention she received. Nevertheless, both parents promoted Schuyler as an interracial role model and as proof of the theory of hybrid vigor.

Though Schuyler briefly fascinated the nation as a mulatto child prodigy, white America lost interest in her as she aged. As a teenager, she began to suffer the injustices and humiliation of racial prejudice. Unable to find a place for herself in the American music community, Schuyler left the country. Her extensive international performance schedule allowed her to explore the dynamics of race in a variety of cultures and settings. She struggled to find a comfortable community and to create a satisfying personal identity. Her failure to do so led to almost constant traveling for the rest of her life. Though she feared she would never feel completely accepted anywhere, she continued to seek a society she could join fully. In *Adventures in Black and White*, a memoir of her experiences traveling worldwide, Schuyler wrote:

> Despite the turmoils, threats, hazards, uncertainties, of this age, I love it, for I realize all human eras have been fraught with problems. I admire the people who are doing their best to shape a new world. I think there is great hope for the human race, and I feel a deep warmth of affection for all peoples, everywhere.[1]

1 Philippa Duke Schuyler, *Adventures in Black and White*, NY: Robert Speller and Sons, 1960, p. 30

PHOTOGRAPHED WITH HER MOTHER, JOSEPHINE COGDELL SCHUYLER, ON JULY 22, 1946

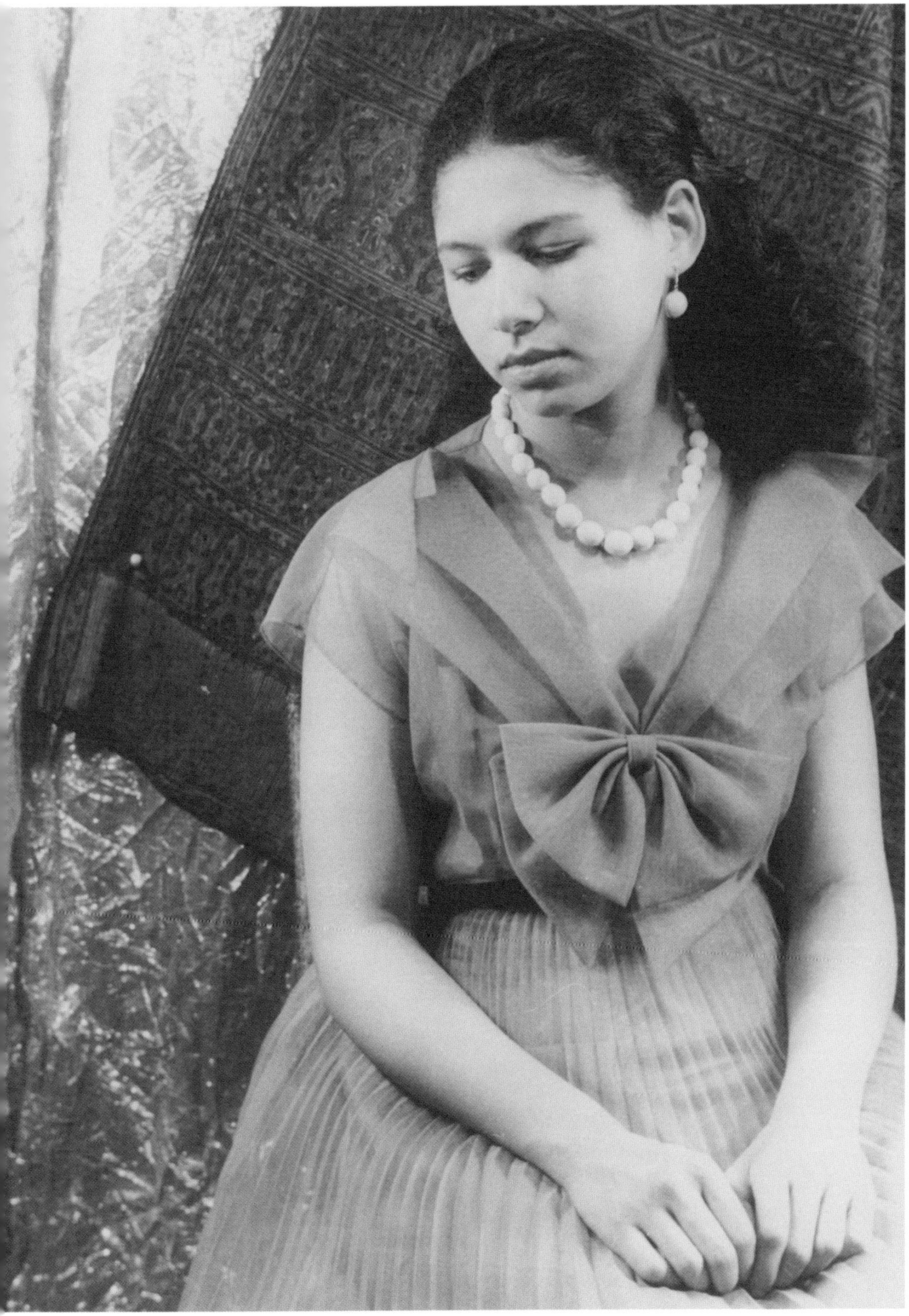

PHOTOGRAPHED ON MAY 9, 1951

## PIANIST, COMPOSER, & WRITER



As a result of her sense of alienation from her native country and in response to the neglect she suffered in the American music community, as a young woman Schuyler changed her name to Felipa Monterro and began to pass as white. She hoped her new identity would free her from being defined by her earlier career. She planned to return to the United States and pursue a new career as a concert pianist. Though this never worked out, as Felipa Monterro she established an international lecture tour, talking on topics related to her world travel.

Though she never gave up performing concerts, as an adult Schuyler also worked as a journalist. Fluent in several languages, she wrote for French, Portuguese, and Italian newspapers, as well as American papers and magazines. She authored several moderately successful books based on her experiences covering international news. It was, in fact, while she was covering the war in Vietnam for an American newspaper that she was killed in a helicopter crash. A posthumous book, *Good Men Die*, collected her writings about Vietnam.

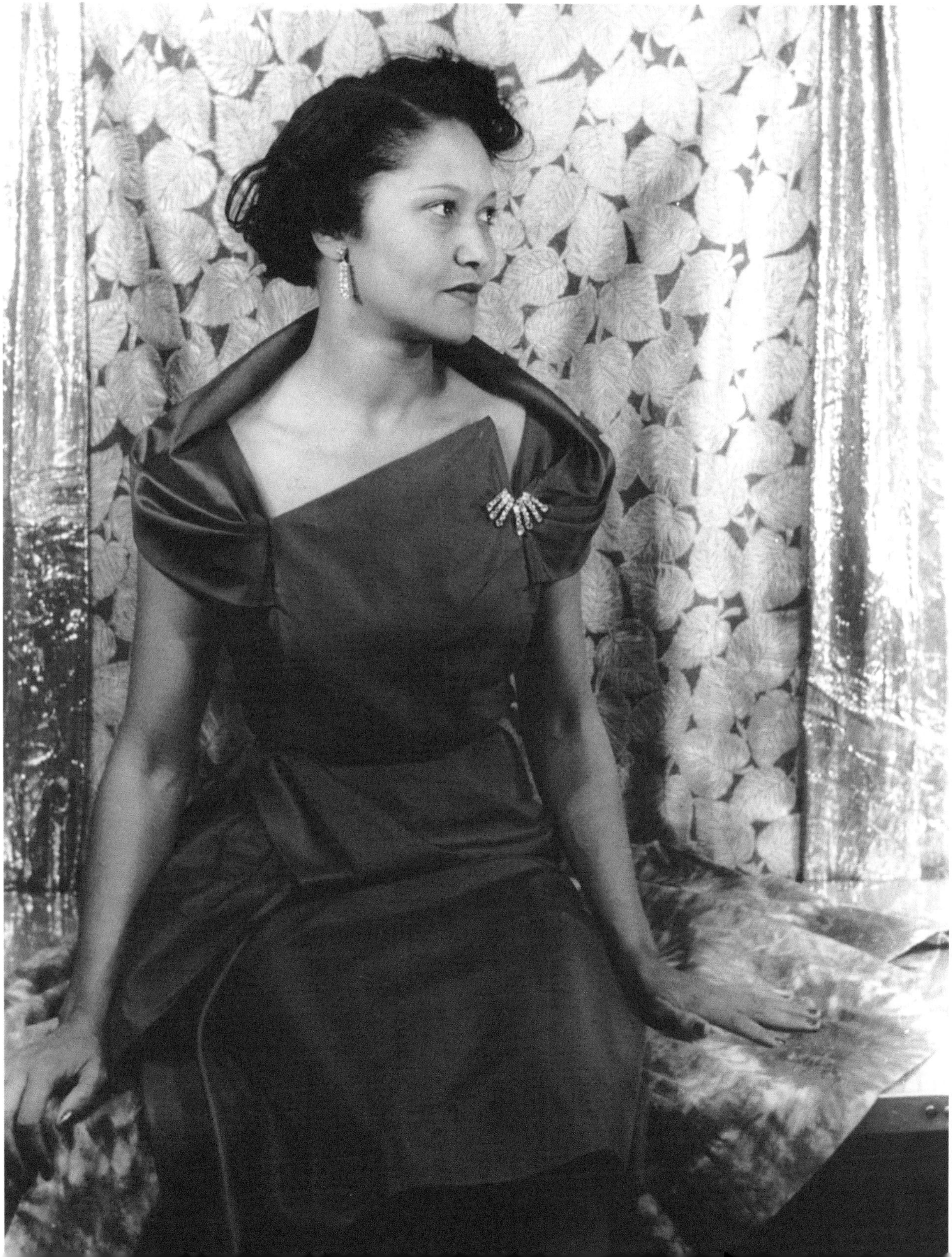

# MAIDIE NORMAN

## ACTRESS



A character actress who played mostly maids, housekeepers, and nurses, Maidie Norman had a long and successful Hollywood career. In spite of the fact that there were few strong parts for African-American women throughout much of her time in Hollywood, Norman was an actress known for making even the smallest parts her own. As a performer of integrity as well as talent, and as a pioneering educator in the field of African-American film and theater, Norman's contributions to her art were considerable. In recognition of her important work, she was inducted into the Black Filmmakers Hall of Fame in 1977.

Norman played her only leading film role in *The Well*, a 1951 drama about the events surrounding the disappearance of a black child and the search for a white man suspected of kidnapping her. In response to the incident, the racially mixed town becomes divided along race lines; racial hatred, fueled by rumor and misunderstanding, results in violence and rioting. Though the film received positive reviews, it did not appeal to audiences and failed at the box office. It did little to improve the roles Norman was offered.

In 1962, Norman played the housekeeper in *What Ever Happened to Baby Jane?* with Bette Davis and Joan Crawford. Feeling the part promoted racial stereotypes, Norman changed some of her lines and updated the speech. Norman's changes made her character more realistic and less demeaning.

In addition to her work in film, Norman was an educator and mentor to young African-American performers. She was an Artist in Residence at Stanford University for two years. She also taught courses at UCLA where she designed a class in African-American film and theater history. It was the first course of its kind at the university and it was among the school's first African-American studies courses. UCLA's Madie Norman Research Award for the best essay on African-American film or theater was named in her honor.

Though she never achieved fame as an actress, Maidie Norman appeared in some two hundred films. She also made many television appearances. Throughout the 1970s, Norman played small roles in some of the decade's most popular television programs, including *Little House on the Prairie, Marcus Welby, M.D., The Jeffersons, Dragnet,* and *Good Times.*

PHOTOGRAPHED ON SEPTEMBER 23, 1951

# NI-GUSTI RAKA

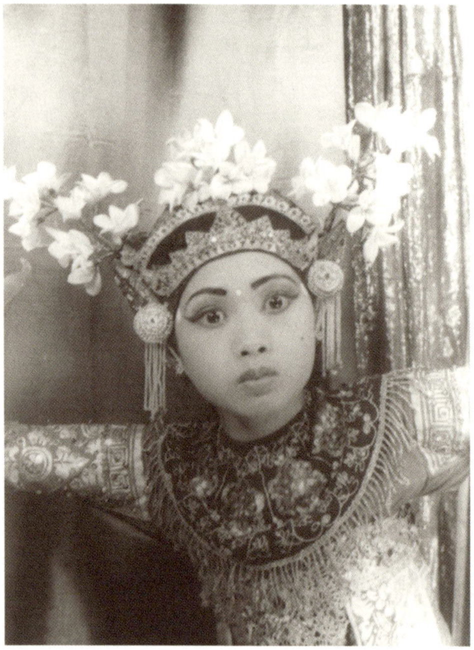

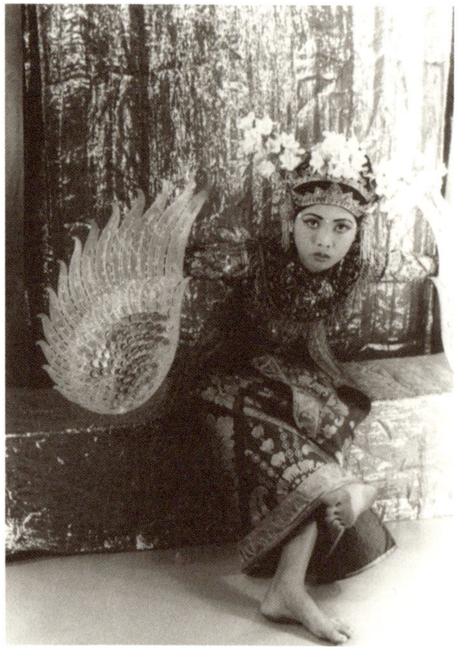

In 1952, Ni-Gusti Raka came to New York as a member of the Island of Bali Dancers, the first company of Balinese dancers ever to perform in the western hemisphere. The group toured the United States for about four months, appearing in several major cities. Their tour was sponsored by a governmental arts agency of the then newly independent Republic of Indonesia in an effort to introduce westerners to Indonesian culture.

Though she was only about ten years old, Raka was the troupe's lead dancer. As such, she performed one of the central dances of the company's show, the Legong, a traditional dance known in Balinese legend as the dance of heavenly spirits. Like many other Balinese dances, the Legong is a highly stylized dramatic narrative performed with the accompaniment of a gamelan, a Balinese orchestra consisting of flutes, strings, and various percussion instruments.

The Legong's three performers, all young girls, enact an ancient tale about a young princess who is kidnapped by a king and locked away. The king chooses to go to war with the princess's brother rather than set her free, but as he rides into battle a bird comes to him and predicts his death. The ornately costumed dancers perform the story through elaborate movements and facial expressions. In addition to dancing this and other traditional pieces, during her appearances with the Island of Bali Dancers Raka performed a new dance, the Tumulingan, translated as the Bumblebee, which had been created specifically for her.

Though Balinese dancers are generally young girls—especially Legong dancers who often cease performing in their early teens—Raka returned to the United States to perform in 1972.

PHOTOGRAPHED ON OCTOBER 6, 1952

DANCER

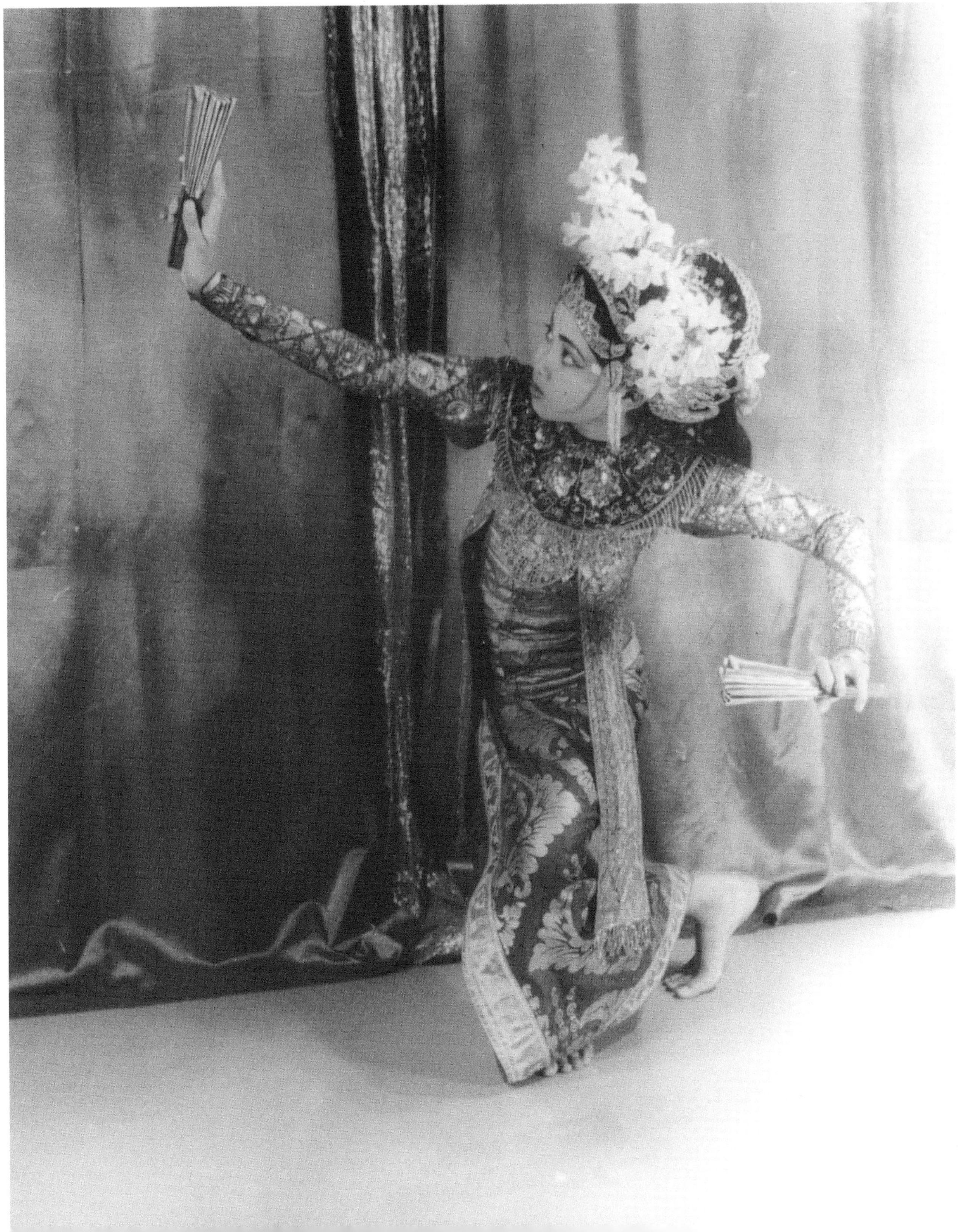

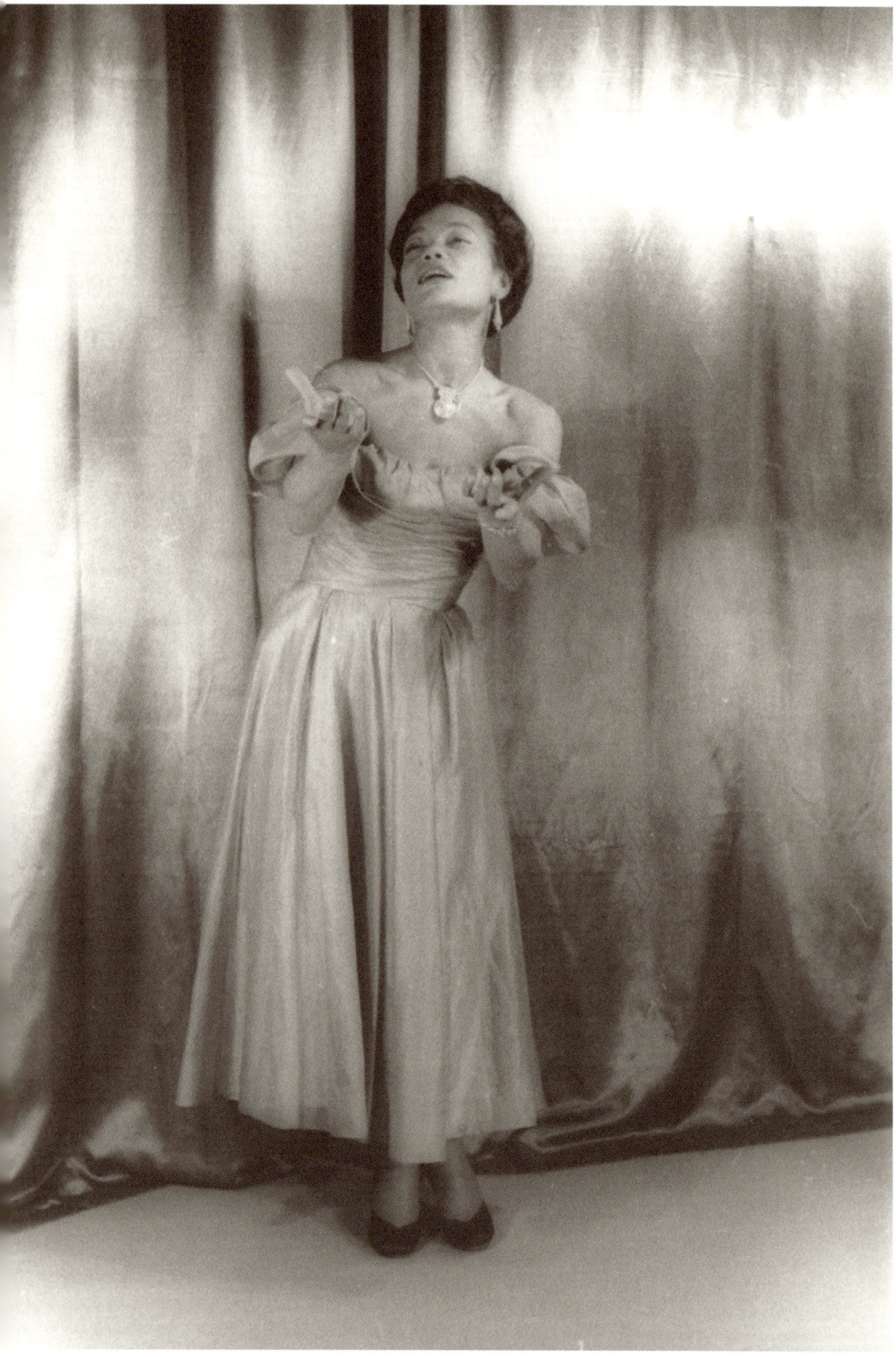

PHOTOGRAPHED ON OCTOBER 19, 1952

# EARTHA KITT

Eartha Kitt has been called "two parts cat and one part woman, sprinkled liberally with dynamite powder."[1] Though she has described herself as "self-reliant, afraid of nothing, even defiant,"[2] she has never forgotten the poverty, abuse, and discrimination of her childhood. Kitt has called her life one "of cotton and caviar," which appropriately characterizes her rise from humble beginnings to her position as one of the most exciting personalities in the entertainment industry.

Eartha Mae Kitt was born in North, South Carolina, to a fourteen-year-old black mother and a white father. She never knew her father, and after her stepfather abandoned the family, Kitt, her mother, and her half-sister wandered from place to place, living with strangers whenever her mother could find work. Kitt wrote of this early period, "Most of the time we lived in the forest, or at least slept there covered with pine straw."[3] When she was six, Kitt's mother left her with strangers and went off with a man who would not accept Kitt into his family because she was half-white. Two years later, Kitt went to live with an aunt in Harlem; however, Kitt ended up running away several times to escape her aunt's abuse.

She finally escaped her aunt for good when she obtained a position with Katherine Dunham's dance troupe. Kitt soon emerged as one of the star soloists of the company, and her beauty, sophistication, and sensuality made her an international sensation. She performed with Dunham's troupe in Paris, but when the company returned to the States, Kitt remained in Paris and began performing in the city's cabarets and nightclubs.

She became the toast of the city, and soon embarked on singing engagements in Turkey, Greece, and Egypt. In 1951, she was cast by Orson Welles as Helen of Troy in his version of *Faust*, and her performance led to her appearance the following year in the Broadway revue *New Faces of 1952.* Her singing in *New Faces* garnered critical acclaim and show-stopping applause every night from the audience.

Soon, she signed a recording contract with RCA Victor and produced hit songs in English, French, and Turkish. She began making movies, appearing in the film version of *New Faces* (1954), as well as in *Accused* (1957) with Sidney Poitier, and *Anna Lucasta* (1958) opposite Sammy Davis, Jr. She also broke into television, playing Catwoman on the *Batman* series and appearing on several game and variety shows.

Her success came to an abrupt end in 1968, after a fateful luncheon at the White House. In January 1968, Kitt was invited by Lady Bird Johnson to attend the first Woman Doers' Luncheon with the theme, "Why is there so much juvenile delinquency in the streets of America?" Kitt took the question seriously. She conducted research that revealed that an increase in street crime might be, in part, a result of the Vietnam War. At the luncheon, Kitt became frustrated with the lack of serious discussion about the topic under consideration. When Kitt addressed the group, she expressed her beliefs about a connection between juvenile street crime and the Vietnam War. "Such graphic remarks," Kitt wrote, "apparently didn't set too well with the peppermint ice cream dessert."[4]

The consequences of speaking out against the Vietnam War at the White House were immediate. Kitt's club contracts were canceled and she was dropped from her television appearances. For years, Kitt was blacklisted in the entertainment industry; she continued to perform overseas, but could no longer work in the United States. She also became the subject of surveillance by several government agencies, including the CIA. After some time, a journalist revealed the government's invasion of her privacy in an article under the headline "EARTHA KITT A CIA TARGET!" Kitt's career began to rebound. She has since returned to the public eye in several movies and live performances.

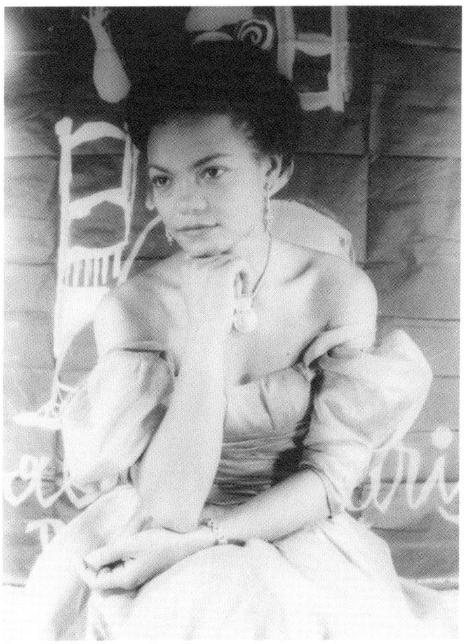

1 Peter Coutros
*Sunday News*
6 Dec. 1953

2 Eartha Kitt
*Alone with Me*
Chicago: Henry Regnery
1976
p. 4

3 Eartha Kitt
*Confessions of a Sex Kitten*
NY: Barricade Books
1989
p. 1

4 *Confessions of a Sex Kitten*
p. 246

SOPRANO



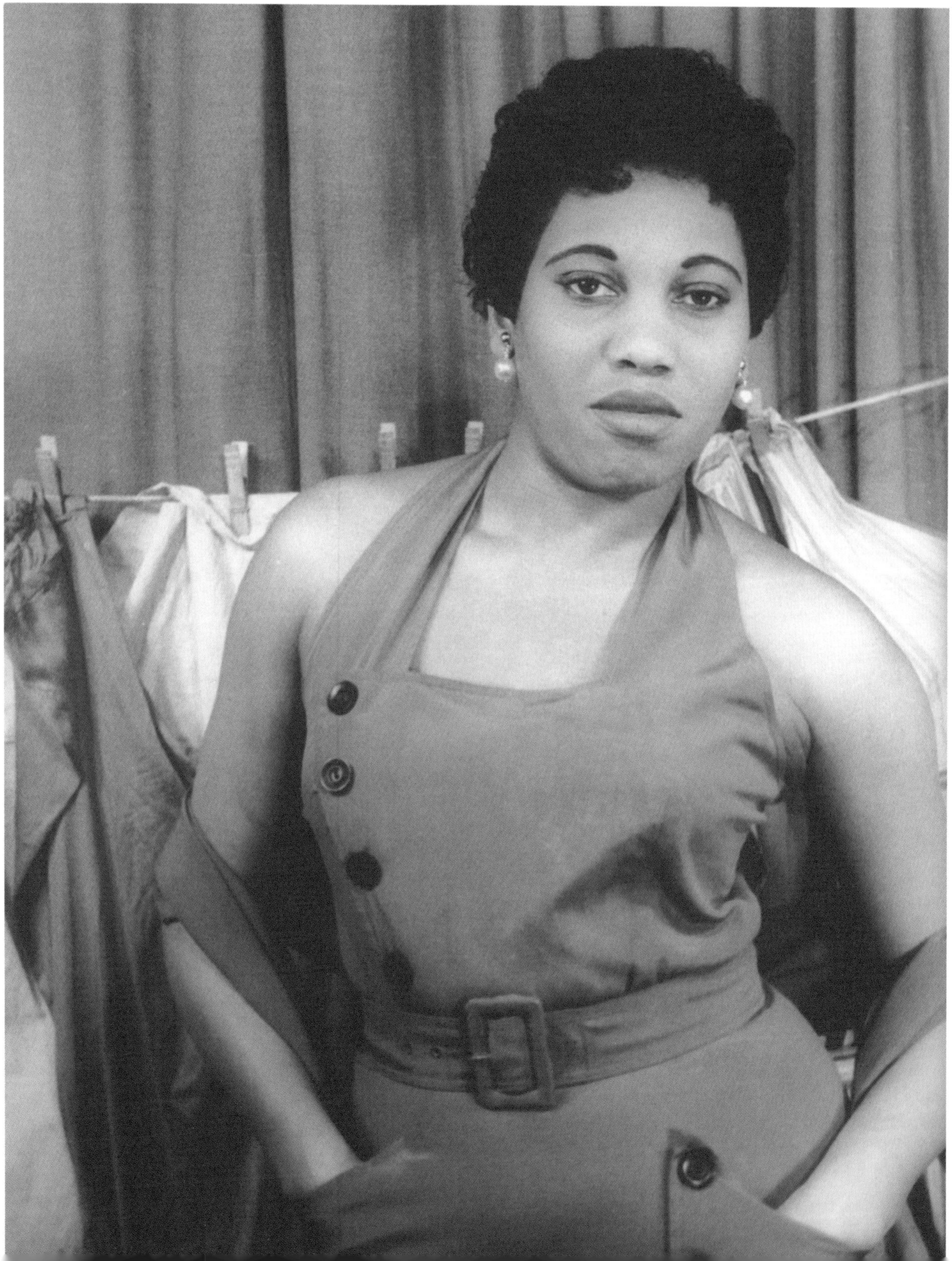

# LEONTYNE PRICE

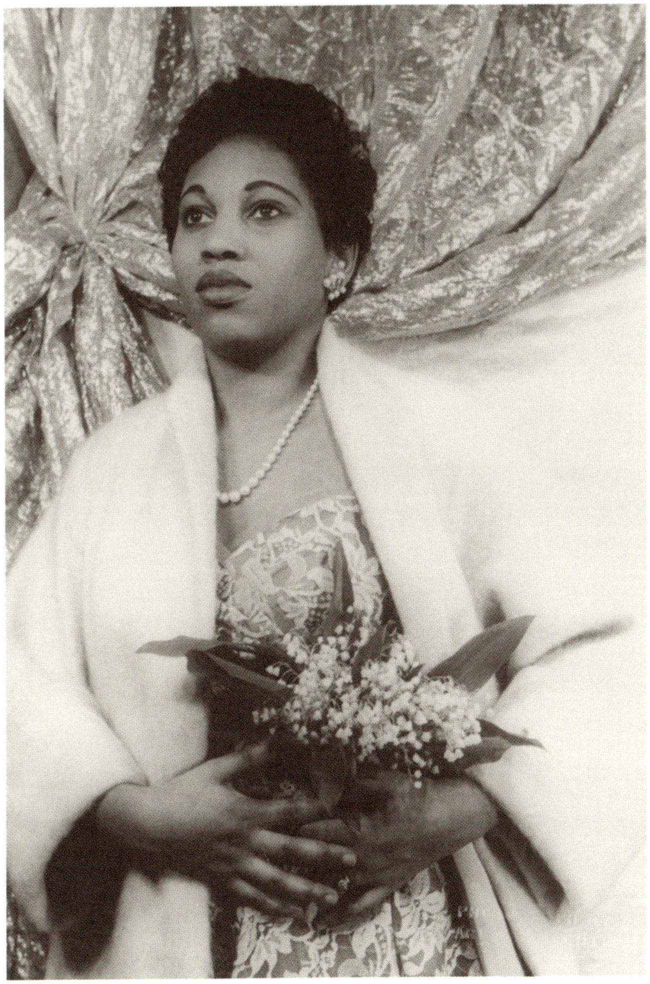



Leontyne Price is famous as one of the first widely acclaimed African-American opera singers. An accomplished soprano, Price performed all over the world. She is considered one of the most important operatic singers of the twentieth century.

Price was born in Mississippi in 1927; her parents—her father was a carpenter, her mother, a midwife—both loved music and were members of their church choir. They supported their daughter's interest in music and singing, enrolling her in piano lessons at an early age. Both children of Methodist ministers, Price's parents encouraged her to sing in their church's choir.

In college, Price started training to be a public school music teacher, but when she received a scholarship to Julliard she shifted her focus, putting all her efforts into her own voice training. As a student at Julliard, Price performed in a number of operatic productions. When Virgil Thomson heard Price sing in one of these operas, he hired her to appear in the Broadway revival of *Four Saints in Three Acts*, the opera he composed to a text by Gertrude Stein.

When she performed *Aida* with Luciano Pavarotti, he remarked, "In the Nile scene . . . Leontyne was so deep into the music that I began to cry backstage before my entrance. She was in superb form."[1] Terry McEwen, once the general manager of the San Francisco Opera, has said, "When Leontyne Price sings *'Vissi d'arte'* it's a spiritual experience."[2]

Leontyne Price was among Carl Van Vechten's favorite singers. He saw many of her performances and followed her reviews in the papers; in 1952 he wrote to Donald Angus, "Leontyne Price has made a sensation in *Porgy and Bess*. With [William] Warfield and Cab Calloway in the company, she has stolen the notices. *The Saturday Review of Literature* gave her a PAGE."[3] A decade later he was still an avid fan. "The excitement of the moment is mostly Leontyne Price who has since I wrote you about her *Trovatore* made an even greater success in *Aida*," Van Vechten wrote to Sandy Campbell in 1961. "This week she sings *Butterfly*. I go to all her performances with rapture. She is *sui generis* and there is no one like her."[4]

1 Harold C. Schonberg
"A Bravo for Opera's Black Voices"
*New York Times*
17 Jan. 1982

2 "A Bravo for Opera's Black Voices"

3 Van Vechten to Donald Angus
12 July 1952
*Letters of Carl Van Vechten*
Ed., Bruce Kellner
New Haven, Yale, 1987
p. 250

4 Van Vechten to Sandy Campbell
26 Feb. 1961
*Letters of Carl Van Vechten*
p. 279

PHOTOGRAPHED ON MAY 19, 1953

# BERTICE READING



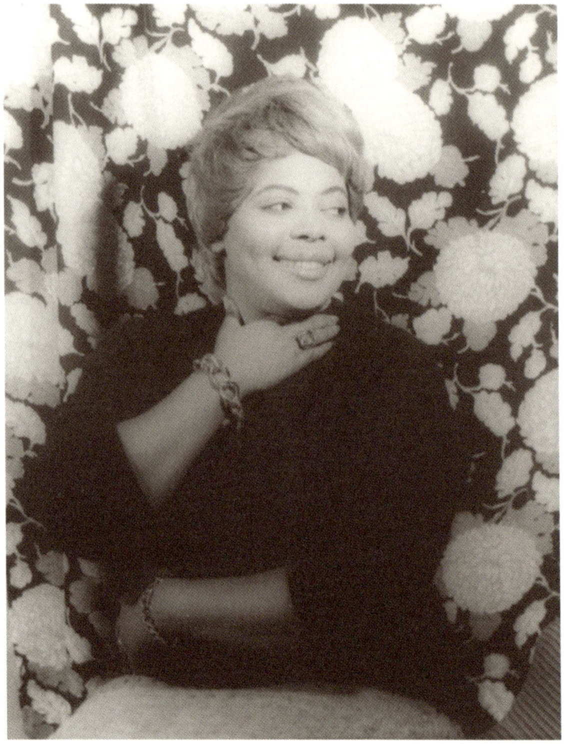

PHOTOGRAPHED ON JANUARY 6, 1954

Born and raised in Chester, Pennsylvania, Bertice Reading began her career in show business when she danced with Bill "Bojangles" Robinson when she was just three years old. Though she met with some early success in the United States, Bertice Reading moved to Great Britain as a young woman, and it was there that her career as a singer, actress, and cabaret performer began in earnest.

An important early European performance for Reading was her appearance in "Jazz Train." "Jazz Train," a history of jazz in performance, began as a nightclub revue in New York during the late 1940s. In 1955, sixty five United States Air Force Officers financed a production of the show in London. The show, which featured an all-black cast, was a huge success. The first show was "wildly cheered" and "all the critics hailed Bertice Reading, twenty-one-year-old blues singer, as a major discovery."[1]

Reading would remain in England for much of her career, returning to the United States for a number of successful performances, including a Tony-nominated supporting performance in *Requiem for a Nun* in 1959, which was, Van Vechten wrote, "a flop save for the performance of Bertice which took all the applause."[2] She also appeared in *Measure for Measure* at the National Theater in 1981. Reading's career included, too, a number of screen credits, among them an appearance as the Downtown Old Woman in *Little Shop of Horrors* (1986).

1 "Jazz Train Hailed in London" *New York Times* 28 Apr. 1955

2 Van Vechten to Fania Marinoff 31 Jan. 1959 *Letters of Carl Van Vechten* Ed., Bruce Kellner New Haven: Yale 1987 p. 272-3

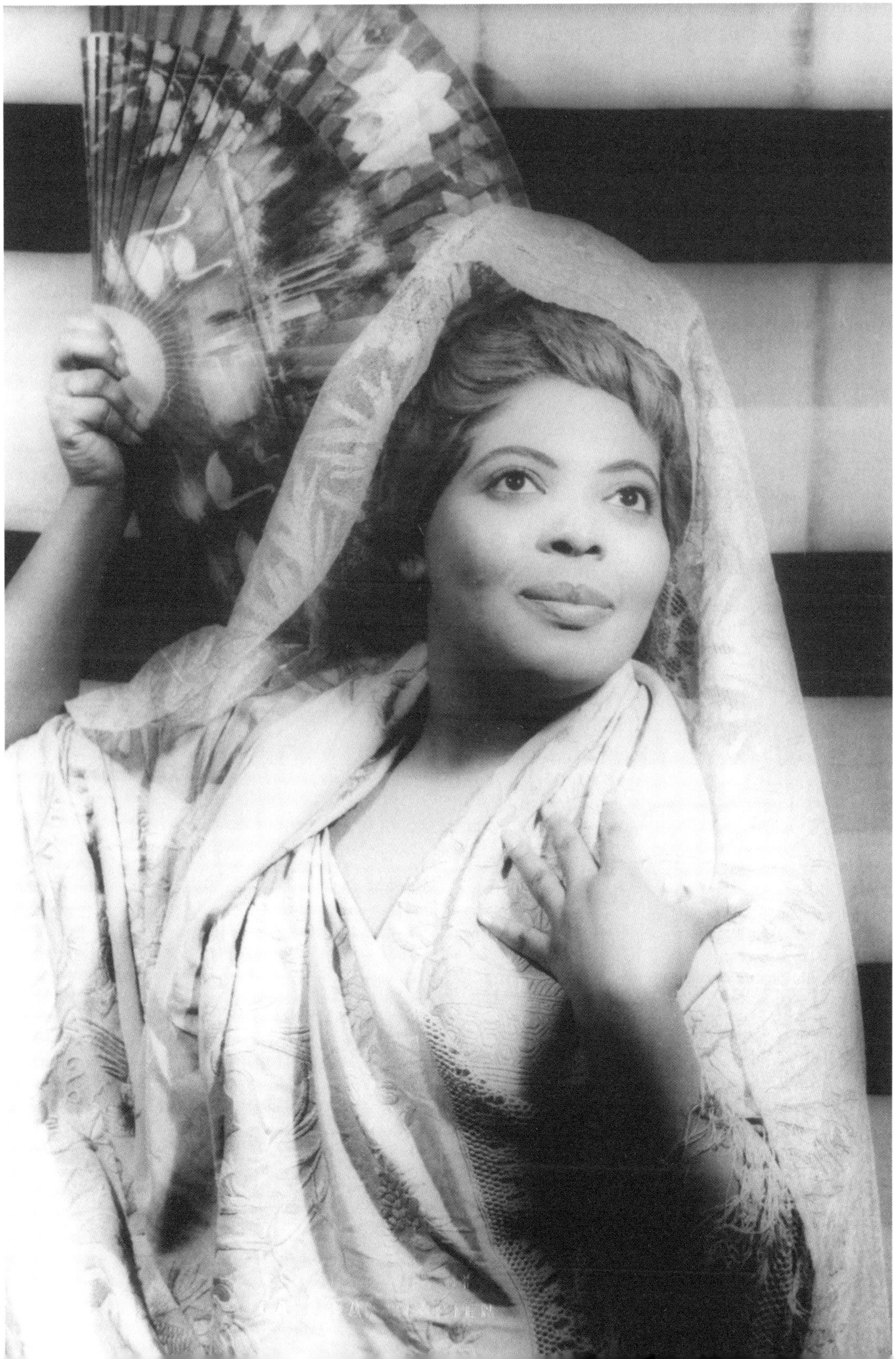

SINGER & ACTRESS

# MATTIWILDA DOBBS

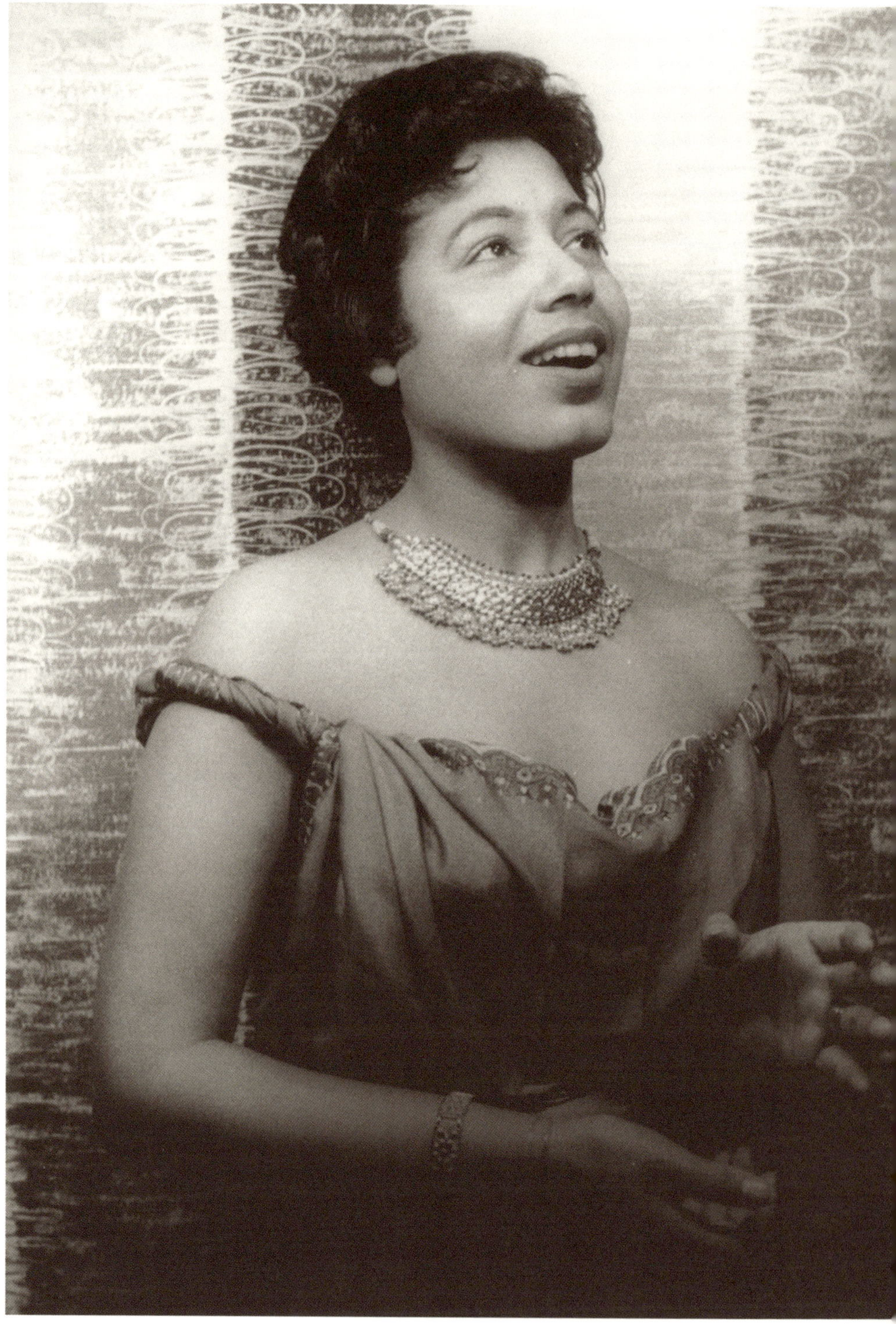



An internationally acclaimed opera and concert singer, Mattiwilda Dobbs has a voice often compared to the clear and resonant sound of a bell and she is known for warm, intimate performances. Only two African Americans sang at the Metropolitan Opera before her, and, appearing in *Rigoletto* in 1956, she was the first African American to perform a romantic lead on that stage.

An Atlanta, Georgia, native, Dobbs was born and raised in the Jim Crow south. Her father, John Dobbs, a railroad postal clerk, was determined that his children should receive a well-rounded education; because the Atlanta public library did not lend books to African Americans, he borrowed books from other libraries on his postal route for his six daughters to read. He also insisted that each of his children study music. Because of his commitment to her early musical training, Dobbs has credited her father with her success as a singer. John Dobbs played a significant role in shaping the future of his community when, in 1935, he founded the Georgia Voters League and began the fight to register southern black voters. He helped to lay the groundwork for future civil rights activists.

While training with some of the opera world's most prominent and rigorous voice instructors, Dobbs earned a number of important scholarships, allowing her to travel to Europe to continue her studies. Among these was the Marian Anderson

PHOTOGRAPHED ON JANUARY 26, 1955

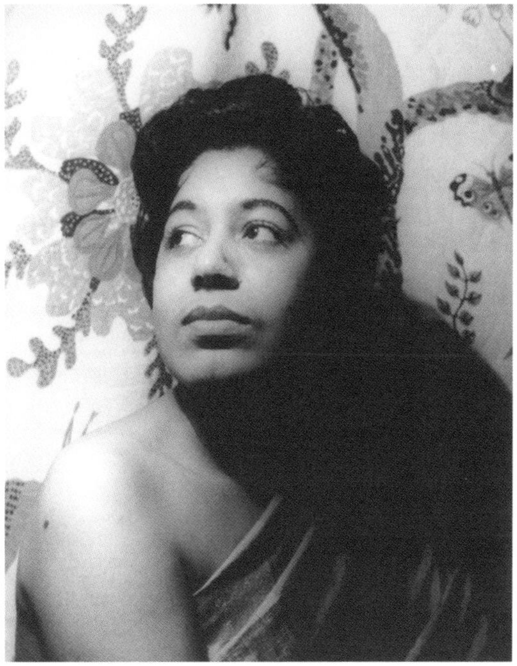



Scholarship, named in honor of the groundbreaking African-American singer. Dobbs was one of the first people to receive this prestigious award. Years later, when President Jimmy Carter awarded Anderson the Congressional Gold Medal, Dobbs, by then a world-class opera star, performed at the ceremony in Anderson's honor.

During the course of her career, Dobbs has received decorations and awards from the international opera community. She won acclaim all over the world—from Israel to Ireland, Scandinavia to New Zealand—in part because of her personal connection to her audiences. For a performance in the Soviet Union, Dobbs learned a song in Russian; when she performed in the United States, she often included adaptations of African-American spirituals, Creole slave songs, and works of contemporary American composers. When she sang at the Municipal Auditorium in her hometown of Atlanta in 1963, she performed for one of the city's first un-segregated audiences. And when her nephew, Maynard Jackson, became that city's first African-American mayor, she sang at his inauguration.

Dobbs was one of Carl Van Vechten's favorite opera performers. "Mattiwilda [Dobbs] was glorious," he wrote of her debut opera at the Met, "a warm and brilliant coloratura and the best Gilda in my experience and I have heard [Nellie] Melba, [Emma] Eames, and Bessie Abott, to say nothing of the current [Hilde] Gueden who always leaves me cold as a sardine in the icebox."[1]

If Dobbs has not received the popular attention her voice and accomplishments deserve, it is likely that she has been overlooked only because of the abundance of fine singers who were her contemporaries. "Sandwiched between the debuts of Marian Anderson and Leontyne Price, momentous and sensational respectively, Dobbs's bow at the house in 1956 was greeted warmly but inevitably overshadowed," *Opera News* critic Ira Siff has said. "The impact was perhaps reduced even more by the advent of the big-voiced coloratura, personified by Maria Callas (who arrived at the Met a few weeks before Dobbs) and later by Joan Sutherland."[2] Still, Dobbs is often celebrated for what Paul Hume has called the "singular purity and radiant texture"[3] of her voice.

1 Van Vechten to Peter David Marchant
Dec. 1956
*Letters of Carl Van Vechten*
Ed., Bruce Kellner
New Haven: Yale, 1987
p. 266

2 Ira Siff
"Arias and Songs"
*Opera News*
64:17 (2000)
p. 81

3 Paul Hume
"Mattiwilda Dobbs"
*Washington Post*
7 February 1981

# DIAHANN CARROLL

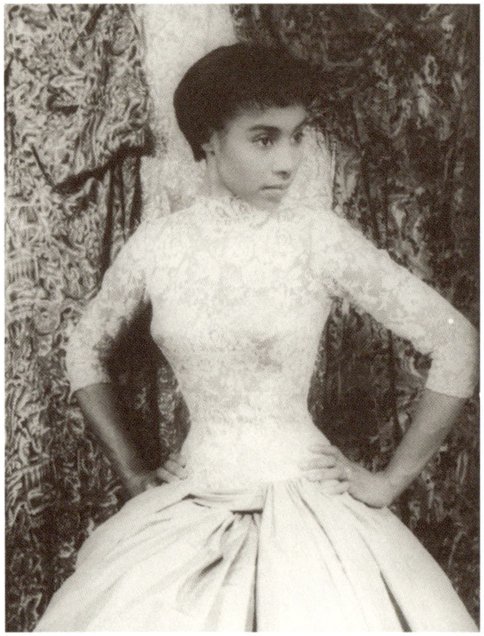



Donald Bogle 1
*Toms, Coons, Mulattos, Mammies, & Bucks: An Interpretive History of Blacks in American Films*
NY: Viking, 1973
p. 211

William Mac Dougall 2
"Minority performers are winning prominent roles and helping to reverse old racial stereotypes"
*U.S. News & World Report*
13 May 1985
p. 70

Diahann Carroll with 3
Ross Firestone
*Diahann: An Autobiography*
Boston: Little, Brown, 1986
p. 244

Born Carol Diann Johnson, Diahann Carroll grew up in New York City. Though she started her career as a model for *Ebony* magazine when she was just fifteen years old, Carroll would go on to achieve fame as a popular and award winning singer and actress. She aggressively pursued a career in entertainment, performing in public whenever possible and entering small talent competitions. Her success in such contests provided Carroll with the opportunity to appear on radio and television, increasing her exposure and her skill as an entertainer. As a result of her early successes, Carroll was able to get an agent and manager by the time she was eighteen years old.

Carroll was soon singing regularly in New York nightclubs. Her captivating appearances in small clubs helped Carroll to get work in films and larger theater productions. She debuted on Broadway with Pearl Bailey in *House of Flowers*, a play adapted from a short story by Truman Capote. Carroll received a Tony nomination for her performance. Songs she sang in *House of Flowers*, including "House of Flowers" and "A Sleepin' Bee," became signature songs that Carroll would perform regularly throughout her career.

In 1968, after many years of success on stage and screen, Carroll became the first African-American woman to star in a weekly television series. The series, *Julia*, was popular with audiences but it was attacked by critics as racist, unrealistic, and degrading to African Americans; Julia, a middle class single mother whose glamorous apartment and wardrobe were entirely out of reach for most middle class African Americans, was an idealized "Doris-Day-in-blackface."[1] In the midst of the contentious public debate, Carroll asked to be released from her contract after just two years. Though short-lived and controversial, *Julia* was a groundbreaking television show and an important part of Carroll's career.

When Carroll returned to television in 1984, she joined the cast of *Dynasty*, a popular evening soap opera; she was the first African-American woman to star in such a show. Carroll's character, the villainous millionaire Dominique Deveraux, was praised by some as one of a growing number of African-American television roles that differed "from the mainly comic roles that have been more typical for blacks" and thus "[helped] to change perceptions about blacks by both whites and blacks"[2] in the entertainment industry. Though it might be argued that Dominique Deveraux represented a different kind of negative representation of African-American women, Carroll called the role "a dream come true, . . . a worldwide successful television series without all the pain and criticism of *Julia*."[3]

PHOTOGRAPHED MARCH 14, 1955

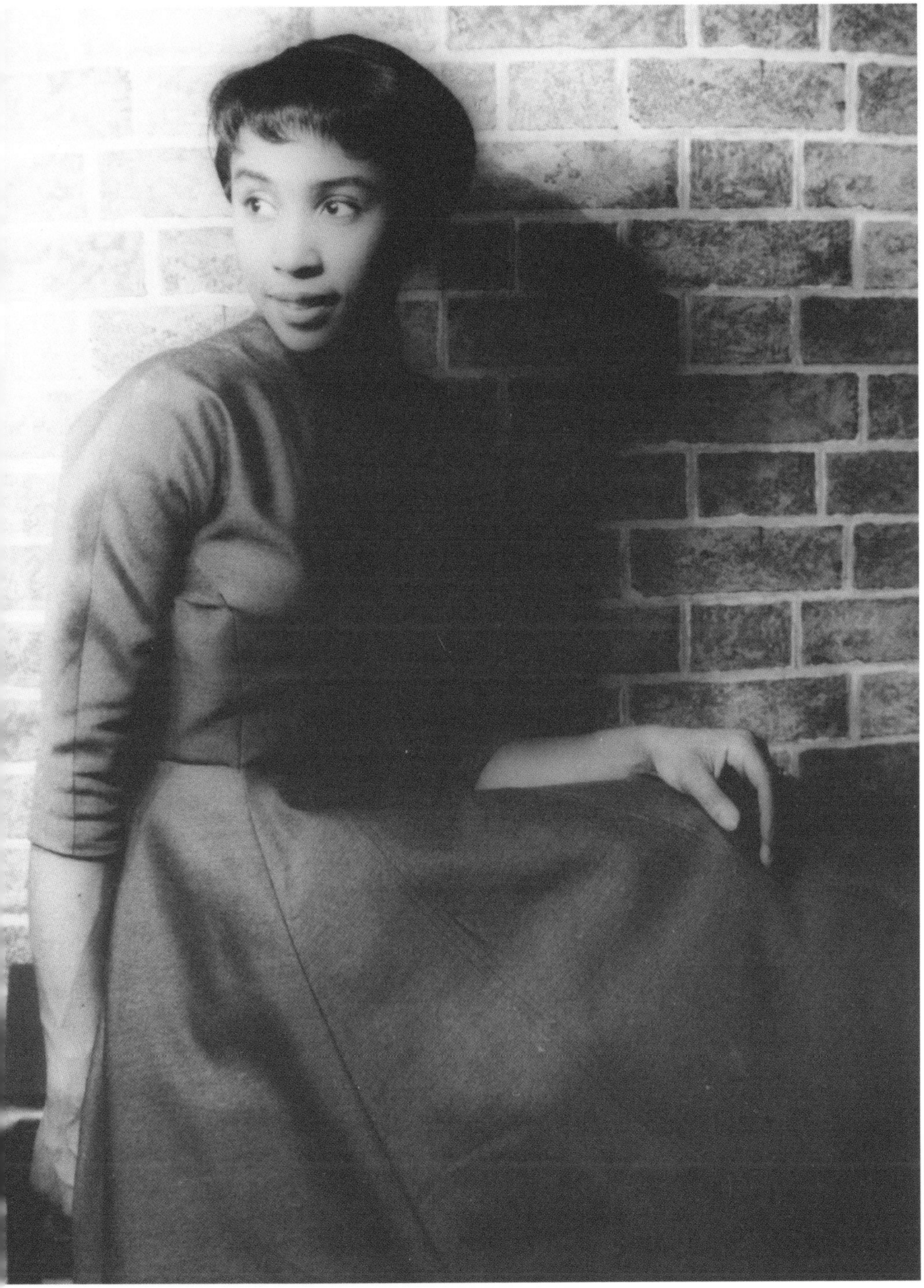

## SINGER & ACTRESS



Throughout her successful career, Carroll has faced many trials in her personal life including several failed marriages and relationships, a controversial affair with Sydney Poitier, and a bout with breast cancer. In spite of the difficulties and disappointments off stage, Carroll has been highly praised as a versatile actress who can successfully play a range of roles—from her Oscar nominated portrayal of a welfare mother in *Claudine*, to her portrayals of glamorous women like Dominique Deveraux. Her many awards offer evidence of her skills as a performer. Carroll is the winner of a Tony award and an NAACP Image award for best actress; her work has received Oscar and Emmy nominations, and she has been inducted into the Black Filmmakers Hall of Fame.

## ACTRESS

The daughter of the famous New York theater and industrial designer, Norman Bel Geddes, Barbara Bel Geddes began working as an actress at New York's Windsor Theater when she was just nineteen. She played small theaters in Connecticut and New York and worked with a USO tour before establishing herself first in the New York theater community and later in the Hollywood film industry. As a stage, film, and television performer, Bel Geddes won the admiration of critics as a bright and charming actress of emotional depth, a skillful performer of complex roles.

After appearing in many popular productions, Bel Geddes was offered the most important part of her career. She became the first woman to act the part of Maggie the Cat in the 1955 production of Tennessee Williams's *Cat on Hot Tin Roof*. The show received glowing reviews and Bel-Geddes's performance as Maggie earned accolades throughout the theater community. Her interpretation of the volatile and complicated Maggie was described as "magnificent . . . vital, lovely and frank."[1] She was praised for her remarkable work in the play's first act, which consists almost entirely of Maggie's monologue. The play, for which Williams received a Pulitzer Prize, has become one of the most important of twentieth-century American literature.

When Bel Geddes appeared in plays that were not well received by critics, she was often singled out for praise. Most critics found her work compelling and convincing, in spite of a

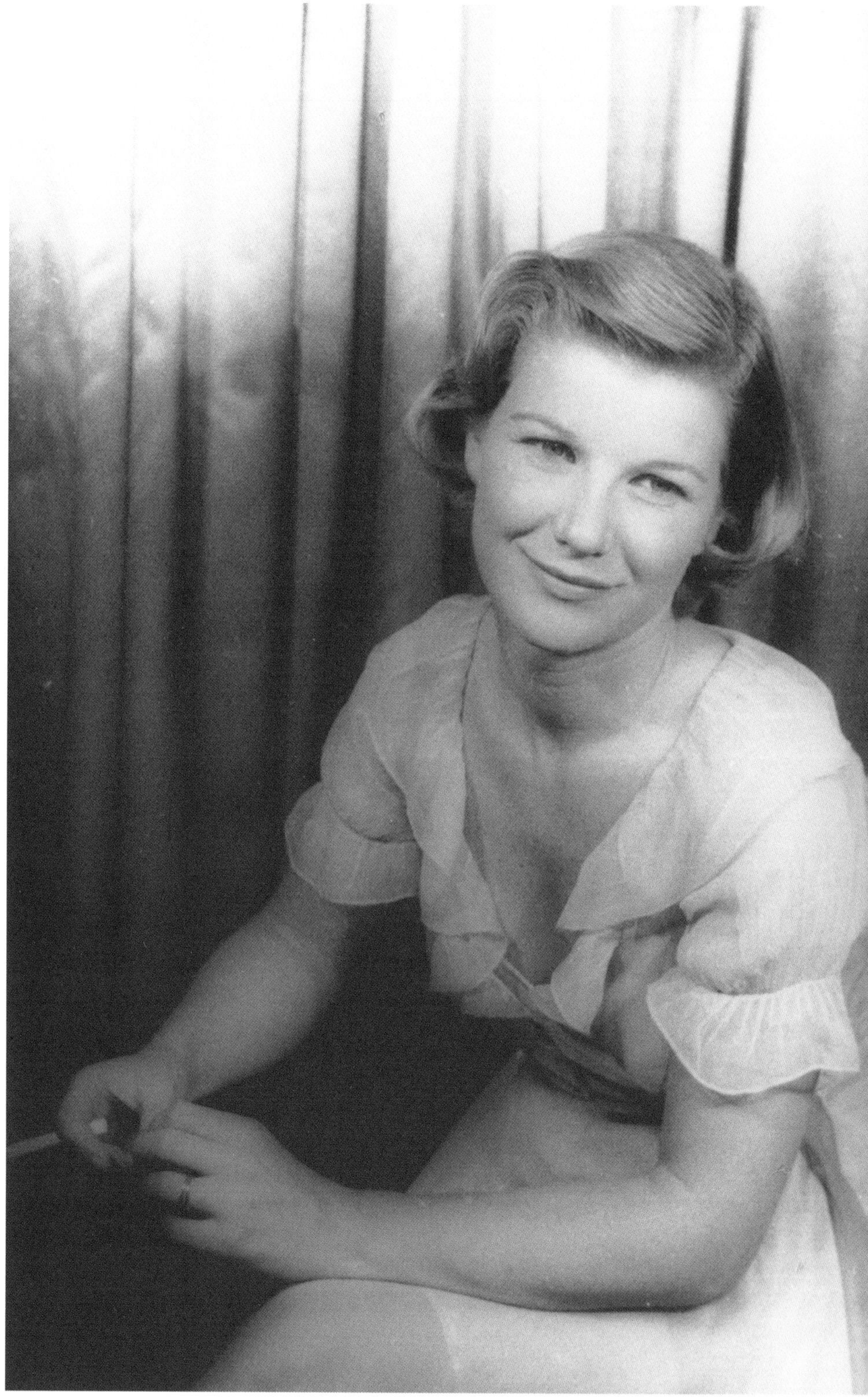

PHOTOGRAPHED JUNE 3, 1955, AS MAGGIE THE CAT IN "CAT ON A HOT TIN ROOF"

# BARBARA BEL GEDDES

second-rate script. In Robert Anderson's *Silent Night, Lonely Night* with Henry Fonda, a play that received only lukewarm reviews, critics noticed Bel Geddes's portrayal of a betrayed wife as a strength of the production. "Even in a mood of grief, she is sunny and beautiful," Brooks Atkinson wrote of her performance, "she speaks her lines with a reticent inflection that is disarming."[2]

Also an accomplished film actress, Bel Geddes appeared in *I Remember Mama* with Irene Dunn in 1948 and the 1950 Elia Kazan noir film *Panic in the Streets* with Zero Mostel. She appeared in Alfred Hitchcock's *Vertigo* in 1959 as Midge, the steadfast Girl Friday to Jimmy Stewart's emotionally troubled private detective.

Like many popular theater actresses of her generation, Bel Geddes is best remembered for a television role and not the theatrical performances that made her famous. As Miss Ellie, the matriarch of a wealthy oil family on the popular 1980s nighttime soap opera *Dallas*, Bel Geddes earned an Emmy Award for Best Actress.

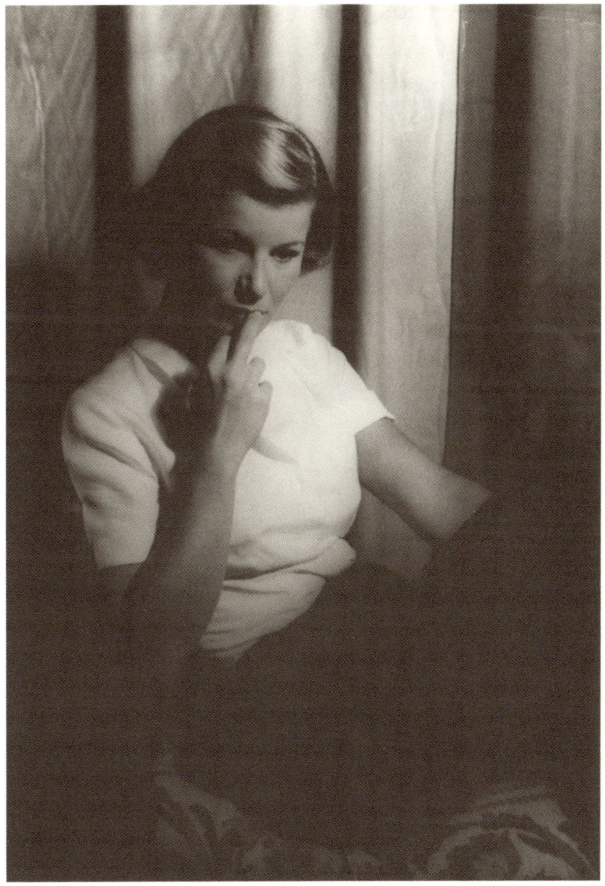

1 Brooks Atkinson "Theatre: Tennessee Williams' 'Cat'" *New York Times* 25 Mar. 1955

2 Brooks Atkinson "Theatre: 'Silent Night, Lonely Night'" *New York Times* 4 Dec. 1959

# CAROL CHANNING

Brooks Atkinson 1
"The Blonde Mantrap"
*New York Times*
18 Dec. 1949

William Tynan 2
"Looking Amazingly Swell"
*Time*
19 Sept. 1994
p. 78

Jack Kroll 3
"Unsinkable Dolly"
*Newsweek*
30 Oct. 1995
p. 78

Carol Channing's unique voice and talent for outrageous and madcap comic performances have made her one of the most popular Broadway performers of the twentieth century. In her most famous roles—Lorelei Lee in *Gentlemen Prefer Blondes* and Dolly Gallagher Levi in *Hello, Dolly!*—Channing's spectacular performances are legendary. Wildly popular touring productions of both shows helped to launch Carol Channing to stardom.

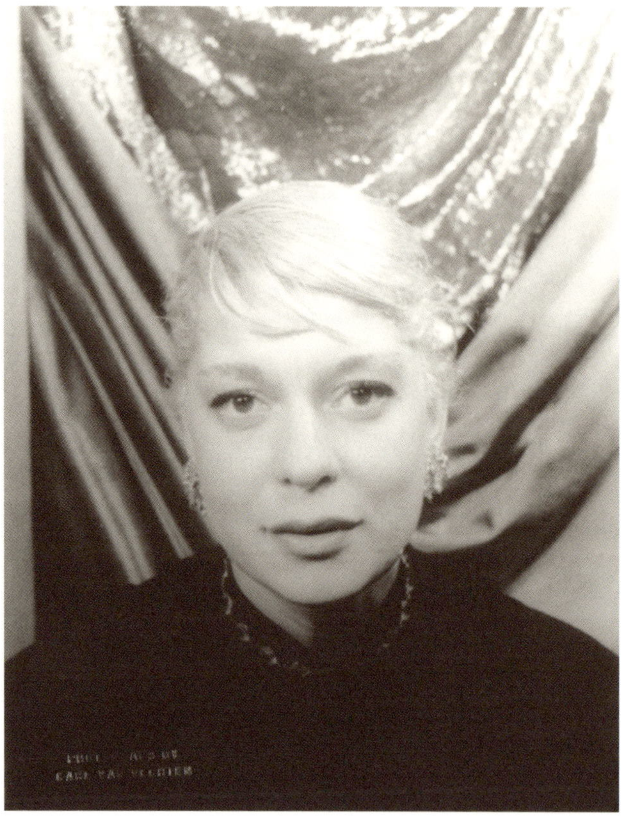

A California native, Channing came east to attend Bennington College in Vermont. In 1940, she spent her winter semester break in New York, performing in her first major show, Marc Blitzstein's *No For An Answer*. Though the show was a failure and closed quickly, Channing's performance was briefly praised in a review; this was enough to convince her to stay on in New York and pursue a career in the theater.

After a series of minor successes, Channing won the role of Lorelei Lee in a stage adaptation of Anita Loos's novel, *Gentlemen Prefer Blondes*. The show and Channing's portrayal of the gold-digging party girl were tremendously successful. "Thanks to the musical version of *Gentlemen Prefer Blondes* we have a new star on Broadway," Brooks Atkinson wrote. "Although the management has not given her celestial billing, it probably realizes, as everyone else does, that Carol Channing is the chief attraction of the production."[1] Ever after, "Diamonds are a Girl's Best Friend" has been a signature song for Channing. In 1974, Channing played Lorelei again in *Lorelei, or Gentlemen Still Prefer Blonds*. Her performance won her a Tony Award nomination.

In 1964, Channing played Dolly Gallagher Levi in *Hello, Dolly!*, the Jerry Herman and Michael Stewart musical based on *The Matchmaker* by Thorton Wilder. The show won the New York Drama Critics Circle Award for best musical and ten Tony

PHOTOGRAPHED ON JANUARY 5, 1956

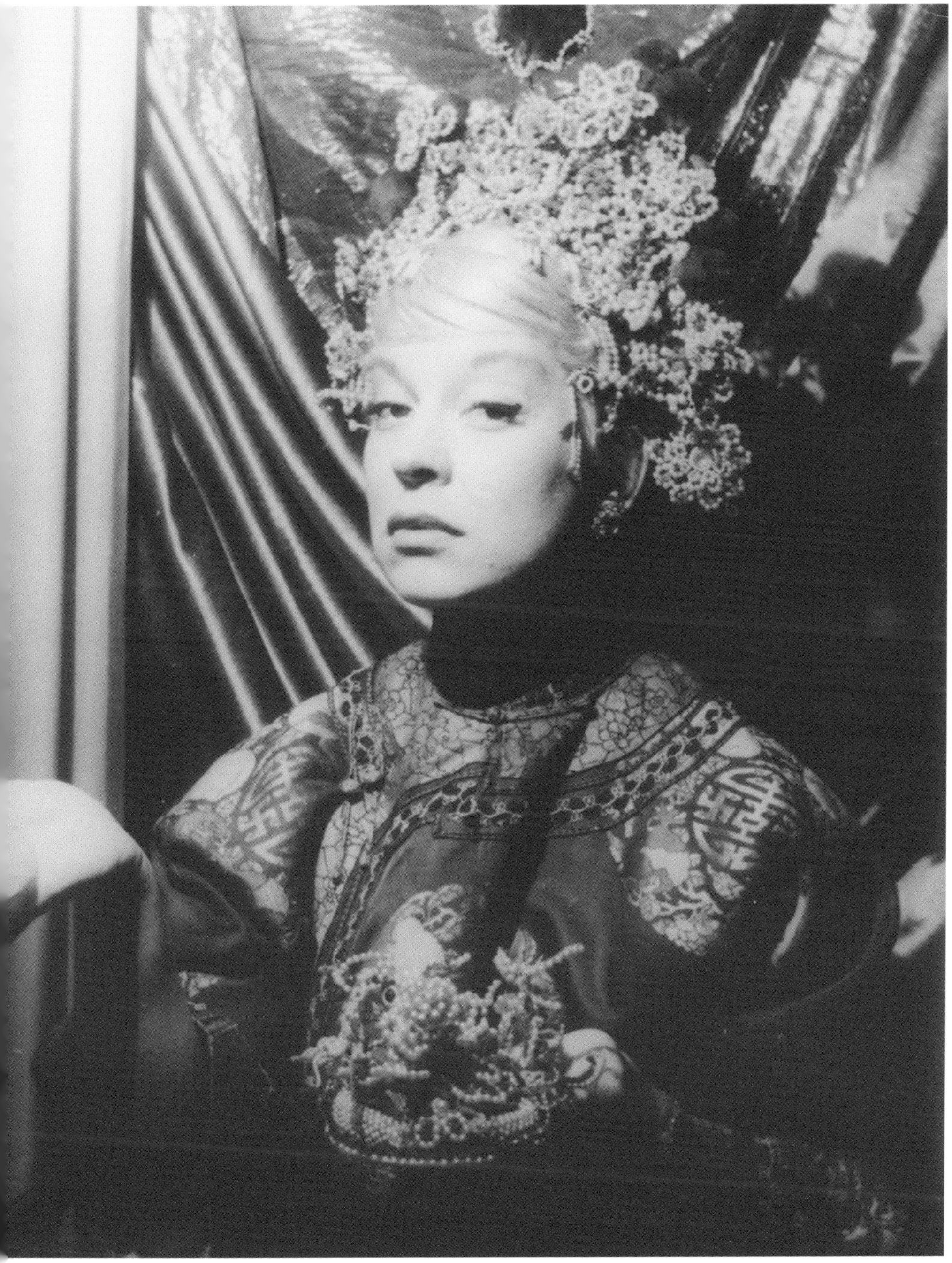





awards, including a best actress award for Channing. The original cast album was so popular that upon its release it beat out the Beatles for top sales.

Channing revived the role of Dolly in 1995, when she was seventy four years old. Though some were skeptical about the project, Channing was in top form, "pitch-perfect and a mistress of timing."[2] "In her red, green and orange turn-of-century outfits," Jack Kroll wrote, "Channing rekindles a straight-to-the-heart, popular theater that's as gone as the show's horse drawn trolley."[3] In all her Broadway and touring productions of *Hello, Dolly!,* Channing, who is said to travel with a separate suitcase for her fake eyelashes, has performed Dolly more than 4,500 times and has never missed a single performance.

Channing has received Tony nominations or awards for every one of her Broadway shows. And though she's made few films, in 1968 she was nominated for an Oscar for her performance in *Thoroughly Modern Millie.* Her television appearances on shows like *Hollywood Squares* and *The Muppet Show* have earned her new fans from a younger generation.

# MOLLIE MOON

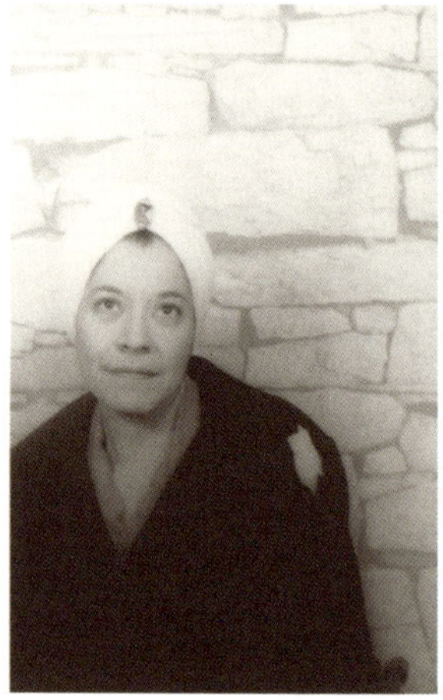



1 Mollie Moon "To You—Our Guests" *Disneyland: The National Urban League Guild's 16th Annual Beaux Arts Ball* New York, 1956 p. 6

2 Quoted in "Mollie Moon, 82, Founding Head of the Urban League Guild, Dies" *New York Times* 26 June 1990

3 "Jazz Greats Jam to Laud Hampton" *New York Times* 18 Feb. 1973

4 "Jazz Greats"

Before beginning a career as a community activist, fund-raiser, and civil rights advocate, Mississippi native Mollie Moon trained as a pharmacist at Meharry Medical College in Tennessee. She also studied at Columbia University's Teachers College, the New School for Social Research, and the University of Berlin. Moon worked only briefly as a pharmacist, and later, as an educator and social worker. Her true life's work was the Urban League Guild, the organization she founded and served as president for nearly fifty years.

Moon described the Guild's beginnings in a 1956 pamphlet:

> In June of 1942, a small, interracial group of young people met and formed an organization called the National Urban League Guild. This group drew on a broad program of educational, cultural, and social activities which it felt, if put into operation, would do much to improve race relations; and it agreed to work on behalf of the National Urban League.[1]

Through her efforts with the Urban League Guild and the Urban League, Mollie Moon worked to improve race relations in New York City and in the United States at large. Moon was an innovative fundraiser whose creative ideas and projects helped to support the Urban League and to raise public awareness about its programs.

The most popular and visible of the Guild's activities was the annual Beaux-Arts Ball. The ball, an extravagant party based on a different theme every year, was first held in Harlem's Savoy Ballroom. It moved downtown to the Rainbow Room at Rockefeller Center in 1948 amidst some controversy. League board member Winthrop Rockefeller co-signed the invitations with Mollie Moon that year. "Nobody was going to buck the landlord," Moon said, "that's how we broke the color barrier."[2]

The ball was eventually moved to the Waldorf-Astoria, where some of the most memorable balls were held. The twenty-fifth annual ball, in 1965, took "Freedom Around the World" as its theme and the sponsoring committee included representatives from the United Nations and the United States House of Representatives. Diana Sands and other popular performers served as judges for a costume contest at this event. A few years later, a "Golden Age" ball included performances by many jazz greats:

> The golden age of jazz was brought back for one fleeting evening at the 33rd annual Beaux Arts Ball Friday night when Lionel Hampton, Benny Goodman, Teddy Wilson, Gene Krupa, Illinois Jacque and Tyree Glenn got together for an unscheduled jam session in the sedate Waldorf-Astoria Hotel.[3]

PHOTOGRAPHED ON DECEMBER 11, 1956

Those in attendance were surprised by the impromptu show, "some danced, some clapped, and some among the 2000 guests stood amazed."[4]

In 1990, Moon received a President's Volunteer Action Award from President George Bush; New York Mayor David Dinkins presided at the award ceremony. Moon's groundbreaking work with the Urban League Guild in the areas of development and volunteerism earned her the respect of the nonprofit and advocacy communities. Her commitment to civil rights and equality, always at the root of her fundraising work, lead her to serve for many years as the secretary of the Urban League Board of Directors, even as she headed up the Guild's work.

The Urban League Guild began as a small, local organization in New York City; under Moon's leadership, the organization grew to include almost 30,000 volunteers working with local and regional Guild chapters. The fundraising and support of the Guild have enabled the continued success of Urban League programs nationwide.

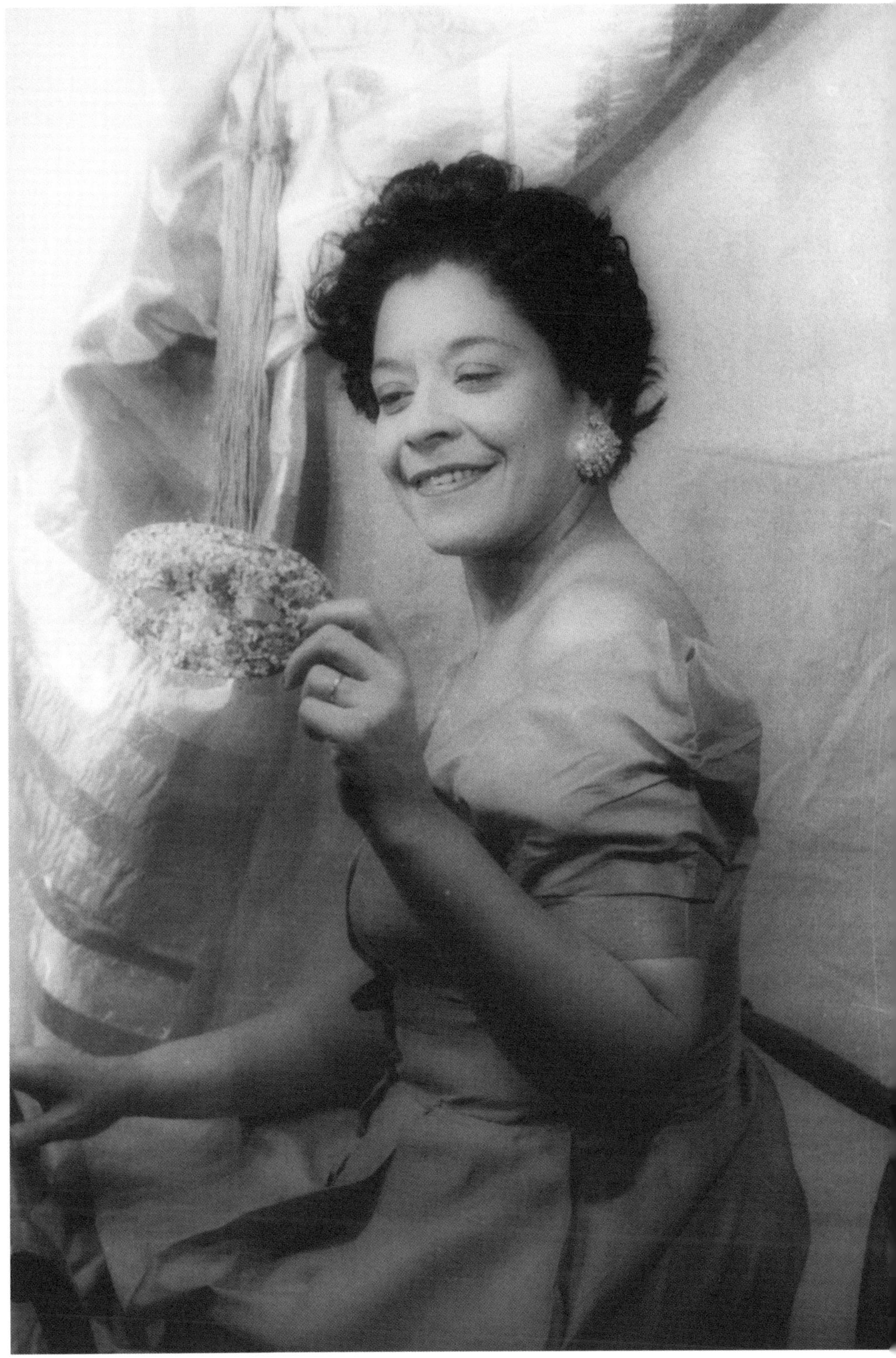

## TENNIS PLAYER



During the 1950s, tennis great Althea Gibson challenged the far-reaching racial barriers of the tennis world to earn many of the game's highest honors. In a sport dominated by wealthy athletes trained at elite country clubs, this was no small feat for an African-American high school dropout raised in Harlem.

Though she was born to sharecroppers in South Carolina, Gibson moved with her family to New York in search of greater economic opportunity. They settled in Harlem where Gibson enrolled in public school. A rebellious girl, Gibson didn't take well to school and regularly skipped classes; when she was present, she found it difficult to get along with teachers. As a result of her truancy and behavioral problems, she was threatened with reform school. Gibson dropped out of school at fourteen. She was unable to hold a job and soon wound up as a ward of the state.

She was introduced to paddleball by a Police Athletic League sports program. A city recreation department worker immediately recognized her innate talent for the game and bought her a proper, if second hand, tennis racquet. He also introduced her to members of the New York Cosmopolitan Club. Members of the interracial club were so impressed by Gibson's skillful performance on the court that they invited her to become a junior member and take lessons with the club's resident tennis pro.

After just a year of lessons, she won the 1941 New York State Open competition. By 1945 she had won two New York State

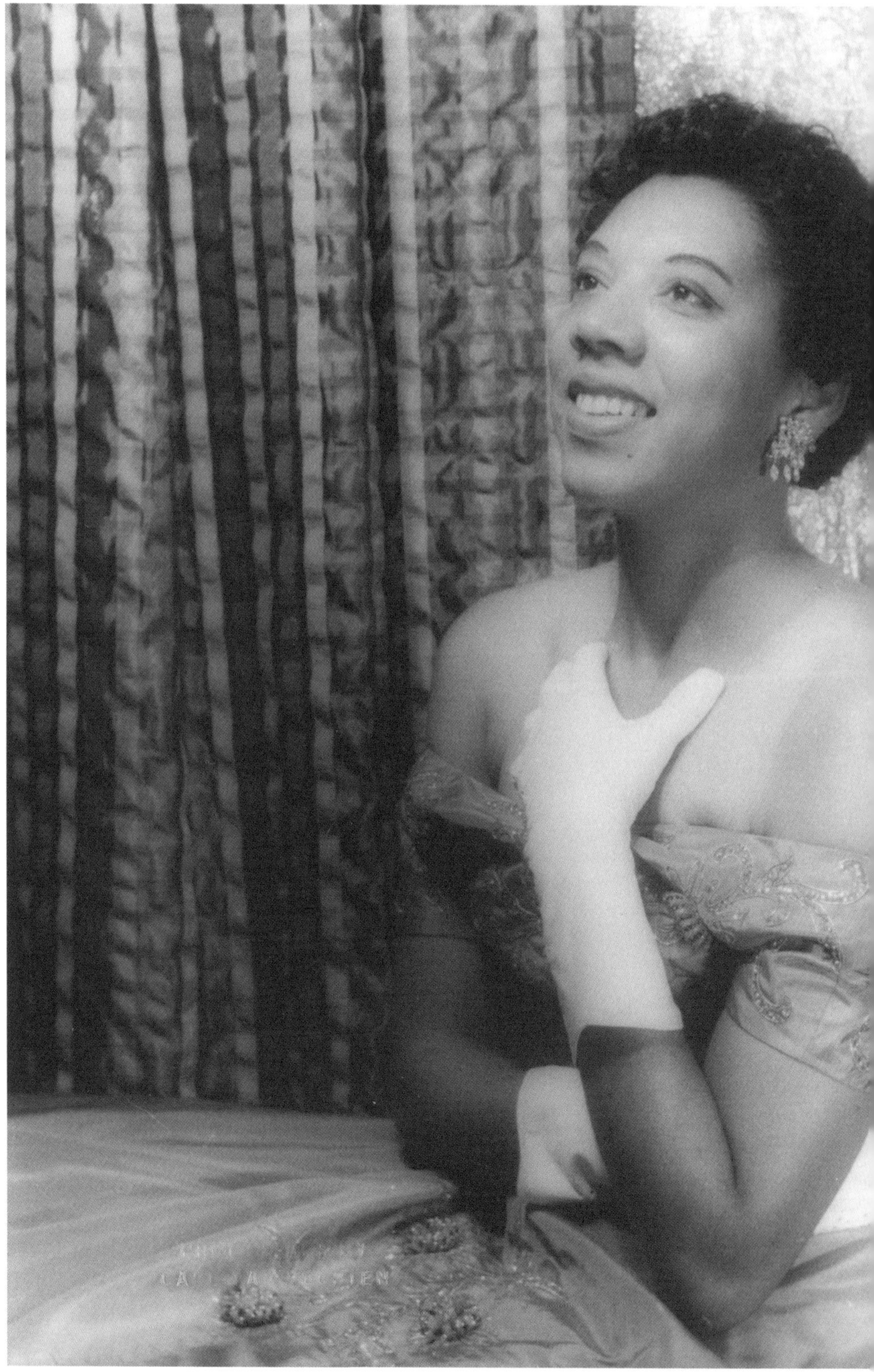

# ALTHEA GIBSON

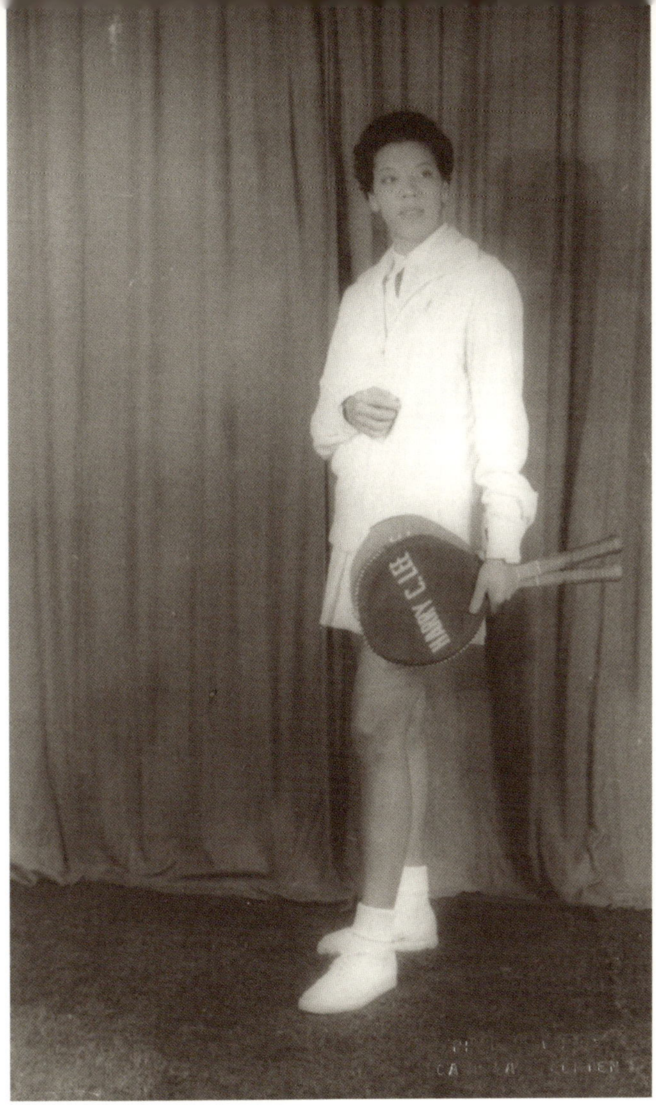

Negro Girls' Championships and her first National Negro Girls' Championship title. Her success earned her the attention of two prominent surgeons who offered Gibson free tennis lessons and room and board if she agreed to return to high school. Gibson accepted and moved to North Carolina where she lived with the family of one of her sponsors and trained on their private tennis court while she earned her diploma. Her play continued to improve and in 1948, Gibson earned her second Negro National Championship. This would be the first of nine consecutive victories in this competition.

Gibson was encouraged to try to compete in major tennis tournaments, though most were open only to white athletes. In 1950, she was denied admittance to the National Grass Court Championship because the host club, Forrest Hills in Long Island, was not open to African Americans. Gibson supporter and prominent member of the tennis community, Alice Marble, wrote an editorial in *American Lawn Tennis* calling for an end to the blatant racism in the sport. The tennis community responded and Gibson was soon invited to many major competitions, including the Forrest Hills grass court tournament.

In 1957, Gibson became the first black player to compete at Wimbledon, tennis's most renowned tournament. She won both the singles and doubles competition that year. Later the same year she won the national tournament at Forrest Hills. She repeated these victories in 1958. Though she was at the top of her sport and only thirty years old, Gibson wasn't able to make enough money to support herself and was forced to retire from competition. After her retirement, her fame led to product endorsements and even a role in *The Horse Soldier*, a Hollywood western directed by John Ford and staring John Wayne.

In the 1960s, Gibson took on another elite sport when she joined the Ladies Professional Golf Association (LPGA) tour. She was the first African American invited to compete in golf's top tournaments. Gibson played well, but she never achieved the levels of success she had enjoyed in tennis. After retiring from professional athletics, Gibson dedicated herself to developing sports programs in her adopted homestate, New Jersey.

PHOTOGRAPHED ON NOVEMBER 20, 1958

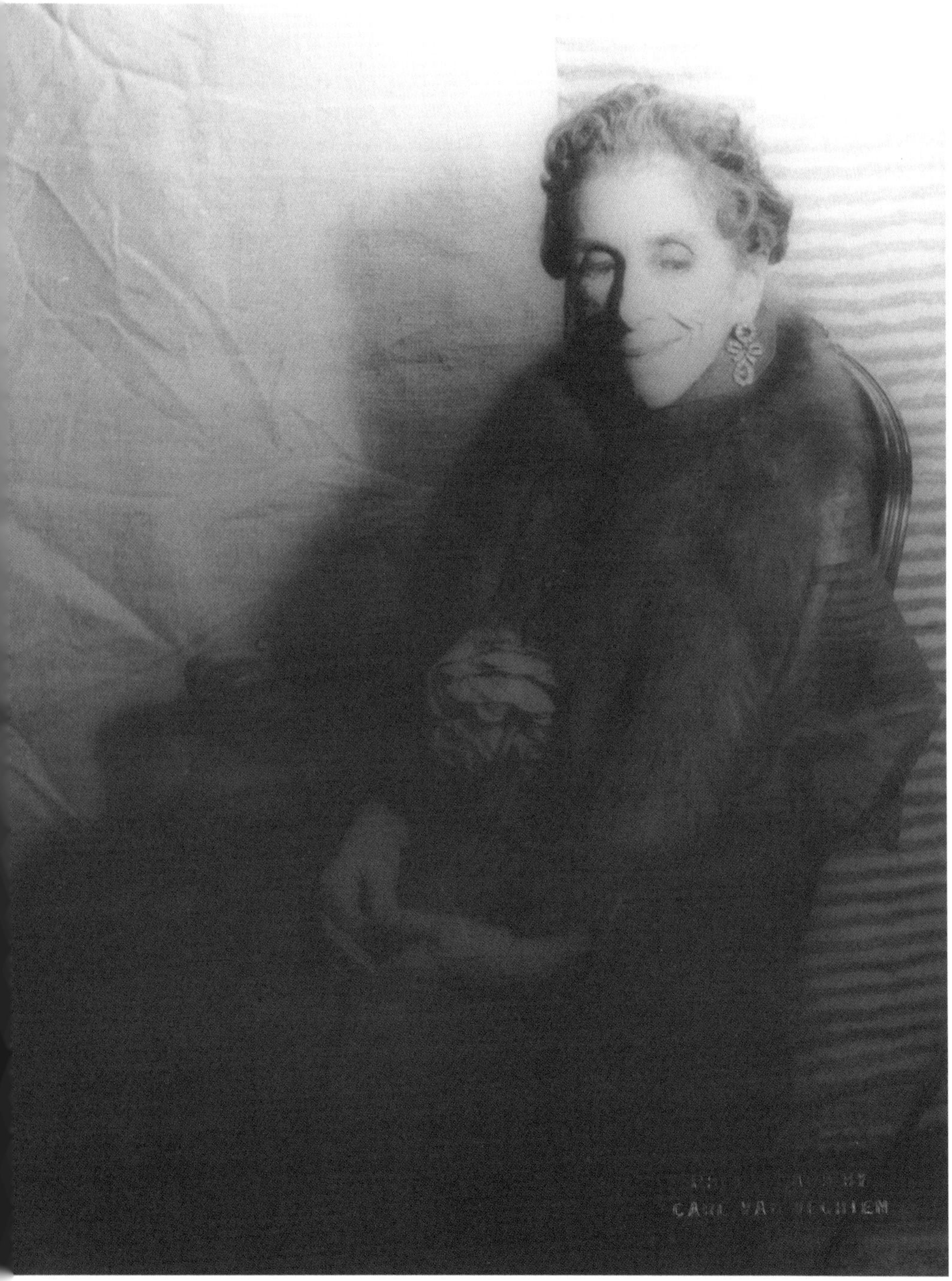

PHOTOGRAPHED ON APRIL 13, 1959

## WRITER

Born Karen Christentze Dinesen in Rungsted, Denmark, Isak Dinesen published her first book, *Seven Gothic Tales* (1934), at the age of forty eight. Now considered one of her masterpieces, the work originally had difficulty finding a publisher; however, once published, it immediately established Dinesen's relationship with American readers.

Influenced by the Gothic and decadent traditions, *Seven Gothic Tales* differs considerably from Dinesen's next book, the autobiographical *Out of Africa* (1937). Employing a more realistic style, *Out of Africa* chronicles the seventeen years that Dinesen spent running a coffee plantation in Africa. By turns a lyrical expression of her affection for Africa, an exploration of her failed marriage to Baron Bror von Blixen-Finecke, and a declaration of love for the Englishman Denys Finch Hatton, *Out of Africa* met with great success in both America and England. Glenway Wescott wrote, "*Out of Africa* is ravishingly written; it is like a love potion, strengthening us in our enthusiasm about our life, whoever we are, whenever or wherever it may be."[1] When accepting the Nobel Prize in 1954, Ernest Hemingway is said to have stated that it should have gone instead to "that beautiful Danish writer Isak Dinesen."

Van Vechten's response was equally strong. On September 9, 1955, he wrote to George George, "I have never enjoyed anything more than *Out of Africa*. . . . I'll never get over it & I am already very different!"[2] Van Vechten then sent a letter to Dinesen

# ISAK DINESEN

herself, writing, "Why I have waited so long to read you, I'll never know, but from the very first words in *Out of Africa*, I understood that I had found an important friend & ally. Never before have I been made to feel so deeply the personal power of the written word."[3]

During a 1959 visit to New York, Dinesen sat for several famous photographers, including Richard Avedon, Cecil Beaton, and Carl Van Vechten. Though he had photographed her the previous year, both photographer and subject particularly enjoyed this session. In a letter to Fania Marinoff of January 29, Van Vechten wrote that the Baroness had been over the night before and stated, "She permitted endless pictures and left only at 10.30. She was excited to be photographed in color, an experience she had never had before."[4] In April, Van Vechten photographed Dinesen again and wrote, "She comes here for MORE photographs tomorrow. There are certain aspects I have missed. I prefer her with her hair showing and in BROWN. Also I think gloves improve her scandalously thin arms. This time I hope that Saul [Mauriber] can catch us together in a fond embrace. I did not manage that in black and white last time, but the color pictures of this sexy scene are magnificent."[5]

Interest in Dinesen later surged with the appearance of the films *Out of Africa* (1985) and *Babette's Feast* (1987), based on her work. Critics have alternately praised Dinesen as a feminist and criticized her as a supporter of colonialism. However, the beauty of her writing and her lasting influence have endured. After her death, Van Vechten wrote, "The impression she made was so deeply indelible that something of her spirit will always endure, even to eternity. This is a belief that I will never lose."[6]

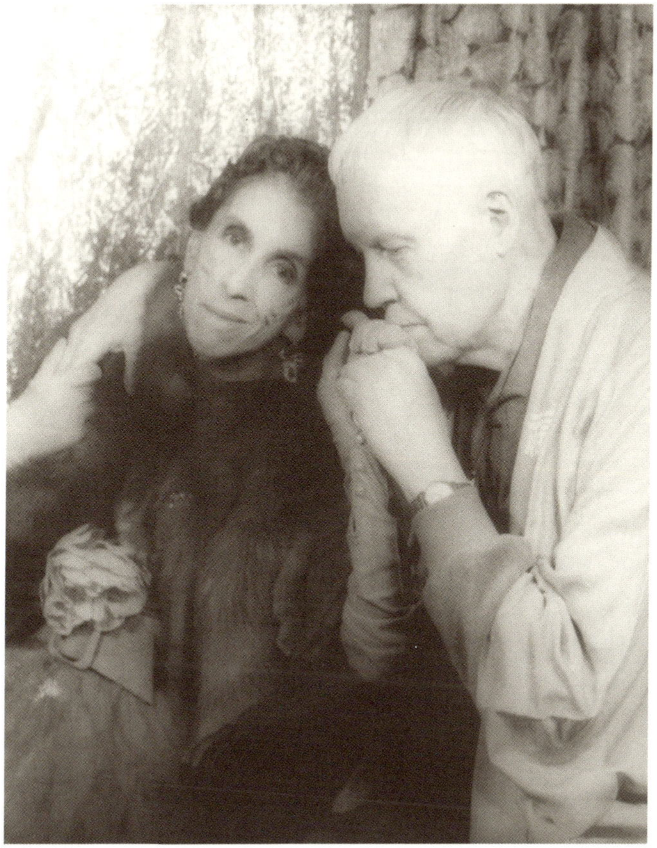

PHOTOGRAPHED BY SAUL MAURIBER ON NOVEMBER 20, 1958



1 Glenway Wescott
*Images of Truth: Remembrances and Criticism*
London: Hamish Hamilton
1963
p. 152

2 Van Vecten to
George George
9 Sept. 1955
*Letters of Carl Vechten*
Ed. Bruce Kellner
New Haven, Yale, 1987
p. 256

3 Van Vecten to Karen Blixen
17 Sept. 1955
*Letters of Carl Van Vechten*
p. 256

4 Van Vecten to
Fania Marinoff
29 Jan. 1959
*Letters of Carl Van Vechten*
p. 272

5 Van Vecten to
Sandy Campbell
12 Apr. 1959
*Letters of Carl Van Vechten*
p. 274

6 In *Isak Dinesen: A Memorial*
Ed., Clara Svendsen
NY: Random House
1965
p. 30

# CARSON MCCULLERS

## WRITER



Carson McCullers burst onto the literary scene at the age of twenty-three with the publication of her first novel, *The Heart Is a Lonely Hunter*, a tale of the lonely inhabitants of a small southern town. The novel was an immediate success, and McCullers was hailed as one of the most promising young writers in America. In her review, Rose Feld wrote, "Carson McCullers is a full-fledged novelist whatever her age. She writes with a sweep and certainty that are overwhelming. *The Heart Is a Lonely Hunter* is a first novel. One anticipates the second with something like fear. So high is the standard she has set. It doesn't seem possible that she can reach it again."[1]

McCullers did reach that standard at least two more times, with *The Ballad of the Sad Café* (1943) and *The Member of the Wedding* (1946). Langston Hughes expressed his admiration for *The Ballad of the Sad Café* in a letter on August 31, 1943, to Carl Van Vechten: "Miss Carson McCullers has a wonderful story in the August HARPER'S BAZAAR. (Or did I mention it to you?) About a hunchback, a criminal, and a woman."[2] At the urging of Tennessee Williams, McCullers later adapted *The Member of the Wedding* for the stage, and in 1950 it appeared on Broadway to widespread acclaim. *New York Times* drama critic Brooks Atkinson said of it, "It is a vivid fragment of the living truth."[3] Starring Julie Harris, Brandon De Wilde, and Ethel Waters, the play won several New York Drama Critics' Circle and Donaldson Awards.

McCullers spent the summer of 1942 at the Yaddo writers' colony in Saratoga Springs, New York, where she met Langston Hughes. Van Vechten, always eager to find new subjects for his portraits, wrote to Hughes, "If you get on with Miss McCullers, tell her I'd like to photograph her some time. I dote on her books."[4] Hughes responded, "I have breakfast every morning with Mrs. McCullers, at which time we unite in damning Georgia. I shall ask her if she would like to have her picture taken."[5]

Although several years passed before Van Vechten photographed McCullers, they became good friends in the meantime. When McCullers was finishing her last novel, *Clock Without Hands* (1961), she asked Van Vechten to read several chapters and give her his comments. Throughout her life, McCullers suffered from ill health, including three serious strokes, the last of which permanently paralyzed the left side of her body. She spent most of 1959 writing *Clock Without Hands*, typing just one page a day using only her right hand.

McCullers has been praised for her sensitive use of language and her compassion for the disaffiliated. Irving Howe, for example, called *The Ballad of the Sad Café,* "one of the finest novels ever written by an American."[6] Some have labeled her a "writer's writer," while Gore Vidal reportedly stated that McCullers's "genius for prose remains one of the few satisfying achievements of our second-rate culture."

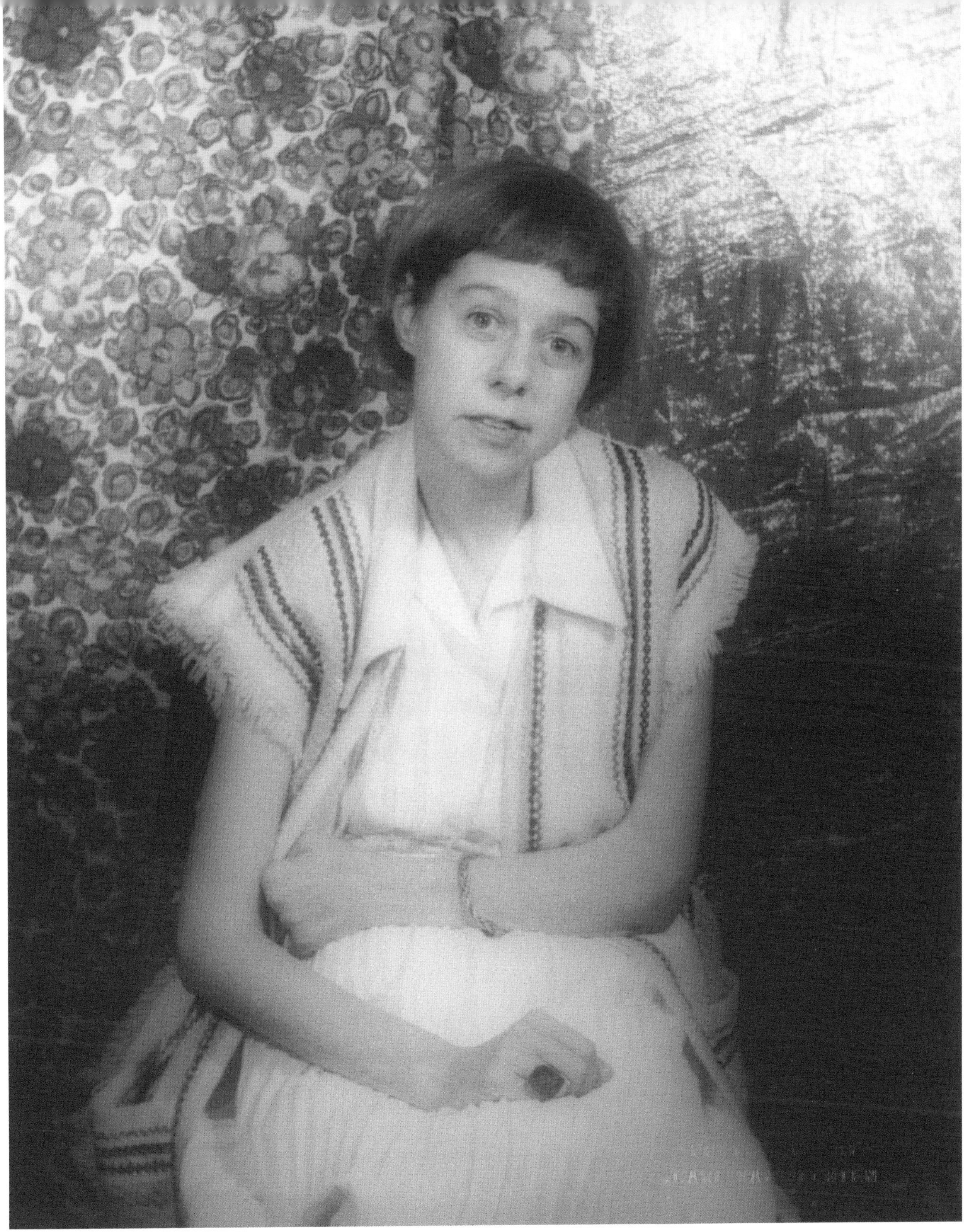

PHOTOGRAPHED ON JULY 31, 1959

1 Rose Feld
"A Remarkable First Novel of Lonely Lives"
*New York Times*
16 June 1940

2 Langston Hughes to Van Vechten
31 Aug. 1943
*Remember Me to Harlem: The Letters of Langston Hughes and Carl Van Vechten, 1925-1964*
Ed., Emily Bernard
NY: Knopf, 2001
pp. 225-26

3 Brooks Atkinson
"'The Member of the Wedding' Superbly Acted by an Excellent Company"
*New York Times*
15 Jan. 1950

4 Van Vechten to Hughes
12 Aug. 1942
*Remember Me to Harlem*
p. 206

5 Hughes to Van Vechten
12 Aug. 1942
*Remember Me to Harlem*
p. 208

6 Irving Howe
"In the Shadow of Death"
*New York Times*
17 Sept. 1961

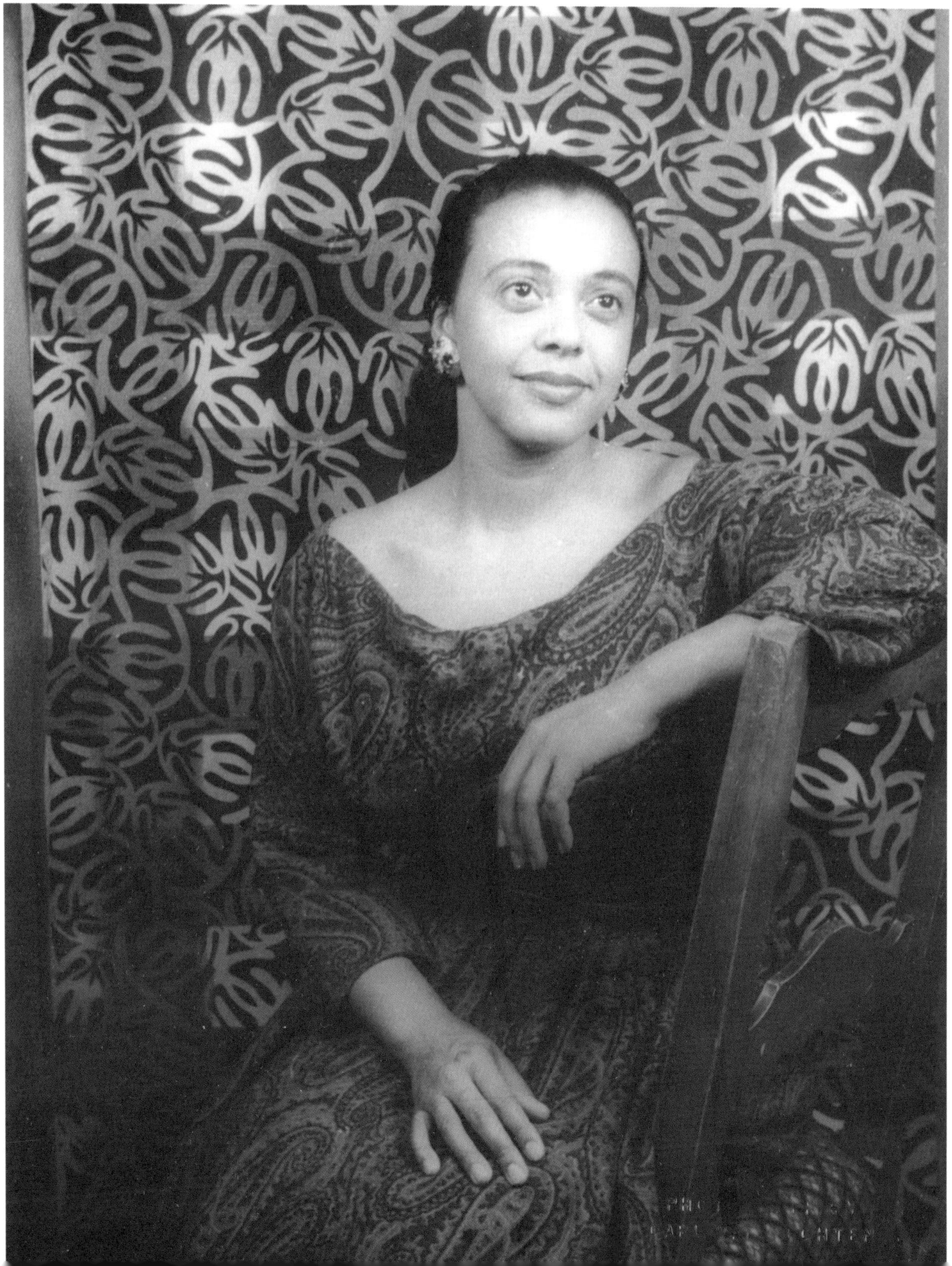

PHOTOGRAPHED ON APRIL 4, 1961

# ADELE ADDISON

## SOPRANO



Though she is not well known today, Adele Addison was an acclaimed figure in opera in the 1950s and 1960s. In 1952, her debut performance at Town Hall in New York was met with excellent, enthusiastic reviews. "The recital season reached a high point last night," one critic wrote, "when Adele Addison, soprano from Springfield, Massachusetts, made her debut in Town Hall."[1] Addison's singing voice was complemented by her performance style, which was rich with emotion and intellectual depth.

Carl Van Vechten photographed Addison in 1955, the year she played Mimi in *La Boheme* at City Center in New York. Adele Addison's performance was highly praised by the reviewer from the *New York Post*, who wrote:

> Adele Addison, young Negro soprano, who made her debut with the New York City Opera yesterday afternoon as Mimi in Puccini's "La Boheme" is about the most appealing interpreter of the little Parisian seamstress yet to appear on the City Center stage. Small, frail looking, and pretty, Miss Addison enhanced these assets by acting and singing with moving poignancy and sincerity.[2]

In 1957, when Addison again performed at Town Hall, Howard Taubman wrote "Adele Addison . . . is developing into an artist of distinction. Her performance last night at Town Hall had high purpose and impressive achievement. . . . [Her] soprano has delicacy of texture and glowing warmth."[3]

Addison, who studied at Westminster Choir College and The Julliard School, made a number of records, including Bach's *Saint Matthew's Passion* and Handel's *Messiah*, under the direction of Leonard Bernstein. She was a voice instructor at several important schools, including the Eastman School of Music and the Manhattan School of Music, where she served as chair of the Voice Department.

1 "Addison, Soprano, Excels in Debussy" *New York Times* 18 Jan. 1955

2 "Adele Addison" *New York Post* 28 Mar. 1955

3 Howard Taubman "Music: Adele Addison" *New York Times* 28 Jan. 1957

# MARTINA ARROYO



Born and raised in Harlem, Martina Arroyo was among the first performers—along with Adele Addison and Leontyne Price—to challenge the color barriers in the opera world. The daughter of a Puerto Rican father and an African-American mother, Arroyo's interest in singing began with a love of 1940s Hollywood musicals. Though she studied dance and piano as a child, Arroyo soon decided she wanted to sing opera.

Arroyo was encouraged by her family to pursue her interest in music, but they insisted on an education in a more practical field, too. Thus, Arroyo trained as a teacher and studied opera simultaneously. She would work as a teacher and as a social worker before becoming a leading performer in the New York and European opera scenes. In addition to her successful stage career, Arroyo has taught at UCLA, the University of Delaware, and Indiana University, and has given master classes at universities all over the world.

Like many African-American performers, Arroyo found early success in Europe, where more opportunities in the opera were available to people of color. Arroyo gained experience performing in many shows, generally playing small roles, or larger roles in small productions. But her powerful voice and dramatic performances earned her increasing visibility and popularity. She performed for several years in London, Italy, and Zurich. When she returned to the United States for a recital at Carnegie Hall in 1957, a *New York Times* critic wrote, "Miss Arroyo's voice is by nature of pleasing quality, with a brilliant, ringing, clarity of tone."[1]

Arroyo's big break came as she was visiting family in New York nearly ten years later. She was invited to substitute temporarily for Birgit Nilsson, then one of opera's leading sopranos, in the Metropolitan Opera Company's production of *Aida*. She debuted in the lead role on February 4, 1965, and though the audience was initially disappointed that Nilsson would not appear, Arroyo earned a standing ovation.

Arroyo has played a part in changing opera's reputation as a stuffy, elitist art form by appearing frequently on *The Tonight Show* with Johnny Carson and guest starring on the popular 1970s television sitcom, *The Odd Couple*. Talking with other singers about opera on a Singers' Roundtable segment of *The Texaco-Metropolitan Opera International Radio Broadcast* in 1970, Arroyo profoundly humanized opera performers when she made a comical slip of the tongue:

1 "Joint Recital: Martina Arroyo, Soprano, and Miss Garcy, Pianist, Heard" *New York Times* 20 Jan. 1957

2 Anthony Tommasini "From the Met, Arias of the Airwaves" *New York Times* 17 Dec. 1999

PHOTOGRAPHED APRIL 4, 1961

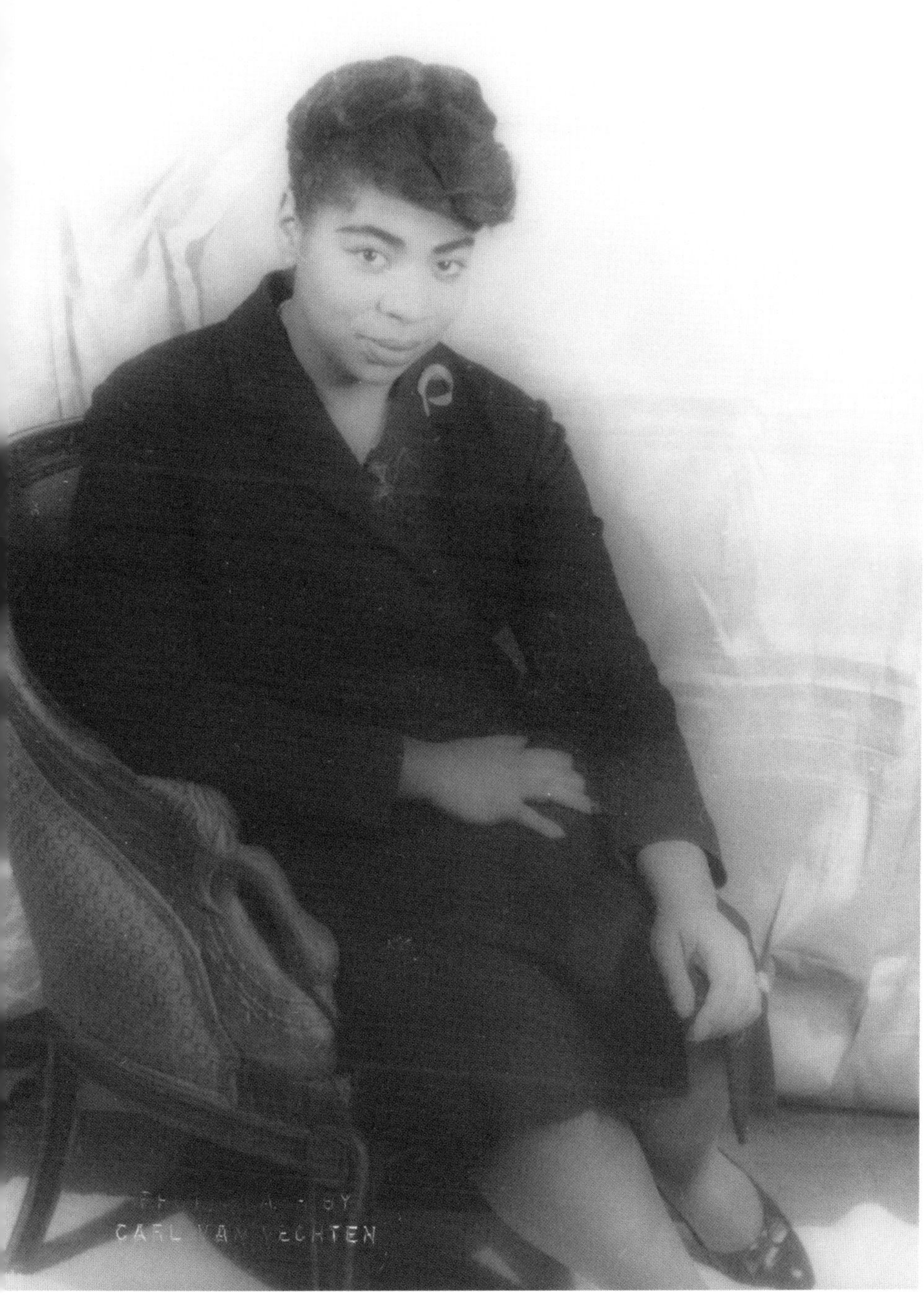

SOPRANO

> At one point the question was posed: Are there any roles that would have suited you vocally but that you choose not to sing for other reasons? Ms. Arroyo, who was not a small woman, answered, in one of the great Freudian slips of all time, "Yes, Madame Butterball."[2]



Martina Arroyo has appeared in every major opera house in the world and she has performed with the finest orchestras. She has made a number of recordings, including Mozart's *Don Giovanni*, Verdi's *Requiem* and *Aida*, Meyerbeer's *Les Huguenots*, and Beethoven's *Ninth Symphony*. Though she formally retired in 1989, she has occasionally appeared for special performances.

## GOSPEL SINGER



The "Queen of Gospel," Mahalia Jackson was the first performer to take African-American gospel singing beyond the religious services where it originated. Beginning her career in small churches Jackson grew in popularity until she became the most famous gospel singer of all time. Her unique, emotional style, punctuated with shouts of joy and moans of grief, and her forceful presentation of traditional spirituals inspired her audiences, often moving her listeners to tears. Using her talent and reputation in support of the civil rights movement, Jackson participated in the Montgomery bus boycott and sang "I Been 'Buked and I Been Scorned" at the 1963 March on Washington, before her friend, Dr. Martin Luther King, Jr., delivered his historic "I Have a Dream" speech.

Jackson was born in New Orleans. Her mother died when she was five and until she was fifteen she was raised by her mother's sister, who lived next door to the Sanctified Church. There, Jackson witnessed the tremendously expressive music the congregation made at their services, singing, clapping, and stomping their feet. Around this time, her cousin introduced her to the blues recordings of Bessie Smith and others. By the time she was a teenager, Jackson had dropped out of school to work as a laundress. She soon left New Orleans and moved to Chicago to live with another aunt.

In Chicago, Jackson joined the Great Salem Baptist Church and began singing in its choir. She and several other young members of the congregation joined to form the Johnson Gospel Singers, a group that sang first in other local churches

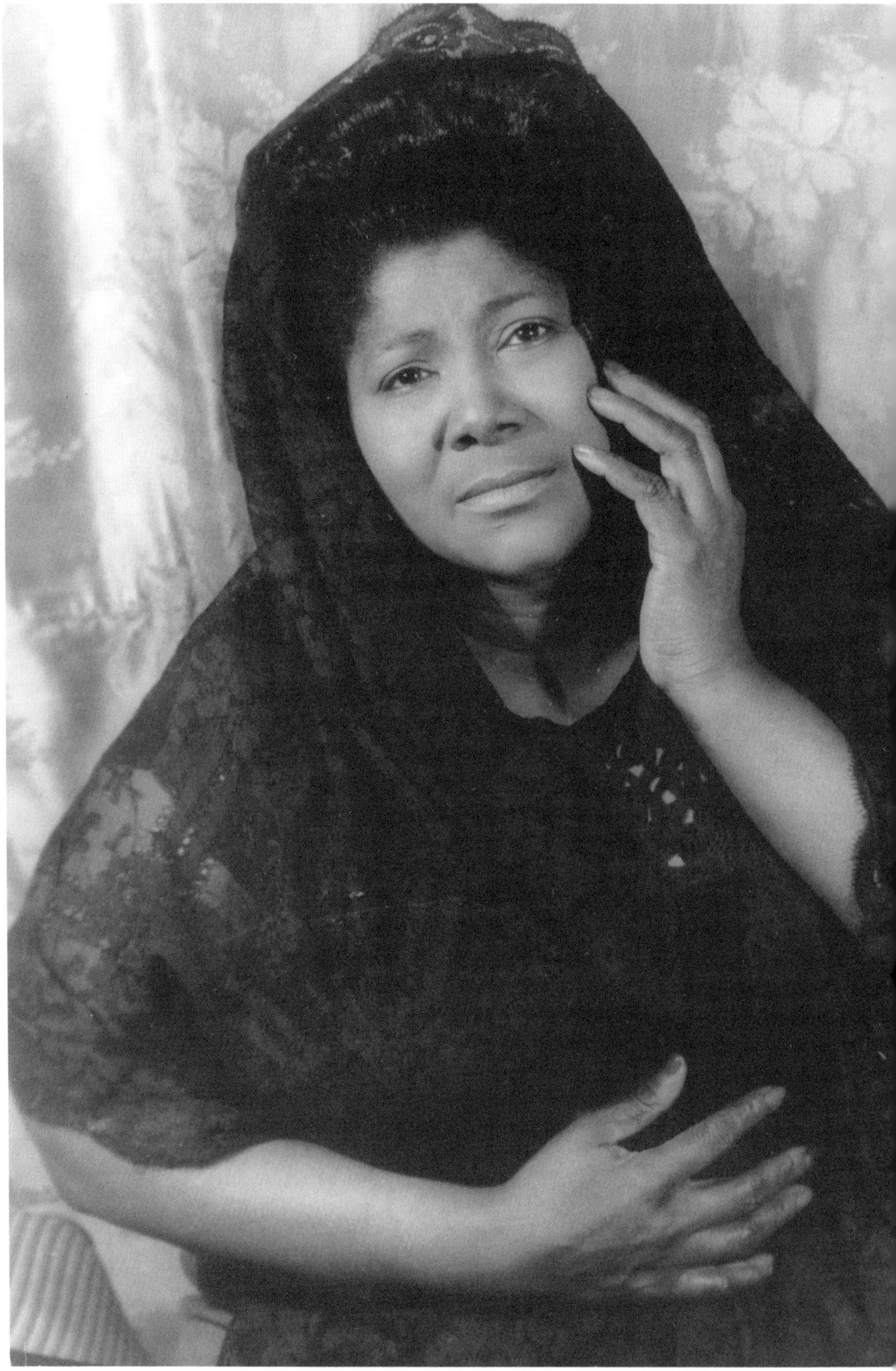

# MAHALIA JACKSON

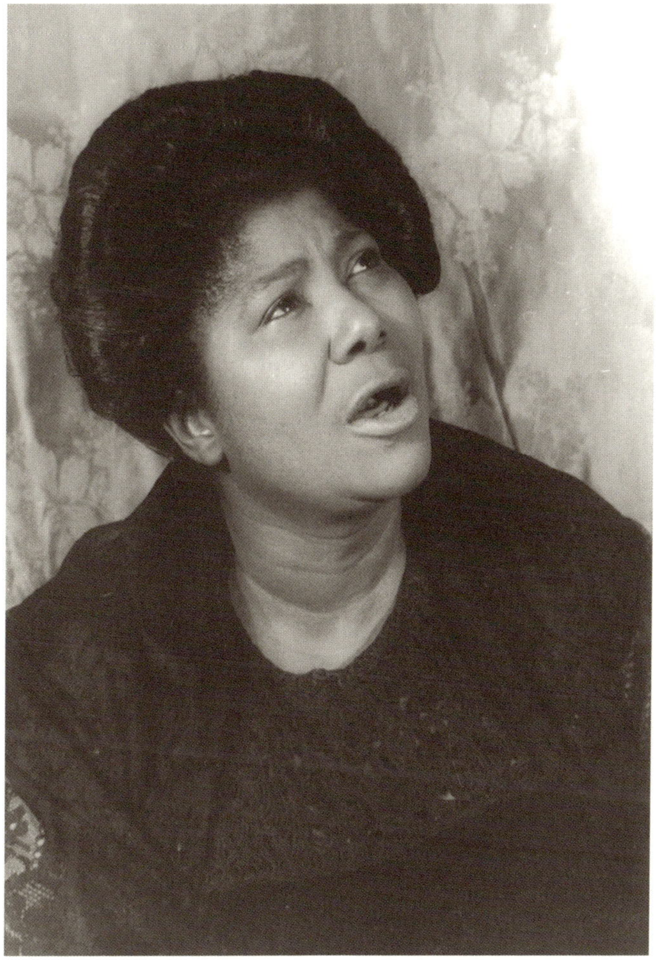

and later traveled throughout the Midwest performing at churches and revivals. The group made very little money, and Jackson continued to do laundry for white families to support herself. After marrying Isaac Hockenhull, a postman who had studied chemistry in college, she opened a beauty salon using her husband's formulas for cosmetics. Her husband pressured her to give up singing in churches and to try to break into the more lucrative jazz and blues music industry. Jackson refused and the couple split.



In 1937, Jackson made her first recording under the guidance of the great gospel composer, Thomas A. Dorsey. She worked closely with Dorsey for the next ten years, traveling all over the country singing. Dorsey wrote songs especially for Jackson and served as her accompanist. Jackson's performances helped to increase the popularity of her recordings; in 1946, her recording of "Move On Up a Little Higher" sold more than two million copies. She became the official soloist of the National Baptist Convention in 1947. Around this time, Jackson was regularly featured on Studs Terkel's radio program; later she would host her own radio and television shows.

During the 1950s and 60s, Jackson appeared regularly in support of the civil rights and anti-war movements. When her home on Chicago's South Side was vandalized by a white neighbor, Jackson appeared on Edward R. Murrow's television show, *Person-to-Person*. She was subsequently invited to appear on other talk and variety shows, including *The Dinah Shore Show* and *The Ed Sullivan Show*.

Jackson performed a European tour in the early 1960s, in spite of her failing health. She became involved in several entrepreneurial efforts, including a chain of stores called "Mahalia Jackson's Chicken System," as well as numerous real estate ventures. She also worked to establish the Mahalia Jackson Scholarship Foundation. By this time, she made few public appearances, though her recordings remained popular. Jackson died in 1971; at her funeral, she was honored by many in the music community and members of the congregations she performed for throughout her life.

PHOTOGRAPHED ON APRIL 16, 1962

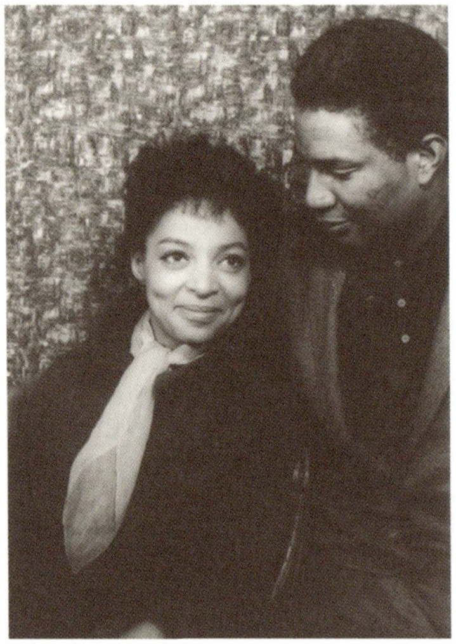

# RUBY DEE

## ACTRESS & ACTIVIST



For more than half a century, Ruby Dee has been a prominent stage, film, and television actress, a dynamic activist in support of civil rights, and a ceaseless promoter of African-American arts and culture. She has successfully married these elements throughout her career by acting, writing, directing, and producing work that grapples with difficult questions about racial and economic stratification in the United States. With her husband, actor Ossie Davis, Dee has been a defining force in the struggle for racial equality. In addition, she and Davis have used their talents and considerable popularity to encourage the creation of politically relevant, socially influential entertainment.

Dee was born Ruby Ann Wallace. She spent most of her childhood in Harlem. Dee's mother, a school teacher, introduced her children to fine music, classical drama, and great British and American poetry, including work by African-American writers such as Paul Laurence Dunbar. As a child, Dee became determined to pursue a career in the arts because of the love of music and literature her mother instilled in her.

At Hunter College, Dee studied romance languages and joined the American Negro Theater, which performed in the basement theater of the 135th Street Library. Within a year of her college graduation, Dee was appearing on Broadway in *Jeb* by Robert Ardrey. Ossie Davis played opposite Dee in the lead role. Dee and Davis appeared together in their next two plays and were married during a break in their rehearsal schedule.

Dee's many stage successes include the title role in *Anna Lucasta,* an all-black play that, soon after its theatrical success, was made into a film with an all-white cast. She appeared with Diana Sands in Lorraine Hansberry's landmark play *A Raisin in the Sun.* Also among her most famous roles is the part of Lena in *Boesman and Lena*, a South African drama by Athol Fugard, in which she costarred with James Earl Jones. Dee has also performed many classical roles, including celebrated performances of some of Shakespeare's most interesting women: Cordelia in *King Lear*, Kate in *The Taming of the Shrew*, and Gertrude in *Hamlet*.

Also well known as a film actress, in 1950 Dee starred in *The Jackie Robinson Story*, as the baseball player's wife, Rachel Robinson, opposite Jackie Robinson himself. In 1958, she appeared in *St. Louis Blues* with an all-star cast that included Eartha Kitt, Ella Fitzgerald, Mahalia Jackson, and Pearl Bailey. Dee has appeared in many popular television mini series and made-for-TV movies and she continues to appear in popular films, as well as documentaries about prominent African Americans, including the controversial director Spike Lee.

Ruby Dee and Ossie Davis have enjoyed one of the most enduring relationships in the entertainment industry. Their artistic partnerships have resulted in some of their most successful dramatic projects, including Davis's 1961 play, *Purlie Victorious*, in which Dee played Luttiebelle Gussie Mae

PHOTOGRAPHED ON WITH HER HUSBAND, OSSIE DAVIS, ON NOVEMBER 15, 1961

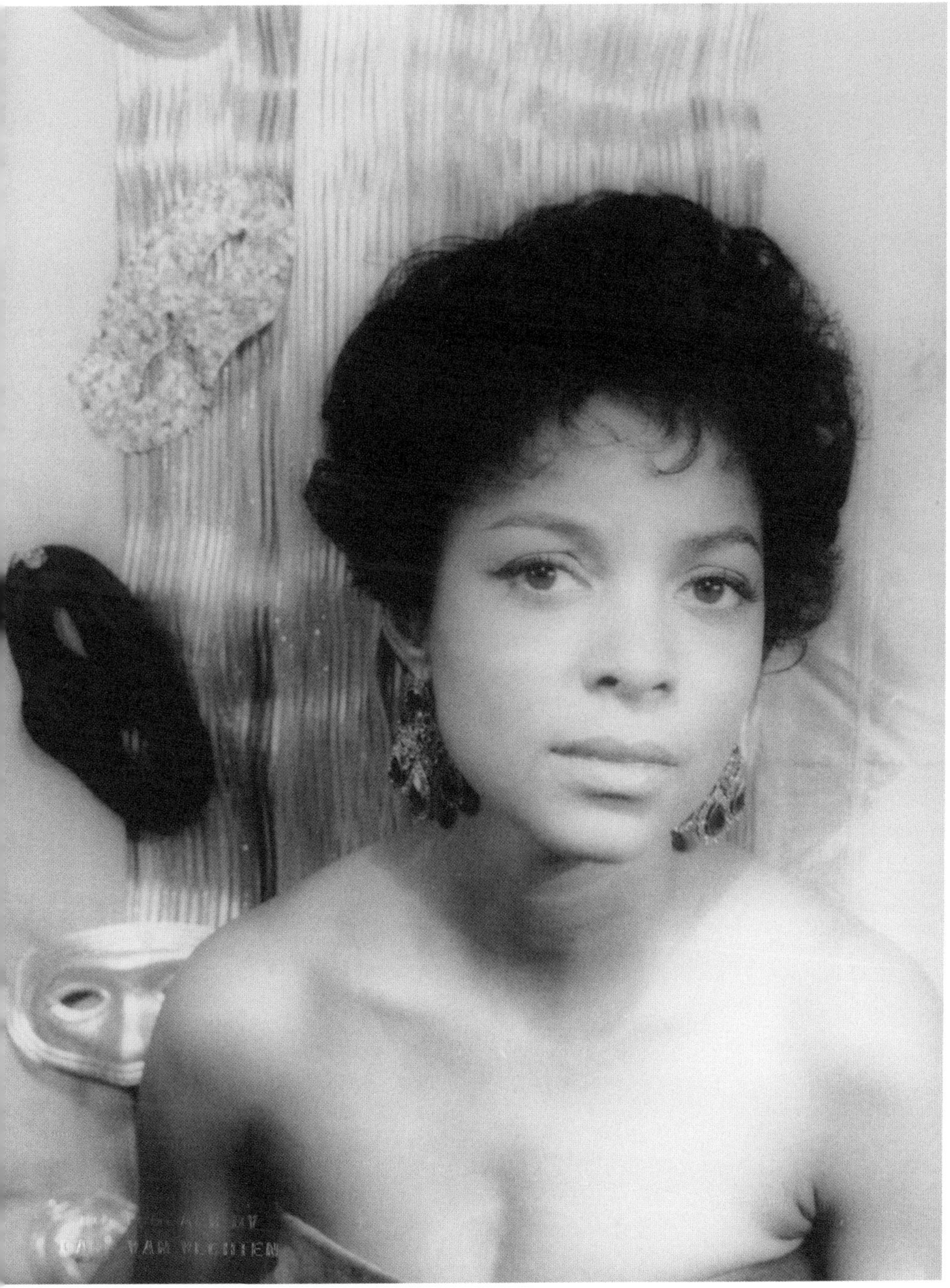



Jenkins, a role that helped Dee shake a reputation as a the "Negro June Allyson." More recently, the couple appeared together in Spike Lee's films *Do the Right Thing* and *Jungle Fever.*

Partners in activism as well as art, Dee and Davis have shared an unfaltering commitment to social justice. Together they spoke out against McCarthyism in the 1950s; Dee, in fact, was blacklisted because of her vocal opposition to the tactics of the House Un-American Activities Commission. The couple's highly visible fight against racism, including their participation as emcees of the 1963 March on Washington and their involvement in more recent public protests, has been an influential force in the ongoing battle for civil rights in the United States.

Their dedication to the celebration of African-American art and culture is legendary. Together they have hosted two television programs, *The Ossie Davis and Ruby Dee Hour* and *With Ossie and Ruby!* on PBS. These programs were devoted to exploring African-American culture and celebrating the contributions of African Americans to the entertainment industry and to American culture.

PHOTOGRAPHED ON SEPTEMBER 25, 1962

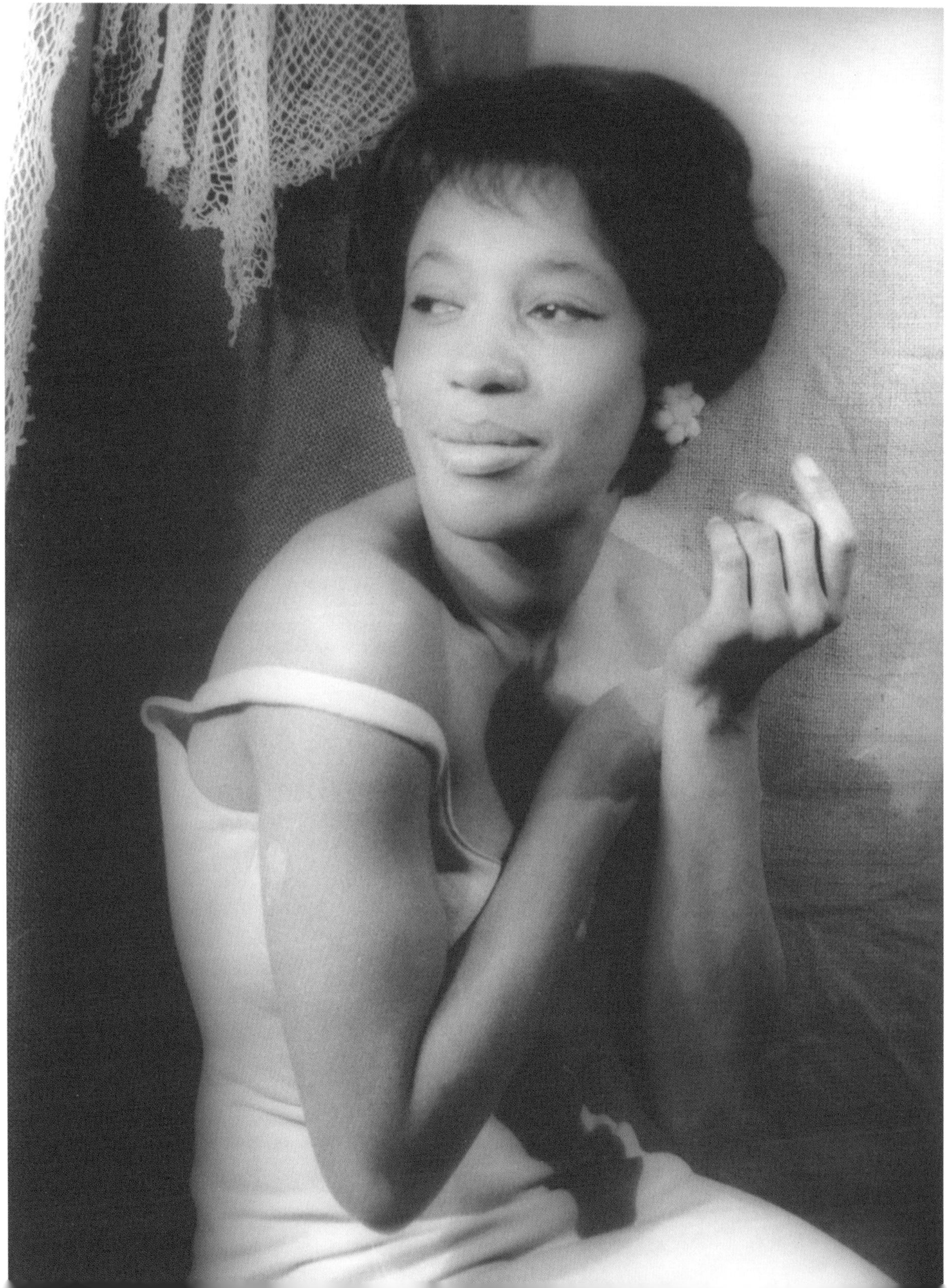

Brooks Atkinson 1
"The Theatre; 'A Raisin in the Sun'"
*New York Times*
12 Mar. 1959

# DIANA SANDS

## ACTRESS

Throughout her career, African-American actress Diana Sands successfully challenged racial barriers in the theater world by pursuing and winning parts that were traditionally played by white actresses. At a time when black actors were offered minor or marginal roles Sands battled for more interracial casting. She also appeared in noteworthy plays about the lives of African Americans.

A native New Yorker who graduated from that city's celebrated High School of the Performing Arts, Sands made her professional debut off-Broadway playing Juliet in *An Evening with Will Shakespeare* (1953) and a year later she appeared in a revival of Bernard Shaw's *Major Barbara*. She had a few minor successes before making her Broadway debut in Lorraine Hansberry's ground breaking play about an African-American family living in Chicago's South Side, *A Raisin in the Sun*. The play was roundly praised as a work that "has vigor and veracity and is likely to destroy the complacency of any one who sees it."[1] Members of the cast, which included Sidney Poitier, Ruby Dee, and Claudia McNeil, were celebrated for their compelling portrayal of Hansberry's vivid characters. Sands was awarded the Outer Critics Circle Award and a *Variety* Critics Poll Award for her performance. She revisited the part in the 1961 film version of the play.

Shortly after the success of *A Raisin in the Sun*, Sands appeared with Alan Alda in a Broadway romantic comedy, *The Owl and the Pussycat* by Bill Manhoff. The two-person play was written for white actors, and race wasn't an element of the story—in fact it was never even mentioned. Such interracial casting was rare and thus was thought by many to be a major step toward dismantling the status quo regarding race in the theater community. Sands continued in this vein when, in the late 1960s as a member of the Repertory Theater at Lincoln Center, she became the first African-American woman to play Joan of Arc in a professional production when she appeared in Shaw's *Saint Joan*.

In addition to performing with touring and regional productions, Sands appeared in films and on television. She was to play Claudine in the 1974 film of the same name, (a role for which Diahann Caroll would eventually receive an Oscar nomination) but Sands, a long-time chain smoker, was diagnosed with cancer and deemed too ill to take the role. She died in September of that year.



PHOTOGRAPHED ON JANUARY 29, 1963, AS ADELAIDE SMITH IN "TIGER, TIGER"

# MABEL MERCER

## SINGER



The daughter of an English vaudevillian and an American jazz musician, Mabel Mercer has been called the most influential cabaret singer of all time. Though her voice was unremarkable, her interpretation of lyrics is legendary. She is said to have been a major influence on some of the most important and popular singers of the twentieth century, including Nat King Cole, Lena Horne, Bobby Short, Leontyne Price, Barbara Streisand, and Tony Bennett. According to show business lore, when Mercer had a regular show at Tony's on 52nd Street in New York, Billie Holiday, who worked in the club across the street, snuck away from work to hear Mercer sing so often that she nearly lost her job. Frank Sinatra once said, "Mabel Mercer taught me everything I know."[1]

After leaving school at the age of fourteen (Mercer's diction training at a convent school is thought by many to be at the root of her precise and powerful enunciation), Mercer joined her aunt's vaudeville troupe and began performing regularly. By the 1920s, Mercer was singing in Paris where she met Ada "Bricktop" Smith, owner of the popular nightclub Bricktop's. Mercer sang nightly at Bricktop's throughout the 1930s, performing for the jazz age elite of Paris café society. At Bricktop's, Mercer was often asked to join guests at their tables and sing for them—she is said to have sung Cole Porter's songs to him while sitting beside him at his table. From this point forward, Mercer sang sitting down, even when performing on stage to a larger audience. This unusual performance style became a trademark, as much a part of her singing style as her personalized presentation of lyrics and the intimate tone of her shows.

Of seeing her in Paris, Carl Van Vechten wrote, "Mabel Mercer was [Bricktop's] leading singer at the time, a Mabel in her thirties, fresh from England, a very dear Mabel; whose singing I have enjoyed so much in New York, especially her interpretation of 'Sunday in Savannah.'"[2] Van Vechten photographed Mercer some thirty years later.

After leaving Paris in 1938 to escape the war, Mercer spent much of the next three decades performing in nightclubs in New York City. She spent her later years living on her farm in upstate New York, and though she still performed frequently, she no longer played the regularly scheduled shows she had in the past. After spending decades away from her home country, Mercer returned to England in the 1970s and was given a warm welcome. During this visit, she appeared in a five-part BBC special, *Miss Mercer in Mayfair.*

PHOTOGRAPHED MAY 28, 1963

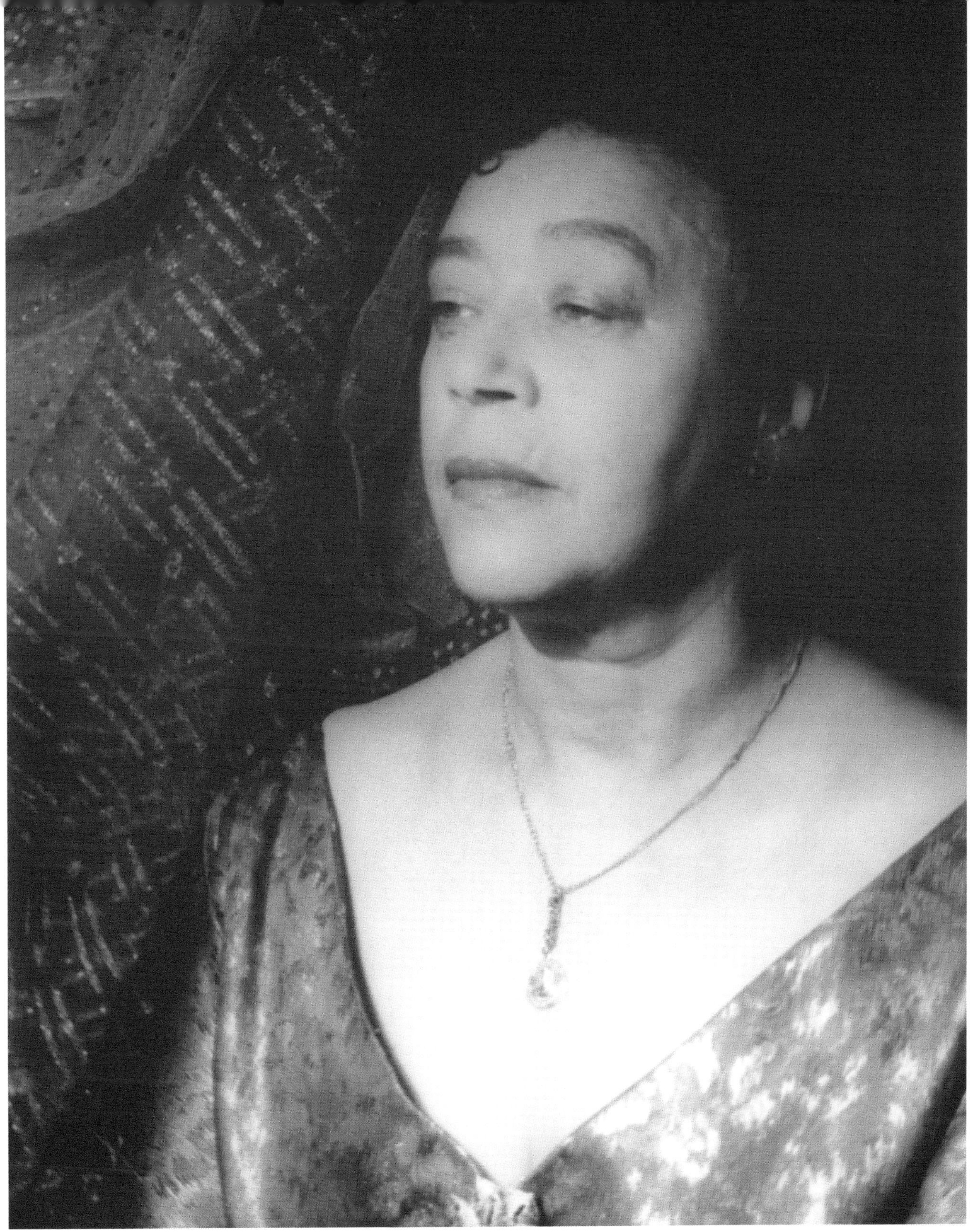



1 John S. Wilson
"Mabel Mercer, Storyteller in Song, Hailed at 75"
*New York Times*
4 Feb. 1975

2 Carl Van Vechten
"Portraits of the Artists"
*Esquire*
58:6 (1962)
p. 257

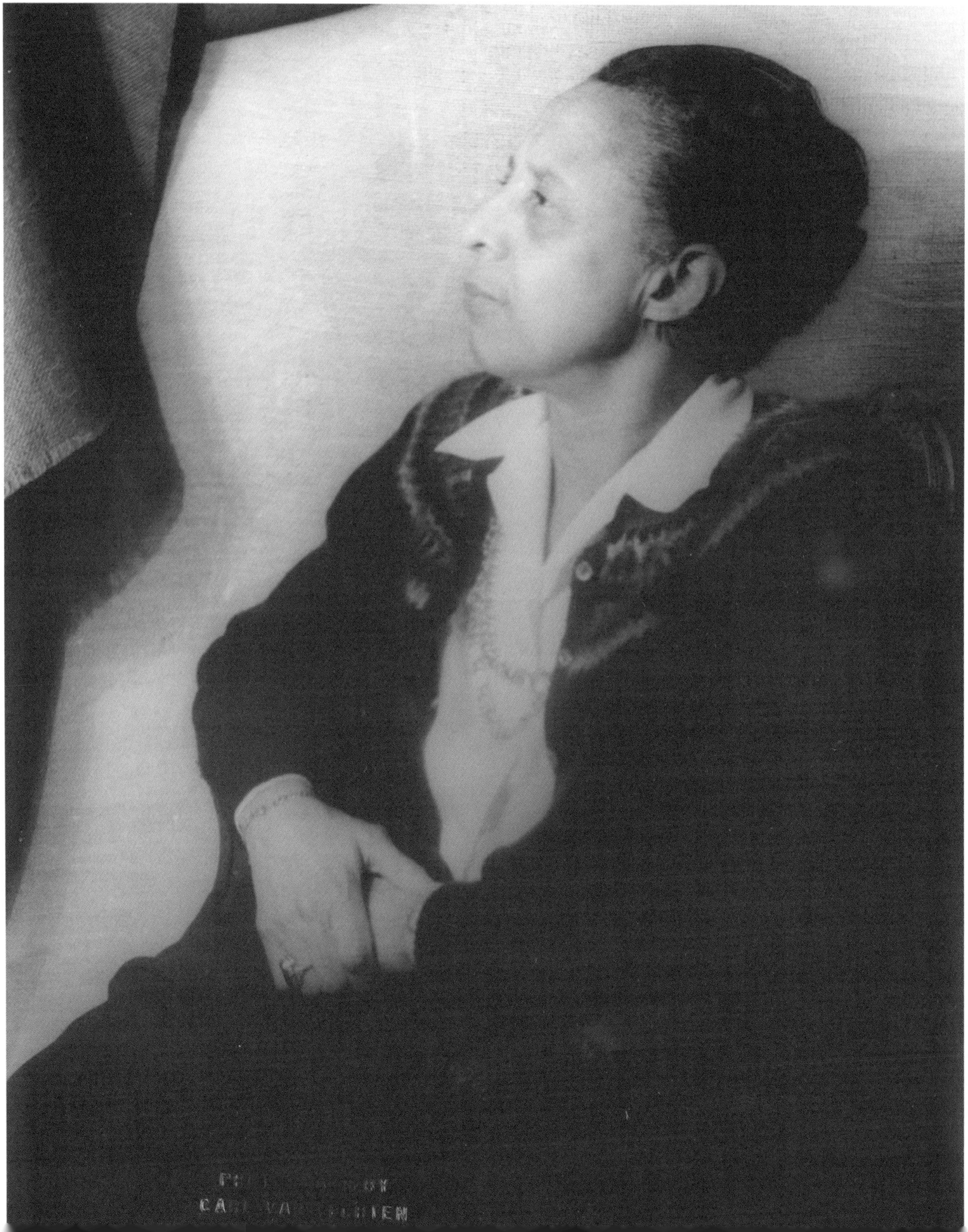

# LOUISE E. JEFFERSON

## ARTIST



Louise E. Jefferson, the daughter of a calligrapher for the United States Treasury Department, was encouraged to draw from a young age. Her father taught her his craft at home and she later studied fine and commercial art in private lessons and at Howard University. She moved to New York to continue her education at the School of Fine Arts at Hunter College.

In Harlem, Jefferson came in contact with other African-American artists and in 1935 she was a founding member of the Harlem Artists Guild, a program sponsored by the Works Progress Administration. Other members of the Guild included Augusta Savage, Aaron Douglas, Selma Burke, Gwendolyn Bennett, and Jacob Lawrence.

During her early years in New York City, Jefferson struggled financially. She earned money by taking free-lance drawing work, including posters for the YWCA for seventy-five cents each. A freelance job with the National Council of Churches' publishing operation, Friendship Press, led to a full-time position. Jefferson eventually became the press's art director. Jefferson was perhaps the first African-American woman to hold such a position in the publishing industry.

In addition to her work with Friendship Press, Jefferson freelanced for major publishing houses, such as Viking and Doubleday, throughout her career. She was known as a designer of both skill and artistry. Jefferson designed pieces for a number of African-American publications, including covers for *Opportunity* and *The Crisis*. For many years, she created publicity materials for the National Urban League Guild's Beaux-Arts Ball and NAACP programs. Her success did not shield her from racist attitudes, however; in 1936, *We Sing America,* a song book Jefferson illustrated with images of black and white children, was banned in Georgia and that state's governor, Eugene Talmadge, ordered that copies of the book be burned.

Jefferson was an accomplished photographer as well as a designer. Carrying a camera with her at all times enabled her to photograph many notable African Americans of her day. Her body of work includes images of a diverse group of individuals—from Thurgood Marshall to Lena Horne.

A number of grants from the Ford Foundation enabled Jefferson to travel to Africa where she studied native decorative arts. Her book *The Decorative Arts of Africa* was the result of her travel and study. The images in this major book on the subject are almost entirely Jefferson's own drawings and photographs.

PHOTOGRAPHED ON FEBRUARY 4, 1964

Bruce Kellner is Emeritus Professor of English, Millersville University, and the author and editor of several books about literature and art. Among them are books about his friend and mentor, Carl Van Vechten, including *Letters of Carl Van Vechten, The Splendid Drunken Twenties: Selections from the Daybooks, 1922-1930,* and the seminal biography, *Carl Van Vechten and the Irreverent Decades.* He is also the author of *The Harlem Renaissance: A Historical Dictionary of the Era* and books about Ralph Barton, Charles Demuth, Gertrude Stein, and Donald Windham, and a memoir, *Kiss Me Again: An Invitation to a Group of Noble Dames.* He is Successor Trustee for the Estate of Carl Van Vechten.

Nancy Kuhl is the Assistant Curator of the Yale Collection of American Literature at the Beinecke Rare Book and Manuscript Library at Yale University. She is the curator of *Intimate Circles: American Women in the Arts*, a companion exhibition to *Extravagant Crowd*. Her criticism and reviews have appeared in *American Studies International, Libraries and Culture, The Changing Culture of Libraries* (McFarland 2001) and *Librarians in the 21st Century* (Greenwood Press 2003). She is the author of *In the Arbor*, a collection of poems published by Kent State University Press. Other creative work has appeared in *Verse, Fence, Poetry Northwest, The Cream City Review, Puerto Del Sol*, and in the anthology *September 11, 2001: American Writers Respond* (Etruscan Press 2002).